To Lady Mackay !
with good wishes
[signature]

15.10.87.

FOR THE
SAKE OF THE
CHILDREN

FOR THE SAKE OF THE CHILDREN

Inside Dr Barnardo's:
120 years of caring for children

JUNE ROSE

Hodder & Stoughton
LONDON SYDNEY AUCKLAND TORONTO

British Library Cataloguing in Publication Data

Rose, June
  For the sake of the children inside
  Dr. Barnardo's: 120 years of caring for
  1. Dr. Barnardo's – History
  I. Title
  362.73′2′0941   HV887.G5

ISBN 0 340 37319 9

For Gabrielle

Illustrations

All the photographs are reproduced by
courtesy of the Barnardo Photographic Archive.

Contents

In his day Thomas Barnardo rescued children from the poverty and brutality of the slums. Now the charity he founded assists thousands of handicapped and needy youngsters throughout the United Kingdom, the Republic of Ireland, Australia and New Zealand.

June Rose's extensive researches into the charity's administrative records, her interviews both with people who were in Barnardo's care and with former and present staff reveal a moving and inspiring story. They show the suffering, the courage and the achievement of many children: they also uncover the charity's frequent struggle to adapt to the changing needs of society.

As President of Dr. Barnardo's I welcome the opportunity to visit the work being undertaken today and to see for myself the care and understanding which the modern organisation gives to children, young people and their families. It gives me great pleasure to be able to continue the Royal Family's long association with Dr. Barnardo's.

Diana.

July, 1987

Acknowledgments

My thanks, first of all, must go to the many children and staff of Dr Barnardo's, past and present, who gave so generously of their time and trust. Some of them are named in this book, others wished to remain anonymous. I am grateful to them all.

Then I should like to thank the Council of Dr Barnardo's for their help, advice and encouragement in my task. I owe a special debt of thanks to Lady Wagner, author of *Barnardo* and *Children of the Empire*. Her original research into Barnardo's background and early life, her analysis of the complicated arbitration case and of the workings of the organisation in the nineteenth century were invaluable in the writing of this book.

I am grateful also to Barnardo's Directors, Mary Joynson, the former Senior Director, and Roger Singleton, the present Senior Director, for making my 'stay' in Barnardo's so rewarding and pleasant. I would also like to record my appreciation of the help and co-operation shown to me by Nick Lowe, Director of Appeals, and Keith Manley, Director of Finance. I am indebted to the Divisional Directors of Barnardo's throughout the country and to their field workers who received me with courtesy and understanding and helped to make my visits to the children and families for whom they care both valuable and enjoyable.

In particular I would like to express my thanks to Barnardo's former librarian, John Nowell, who, from the beginning, guided me so knowledgeably through the maze of records and information. Without his help and the outstanding co-operation from the library staff and the present librarian, David Potter, my task would not have been possible. I am grateful, too, to Roy Ainsworth for sharing his encyclopedic knowledge of Barnardo's photographic records with me. Special thanks are due too to John Ruffels of Barnardo's Australia for the generous loan of his extensive archive material.

My thanks, too, to Michael Cook, the Archivist of Liverpool University, and his assistant Adrian Allan, for facilitating my research. Many other people helped me. I am grateful to Mrs B. Howlett, GLC Archivist, for her guidance in the use of the Barnardo papers in her collection, to Alan Little of the Wimbledon Lawn Tennis Museum for unearthing the early story of the Barnardo ball boys, to Winifred Stone of the Children's Society and Brian Parnell of the National Children's Home for their help and advice and to the librarians of the NSPCC, of MENCAP and the Spastics Society. I would also like to express my appreciation to Professor Burnett of the Department of Government, Brunel University, for help and advice, and to Dr Mayall of the Department of History, De la Salle College, Manchester. I am grateful to Miss Hartwill, the Librarian of the Department of Education and Science for her help.

I am indebted, too, to Muriel Glynn Jones, former Senior Inspector of the Home Office, and to one of her team who wished to remain anonymous, for explaining the post-war child care scene.

Finally I must publicly thank my many friends who bore with me, encouraged and helped me during the preparation of this book. In particular I would like to mention Renata and Otto Koenisberger who went further and read the manuscript and made valuable suggestions.

Gabrielle Morrison typed and retyped the manuscript with enthusiasm and expertise; she was always a valuable source of advice.

Finally I should like to express my thanks to my editor, Christine Casley, for her perceptive and painstaking comments and to Christine Medcalf who selected the photographs.

J.R.

Prologue

In the beginning an unknown medical student in the East End of London brought the children of the slums to his home. Thomas Barnardo rounded up boys sleeping in the streets to house and teach them; within ten years he had raised sufficient funds to build homes, a hospital, a separate village for girls and to provide industrial and domestic training for his charges. By the twentieth century his name had become synonymous with orphan homes; a network of Barnardo homes covered the UK and his personal influence on the upbringing of destitute children spread as far as Japan, China, India, Argentina and North America.

In Barnardo's day, in the 1860s, child life and labour were held cheap; the numbers of children who died through cruelty or neglect were too numerous to remark. There is no cause for complacency in our own time and fresh evidence suggests that the problem of protecting vulnerable children demands constant vigilance. Yet in the mid-nineteenth century the law was powerless to protect children from parental abuse. As for pauper children, the only state protection offered to them was the regime of discipline and punishment found in many workhouses. Children with spirit often preferred to peddle or beg in the streets. Only if they were caught offending against the law could they expect to provoke public concern. Then they might be sent to an industrial training school or to a reformatory. Charitable bodies offered the children of the streets their best hope of refuge.

The terminology used to describe stray children tells something of the development of the work. In the nineteenth century, before philanthropists like Barnardo had transformed the care of destitute children into a national concern, they were regarded as little more than child refuse. Barnardo himself described them as street arabs or little rescued gutter lads. By the 1920s and 'thirties boys and girls entering Barnardo homes were termed 'lonely little children'. Today the charity cares for children with special needs.

Barnardo's claimed to be 'the largest family in the world' in the past, and as in every family there were children who grew up with a profound sense of injustice as well as those who were content with their lot. Despite pious hopes, some rescued children found institutional life oppressive. Deprived of freedom and cut off from former haunts and contacts, they had to learn the skills of group survival. As late as the 1960s, the work had a missionary purpose and a missionary zeal. In certain homes, boys and girls grew up under a strict Victorian regime with the waxwork figure of Dr Barnardo still in command at headquarters.

Today the old possessiveness has gone. Barnardo's cares for children in a modern and professional manner, helping the disadvantaged to attain their full potential and working within the community as far as possible. Over a quarter of a million children have passed through Barnardo's hands in a remarkable record of child care. Despite the suffering some children endured in the past, the vast majority remain loyal to Barnardo's, drawn by the strong identity of the homes and the magnetism of the founder.

1

Origins

'Character is better than ancestry.'
Thomas John Barnardo

Thomas John Barnardo, the founder of the orphan homes, mounted a remarkable crusade to rescue poor children from the streets. Part of his success sprang from his gifts of preaching and writing. Through his eloquence Barnardo was able to provoke a concern for the most damaged and downtrodden children and by his championship of them he created a new image of the children of the slums.

The story of his own childhood is blurred. As his fame grew, so did the anecdotes and legends about him until they became folklore. Much of the early history of his life and of the homes he wrote himself, but where his father's family came from and how he spent his first years in London remain uncertain. For want of more concrete evidence the photographs of him provide an interesting commentary on his character.

He looked extraordinary with a lofty forehead set in a large head, his gaze stern or beaming, his squat body stiff, even in family photographs. The dapper figure with military moustache, smartly trimmed and tweaked sometimes, has the air of a ringmaster at a circus or a magician in a fairy tale.

Three portraits from childhood suggest, even more clearly, the complexities of his character. In the first, when he was a boy of eleven, he looks tight-lipped and dangerously angry; in the second, he appears a cheeky, likeable youngster; and in the photograph taken when he was twenty-one, he emerges as the public figure, his grey eyes hooded by the thick blue-tinted glasses he had to wear for short sight, his expression enigmatic, clearly a powerful personality.

The public image of the tiny 'doctor' (he was just five foot three), spectacled, a stern father, dominates so that it is hard to imagine that Thomas John Barnardo was ever a child himself.

The first official biography was written by his widow and James Marchant to raise funds for a national memorial.[1] The book furnishes him with a romantic background, a father of Spanish origin, born in Hamburg with aristocratic connections in Venice, and a mother from a well-respected Anglo-Irish family.

In the latest, carefully researched biography, the author suggests that the anti-Papist Protestant was the son of a German Jewish father and a mother of partly Catholic origin.[2] Until the 1950s the Catholic connection was suppressed. Barnardo's grandmother, a Drinkwater from a Quaker family settled in Ireland, had scandalised her parents by falling in love with Philip O'Brien, a Catholic from County Clare. The couple eloped and after the marriage her family refused to see her again, but Elizabeth was a woman of strong character who brought up her own daughters to be staunch Protestants.

Barnardo's father's family remains even more elusive. Nothing is known of his paternal grandparents. His father, John Michaelis Barnardo, was born in Havelberg, Prussia, in 1800. Jewish historians infer that his name and his trade (he was a furrier) point to a Jewish origin and the author Somerset Maugham, Barnardo's son-in-law, corroborated that version.

In the realm of fact, it is certain that John Michaelis settled in Ireland in his early twenties, bought himself one of the new Regency terrace houses in Upper Gardiner Street, Dublin, and set up his own fur business. By the time he was twenty-six, he was sufficiently established to seek a wife. On New Year's Day, 1827, he married Elizabeth O'Brien. Three years later the family moved to a solid four-storey Georgian house in fashionable Dame Street, a better address for his business, where they lived over the shop. Meantime the family and their expenses increased and the young Barnardos took in a lodger. By the winter of 1835, after eight years of happy marriage, Elizabeth had borne her husband six children, four boys and two girls. She died in August 1836 giving birth to her seventh child who survived her by only a month.

Left a widower at the age of thirty-six, with a business to run, a young family to support and no relatives of his own in the city, John Michaelis turned to his wife's younger sister, Abigail. Almost inevitably the couple grew close and within a year of his wife's death, John Michaelis asked Abigail O'Brien to marry him. The woman who was to become Tom Barnardo's mother appears determined, comely, with features too strong to be conventionally good-looking. Her portrait reveals a distinctly worldly young woman, with a low décolleté, earrings and a fur-edged shawl.

Before they could be married there were practical difficulties to circumvent. Marriage to the sister of a dead wife was still forbidden in British law so John Michaelis took his young bride to the German Church in London to have their union sanctified. A German pastor married them in June 1837, the month the young Queen Victoria came to the throne.

The marriage, so soon after his wife's death, to her sister must have set neighbours chattering particularly in Dublin, a city nourished by gossip. The Barnardo family, however, lived a busy, self-contained life in the heart of the city. The 'carriage trade' came to shop in Dame Street for silks, perfumes and furs; there was even a well-known shop which supplied the young bucks with specially carved walking sticks.

The second marriage proved as fruitful as the first. A son, Adolphus, was born but survived only until the age of two. Two more sons followed, George and Frederick, and on 4 July 1845 Abigail gave birth to her fourth son, Thomas John Barnardo.

Thomas was born when John Michaelis was middle-aged and beset by business worries. A few hours before the baby was delivered, the Wicklow and Wexford Railway Company, in which Barnardo senior had formerly invested successfully, went bankrupt. It was also the year of the great potato famine. From the autumn of that year until young Tom was almost four years old, more than a million Irish men and women died of starvation or emigrated.

More immediately at 4 Dame Street, the family was in confusion. Abigail, too weak to nurse the baby and pregnant yet again, was sent to relatives in the country to recuperate from the cares of family life. Protestant families in Dublin, who were greatly in the minority, felt more secure with servants of their own faith in that restless time but the need for a wet nurse was too pressing and a Roman Catholic girl was found to suckle the infant. She took the baby to the suburbs where she lived.

Tom's half-sister Sophia, by now seventeen and temporarily in charge of the household, visited him frequently. One summer's day she called and found the wet nurse had gone out and left the new baby lying dangerously close to an open window. Sophia bundled baby Tom into her arms and carried him back home to Dame Street. When the nurse, frantically worried about the missing child, came to the Barnardos' home, Sophia informed her indignantly that if she wanted to keep her job she must live in, where she could be supervised. Sophia became Tom's lifelong friend and protector.

Even in well-to-do families child mortality was high and Thomas was an unusually delicate baby. At the age of two, according to a family story, he fell gravely ill and after weeks of sickness was pronounced dead by two physicians. With the embalmer called in, the little body stirred and was snatched back thankfully from the grave.

The ravages of famine, a typhus epidemic in 1847 and rebellion in the streets reached even Dame Street where 'red jackets' were drafted into Trinity College to quell the starving Dubliners, armed with pikes and penknives.[3]

Business must have suffered too, for in August 1849 when Queen Victoria paid a state visit to the city, Dublin was in sombre mood. According to the *Evening Mail*, 'the greater number of good houses in Dame Street, Grafton Street and other principal thoroughfares are in a dirty and dilapidated condition, the windows broken, patched with brown paper or here and there studded with an old hat, the shops closed and the wooden shutters covered over.'[4]

Another more commonplace occurrence marred Tom's childhood. A baby brother, Henry Lionel, born a year later, soon took Tom's place as favourite. Visitors found Henry Lionel with his fair curly hair and his sweet singing voice an enchanting child and the little fellow was often sent for in the drawing-room where he would delight the company with his piping songs. Afterwards, to his brother's disgust, he would scamper downstairs beaming and scoffing the chocolates he had been given.

Young Tom's patience wore thin after these performances and one day he lashed out at Henry: 'Take that for showing off in the drawing-room and that, you pig, for eating all the chocolates yourself.'

As a philanthropist Barnardo wrote prolifically and sentimentally about poor children, published children's stories with a strong moral content and described his work, his life, his Christian faith in many different versions. Yet he rarely alluded to his own childhood and when he did it was with a cold anger. From a man given to weave stories the omission must be noted. Hints from other sources suggest that his childhood was stormy and far from happy.

According to the mores of the times, the family were outsiders, foreigners of mixed blood with a marriage which was barely acceptable. Thomas John Barnardo, the founder of the world's largest family, grew up in a household in which a habit of secrecy must have been second nature. He was also a small, sickly, rather plain-looking boy who did not go to school until he was ten years old. Fortunately his first experience of the classroom suited his temperament.

He began his studies at St Ann's Sunday school. Old-established, well run and small enough to offer the children individual stimulus and encouragement, the school was just what Tom needed. With his quick, natural understanding he flourished under the cheerful guidance of the rector, Mr Dickinson, and his curate, Mr Sanders. At home, Sophia proved a sympathetic teacher for his lessons.

At his first day school round the corner, St John's parish school, he was subject to more discipline and the experience was less happy. 'He gave no end of trouble,' wrote one of his brothers. 'He was never one of those very goody-goody boys who die early and go to heaven. He was full of fun and mischief, thoughtless and careless. He gave a great deal of trouble at home and he had a very strong and determined self will.'[5]

From St John's Tom transferred to the large, well-established St Patrick's Cathedral Grammar School which prepared boys for the university. He hated this school and his feelings for his headmaster, 'one of the biggest and most brutal bullies', carry forcefully across·the years. 'The Principal was a clergyman and a Doctor of Divinity,' he wrote years later, 'nevertheless the most cruel man as well as the most mendacious that I have ever in all my life met. He seemed to take a savage delight in beating his boys . . . I often wondered why those unhappy lads . . . ever had the courage to return, day after day. I am sure if I had been one of his victims . . . I never could have returned to school and awaited the torture.'[6] His headmaster's cruelty, he wrote, bred in him an 'intense disgust and loathing' for harsh treatment to children.

With his independent spirit Tom Barnardo was regarded as a trouble-maker. He mastered his lessons quickly and soon became bored with formal learning. Handicapped by his build and short sight, he disliked cricket and football and he took to reading voraciously, anything he could find, 'Not', according to his brother, 'always the best and most suitable books for his years.' Evidently his eloquent tongue, which was to prove such an asset in his philanthropic work, was a source of annoyance at school. His form was nicknamed 'Prater's Row'.

Nor was home life without trials. Tom was a natural rebel. In a revealing remark his brother recalled that young Tom 'always respected his father; to his beloved mother he was deeply attached with very true affection even from his earliest days'. All his life Tom's relationship with his father remained uneasy.

Perhaps the radical books that the young Barnardo read so eagerly, the writings of Rousseau, Voltaire, Thomas Paine, fired his mutinous spirit. But his wide reading could not substitute for textbook learning. Unlike his two brothers, George and Frederick, who had done well at St Patrick's and gone on to study medicine and theology respectively, Thomas John, the ablest of the three, did not distinguish himself at school. He did not even pass the public examinations. At the age of sixteen, Tom was apprenticed to a wine merchant, Robert Anderson, who years later was to support Barnardo in his work for children. Anderson knew Tom in his schooldays and remarked that he had rarely met a more self-centred individual or one 'less likely to do anything for anyone else, particularly for a dirty or diseased child'.[7]

The transformation process from wayward youth to born-again Christian remains a mysterious one. Until his conversion Thomas Barnardo gave no outward sign of a religious nature. He delighted to shock and boasted of being an agnostic. His parents attended church twice on

Sunday but although an office holder in church his father disliked 'public display' in religious matters. As an alien businessman, he was probably concerned to uphold his position in respectable society. (In 1860, when Tom was fifteen, his father became a naturalised Irishman and was appointed furrier to the Vice-Regal Court the same year. The appointment was important since the court led the fashion.)

As she grew older, his mother became more religious and she and two of her sons, George and Frederick, responded with ardour to the surge of religious feeling which swept across the Atlantic and from Ulster to the south. The revival, the 'old time religion' which had its roots in the American holiness camp fire meetings, aroused deep yearnings in the crowds who gathered to hear 'the Good News'. The Evangelicals distrusted formal religious teachings. They put their faith in the message of the gospels, in piety and repentance, and warned of the perils that faced sinners who would not mend their ways. Death figured largely in their imagery and the presence of death was very real in a city ravaged by poverty, famine and disease.

Two or three times a week, huge numbers gathered in the Metropolitan Hall, a large building in Abbey Street in which the crowds had once thrilled to the delights of the circus. Fervent preachers, the spiritual ancestors of Billy Graham, exhorted their audience to repent, to enlist for service in the Kingdom of God. Mrs Barnardo and her sons came home from those meetings charged with religious fire and zeal. Her husband remained unimpressed by the enthusiasm generated at the mass meetings; in court circles they were not fashionable. At first Tom could not be induced to join the 'hysterical' gatherings.

He mixed on the fringe of those who enjoyed the gay social life of the capital thanks to his work and adopted a cynical attitude to the religious fervour of the day. He dressed with care, ordering his suits from Dublin's best tailor, and affecting a silk hat, spotless white shirts and natty and carefully chosen neckwear.

The contrast between the gaieties of the Dublin social round, with fancy dress balls and theatres, and the appalling poverty of the slums was particularly stark in such a small city. The housing conditions were probably the worst in Europe, with the wretched hovels just a street away from elegant Georgian buildings. The Evangelicals promised the poorer classes salvation if they would repent and cling to their Bibles and exhorted the well-to-do middle class to seek moral regeneration.

Both his mother and his two brothers urged 'dear Tom' to accompany them to prayer meetings. They persuaded and cajoled. Flattered perhaps, he reluctantly agreed. At first he found the gatherings ludicrous. His family always stayed on after the meetings, to talk excitedly with other worshippers. Enthusiastic Christians would come up to young Tom and ask him if he had found Jesus.

'I used to think these people were mad,' he wrote to his sister,[8] but gradually, almost grudgingly, young Tom Barnardo began to respond to the religious fervour and to feel that there was 'some reality' in the Revival movement. For weeks he wrestled with doubts about the inspiration of the Scriptures. The large public meetings, with crowds verging on hysteria, left him unmoved. However, meetings were also held in private houses and in the more intimate, encouraging atmosphere of the drawing-room, Tom was susceptible to personal influence.

One evening he was induced to visit the home of William Fry, a wealthy Dublin solicitor. William Fry evidently saw beyond the cocky, irritating exterior of the young man and in a letter written to him years later, Barnardo recalled vividly what happened:

> I did not half like to go but I went there and in that meeting Rocheford Hunt spoke to me and so did you. I know I behaved very badly. I was just as cheeky as a young fellow can be, and I thought you looked at me as if you would say: 'If I had that young fellow alone for five minutes I would take down his conceit, I'd give him a good hiding.' But somehow your words were very kind and not in harmony with what I thought your looks meant and that was the beginning.[9]

Often the speakers were laymen, 'converts' who spoke in ringing tones of former sins and new-found grace. One of them, John Hambleton, a former tragic actor and repentant drunkard, was an orator of great passion and eloquence. After hearing Hambleton speak at a private prayer meeting, young Tom Barnardo was deeply impressed. He walked the mile to his home in silence.

'After coming in from prayer meeting, still dark and cold and dead within myself,' he recalled six months later, 'Fred asked me to go into his room after he went to bed. I went and he was in bed. He caught hold of me and remained in earnest entreaty with me for about an hour . . . It pleased the Almighty there and then to remove every doubt and difficulty.'[10]

Forty years later, Barnardo wrote another account of his conversion, stressing that his brother Fred and Dr Hunt were of great help to him, 'but I actually found Christ without any human intervention when alone, some days after a special interview with my brother Fred and Dr Hunt'.[11]

Whatever the circumstances, the conversion took place on 26 May 1862 when Tom was approaching his seventeenth birthday. His burning faith would change not only his own life but the lives of generations of destitute children.

Once converted, young Tom became a red-hot Evangelical, impatient to convert others, urgent for action. He obtained permission to teach a Bible class in the appropriately named ragged school, which singled out the most wretched and filthy of children for tuition on Sunday mornings. The fastidious young man shrank from the stench of the children and the bedlam that they created with the bawling of the babies, the cat-calls of their parents and the hooting and jeering of his pupils. He also held a smaller, more decorous Bible class for children of the well-to-do.

It was in the slums of Dublin, the notorious Liberties, 'the infernal regions', densely populated and regarded as dangerous by respectable citizens, that Barnardo began to prepare for his life's work. He visited the parents of his pupils, weeping with emotion as he prayed with them, leaving tracts and little packets of tea as he left their dingy, lice-infected hovels. Some responded to his preaching; most were steeped in 'super-stition, ignorance and whisky'. Gradually he gleaned an understanding of their privations. 'Had I a dog I would not kennel it where I found these immortal souls,' he said. This belief that they were souls in danger sustained him. The studious young man held classes for the large garrison of troops stationed in Dublin Castle and for the local police. He filled his bookshelves with religious books and commentaries and his leisure with pious duties. Yet he felt dissatisfied, with a growing belief of his God-given mission, in his power, and with an increasing knowledge of the physical and spiritual poverty in the city.

His mother and brothers had already become members of the Ply-mouth Brethren and he too became interested in the strict fundamentalist sect, and through them in George Muller, a German immigrant like his own father, who had settled in Bristol and founded an orphanage for boys. Muller was much admired in Brethren circles for his charitable work and for his deep, quiet faith.

In the autumn of 1862 Tom Barnardo, converted only a few months, wrote to the great man:

> I have for some time endeavoured to put by a little weekly out of my pocket-money for the Lord, and I am now desirous of your advice and counsel. Living in the heart of the city of Dublin I see daily around me numbers in a dying state, dying because they have not life eternal, and I am anxious with God's help to do something to arrest them on the brink of ruin, but I am so very young, being a lad of only seventeen years; but I have been thinking lately that if I, in connection with young Christian friends were to hire a room for one night in the

week and there with those friends hold a revival prayer meeting the Lord would bless us. I have been bringing the matter for some time back before the Lord and today after rising from my knees the finger of the Lord appeared to point me to you and to abide by your advice.[12]

The letter has a touching sincerity and a rare note of humility but Muller was not impressed. He replied coolly, advising the boy to study the word of God in private. That sober advice was not what young Barnardo wanted to hear.

About that time he was seeking to deepen his faith. In a notebook he kept a spiritual journal which opened with a prayer in October 1862: 'Oh Lord God! Grant that nought but the word of TRUTH may be written in these pages and . . . that . . . I may seek THY GLORY rather than my own, THY PRAISE rather than the praises of men. "Blessed is he that considereth the poor." '[13] He prayed to be protected from the frivolity of thoughtless companions (probably colleagues in the wine trade). He prayed for his father and brothers and sisters who were not saved and invoked divine mercy for them in their 'terrible condition'.

All Evangelicals, whatever their religious status, had to be 'converted'. Now Tom Barnardo wanted to demonstrate his commitment even further by undergoing a 'believers' baptism'. His spiritual journal records his misgivings at telling his father about the forthcoming ceremony for John Barnardo had little patience with what he considered as his son's excessive religiosity. He did not withhold consent but would not accompany Tom to the ceremony. His mother and his elder brothers, Fred and George, escorted him to church as well as his sister Celia.

Not long afterwards Tom left the Church of Ireland to join the Brethren. At their centre, Merrion Hall, he became a Sunday school teacher and worker, speaking to the boys with such intensity and energy that one lad was converted on the spot.

He also joined the Dublin YMCA in Sackville Street and often addressed them. In his teens he was as pugnacious as a preacher as he had been truculent as a schoolboy. On speaking to a sinner who took little notice, Tom prayed that his words would 'cleave to him and give no rest either day or night till the matter is finally settled between him and his God'. Years later, one of the young men drawn to the work, John Johnston, recalled the 'strongly marked and aggressive quality of Tom Barnardo's religious life'.[14]

Evidently young Barnardo had to work hard to keep his hot temper in check. A colleague from the Swift's Alley Mission, Richard Owens, always carried a cane or umbrella with him. Tom Barnardo remarked on the habit and confessed one day that he had recently decided to leave his walking stick at home when he visited the slums because 'the boys so annoyed me, gathering round me in the street that I lost patience and had all I could do to keep from striking them with the walking stick. If I had, it would have killed my work with the Lord, so I left it at home after that.'[15]

That same colleague who guided Tom Barnardo on his first visits to the slums was struck by his sincerity: 'When I called to go with him, he took me into a room in his father's house and having talked with me he knelt and prayed earnestly, not only for those we were to visit but for wisdom and grace for ourselves.'

When he was not at business, he was hurrying out to visit the poor or attend a prayer meeting. When he was at home, he would retire to his room straight after dinner, to study, meditate or engage in prayer. What Tom's father made of the fanatical attachment to the Scriptures and good works in his household is not recorded. A photograph of his wife, Tom Barnardo's mother, taken in middle age, shows her as a decorous lady with lace collar, bonnet and shawl, a book, very probably the Bible, clutched in her hand, a great contrast to the dashing young woman Barnardo had married. The household at that time was deeply divided.

Meantime young Tom applied himself to his Christian social work with a diligence that had been totally lacking in his school work. Despite Muller's advice, he did hire rooms in Aungier Street with his brothers and held prayer meetings there. He even took a hall in the Liberties, where his gospel meetings met with jeers and cat-calls from the ribald audience.

When he went to hear other Evangelical preachers address an audience he took a note pad with him. He studied the Old and New Testaments with intense application as his sermon notes, made years later, reveal. His detailed knowledge and love of the sonorous language, the vivid imagery, the powerful stories in the Bible proved one of his most potent weapons in his crusade for children. By the time he was eighteen years old, young Barnardo had found a platform, a voice, a cause.

Nothing is known of his work in the wine trade; he never referred to it. For four years, from sixteen to twenty, he went to business every day, including Saturdays. By now, he certainly knew that his real apprenticeship lay in his visits to the poor and his study of the Scriptures. Influential men in the missionary movement marked him as outstanding, and as his missionary work grew so his interest in his daily occupation flagged.

Dr Grattan Guinness, a leading evangelist who had campaigned all over the world to prepare young men for Christian work, held a small theological class at his home and Tom joined the élite group. In February

1866 Dr Guinness travelled to Liverpool to hear a young missionary, Hudson Taylor, speak on the Inland China Mission he had founded. Hudson Taylor was in England to raise money for his mission and to revise the Ningpo New Testament. Greatly impressed with the man and his message Dr Guinness invited him to Dublin to Merrion Hall to address Evangelicals on his mission. He also asked his own class whether they would like to hear the missionary from China in a private setting. The young men were all would-be missionaries and they responded enthusiastically.

Before the visit they read Hudson Taylor's pamphlet on his work, 'China's spiritual needs and claims'. On the appointed evening the young men waited in a buzz of excitement until Dr Guinness entered the drawing-room, followed by a slight, fair-haired, unassuming stranger, even smaller in stature than Tom Barnardo.

'Is he the great man?' Tom Barnardo whispered to a fellow student, John MacCarthy. When Hudson Taylor was introduced, Barnardo turned to murmur to MacCarthy, 'Good, then there's a chance for me.'

They listened to the missionary's account of China's national disintegration, the staggering social problems, and lack of spiritual leadership, and when Hudson Taylor spoke of 'a million a month dying in China without knowing Christ' they felt the inspiration of his words. At the end of the evening four young men stayed on to meet Hudson Taylor and volunteer to serve in China, Tom Barnardo among them.

Tom's father was horrified at the outlandish plan and made it clear that Tom could not expect financial support from him if he really meant to go to China. But the converted members of his family gave him their support and three of the elders among the Brethren agreed to provide him with a small subsistence allowance. The plan was that he should first study medicine; friends from the YMCA gave him a letter of introduction to the London Hospital.

Tom Barnardo's lively imagination soared at the prospect of foreign service. He saw himself there already and wrote a poem, 'God's Call to China':

> Speed away, speed away
> To the lands that are lying in darkness and night.

Even his father's displeasure could not dampen his enthusiasm. He wrote in his Bible: 'Tom Barnardo: China'.[16]

2

The Opportunity

'There exists ... in this city ... vast numbers of children who can only be spoken of as "arab" and "gutter" children.'

Annual Report, 1874–5

In the spring of 1866 Tom Barnardo arrived in London buoyed up by religious fervour and personal ambition but with little else to sustain him. Three elders of the Plymouth Brethren provided him with a small allowance and he held letters of introduction to the Brethren in Stepney and from the Dublin YMCA to Christian workers in London. He settled in the swarming East End, close to dockland where children in tattered clothes peddled fruit, matches and newspapers or begged for a night's shelter.

In the East End the new railway lines cut through former residential areas and pitched out thousands of families from their homes at a time when the dispossessed from rural areas and Irish immigrants fleeing from starvation were flooding in. The sheer numbers involved (London had a higher illegitimate birthrate than anywhere else in the world) defeated the Poor Law authorities and caused chaos.

A growing social segregation, aided by new public transport, the horse bus and the railway, distanced rich and poor. Fashionable ladies from the West End of town, who flocked to see Henry Irving's debut at the St James's Theatre that year, knew nothing of life in the East End. Only sensation seekers went slumming to see the cock and rat fighting or visit the prostitutes in the area. Respectable people with means, however small, moved out.

By the 1860s an increasing number of individuals, church workers, missionaries, philanthropists, had moved in to settle among the poor, to visit them in their own homes and to found missions, schools and churches and to relieve the moral and physical degradation of the slums. For them, it was an opportunity. Tom Barnardo lodged with fellow students at the house of a Mrs Mary Parsons of 30 Coburn Street, Stepney, amongst paupers, parish authorities, Poor Law Guardians, seamen, labourers and preachers. In Dublin, he had been able to slip back to his comfortable home after visiting the poor, but in the vastness of London he was penned in by the slums. On the streets, the clatter of ironshod horses, the shouts of street vendors, the rumble and roar of the railways met his ears; the stench from the 'stink factories' in the area, rubber, chemical and manure, as well as rotting refuse and open sewers, fouled the air. Yet for Tom Barnardo the vast city of London, 'the emporium of crime and the Palladian of Christianity', was a backcloth. At the time he could afford to ignore it all, caught up in the exciting prospect of a future in China. With fellow students he embarked on an intensive course of study and prayer preparatory to the mission led by Dr Hudson Taylor.

In his sermon notes on St Paul's letters, Barnardo commented: 'If we read the New Testament carefully we must see that the writers of it were men terribly in earnest.'[1] Barnardo underlined those words. He himself was 'terribly in earnest' but his very intensity made him intolerant, unable to accept guidance. He openly criticised Hudson Taylor's methods of running his mission to China. The audacity of the young man was a source of 'great amusement' to the missionary but made him an unpopular candidate.[2] Tom Barnardo was a protégé of the Brethren and he upheld their principles with uninhibited ardour. The sect strictly forbade members from falling into debt and Tom Barnardo had the gall to criticise Hudson Taylor for his mismanagement of the financial affairs of his mission. That irritated as well as amused the founder of the Mission to China and before long he decided that the young man needed to gain more experience and maturity before undertaking missionary work abroad.[3] A plan was tentatively drawn up for Barnardo to begin his medical studies and go to the East later.

In May 1866, six weeks after Barnardo had arrived in London, Hudson Taylor sailed back to China aboard the SS *Lammermuir*, taking a party of 'fine young men', Barnardo's fellow students, with him. When the ship was out of sight, Tom Barnardo realised that he was now really alone, his hopes of a foreign mission deferred, his business career jettisoned, living in Stepney on a very tight budget.

The true story of Tom Barnardo's life in his first year in London remains misted over. In later years he studiously dated his rescue work with children and his medical studies from 1866. For over a century the Barnardo charity accepted that date as authentic until Gillian Wagner's authoritative biography proved otherwise. However, Barnardo himself wrote in his first Annual Report (1867–8): 'I put forth an appeal in *The Revival* [a Christian journal] in which I stated my desire to reach by extraordinary and special methods some of the young tough lads and boys and also the girls and young women of Stepney.'[4] That appeal appeared in July 1867. From May 1866 until the summer of the following year we have only Barnardo's evidence of his activities. Certainly he was not registered as a medical student until 1867.

As he grew in age and reputation he embellished and elaborated his early history. The first hint of his activities after the China party had left London lies in a letter from his mother written in the spring of 1867: 'I dare say you remember that when you were in Paris last spring I wrote to you an earnest, anxious letter, because of the dangers by which you were surrounded. You replied in so satisfied a manner, saying that you were never more happy in soul, that my lips were closed on the subject and my pen stopped – yet my heart was not glad; the very reply only increased my anxiety.'[5]

No trace of that first visit exists or has ever been found. Barnardo himself often referred to the cholera epidemic which broke out in July 1866 and brought a terrible toll of death to Stepney. Every morning a Pickford's van pulled up at the London Hospital near his lodgings, to carry away the dead. In three months the outbreak had claimed over 3,000 victims. In the hospital the wards were strewn with sawdust soaked in carbolic, and even the doctors were at a loss to treat the dying. Barnardo had no medical qualifications but, according to his own account, he made house calls in the fever-stricken streets to comfort and preach to the dying. To hurry through streets stinking of decay to hovels where the dying lay vomiting took great courage. But courage both moral and physical he possessed, and he seemed to be driven to the task. Perhaps he was able to purge his very marked sense of sin through those grim visits. One day he witnessed sixteen people die. The experience served as his university in social work. 'But for that epidemic I should never have known Stepney and all its horrors,' he wrote later.

The cholera epidemic helped to 'solemnise' men's minds, Barnardo wrote. At that time he was greatly influenced by the belief of the Plymouth Brethren in the Second Coming of Jesus Christ and the need for men to repent before Judgement Day. He did not hesitate to preach the perils of eternal damnation to crowds of half-starved East End no-hopers. 'There are many here who will never see the first Sunday of 1875,' he thundered in a sermon eight years later. 'Yet you have heard the truth for twelve months and you are still unconverted and God has suffered you to live unpunished ... do you think it will always be thus?'[6]

His sermons with their immediacy, their reference to the Bible, to contemporary events, mesmerised the crowds. 'I was in East London unknown, comparatively friendless and without influence,' he wrote later, 'yet all around me were men and women, boys and girls steeped in ignorance whose souls needed the illumination of the Gospel.'[7] In the early days of his work, it was his preaching and his sense of drama that made his name.

In the spring of 1867, he was again due to visit Paris accompanied by ten other missionaries to distribute Bibles on behalf of the Brethren at an international exhibition. Mr Berger, Hudson Taylor's London agent, felt misgivings about Barnardo and disapproved of the excursion despite the pious purpose. But Tom Barnardo, as usual, went his way.

His mother followed his work from Dublin with anxious concern and wrote to warn him of the dangers of working in the limelight:

And now dear Tom: I charge you in the name of Jesus to go alone to God and ask Him in humble earnestness to lay bare your own heart before Him. Are you seeking the praise of men? Do you love to be approved by them? Do you indulge the flesh as to food, dress, frivolity, excitement? ... The very work which you have undertaken makes you, as it were, 'a city set on a hill'. Oh! my son! See to it that the light which proceeds from that city be not a false light. You are one of those who should work for Jesus; do it faithfully for His sake – not for your own sake – for the sake of those precious souls who gather round you Sunday after Sunday.[8]

What his mother had sensed, perhaps rightly, was that the gifted young man was gaining awareness of his own power, of the heady experience of holding an audience. Back in London in 1867 Barnardo scavenged for souls in his eagerness. He foraged in beerhouses, among the festering courts and slums of Stepney. One day he was roughed up by a rowdy crowd, suffered two broken ribs but refused to prosecute his assailants. That gained him respect from the East End rowdies. He also haunted the penny 'gaffs', the gaudy little 'theatres' which offered children lurid tales of swaggering highwaymen and cringing victims. He came to know and loathe those dens and one night he paid his penny and leapt on the stage, offering the children cheap Bibles for sale and the solace of religion instead of the cheap melodramas they had come to see. So eloquent was the small Irishman that when the manager forced him off the stage, a fascinated crowd followed him to the front of the house.

His first public announcement of his preaching was in *The Revival* in July 1867. The young preacher, earnest, impassioned, his eyes closed in devotion as he chanted psalms, must have presented an irresistible target to the street people. Rotten eggs and mouldy fruit were often pelted at him, refuse and chamber pots emptied from tenement windows. One young marksman kneaded pellets out of mud and shied a mud egg straight into Barnardo's open mouth, effectively plugging him. 'We were not discouraged,' Barnardo wrote in *The Revival*. 'We laboured chiefly on the Lord's Day sometimes giving four or five addresses in different localities, on the same day.' What struck him, he wrote, was that half of his audience were children, a quarter their parents and the remainder 'thieves and lost women', in effect young men and women between the ages of thirteen and twenty-eight.[9] Those early experiences convinced him of the desperate need of poor children.

He learnt other lessons, too. He often stopped to stand and listen to William Booth, founder of the Salvation Army, preaching on a text on Mile End Waste on behalf of his 'Christian Mission to the Heathen of our country'. Barnardo took note of the military style and insignia, the music and the slogans of the bearded preacher who offered 'soup and salvation' to the benighted poor.

In his first year in Stepney Barnardo found work teaching poor children in a ragged school in Ernest Street off the Mile End Road. The school was small, with low ceilings; the children were taught in a narrow and badly ventilated room which seated eighty-six. In summer it was stuffy, in winter overcrowded.

He was a gifted teacher and soon gained a reputation for being able to hold his own among his pupils. The hardened children (a third of his class at least had been in prison) thought at first that their new teacher would prove an easy target. A group of them ganged up on him one Sunday and dumped him out of the first-floor window. Barnardo merely dusted himself down and made a dignified return. Though small, he had a formidable presence which won the children's respect. He knew that many of them lived in squalid lodging houses or with their parents, crowded eight to ten to a room; others found the streets an escape from the grim charity of the workhouse. He knew, too, that the authorities would only concern themselves with the children if they committed a crime or loitered in the streets.

At the school his diligent work was soon recognised; he was promoted to superintendent and given a place on the school board. In his eagerness to press further with the work for the children he over-reached himself. In July 1867 he wrote to *The Revival*, heading his letter 'Important Ragged School Work in the East End'. In it he outlined a plan to rescue the boys and girls he had to turn away from his ragged school each week. He proposed, he wrote, to hold a large tea-meeting service on Sunday evenings for boys and girls at risk and asked forty or fifty Evangelicals to join him and made his first public appeal for funds. His letter brought him donations of £90 and an offer of rooms for his tea but it also cost him his job. He had not asked the school committee for permission to raise funds or to use their name. To Barnardo, this merely presented another opportunity. He learnt to use the press very early, for he wrote another letter to *The Revival* announcing his resignation from the ragged school and informing the public that he had decided to concentrate his energies on the larger enterprise. Impatient as always to begin he decided to hold his first tea before he had reached his financial target of £200.

On 5 November 1867, twenty-two-year-old Barnardo entertained the remarkable number of 2,347 children, 'a large proportion of the older ones being thieves and poor lost girls', in the assembly rooms over the King's Arms at the corner of the Mile End Road. At his first independent effort at youth work the children scoffed the tea and buns and drowned the missionary's preaching. However, he persisted until most of the crowd had drifted out and left a handful of older lads. Eventually he succeeded in making himself heard above the din. 'More than one poor wanderer professed to find peace in believing,' he noted.[10]

For six successive Sundays Barnardo and his helpers paraded the streets of Stepney singing hymns, carrying banners and drumming up the recruits (about 600 each time) for the meeting and free tea. On the seventh Sunday, with the tea and buns already paid for, a new landlord at the King's Arms refused Barnardo and his helpers admission two hours before the tea was due to begin. The publican was afraid that Barnardo's mission was enticing his customers away from the bar. Once again his extraordinary efforts to establish himself as a missionary had failed. Tom Barnardo had poured his creative energy, his future hopes into it. Now that he had failed, he fell ill with a mysterious ailment which was to recur at times of great disappointment.

Some weeks earlier, in September 1867, Tom Barnardo had travelled to Durham to take the registration examination for medical students, presumably as a safeguard if he failed to gain a place at the London Hospital. By November he was registered as a student at the London Hospital, and began his studies. Early in January 1868 he wrote to Hudson Taylor's agent, Mr Berger, pouring out his deep longing to go to China and assuring Mr Berger of his progress: 'I am now in my *second* winter session,' he wrote, 'and with God's help I have worked hard, having up to this been enabled to dissect two complete subjects.' He had also, he said, 'attended all lectures, including special courses upon eye and skin diseases and attended sixty-four maternity cases for the hospital.'[11] He explained that at the end of their second winter session, students had to pass the anatomical and physiological examinations at the Royal College of Surgeons and could then go on to study surgery and medicine. However, he confided to Mr Berger his plan to circumvent the system. He would 'read up with all the men and attend the special classes for them during the coming three months as if I were indeed going up with them at the April exam. In this way I will, with God's help, know as much as those who do go up, the difference simply being that they will have been examined and I will not.' Then he hoped to 'get or pay for' three months' in-patient dressing in the hospital, a few months at the ophthalmic and skin disease hospitals, attending at the same time the physicians' and surgeons' wards and clinical instruction. By November 1868 he confidently hoped to be ready to go to China. In other words Tom Barnardo had decided to slide over the slight matter of examinations and concentrate four years' work into one. Undoubtedly a large element in Barnardo's success was his audacity. Berger acknowledged his talent yet found him personally obnoxious. 'He is so overbearing that it tries some of us a little,' he wrote to Hudson Taylor in China. 'He is doing a great work in the East End of London and gaining valuable experience, especially in the wise use of money, for he is naturally fast and spends his money far too freely and unthinkingly . . . and gets behind in his payments, so he will not be so forward to judge others who do likewise.'[12] Fortunately Berger did persuade Tom Barnardo to take his preliminary examination. By the end of 1868 Barnardo still yearned to go to China but felt he could not give up his work until he had found a successor. He moved to a terrace house in Bromley Street and took lodgings with a Mrs Johnson, a sailor's wife. That was to be a significant move.

After convalescing from his illness in March 1868 he first rented a small room in a poor street, then found two four-roomed cottages in a 'nice retired court' in Hope Place, Stepney, a blind alley. This location was useful for his purposes with 'hundreds, if not thousands, of poor little ones living almost within the sound of one's own voice'. That was the beginning of his systematic work with children. He immediately segregated the sexes, with one house as a school for boys and one for girls. Barnardo himself wove an elaborate web of folklore, with Christian overtones, around his early work. His work began in a donkey stable, he wrote in 1900, but his most recent biographer found no evidence for that story. A contemporary account of his work by George Holland, a sympathetic fellow worker, provides more reliable evidence. After attending a meeting at Hope Place, Mr Holland described the busy mission: 'there are held weekly special services for children; Bible classes for men, women and children, mothers' meetings, girls' sewing classes, a special service attended every evening of the week by an average of 130 lads. A little church has also been formed, numbering to this date nearly 90 souls (adult) . . . The total weekly expenses are about £4 10s.'[13]

Barnardo also instituted a penny savings bank (depositors of one shilling were entitled to free use of the library) and a shoeblack brigade.

In his first Annual Report, 'The first Occasional Record of the Lord's dealings in connexion with the East End Juvenile Mission', he made full acknowledgment to the Limehouse shoeblack brigade who took the boys he recommended. He also announced his intention 'to provide our own uniform and badges with the distinctive name of our mission'. From that day to this, the organisation he founded has been insistent on labelling, formalising and maintaining a distinctive and flamboyant Barnardo identity. The name of Barnardo has served them well.

Tom Barnardo's plans bore the mark of a fertile mind. He knew from his own experience the value of a good story. His 'Boys' Reading Room' which, he claimed, was unique, tempted boys into a bright, warm room to read improving and entertaining books and illustrated papers. He soon discovered that many of the street lads could not read. Resourceful as ever, he enlisted a helper to read to them. Around the fire, sixty or seventy boys would huddle to listen, with varying degrees of attention, to suitable stories from *Uncle Tom's Cabin* or *Pilgrim's Progress*.

He arranged for boys in work to subsidise, to some extent, their less well-off brothers. Many of the lads who were employed during the day joined his evening school and he charged them one or two pennies a week for four nights in winter. (Tuition was free in the summer.)

Barnardo's observations on the privation and poverty in the East End at the time reveal a growing involvement in the social as well as the spiritual conditions of the poor. He had entered the work for missionary purposes to wage a 'fight with London's sin and vice', to pluck souls from the flames. Faced with the reality of poverty and unemployment, he was anxious to help the wretchedly poor to retain self-respect. He advocated a form of sheltered workshop rather than dole money, a penny savings scheme and the sale of cheap food and clothing, rather than handouts. Imagination always informed his work and he employed funds given to him to relieve distress in redeeming workmen's tools from nearby pawn shops.

The wretchedness, the hunger, the despair were present for all to see and many preachers and reformers had drawn attention to them. Barnardo dramatised and personalised the poverty. He almost invented the street waif. Although today his style may seem histrionic and sentimental, it was largely this style that saved the children. He conveyed a sense of urgency and solemnity in his stories of the dying who repented at the eleventh hour, of tiny children, naked and starving, snatched from the gutter. Barnardo was liberal in the use of capital letters, italics, exclamation marks, phrases that captured the imagination; he also had a useful journalistic instinct for using his material in different forms for different audiences. He wrote prolifically, effortlessly, and had begun to earn a small income from writing in religious papers and from preaching engagements.

Other settlers in Stepney, concerned to reform social conditions rather than rescue individuals, wrote in more sober tones of the district. For Edward Denison, the son of a bishop, later an MP, it was spiritual poverty rather than lack of food or disease that afflicted his Stepney neighbours: 'What is so bad is the habitual condition of this mass of humanity in its uniform mean level, the absence of anything more civilising than a grinding organ to raise the ideas beyond the daily bread and beer, the utter want of education, the complete indifference of religion.'[14]

From the beginning Barnardo made a direct and very forceful appeal for funds. Despite criticism, he was not content to imitate his boyhood ideal, George Muller of Muller's Orphanage, who relied solely on prayer to supply his needs. He told the public boldly what he wanted: £3 a week, or £3 10s. in winter, would meet the needs of the mission. He also appealed for old clothes, tracts and books for the library. His first Annual Report showed that the East End Juvenile Mission had received £214 15s. and Barnardo was able to balance the books.

At that stage of his life, just turned twenty-three, he was preaching frequently and fervently, teaching, supervising, visiting the poor as well as studying medicine. If he had any time for personal life, as a single man in a big city, it was never mentioned. He drove himself and his sheer energy imbued his supporters with a sense of urgency. From his report it is clear that the work was beginning to fill his life, despite his original intention of going to China. He was excited by the opportunity to enlarge the work and the buildings.

> I ought to say that great sorrow often fills my heart as I see the people who come to the preaching compelled to go away because we have not sufficient space . . . A builder has assured us that by an expenditure of £65 we might so alter the premises as to obtain a hall capable of seating about 250 people. And if we add £30 to this sum for gas-fittings, seats, etc. the whole would come to but £95. We look forward to this small sum soon being received.[15]

Barnardo followed up his appeal in his report by a notice in *The Revival* asking for money for a hall and by a second announcement appealing for a successor to take over his work so that he could, at last, take up his missionary work in China.

Evidently his threat of leaving the work touched the conscience of at least one reader of *The Revival*. Samuel Smith, a wealthy Liverpool businessman, who was later to become Member of Parliament for that city, wrote to Barnardo offering him a large sum of money if he would give up any idea of going to China and concentrate his talents on working for the poor in the East End of London. The money was intended for a hall for his evangelistic work but, in the course of time, as the name of Barnardo became synonymous with children, the sum grew larger and the money was said to be earmarked for a home for orphan children in Barnardo's reconstruction of his past. In his make-up business acumen blended with Evangelical fervour. He saw in that unexpected offer from Liverpool a sign, the sign, perhaps, that he had been waiting for, that he must give up China to work among the children of East London.

Again the sequence of events is overlaid by Barnardo's weaving of tales. What is certain is that in his very brief Annual Report on the East End Juvenile Mission, 1870–1, T. J. Barnardo announced that he had 'clearly seen his way to give up all hopes and prospects of labouring in a foreign mission'.

In the summer of 1870 he finally achieved his ambition of lodging children of the streets. He rented a house in a mean street, 18 Stepney Causeway, for £57 a year including rates. In his dealings with property he was immensely practical. He hired a carpenter, painter, plumber and gasfitter to make the house habitable for fifty boys and furnished it with dormitories, bathrooms, a kitchen and wash-house and a private room for the 'godly brother and his wife', a schoolmaster and his wife who were to manage the home. In a very short time he ran out of money and dismissed the builder and the workmen, making sure that his influential Evangelical friends heard all about the half-completed work. (At that time Barnardo was still convinced that to fall into debt was morally wrong.) The editor of *The Christian*, a personal friend, appealed for funds to finish the work and Barnardo wrote later that he and his friends spent 'many a happy hour in whitewashing walls and ceilings, scrubbing floors and otherwise making the place habitable for a family'.

By December 1870 he had opened his first residential home and installed thirty-three 'bairns' in it. At the opening ceremony Barnardo 'asked no outside friends, invited no subscribers but held a simple service of dedication with the boys'.[16]

His 'bairns' were grown youths divided into three categories: good, steady, respectable lads who needed a comfortable home and could afford to pay for it; unemployed youths who were given work in the home and taught self-reliance; and wholly destitute boys who were clothed, fed, housed and taught simple trades. According to the accounts, Barnardo received a total annual payment of £53 2s. 6d. from his lodgers. He naturally highlighted the most sensational work among the utterly bereft.

Later the accounts of the good steady respectable lads who helped to pay for the cost of the home were dropped from Annual Reports. Presumably the boys left the home.

As an entrepreneur, Barnardo proved brilliant. He borrowed money to buy wood for his woodchopping brigade before he opened the Boys' Home, and advertised their wares; in the first year the boys gained an occupation and an income and the home a modest profit.

During that first year in the Boys' Home, Barnardo again suffered an illness for four months and was unable to compile more than a two-page report, he explained. Donations in 1871 amounted to over £3,000. He was selling his first Annual Report (originally priced 4d.) at 6d; he had written a little booklet 'Labours of Love among our East End Arabs' for 1d. These sales, together with his novel idea of selling packets of photographs of his 'waifs', began to produce an income and interest in his work.

Until he opened his Boys' Home, Barnardo had been a teacher and missionary, known only to a small circle. Every year his reputation grew and every year in his Annual Reports he outlined plans to expand the work, to house yet more children. His first account of the inspiration for his work, 'How it all Happened', appeared in 1872. He told and retold the story in different versions in his lifetime and generations of children came to know it after his death, yet it still holds appeal.

One winter's evening at about half past nine when he and his helpers were about to leave the ragged school to go home, they noticed a little boy by the fire. When asked where he lived he replied 'nowhere' and pleaded to stay in the warm all night.

> It was a very cold night, for although there had been no snow or wet during the day, the sharp and biting wind seemed to penetrate every joint . . . and as we looked at the little lad whom the Lord had sent to us and noticed how ill-prepared he was to resist the vicissitudes of the weather our heart sank as we silently reflected: if all this boy says is true how much he must have suffered! Then for the first time we asked ourselves the question. Is it possible that in this great city there are others as young as this boy, as helpless, as ill-prepared to meet the trial of cold and hunger and exposure of every kind?

That night the boy, Jim Jarvis, took Barnardo out to see for himself one of the 'lays' where homeless children huddled for warmth, astride the iron roof of an old clothes market off Petticoat Lane. The sight of them 'with their heads upon the higher part of the roof and their feet somewhat in the gutter' haunted Barnardo all his life: 'At that moment, standing there alone, in the still silence of the night with sleeping London all around me, I felt so powerless to help these poor fellows, that I did not dare to interrupt their slumbers. It was to me a revelation and a message.'[17]

Another revelation came to Barnardo when he questioned Jim Jarvis about his religion. He asked the orphan if he had ever heard of Jesus. 'Yes, sir,' came the reply, 'I knows about him . . . HE'S THE POPE OF ROME.' Barnardo was appalled, gave up his questioning and 'drawing his chair and my own close to the bright fire, I told him slowly and in the simplest language . . . the wonderful story of the Babe born in Bethlehem'. At least twenty years earlier, Lord Ashley had roamed the slum district and written of the 'squalid and half-naked groups' of children in the courts and alleys. But he lacked Barnardo's illuminating pen, his talent for telling a story.

Dates and details of that night with homeless children can, perhaps, never be traced, but Barnardo was deeply affected. He was to repeat the story many times but never with more effect than at his first public meeting. One Sunday evening Barnardo, a missionary medical student still in his early twenties, was invited to sit on the platform at a conference on foreign missionary work held at the Agricultural Hall, Islington. During the meeting two or three of the main speakers sent word that they were unable to attend. The chairman, the Reverend Thain Davidson, turned to Barnardo who was sitting beside him and asked him to tell the audience about his ragged school in the East End of London. Tom Barnardo almost froze with fright. Since he was a youth he had spoken in public to small groups of poor people or children, but he had never before addressed a large formal gathering. However, as soon as he began to speak he sensed the audience's response to his oratory and his passion. He described 'the most pitiable children one can imagine, homeless and friendless, foodless and clad only in rags. And I dwelt on the pity of it and the sorrow of the fact that no one seemed to care for the souls of these outcasts.'[18] When the meeting was over a young servant girl came up to the platform and shyly thrust a brown paper parcel at Barnardo. She had been saving up from her earnings for months for heathen children in far-off lands, but after hearing Barnardo speak of children in the East End she begged him to accept her money, twenty-seven farthings, for 'his poor children'. Never before had Tom Barnardo had money pressed into his hand and he felt awkward. That, too, became a sign to him that the work must go on and the story of the twenty-seven farthings became part of the folklore of the great Barnardo charity.

The mission boys in their smart uniform of indigo tunic and trousers piped with scarlet, with matching cap, soon became known in the district.

Two or three nights a week Barnardo, lantern in hand, his pockets stuffed with buns and halfpennies, would go out at midnight to their haunts in the slums where he could 'catch' destitute boys. When he had gathered up two or three and persuaded them of the benefits of life in his home, he would take them back to Stepney Causeway. There each child would be photographed before his filthy rags were soaked or cut off and, again, in his new uniform and cropped hair. The photographs tickled the public's interest with their novelty. The following day each boy was allotted a household task.

By 1870 when Barnardo opened his home for destitute boys, charitable activity was flourishing throughout the country. In London alone there were over 640 different charitable bodies with an annual income of nearly two and a half million pounds.[19] London also housed fourteen asylums for orphan children. Barnardo was not so much a pioneer as a brilliant entrepreneur who took over ideas and adapted them on a scale and in a style which made them uniquely his own.

Within a year of opening his Boys' Home he had doubled his activity and the income of the home. He built workshops, fitted workrooms, started a city messengers' brigade, brushmaking and bootmaking departments and a tract department for the sale of improving literature. He opened up a new branch ragged school in Salmon's Lane and employed twenty-four 'staff' including cook, drill-master, trade manager and two schoolmasters in the home and teachers, door keepers and a sick visitor and Bible woman in the mission. His hot dinners and soups were famous in Stepney. And both the boys' work (the woodchoppers sold wood to the value of £765) and the tract shop were 'driving a fair business'.

In the 1871–2 report he reiterated his principles: we never beg for money for the Lord's work; do not go into debt; do not publish the names and addresses of donors. However, he did permit himself to publish what he described as 'suggestive possibilities'. £15 would keep a street boy in the home, fed, clothed and taught for a year; £1 5s. would do the same for a month; 6s. for a week and 13s. 6d. would give a good hot dinner to 100 little ragged boys. Nothing was left to chance. He gave explicit instructions about making up parcels, making out cheques and ordering goods; he even included a form of bequest 'to be paid with all convenient speed'.

For the first years the mission activities and Barnardo's preaching in particular provoked the greatest interest. In the summer of 1872 he set up a huge tent to seat 3,000 outside the Edinburgh Castle public house. Nightly, 200 people in the heated assembly would profess conversion. 'The scenes we are permitted to witness,' Barnardo wrote, 'are such as

I never remember beholding during any previous period of my spiritual life. Last Lord's Day evening twenty-five hundred persons crowded to hear the word of Life and for hours afterwards we were occupied in dealing with anxious souls, pointing them to Jesus and in meeting the wants of those who thronged around to touch his garments.' By contrast, at the pub across the way which he visited with two fellow workers, 'the scene that met our eyes burned itself deep . . . A roaring drink trade was going on and, on the stage, songs were being sung which won applause in strict proportion to the filthy *doubles entendres*. Round the room in niches of the wall were statues of the nude, which I suppose would be considered all the more artistic in that they were disgusting to decent people.'[20]

Through his experience with his lost boys, Barnardo was convinced that the 'drink curse' lay behind much of the family distress in the East End. To counter the attractions of the pub, Barnardo enlisted Fiddler Jos, 'free and easy on the violin', and his wife Mary, whom the reformed drunkard had once knocked into the gutter. The trio attracted enormous crowds during the summer. By October 1872 as a result of the counter-attractions of the tent services, the Edinburgh Castle was up for sale. In a letter to *The Christian* Barnardo pointed out that the building, 'a splendid house containing eighteen rooms . . . and ground sufficiently large to enable us, if necessary, to hold open-air tent services in fine weather', was for sale for £4,000. He was fearful, he wrote, that it would be re-opened as a concert and music hall. He prayed that the Castle would be bought instead for holy service. The Chairman of the Stock Exchange, Samuel Gurney Sheppard, was so moved by Barnardo's argument that he subscribed £1,000; others followed suit. On the day of the sale, Barnardo was short of over £1,100. He felt impelled to take a risk and paid the deposit. His faith was justified when within the fortnight's grace period he had received the balance in donations. His trustees included a number of leading Evangelicals, so that he now had supporters among wealthy and influential individuals.

His work in converting the Edinburgh Castle into a coffee palace and church, although not, perhaps, as original as Barnardo claimed, certainly outshone the tame temperance houses and mission halls. He retained the pub's sign but hung a signboard outside the Castle bearing the slogan 'No drunkard shall inherit the Kingdom of God'.

Inside, the coffee palace was fitted up 'in the style of a first-class tavern'. Lit brightly by gaslight, the original bar was retained and the Castle refurnished with 'mirrors, bright paintings, comfortable and snug little corners at the bar' and 'Friendship, Sobriety and Happiness' over the doorways. The coffee palace offered 'hot coffee, strong tea, rich cocoa' for a small sum; newspapers were provided and tables for domi-noes and draughts. Every Sunday 100 smart lads from Dr Barnardo's Home marched to the music of their band, following Barnardo to the coffee palace where he preached in the former music hall to audiences of thousands. The seal was set on the venture in February 1873 when Lord Shaftesbury, the social leader of Victorian philanthropy, formally opened the Castle, although, later, Shaftesbury was to feel misgivings about Barnardo's management and judgement.

From the opening and success of the Edinburgh Castle Barnardo now looked unstoppable. To further his work he needed a wife. In the autumn of 1871, Syrie Elmslie, the daughter of a city businessman living in Richmond, had invited Barnardo to speak at a large meeting and enter-tainment for poor boys in Richmond. She was an Evangelical, like Tom Barnardo running a ragged school, and she had read with admiration of his activities in the Christian press. The meeting went well but the couple did not keep in touch until they met by chance in 1873 at the funeral of an Evangelical minister. This time Tom Barnardo seized the opportunity to get to know Syrie better and very soon afterwards proposed to her. The couple had much in common and were both devoted to their Christian social work. However, Barnardo was twenty-eight, living in lodgings and without family connections or a fixed income. Syrie's father opposed the match and at first she refused 'the little rascal'. Tom Barnardo persisted, his enthusiasm and eloquence were hard to resist, and by then Syrie was twenty-six and in need of a husband. She accepted him and within a month became a wife dedicated to her husband's interests; it was an entirely suitable marriage, although on both sides the union seems to have been lacking in warmth.

Syrie's family naturally wanted the ceremony to be held at their own church in Richmond. The groom, however, insisted that they must be married in the East End, so that his own congregation and his helpers and supporters could be present. The wedding, Barnardo urged, should be held 'in an ordinary way, in an ordinary dissenting chapel'. They were married in the great Metropolitan Tabernacle, Newington Causeway, which could seat 6,000, and the wedding ceremony developed into a demonstration of support for Barnardo's work. As a wedding present, John Sands, a wealthy Evangelical solicitor, presented the couple with the lease of Mossford Lodge, Barkingside, to be used as a home for girls.

Since he had first begun scouring the streets for stray children, Barnardo had felt a zealous urge to reach out to the little girls he met there, the sisters of his boys 'prepared for sin'. He had started a fund for girls as early as 1870.

After six weeks' honeymoon he launched the scheme with Syrie's help. The couple went to live in Mossford Lodge and Syrie Barnardo wrote to *The Christian*:

> Through the great goodness of God, a Home has been placed at our disposal at Ilford in Essex in which it is our united desire to receive such little female waifs and train them after a fashion not, so far as we know, adopted anywhere else as domestic servants of the better class . . . aided by thoroughly good servants and the voluntary help of some Christian ladies, I hope to train up a band of kitchenmaids, housemaids, parlour-maids, laundry maids, dairymaids and cooks to meet the great demand existing everywhere for cleanly and instructed female servants.[21]

In this way, Syrie intimated, by drawing girls away from low lodging houses, the couple would be helping to tackle 'our greatest social sin'.

In October 1873 twelve girls came to live in the adapted coachhouse adjoining the Lodge and at first Barnardo made the home into an imitation of Stepney with accommodation for sixty girls. Like the boys, the girls were all dressed alike and subject to a disciplinarian life under the 'barrack' system. He left the supervision of the girls, who came from squalid homes and were 'ignorant in mind and stunted in body', to his wife. Syrie soon became pregnant. With a new home to care for and a household to run on a very tight budget, she found the girls impossible to manage. 'The Home for Orphan and Destitute Girls', Barnardo wrote in his Annual Report for the year 1873–4, had not reached 'that degree of success in the undertaking that was contemplated' although the number of girls had grown to fifty-four. Coming from Barnardo that was tantamount to a confession of failure. The home proved disastrous. Despite Barnardo's hopes that the girls would reform under the influence of Syrie and the other Christian ladies, he was soon disappointed. One night he overheard the girls talking and was horrified by their 'vile conversation . . . in a moment I realised what were the hidden forces of evil at work, undoing all we hoped had been attained. Indeed I was made to feel, as I listened with horror, that probably I had done harm, not good, and that by our system of aggregating these girls I was but propagating and intensifying evil.'[22]

The work he cared about so desperately had failed; it was clear that he had not succeeded in reforming the girls and if they were placed in Christian households as domestic servants they would damage the reputation of all his work.

In the face of failure he was resilient; it was one of his greatest qualities. In a letter to *The Christian* he announced that he had closed the Girls' Home. He turned the humiliation into an opportunity just as he had when forced to resign from the ragged school. He announced new plans for caring for girls, a new Girls' Village Home which, he revealed, had appeared to him in a dream, 'a vision of the night'. Instead of a large house with sixty motherless girls herded together 'clad in some dull uniform generally divested of all prettiness . . . little cottages should arise, each of them presided over by its own "mother"'. The girls would be of all ages from babies to growing girls.[23]

Difficult to believe that Barnardo, who kept himself informed of work with poor children, had not heard of the Raue Haus experiment in Hamburg, where delinquent street boys were housed in cottages in 'families'. A similar experiment was founded near Tours in France and in England Mary Carpenter and other social reformers had urged the need for a place where young delinquents could be trained in an atmosphere of discipline and love.

He appealed in *The Christian* for £13,500 to build thirty cottages. In each cottage a Christian housewife would mother and care for a family of twenty girls. His plans, if fulfilled, would increase the numbers of girls at Ilford from sixty to six hundred. The response was slow, it was not long since Barnardo had made his last appeal for his girls. When no help came, he was downcast for weeks but a 'miracle' restored his faith. On a visit to Oxford to attend a religious gathering a stranger tapped at Barnardo's door and asked briskly to subscribe to the first cottage in the Girls' Village Home. The early morning caller had read Barnardo's appeal in *The Christian* some weeks earlier and had intended to write offering him £450 to erect a cottage in memory of his little daughter who had died. Once again providence had come to Barnardo's aid and he did not fail to apprise the readers of *The Christian* of it, with excellent results.

That Barnardo was a visionary seems clear from a scrutiny of his sermon notes; that he employed his inspiration and imagination to attract publicity and finance seems equally evident from a reading of his Annual Reports. Impatient of the rules that governed other men's conduct, he cut corners for the cause. Sometimes it seemed that his own self-importance, as much as his sense of compassion, propelled him to grandiose schemes and buildings in which to house them. His instinct for gauging the public mood never failed. In the 'seventies the mid-Victorians were in terror of the 'dangerous classes' and of the breakdown of law and order, of mobs of juveniles threatening their peace and security. Barnardo played on those fears and promised the public the reform and rescue of young children on the road to ruin. The public had no choice, he stated roundly. They could either subscribe to his mission (or similar bodies) or pay their money in 'rates and taxes for the support of police, magistrates and Justices, houses of detention, convict prisons'. His brilliant propaganda, his somewhat simplistic arguments, commanded attention and support but also antagonised many colleagues working with considerably less success to improve the condition of the poor and to bring them the solace of religion.

Since his marriage, Barnardo's fortunes had soared. In 1871–2 his receipts were £9,190 4s. 5d. By 1875 they had reached £23,312 6s. 8d. In the course of those years Barnardo had increased the children in his care from 135 to more than 400, had opened a Girls' Home, taken a 'Citadel of Satan' (the Edinburgh Castle public house) and converted it into a coffee palace, and built another coffee palace (the Dublin Castle) in the East End.

His Annual Report for 1874–5, like all his Annual Reports, was published late; although 'fully set-up in type in October 1875', what Barnardo described as a 'variety of events' compelled him to hold it over until January 1876. Entitled 'Rescue the Perishing' the report was the most ambitious he had ever published with a long text, ten wood engravings and two 'photographs from life' illustrating his work. Barnardo's unbounded confidence for the future was to be found on almost every page.

'My accountants say I shall need so many thousand pounds for the work of the ensuing year; but what is that to HIM . . . I know I shall need more, yea, much more, that money may not, cannot buy heavenly wisdom, grace from above, singleness of eye and power for service. But I know from whence it all comes and I have the promise.'

In order to expand the Boys' and Girls' Homes, build a training ship (a favoured project, never realised), Barnardo revealed that he needed about £15,000 as well as funds to support the 400 children under his wing and carry on his mission work.

In the same report he claimed that within twelve months he would have nearly one thousand children under his training and care. There were many who read his 1874–5 report, men of the cloth among them, with a measure of scepticism. His admirers wondered at the boldness and sweep of his enterprises. His detractors were convinced that this time Barnardo had gone too far.

3

An Uncharitable Affair

'Why will you not come with me to the HOME, where you will get a comfortable bed, and be taught a trade, and learn to read and write?'
'I don't want none o' yer 'omes! I prefers to be left alone, I does, and to mind my own business.'

Annual Report, 1874–5

Many of Barnardo's stories of his midnight sorties in search of stray boys reveal that he admired, and perhaps recognised, the independent spirit in the children of the slums. Before he married in 1873, he scoured the common lodging houses, the courts, the alleys and the markets almost every night. He claimed to be the first to seek out destitute children by night and was certainly a pioneer of street rescue. Other missions labelled his methods sensational but when they saw his results they soon followed suit.

His enterprise was in evidence everywhere in Stepney. In seven spectacular years, from 1868 to 1874, Tom Barnardo had risen from unknown medical student to East End philanthropist of standing. At the age of twenty-nine he led a rapidly expanding mission church, a home for street boys and a sister home for girls, a new-style coffee palace for working men, an employment agency for his boys, and a depot for religious literature. During 1874, he also bought up a children's magazine, *Father William's Stories*, changed the title and the content to *The Children's Treasury*, 'an advocate of the Homeless and Destitute', and wrote and edited it himself. To house his numerous activities he had acquired over a dozen properties in the East End and his receipts had risen by over £12,000, from just £214 15s. in 1868 to £20,055 9s. 9d. in 1874.[1]

He took sole responsibility for the 400 children in his charge and for all the public money donated. Although he employed both paid and voluntary staff, Barnardo worked without a treasurer or committee and awarded himself neither salary nor expenses. Each year his Annual Reports were published, but published very late.

No sooner had he launched into one scheme than he would discover a burning need for another. Even in his earliest days he kept a profusion of plans and funds alive and an air of business and importance about his mission. With his great talent for publicising his work and the grandiose plans he unveiled, it was inevitable that he would provoke gossip and speculation in the East End.

The very excesses of his style which served him so well in appealing for funds could arouse suspicion. By 1875, his Annual Report, 'Rescue the Perishing', revealed an astonishing record of achievement: boys snatched from 'low lodging houses, courts, alleys, the markets, the waterside ... to rescue, shelter and training; the most numerously attended ragged schools in London', industrial schemes for poor boys with Barnardo acting as employment agent for young woodchoppers, city messengers, shoeblacks. Although he had 'absolutely not one pound in hand' Barnardo confidently appealed for funds to build twelve more cottages for girls, acquire a man o' war training ship, expand his Boys' Home and build new premises for his ragged schools.

During 1874, D. L. Moody, the well-known American Revivalist, a spiritual ancestor of Billy Graham, had visited London, preached at Barnardo's Edinburgh Castle and publicly praised his new work for poor girls. The American style suited Barnardo and his standing grew from the association. He also learnt new methods of management, fund-raising and, above all, publicity.

Since 1869 his own appeals operation was becoming more sophisticated. He had sold leaflets and packets of photographs 'comparing the past and present condition of destitute lads', wonderfully effective propaganda for his homes, since they were such a novelty. Barnardo's list of donations now took up almost seventy pages in his Annual Report and the gifts from wellwishers made lively reading. The inventory ranged from antimacassars, an officer's scarlet jacket, trousers and waistcoat to framed texts, woollen comforters, half a gallon of cod liver oil and fifty-six pounds of pearl barley.

Even his detractors had to concede that his frenetic activity had eased the hardship of the children of the East End. In 1874, he had opened an all-night refuge for homeless children at his Stepney headquarters after finding 'Carrots', John Somers, an eleven-year-old urchin who had begged him for a bed the week before when the home was full, dead in a sugar barrel. After the death a large wooden sign 'NO DESTITUTE BOY OR GIRL EVER REFUSED ADMISSION' was hung outside the home and a light was left on all night. Later, he established Ever-Open-Doors in provincial cities. Hundreds of hungry children in the East End came to reverence his name through the hot breakfasts and dinners he provided. In the Edinburgh Castle, his great pop mission offered poor men cheap and nourishing food and thousands of them signed the pledge.

As an orator, as a preacher, he seemed able to sense the temper and understanding of his audience. The wealthy and influential, as well as the poor wretches of the slums, felt the urgency of his words. Through the power of his preaching, and his brilliant advertising campaigns, knowledge of his work spread throughout Stepney and to the wider circle of Evangelicals in the country. If he was ambitious, if he was thrusting, he justified it all for his God-given mission.

Yet, as the scale of his operation grew, so, too, did misgivings about the propriety of one man assuming responsibility for so many young lives, so much of the public's money. In Stepney, they remembered Barnardo as a struggling young medical student putting up in poor lodgings. His success, accompanied by his marriage and his new status in Evangelical circles, was mirrored by a change of lifestyle. Now Tom called himself 'Dr Barnardo' and had acquired the paraphernalia of middle-class respectability, with a house in town and three rooms in his country residence, the Girls' Village Home in Ilford. He travelled by coach, employed servants and instead of scouring the streets at night for stray children, he employed a beadle, a former police constable, to do the work. Barnardo himself did occasionally venture out into the streets.

Nevertheless, many envious individuals gossiped about the extraordinary change in his fortunes and Barnardo himself was not helped by his pride. He stated very clearly that he did not receive any salary or payment for his services; that he had a 'sufficient private income' to enable him to do that.[2] Although his wife may have had a small income, it later emerged that he himself could lay no claim to substantial private means. However, he worked extraordinarily hard and earned an income from both his preaching and from his journalism, from the children's magazine he owned and edited. In all probability influential friends who gave so generously to the homes helped him personally, since the East End Juvenile Mission was, in effect, Tom Barnardo. If he did draw expenses from the mission (and that is now impossible to know) the amount of work he did would have justified him fully.

However, his cavalier attitude invited criticism, at a time when indiscriminate charity was looked upon as an evil. From the 1830s onwards statistical societies were beginning to 'collect, digest and publish facts illustrating the condition and prospects of society'.[3] More and more professional people believed that only by systematic study of a social problem could solutions be found. In 1869, the year after Barnardo founded the East End Juvenile Mission, the COS, Charity Organisation Society, a body of urban business and professional men, joined together to try to weld the numerous charities into a system, by weeding out the fraudulent and the overlapping and co-ordinating the remaining charities. They soon attracted support and grew in authority.

Barnardo's personal style of fund-raising, his vivid dramatisation of the plight of the children of the street, aroused distaste and distrust in the members of the society. Like most Victorians of their day, the COS saw poverty as an individual character defect and drew a stern distinction between the deserving and the undeserving poor. The latter, the feckless and the bad, the old and the sick as well as the children, should, in their view, be sent to the workhouse and live there in considerable discomfort in order to discourage other 'shirkers'. Only the poor who could be helped to help themselves by individual visiting (the casework of the day) were their concern.

Barnardo's own practice and convictions were in direct opposition. He believed that children deserved a chance, whether they were legitimate or illegitimate, healthy or diseased, sons and daughters of criminals, prostitutes or vagrants. They were 'his' children, boys and girls on the run from the workhouse, the courts or the brutality of parents. As a keen Evangelical, he naturally wanted to 'save' the children; but he also planned to transform them into sound working men and women with a trade and a sense of their own rightful, if modest, place in society.

The brilliant, unqualified preacher represented everything the COS most disliked. However, it took a rival more directly involved to provoke them into action. It was George Reynolds, a little-known Baptist preacher, formerly a railway porter from Wales, who ignited the opposition to Barnardo. Reynolds preached to a tiny congregation of less than a hundred in a chapel in the Mile End Road, near to the Edinburgh Castle. Once the 'Castle' was converted, many of Reynolds' congregation had drifted away, and overflowing audiences assembled on Sunday mornings and evenings, drawn by the appeal of the erstwhile pub and its magnetic preacher. During 1874 whatever influence Reynolds possessed had diminished and he had little to do but dwell maliciously on the man he looked on as the author of all his troubles.

By coincidence Reynolds lived in Barnes Street, opposite a former landlady of Barnardo's, a Mrs Johnson, wife of a sea-captain. In the years since Barnardo had lodged with her, Mrs Johnson had separated from her husband and gone on the streets. According to local gossip, she was never seen sober after midday. She and her children had joined Barnardo's church and, again, rumour reported that Barnardo was seen arm-in-arm with the abandoned lady. When Reynolds discovered this tit-bit he wanted to know more and one day during 1874 invited Mrs Johnson to his house and egged her on to gossip about her former lodger and to boast that she had granted Barnardo sexual favours. After that

Reynolds saw to it that the story spread round the district and even reached the ears of the deacons of the Edinburgh Castle.

Reynolds had not taken the trouble to verify the rumour and one can only imagine the indignation and efficiency with which Barnardo dealt with the situation. His church deacons from the Edinburgh Castle bore down on Mrs Johnson one day, accompanied by her own mother and a doctor, and challenged her story. They satisfied themselves that Mrs Johnson was suffering from what they described as 'sexual hysteria'[4] and could not therefore be trusted as a witness. But the 'wicked woman' scandal had made delicious gossip for those who found Barnardo's manner arrogant and his rapidly growing popularity an irritant. Frederick Charrington was a young man whose religious life had led him on a similar path to Barnardo. He, too, had experienced a profound conversion, joined the Evangelical ranks and taught in the poor schools of Stepney. He, too, ran a boys' home and mission and the two men naturally knew each other. He came to the temperance cause in a typically Victorian fashion, heightened only by his family connections. One day he witnessed a lout outside a public house in the Mile End Road boot his wife to the gutter. When he looked up and saw his own family name 'Charrington' on the sign of the Rising Sun Inn he is said to have renounced his inheritance and the family business to concentrate on missionary and temperance work. But Fred Charrington still bore the family name and looked on the Mile End Road, the headquarters of his family's brewery, as his own natural territory. After the success of Barnardo's Edinburgh Castle Charrington was eager to build his own mission hall. He was furious when he heard that Barnardo had acquired a site on the Mile End Road to build a second coffee palace and tried, by somewhat devious means, to frustrate the enterprise, but he failed to stop Barnardo.

Almost inevitably the two embittered Stepney missionaries, Charrington and Reynolds, met and drew together during 1874. Charrington seized on the 'wicked woman' story and arranged for a friend to write a letter about it to Barnardo's private address; he was a man of means and he paid for handbills and literature to distribute the smear.

By 1875 the squabble amongst the East End preachers reached the press and the little local scandal assumed larger proportions. Reynolds started it: writing under the pen-name of a 'Protestant Dissenter' in the *East London Observer*, he attacked Barnardo's soaring success and his new lifestyle. 'Few dissenting ministers,' he commented, 'can afford to keep a country seat equal to Mossford Lodge or a town residence equal to Newbury House, Bow, the residence of the self-denying Dr Barnardo . . . Let the truth be told, far from having sacrificed all for the Lord's sake, he has raised himself on the pedestal of his work.'[5] He closed the letter by calling on the Charity Organisation Society, who were eager to probe into Barnardo's affairs, to investigate the work.

Barnardo had publicly announced that he would not permit himself to become embroiled in a newspaper scandal but the insults could not be allowed to go unchallenged. Two weeks later, an ardent champion of Dr Barnardo, one 'Clerical Junius', sprang to his defence in the same newspaper. His self-appointed task: 'to draw aside the curtain which has hitherto shrouded from view the whole life-work of one of the truest philanthropists that ever blessed the East End or any other part of the Metropolis with his presence'. The writer, professing himself a Church of England clergyman and would-be biographer of Barnardo, had fulsome praise for his subject, 'a man of private means and ancient family' who lived in the East End by choice, 'dispensing on every side of his bounty'.[6]

Reynolds replied, in his own name this time, by pressing further charges against Barnardo in the paper.[7] He questioned Barnardo's right to assume the title of 'Doctor' and promised more details of the 'wicked woman' scandal. This stung Barnardo into taking out a writ against Reynolds. Then the mysterious Clerical Junius stepped in again, writing this time an immensely long letter to the *Tower Hamlets Independent*. In this letter the writer defended Barnardo and baited Reynolds for his envy of the success of the Castle, 'it might be too much for his weak nerves to really know how much the Church collects', and also teased the writer for the suggestion that Barnardo might have no right to assume the title of 'Doctor'. 'May not my friend be a Doctor of Laws, why not? DD and LLD are nowadays regarded as honorary and honourable distinctions ... and as to Physics, he may be a Doctor of Physics for aught I know.'

Towards the middle of the letter, the tone changed and the author invited his readers to share a reverie: 'I was in dreamland, transported to a theatre ...' From a curtained box the dreamer saw the play. Among the dramatis personae he pointed out a certain Dr Dogood (Barnardo), Mr Brewgoose (Charrington) and the Rev. Swino Reynard (Reynolds). On stage Dr Dogood was shown as a public benefactor, feeding ragged children, distributing warm garments to the poor and sheltering the homeless. Having enough money of his own to live upon, Dr Dogood gave up all his time and his services to his work gratuitously. In the dream 'everybody was talking of Dr Dogood'. 'He never spoke himself but every one did it for him.' Mr Brewgoose by contrast gave up his father's 'naughty business', 'but this good young man, so self-denying, did not give up the little income derived from the said naughty business but continued to rear his head as high as ever in the parish as the son of the well-known house of Brewgoose.' Mr Brewgoose also let it be known that he had a fortune of £60,000 although he really received £400 a year from his father's share in the naughty business which he had renounced. 'The desire for religious fame grew into a mania with poor Mr Brewgoose and at last produced a disease which physicians call chronic jealousy of the mind . . .'

'It so happened that one day the Rev. Swino Reynard was conversing with a very wicked person . . . a person so wicked that . . . respectable people would not like to be seen talking to her; and she told the minister a story about Dr Dogood, which, if true, would prove that the latter must be a very naughty man.' In this vein the reverie and the letter continued until, in the end, 'Dr Dogood was proved to be what everybody had always known him to be, a hard-working, earnest, good man'. After a libel case 'the mean treachery and sordid aims of his traducers were fully exposed in open court'.[8]

This sparkling piece of faction caused an uproar when the newspaper appeared and Barnardo sold copies of the newspaper at the Edinburgh Castle. Within days he realised that the Clerical Junius letter itself was creating scandal by its language and implications, particularly since the author was said to be an Evangelical Church of England clergyman. He fired off a shot to the *East London Observer* condemning 'the abominable epistle' written on his behalf, indignantly denying its authorship, whole or partial, and stating that he was instigating legal action against Reynolds and Charrington.[9]

Even when he was seeking to appease, Barnardo's intemperate language served to provoke. Church of England clergy saw his denunciation of his 'friend' as a slur on them and curiosity about the true identity of Clerical Junius intensified. It emerged that the name given as a guarantee to the newspaper was that of S. W. Walrond of Lowestoft but no Church of England clergyman of that name living in Lowestoft could be traced. A clergyman of the same name wrote indignantly to the press stating that there were only three Church of England clergymen of his name beside himself and none of them had written the offensive letter. Mr Walrond, who was a founder member of the Charity Organisation Society, also wrote to *The Recorder*, a national Church of England newspaper. By now the name of Barnardo had, as Walrond wrote, a notoriety. The COS, more than disinterested bystanders in the scandal, were already gathering ammunition against him.

The timing of the affair could hardly have been more damaging to Barnardo. His cherished dream of opening a Village Home for destitute girls where they would be mothered in cottages and taught essential domestic skills had already attracted support from leading members of society in the Evangelical movement. In June 1875, only two months before the letters appeared, Lord Aberdeen, a grandson of the Prime Minister, had laid the foundation stones of eleven cottages and the Lord Chancellor himself, Lord Cairns, had already demonstrated his interest in Barnardo's philanthropic work.

By now Barnardo was so enmeshed with the Evangelical cause that any attack on him cast a shadow over the whole movement and even reflected on the Government and its leaders who had welcomed him so warmly. Efforts were made to settle the matter discreetly. Thomas Stone, a well-known Evangelical, persuaded Barnardo to withdraw his writ and extracted a signed agreement from all three involved, Reynolds, Charrington and Barnardo, to let the matter drop, but the rumours rumbled on throughout 1876.

That was a crucial year for Barnardo. The previous autumn he had been challenged in the press about his claim to the title of 'Doctor'. He later insisted that he had obtained an MD (a degree by mail order) from the University of Giessen but 'the letter he produced to support the claim was a forgery'.[10] Now it was imperative that he should obtain a professional qualification to silence his critics. In January 1876, he travelled secretly to Edinburgh and spent four months studying at the Royal College of Surgeons to gain his diploma, while making it known in his magazine, *The Children's Treasury*, that he had been ill from January to March. By April, he had registered as a medical practitioner in London. Legally, at least, he was within his rights in styling himself 'Doctor' (although the Royal College of Physicians allowed the title only as a courtesy to graduates of medicine of a university).

Perhaps it was just as well because, within three months, Dr Barnardo was to welcome Lord Cairns and his wife to the opening of thirteen cottages of the Girls' Village Home, an event which brought more publicity and acclaim to his East End Juvenile Mission. Meanwhile, his enemies were even more incensed at the publicity and popularity Barnardo enjoyed. Despite the agreement they had signed, Reynolds and Charrington conspired to produce 'anonymous' pamphlets and leaflets. By December 1876, Reynolds had encompassed all his venom in a sixty-two-page shilling book under his own name, *Dr Barnardo's Homes: Startling Revelations*. In it he repeated all his former allegations against Barnardo and included the full text of the Clerical Junius letters as well as a documented accusation purporting to prove that Barnardo was the author of them. The pamphlet also specified charges of sexual misdemeanours; cruelty to children; incompetent management; obtaining money under false pretences; failure to instruct the children in religion; using false photographs and misrepresenting himself as a Doctor

53

of Medicine. The first brief paragraph of the *Revelations*, however, contained sober and constructive criticism of the management of the homes; the suggestion was made that all the properties belonging to Barnardo's East End Juvenile Mission should be vested in trustees; that a committee of management be constituted and that a treasurer, as well as an independent auditor, be appointed.

By foresight, or prior knowledge, that course had already been taken as far as the Girls' Village Home was concerned. In November, a month before the publication of *Startling Revelations*, John Sands, the solicitor who had presented Barnardo with the leasehold of Mossford Lodge, Ilford, as a wedding gift to be used for his Girls' Village Home, changed the status of the land. With Barnardo's agreement, the solicitor transferred the leasehold into a freehold and vested the property in trustees who would manage it. Barnardo was appointed Director for his lifetime, accountable to the trustees, a distinguished body of Evangelicals under the chairmanship of Lord Aberdeen. Only the dangerous position that Barnardo and his homes found themselves in could have persuaded him to allow his own position to change from private philanthropist to Honorary Director. The timely action probably saved Barnardo and his work. Similar trust deeds were drawn up in January 1877 for the Boys' Home in Stepney.

Almost immediately after *Startling Revelations* was published, subscribers to Barnardo's homes began to write in to the Charity Organisation Society asking for guidance. The COS now interested themselves officially in Barnardo's affairs, blacklisted the charity and in a cautionary circular warned would-be subscribers against donating to the homes.

In addition to resources diminishing, the trustees, as well as Barnardo, were now in great difficulty about the reputation of their charity. They were constantly being badgered by the COS to answer questions.

Soon after the publication of *Startling Revelations* the trustees called a meeting and questioned their new Director closely about all the accusations levelled against him. They also instructed an independent firm of accountants, Messrs Turquand, Young and Co., to make an audit of the past year's accounts.

The issue at stake was not only Barnardo's management of the mission but the idiosyncratic nature of the man himself. The very qualities which enthralled the Evangelicals, his religious fervour, his flow of language and his confident assumption of divine approval of his activities, were those that disturbed the Charity Organisation Society. They were the qualities that had enabled him to accomplish so much and yet they were dangerous.

Barnardo's trustees were men of the world and realised that a means had to be found to settle the matter and to silence Barnardo's accusers once and for all. Clearly they did not want the affairs of the homes bandied about in the criminal courts. Once they had received a satisfactory report from the accountant, the trustees decided to submit the matter to arbitration. This discreetly narrowed the dispute to the parties immediately involved and prevented a confrontation between the Evangelicals and the Charity Organisation Society on much wider issues. Now it was Barnardo versus Reynolds, two East End preachers engaged in a singularly uncharitable dispute. Barnardo now had no chance of retrieving his costs which were substantial. An appeal was launched and Barnardo's supporters, headed by the Lord Chancellor, responded generously. Thanks to his influential connections, he was represented by a leading counsel, the Hon. Alfred Thesiger, QC, who was himself the son of a former Lord Chancellor, assisted by two juniors. Reynolds, on the other hand, was represented solely by his solicitor, St John Wontner. The hearing was not held until the summer of 1877. For the whole of that year Barnardo, who had courted publicity so assiduously, now found his private life, his origins, his income, as well as his mission work brought into the glare of public scrutiny in an extremely uncomfortable way. He used his new journal, *Night and Day*, intended as a record of his own and other Christian philanthropic work, to explain and defend himself. In the March issue he answered a reader's query about the management of the homes by stating that it was the trustees who held responsibility for the management of the homes and for their finances: 'The Editor is only a Director appointed by the Trustees, without salary and may be dismissed at any time.' The humble stance did not suit Barnardo. By May 1877 he was defending his homes in his usual style: 'I believe there is no institution in this country or in this world whose accounts are more minutely accurate . . . for any friends to withhold support is, in this case, practically to condemn . . .'[11]

When the Reynolds-Barnardo arbitration hearing opened in June at the Institution of Surveyors, the prosecution paraded their witnesses in front of the arbitrators: disgruntled former employees of the homes, disenchanted parents, one or two of the old boys. In the witness-box Reynolds himself proved bold and unshakeable, proclaiming his scepticism of religious philanthropy. Charrington, by contrast, played a covert and rather cowardly part in the affair. Although he had paid for the publication of anti-Barnardo pamphlets and fuelled Reynolds' enmity with his own intense jealousy of Barnardo's work, he had at first refused to give evidence until Reynolds had the scope of the inquiry widened to include him specifically. By now the arbitration had become, for those in the know, a struggle between the 'indiscriminate charity' which

Christian charitable work was accused of, and the regulated charity that the Charity Organisation Society was trying to impose upon voluntary charities at the time. As a mission leader and an Evangelical, Charrington did not relish appearing on the 'wrong' side.

In August, when Barnardo began to give evidence, Reynolds published a strange photograph of Barnardo in tall hat with rolled umbrella in both hands, looking somewhat alarming. To counteract the damage, Barnardo wrote to the *Tower Hamlets Independent* enclosing 'a *carte-de-visite* which shall faithfully depict my phiz for the satisfaction of those who are kind enough to care for the same'.[12] In this 'authorised version' he appears sober, thoughtful, kindly. As in childhood, the two faces of Thomas Barnardo provide an interesting commentary on his character.

In the witness stand, Barnardo, a tiny figure, stood dignified and erect. Under cross-examination by Reynolds' solicitor, he was asked point-blank for the name of the writer of the Clerical Junius letters. By now Barnardo's good name and his credibility as a person of standing rested almost entirely on the wretched letters which had assumed a disproportionate importance due to the publicity. Under cross-examination it emerged that he was more implicated in the affair than he had admitted. He himself had taken the second 'dream' letter to the newspaper office. But although St John Wontner, Reynolds' solicitor, asked him three times for the name of the letter writer he stubbornly refused to give it. 'I distinctly and fully accept the entire authorship of the letter but I decline to inflict an injury upon the real author by giving up his name.' The refusal to confirm the material question discomfited Barnardo's supporters and gave ammunition to his enemies. The arbitrators were extremely displeased with Barnardo and even his own counsel admitted his embarrassment. Significantly, Thesiger pointed out that 'great interest has been taken by those who are the Trustees of those Institutions and by persons who are behind the Trustees, subscribers to these institutions'. In effect, the Evangelical Establishment, as well as Barnardo, was on trial.

The court adjourned until the following day but the star witness still would not answer the material question, the authorship of the Junius letters. After Barnardo's point-blank refusal Reynolds' solicitor declined to continue his cross-examination since Barnardo was withholding crucial evidence. He left the court with his client. The arbitrators and Barnardo's supporters were considerably disturbed. One of the three arbitrators, Canon Miller, stated that in the circumstances he would find it impossible to make an award. The lengthy and expensive court proceedings to clear the reputation of Barnardo and his homes seemed destined to fail. But it could not be allowed to happen. Thanks to

Thesiger, Barnardo's brilliant counsel, the arbitrators were persuaded to allow an unopposed summing-up of the complex case. Reynolds' solicitor did not pronounce.

For six weeks no award was announced. In the meantime the Charity Organisation Society lost no time in publishing a cautionary circular on what they saw as the main point of the arbitration: 'Barnardo's credibility and trustworthiness'. The COS sent copies to all newspaper editors.

Barnardo's friends in high places did not desert him. Before the award was announced Barnardo received 'a private message to the effect that if, after the arbitration is concluded, you wish to be helped by a committee and are desirous of choosing one, the Lord Chancellor will be very pleased to show the confidence he has in you and your work by taking the post of President'. Barnardo revealed later that Lord Cairns had been following the arbitration closely.[13]

When the arbitrators made their award in mid-October, Barnardo was vindicated of the most serious charges brought against him. They cleared him entirely from charges of 'improperly appropriating donations for his own use'. They could find no evidence of cruelty to children, although they did criticise Barnardo for locking his boys up in solitary confinement in a cell, a practice he no longer continued. Not surprisingly, they absolved him of the charge of lack of moral and religious training in the homes. Such training, they concluded, was given a prominent place. The charge that children were kept in the homes against their wishes was dismissed. (When children were admitted to the home, either relatives, friends or the children themselves had to sign an agreement stating that they would not leave without permission from the Governor of the home. In those days before Government assumed responsibility for destitute children, Barnardo himself would decide whether parents were capable of assuming the obligations of parenthood.)

On the charge of misrepresenting the homes to visitors by dressing children up for show, or displaying rugs, sheets and counterpanes when company called, the arbitrators found the evidence 'very shadowy'. Methods of advertising the homes, however, came under sharper criticism. In order to dramatise his work, Barnardo took 'before' and 'after' photographs of the children and liked to portray his charges as utterly wretched on admittance. One example cited by the arbitrators as typical was of Mrs Holder's daughters, Florence and Eliza, sent to the homes by their mother 'poorly but decently clad'. In a photograph Barnardo used of Florence she was shown with 'bare feet and head, dishevelled hair and tattered dress, selling newspapers in the street. In this condition and employment she never was.' The photograph of her younger sister used on a collecting-box with the caption, 'A little waif, six years old taken from the streets', was equally misleading. Eliza came from a poor but respectable home. The mother who appeared in court was furious at the slur on her good name. The arbitrators cited other instances and commented, 'The use of artistic fiction to represent actual fact is, in our opinion, not only morally wrong . . . but might in the absence of a very strict control, grow into a system of deception dangerous to the cause on behalf of which it is practised.' That was the most stringent criticism of Barnardo made by the arbitrators.

On the count that he had assumed 'the style and title of Doctor', the award was less censorious. They noted that as a medical student he had been known as 'Doctor' and added that it was 'strictly true that he had no legal or real right to the title and style of Doctor'.

Over the delicate matter of the Clerical Junius letters, the award left a question mark. With the evidence incomplete, they reported themselves 'unable fully to determine the question' but gave their opinion that although Dr Barnardo was not the actual writer, he had supplied the data, had both letters submitted to him before publication and took the second letter to the newspaper himself and was 'as much morally responsible for them as the writer'.

The paragraph of most significance came towards the end of the lengthy award. The arbitrators judged that 'these Homes for Destitute Boys and Girls called the Barnardo Institutions are real and valuable charities and worthy of public confidence and support'. They did strongly recommend that 'the trustees appoint a working committee of gentlemen as soon as possible to avert further difficulties and increase public confidence'.[14]

What mattered was the work. As *The Times* commented: 'If any curiosity which may be felt as to Dr Barnardo's career or personal character is not fully satisfied, yet we have what is much more important, independent testimony to the value of the work.'[15]

The public, who in the beginning had been amused by the scandal, ended up by being thoroughly discomfited at the spectacle of religious philanthropists, who professed to guide others, squabbling in a highly unedifying manner. The judgement for the homes was reassuring and popular.

To come out relatively unscathed after being accused, as a missionary, of immorality, cruelty, embezzlement and dishonesty, was an extraordinary feat. In remarking on it, the *Morning Advertiser* of 20 October 1877 noted: 'The general effect of the award is to exonerate the Doctor who may, therefore, congratulate himself on having got, as he has got, out of a serious and delicate position.'

The affair was costly and both Barnardo personally and the homes incurred a substantial debt. The Arbitration Fund fell short by £2,200 of the costs of the case and the Finance Committee transferred the remainder of the costs to the General Fund. Some of Barnardo's plans had to be delayed and the training ship was abandoned. But it had its compensations. As a result of the sensational case Dr Barnardo's name and his homes had become known throughout the country. Despite some dissent by his new Committee (which Barnardo had reluctantly agreed to appoint) he continued to sign himself 'Dr Barnardo'. Since the homes were now so well known through their founder, the name was changed to 'Dr Barnardo's Homes and East End Juvenile Mission'. A lingering doubt remained in some people's minds about Dr Barnardo. Lord Shaftesbury himself was uncertain whether the verdict was the correct one.[16] But gradually subscriptions picked up and the sheer volume and momentum of the work brought Barnardo's homes into public favour more prominently than ever.

4

A Dream Home

'Each girl saved from a criminal course is a present to the next generation of a virtuous woman and valuable servant.'

Night and Day, March 1879

In his Girls' Village Home at Barkingside, Barnardo created a world in miniature which gave rein to his fantasy of childhood. The ivy-clad doll's house cottages clustered round the village green and the girls in white pinafores who lived in them captured the imagination of the public. In his photographs the Doctor himself, small, dapper and fastidious, bore an unmistakable air of toy town.

In Barnardo's vision all his waifs were to be transformed into industrious women of virtue and the Village Homes were to mould them to his ideal. His dream Village was destined to remain virtually unchanged until well after the Second World War; even now the spell of his dream lingers. For some, the reality of the dream was a safe and happy childhood, whilst others were overshadowed by its power.

Doctor Barnardo described the Village as 'the desire of my heart' and named the original cottages after flowers and plants, Forget-me-not, Myrtle, May, Lily Rose. Later, cottages had more prosaic names to commemorate donors or donors' home towns.

Barnardo himself decided on the colour of the paint and paper in each cottage and on his girls' dress and diet. The girls wore a ribbon in their best Sunday hats to match the colour of their cottage, Rose, Forget-me-not, or in the case of cottages named after patrons, some chosen hue.

In the Village in the 1870s neglected girls from the streets were brought into the neat little cottage homes to be transformed. Children with street cunning, some half-naked and starving, were trained to become industrious, respectable, God-fearing servants. Some had learnt already to beg or thieve; some were on the brink of a life of prostitution, others were unfortunate children from desperately poor families. Whatever their background, in the Village, Christian influence, stern love and industry would mould the children.

In spite of his delight in charming children, Barnardo showed a wonderful compassion for the physically maimed and the mentally retarded and they, too, found a niche in his dream Village.

In building the Girls' Village, Barnardo transformed the whole environment. Until he came to Barkingside, open ditches in the ploughed fields had served as drainage; he constructed a drainage system which benefited the entire district. To ensure that his girls would enjoy a supply of pure water, he had an artesian well, three hundred feet deep, bored into the ground.

Barnardo relied on Christian lady volunteers, the 'mothers' of individual cottages, to perform the miracle he sought, the transformation of the children from street urchins to serving maids. He wanted to attract dedicated Christian ladies and, unlike other similar charities, offered no salary but promised a 'small yearly sum for clothing' to applicants without private means. He required the 'mothers' to be 'strict total abstainers, attached members of some Evangelical body'. He called for earnest-minded, educated ladies and suggested that 'Christians in good health and without family ties of their own would find the work satisfying'.[1] Thus Barnardo created the expectation that the work would become a way of life for his 'mothers'. As indeed it did.

Those spinster 'mothers' placed in charge of a 'family' of between sixteen and twenty-five girls from babyhood to teenage held almost total control of the children. Once a girl was handed over she was, in Barnardo's words, 'wholly surrendered to our care for a term of years to be agreed'. Parents were permitted to apply for a visit once every three months and the children were allowed to write home monthly.

For the rest, the girls lived in a walled and totally feminine world, sheltered from any influence considered undesirable and from the male sex. The children received an elementary education in the Village and worshipped regularly. Early on the Village had its own laundry where the girls (under adult supervision) washed over 6,000 sheets and garments a week for all the homes. They also baked bread, grew vegetables and kept goats and a pony. Every hour of their day was carefully planned and ordered.

For children who had known only wretched lodging houses or crowded hovels, the creature comforts of the Village must have been overwhelming: plenty to eat, a warm bed at night, clean clothes, fresh air. Undoubtedly some rescued girls would have died or become permanent invalids or perhaps criminals without Barnardo's beneficent intervention. Compared with many workhouses where 400 to 500 children lived side by side, ticketed, drilled and numbered, Barnardo's Village was a paradise. Workhouse children were marked by a drab uniform; Village girls wore simple, neat clothes of varied design, often given by well-wishers. In the

Village, the girls ate meat twice a week, had a 'basins or plates' one-course dinner and unlimited bread. The staple fare in many workhouses was bread and gruel.

In nearby Epping workhouse, girls shared a double bed. At Barnardo's, by contrast, each girl had her own bed with mattress, straw palliasse underneath, sheets, pillow and pillowcase. The sheets were changed once a week and a snowy white quilt covered the green iron bedstead. Under the bed two important articles were stored, a bed basket for clothing and a round white chamber pot with the girl's name painted on the enamel underside. Cleanliness of person and property was an early and important lesson girls had to learn. In huge workhouses, however, it was impossible to supervise the children so closely. In the cottages, the whole tone of a child's upbringing depended on the disposition of her 'mother'. General rules applied, of course, but the way in which the individual 'mother' interpreted her duty varied greatly. The children were nearly always under her eye, in the morning, in the evening and at mealtimes:

> Make us Thy creatures thankful, Lord,
> For this our daily food,
> Our deeds to Thee how ill they are
> And Thine to us how good.

This thankfulness to God instilled into the girls became, in time, translated in part to a thankfulness to his agent, Barnardo's. From 1903, girls were encouraged to join 'The Guild of the Grateful Life', an old girls' league which kept them in touch with each other and the homes and encouraged them to support the work.

Undoubtedly one reason why the Village remained popular with the public for so many years was that it provided a source of well-trained, docile, domestic servants. With his flair for anticipating public demand, Barnardo started the Village at a time when the ratio of domestic servants to the population reached its peak.[2] In the late nineteenth century, employing servants became increasingly a mark of status. Barnardo foresaw that good plain cooks and maids-of-all-work would be needed for generations. In the early days the target for the Village was to turn out between 100 and 200 servants a year.

His supporters found great satisfaction in both upholding the work and assuaging their fear of the 'dangerous' classes whilst assuring themselves of a servant corps for the future. 'I hope your girls are being trained for domestic service, good servants are so difficult to obtain now,' wrote a lady to Barnardo in 1879.[3] It was, he commented, a topic that cropped up frequently and was to recur forty years later after the First World War.

At fêtes and on special occasions selected children demonstrated their prowess. Barnardo lent six little girls from the Village to give a display in the drawing-room of Earl Fortescue's home in Belgrave Square.[4] 'My little girls,' Barnardo reported proudly ' . . . set to work singing all the time to set the tables and afterwards to clear away the things. Thereafter washing day was set up and they demonstrated that they were conversant with all the mysteries of that dread operation.'

The girls used toy samples and sang work songs to the delight of the aristocratic audience. Their instructor, Miss Heddon, explained that the children learnt how to make beds, lay and light fires, clean grates, scrub floors, sweep, wash and iron and show in visitors.

Rigorous insistence on cleanliness Barnardo demanded in all the homes. New girls were given a thorough medical examination and had their hair cleansed and cut short. They also learnt how to use a toothbrush. This emphasis on hygiene proved vital both in training for the future and in maintaining good health. Just after Christmas in 1879, an attack of scarlet fever broke out in the Village. At first the cases were so slight that they were barely noticed but by January twenty-one new cases were reported within twenty-three hours. The Doctor himself hurried to the Village, called the staff together in prayer and contacted the Local Government Board at Whitehall to ask for help. A Medical Inspector, a Dr Thorne, arrived and after inspection agreed with Dr Barnardo that a gift of contaminated second-hand clothing was the most likely source of the trouble. Barnardo hired extra nurses and constructed a baker's oven to disinfect girls' clothing, bedding and books. His prompt and practical action prevented disaster. Not one of the 171 children and adults affected died of the disease which, as the Medical Inspector duly reported, was a remarkable result. The Inspector was favourably impressed with the space, ventilation and scrupulous cleanliness in the cottages and left a detailed account of the sanitary arrangements. 'In a semi-detached outbuilding is an ordinary water-closet and a trough water-closet for the use of the children, emptied, cleansed and refilled with water twice a day.'[5] The Doctor's dream of saving the children was entirely vindicated.

In the cottages the girls learnt to elevate neatness of person, nimbleness of fingers and a proper sense of their station into spiritual attributes. The 'Song for Our Little Servants' appeared in Barnardo's magazine *Night and Day* in June 1878 and was sung by his girls at the Annual Fête the following month:

For the Sake of the Children

When I go to service
I must watch and pray
That my Heavenly Father
Will direct my way.

May the love of Jesus
Fill my heart and mind
And his Holy Spirit
Make me good and kind.

Keep me strictly honest
Steady and upright
Thoughtful of my mistress
In and out of sight.

If her things are broken
By my carelessness,
Let me mind 'tis better
Always to confess.

I must be good-tempered
Always neat and clean
Civil in my manners,
Never pert or mean.

Then my fellow-servants
Will respect my ways,
And I need not mind it,
If I get no praise.

For my Heavenly Father
Will be pleased with me,
With His love and blessing
Happy I shall be.

The pious little maids-in-waiting, snug in their cottage sanctuary, proved an irresistible attraction to visitors:

My guide opened her hall door into the cleanest of passages. To our left are the children's playroom and nursery opening out of each other and ending with the mother's little sanctum . . . each child's toys are carefully arranged in a nest of pigeon holes . . . Both the children's rooms are of course uncarpeted but the floors and tables literally shine with cleanliness and the walls are enlivened with pictures (of a religious nature) and the mantelpieces are ornamented with a selection of cups and saucers of the dolls' house order . . . The mother's room is tiny but cosy and large enough to hold its armchair and sofa. The floor boasts a neat carpet and there are flowers in the window and on the table.

As well as two windows 'mother' had a peephole pane of glass overlooking the kitchen so she could peer out at the older girls. Her provisions were kept separate. 'She had her own little loaf, a weekly allowance of butter and a daily meat dinner. The cupboard in her sitting room contains a select stock of small delicacies . . . Eggs or a cabbage for the mother was brought to the door and kept separate from the "family's" food.'[6]

At first Barnardo provided all girls who graduated to service with a complete outfit of clothes. By the 1890s, outfits were awarded on merit, in a complex system of grading. When they reached their thirteenth birthday the girls were divided into four classes according to character and conduct, and transferred or demoted according to behaviour. At sixteen 'first-class' girls received an 'outfit of the first class value £5' which they could keep, provided they did not change their job for a year. Those who stayed the course received a special prize. Second-class girls, guilty of 'ill temper, disobedience, insolence, laziness or other grave faults' were given an outfit worth £3 10s. Girls in the third class were placed out in the third division, the mistress being informed of 'their faults'. They received a third-class outfit, costing £3, and had to pay the cost out of their own wages. Fourth-class girls, 'dishonest, habitually untruthful, violent and uncontrolled in temper, vicious, unclean in their personal habits' were sent from the Village in disgrace or to a school of punishment. No record exists of how many Village girls fell into each category.[7]

These grades reveal that not every girl in the Village grew into Barnardo's ideal of a Christian domestic servant. In his publicity he stressed that he took in the worst cases 'rejected at every other door' and that, for many years, has been a proud Barnardo tradition; however, he was not always consistent in his claims. The anecdotes, understandably, told of appalling cases: a six-year-old whose mother 'was a lunatic as a result of drink and other excesses', or a girl of eleven and a half 'found by a Bible-woman in a house of ill-fame in the provinces', and he waxed eloquent about the numbers of girls snatched 'from actual hot-beds and forcing houses of vice and crime'. However, from time to time he would assert that many of the girls in the Village came from 'widowed mothers in circumstances of the very greatest poverty'.

But the appeal of the sensational transformation of soiled child into spotless Christian servant won him fame and support. At his Annual Meeting in Exeter Hall in May 1888, he presented a large audience with an 'object lesson'. 'I think you would like to see one of the children we take,' he announced, as a little girl of seven years, neatly dressed and 'safe and happy in the Village Home', stepped up on to the platform. 'This is a very dear little child from our Village,' Barnardo beamed, 'I will venture to say that she is very good. I hope she is not frightened; we are not going to do anything to her that is unpleasant. Now,' said Barnardo with the flair of a showman, 'I am going to show you another little girl.'[8] A small child, clean but dressed in the rags she wore on her admission to his all-night shelter a few days before, came up timidly to the platform to be presented to the audience. 'This child,' Barnardo intoned, 'is five years of age. Her eyes are so badly affected that there is some fear she may become blind. Her story is a dreadful one which I cannot tell, even before her and the other children here, because although she would not understand it, the others would. The cruelty that child has suffered is such that I cannot repeat it. The mother was a person of degraded life. The child has just been admitted. May we not hope that she will some day be like this one. Do you not feel you are doing God's work in this wonderful alchemy of love? In helping turning this into that . . .' Even for Barnardo parading human examples of 'before' and 'after' was extreme, but for his audience he could do no wrong and they demonstrated their approval with loud cheers. In 1889, the dear little mite, now six and looking neat, shining and healthy, was triumphantly presented to the audience again: 'She is one of my little daughters now,' Barnardo proclaimed.

At the time the homes were over £12,000 in debt and it would seem that this was yet one more desperate bid to raise funds. In his eagerness, Barnardo singled out the individual child and sacrificed her self-esteem for the image of the work – not for the first time. He himself seemed split in his roles, caring, sensitive philanthropist on the one hand and ruthless showman and publicist on the other. But by then Barnardo considered himself the champion, almost the inventor, of the destitute child. Compared to the wilful neglect, the cruel anarchy of the streets, his rescue operation was a lifeline. But how much the writing off of a child's parents and her past, the turning of 'this' into 'that', crushed the spirit of the boy or girl is a question at least worth asking. For all his great work in rehabilitating poor children, Barnardo, the brilliant publicist, helped to condemn parents who were often as hapless as the children they had bred.

In the Village 'mothers' deliberately drew 'the dark curtain of the past' over the girls' early memories of homes, parents, relatives and friends. The difficulties involved in this bold piece of social engineering are hinted at in cosy accounts of Village life: 'Imagine a household composed of a dozen small servants for the most part intent on doing as little work and making as much commotion about it as possible,' wrote a holiday 'mother' in 1881. 'A kitchen girl (an older child) stirs at 5.40, prepares breakfast and at 7.30 the mother holds a simple morning service. Breakfast is served by a girl in mother's cosy parlour but alas, she is to learn that patience is needed since she is offered toast as tough as leather, though the young cook has been told over and over how to make it.'[9]

The Honorary Secretary to the Girls' Village Home, a Miss Margaret Stent, wrote in more general terms of the difficulties of those cottage 'mothers', especially when their 'family' consisted of new girls with no Barnardo training:

> The result frequently makes large demands upon the patience and perseverance of the 'mother' for the sixteen or twenty inmates often come from utterly loveless and unhomelike homes . . . Many of the young girl waifs have no idea of order or of method, no notion of cleanliness or of comfort. All has to be begun afresh and the mother has need of all her energy. If anyone thinks it is an easy thing to win the confidence of, or to make obedience a pleasure to these poor little girls who have been accustomed to distrust everybody, or to reconcile with an ordered life, young people who have been accustomed to run wild and to claim the liberty of turning day into night – well, let him or her try it! . . . we are our own servants at Ilford, our own chambermaids and charwomen, our own cooks and nurses; we sew, and mend, and darn, and sweep, and dust; and positive training in all these feminine arts is no light task.[10]

The experiment in creating a substitute family based on maiden ladies acting as 'mother' was courageous. In many, perhaps the majority of cases, 'mothers' displayed a heroic and touching devotion to their duty.

Not all the girls, however, responded to the treatment with the grace and gratitude expected, to the astonishment of their betters:

> Occasionally some little girl appears as if she were actually possessed by an evil spirit so painfully do the lack of self-control and the spirit of disobedience manifest themselves. Unspeakably sad, for instance,

are the occasional outbreaks of little Florrie, a tiny slender mite of five with a clinging affectionate manner and a sweet wee face ... Cross the small maiden's will or reprove her for a passing fault when, alas, issues a volley of foul language such as only a hardened reprobate would dare to use ... Florrie is new to us but already shows signs of improvement ... gradually the quiet, fireside Christianity of our Cottage sinks deeper into the minds and hearts of the little rescued inmates.

The literature, understandably, concentrates on the successes, and Barnardo regularly published letters of gratitude from his girls: Caroline A. (South Hampstead):

I have been thinking so much of you all since I left ... Every time anything is said to me about the home and all my friends there, I feel as if I shall be choked. The tears want to come; but I am trying to do my best and bring credit on the home. I look back, and am getting into the way of thinking and talking of Ilford as my home.

Ellen S. (London SE):

I found out a great deal of difference in smoky London to the Village Home ... I miss my companions very much ... Dr Barnardo gave me a Bible and a pledge card. How often I think now of what he said to me! I did ask him if he would still call me one of his daughters. And he said, Yes, of course he would. Oh, ma'am! how can I thank him enough for what he has done for me – or rather, thank God, who put it into his heart to do so? I mean to do all I can not to bring discredit to the home.[11]

Despite the purple prose of persuasion, it seems clear that Barnardo did feel a special affection for 'his girls'. After they left the Village, he remained in touch, possessive, protective and deeply interested. A rare letter survives which shows him dissatisfied with his 'mothers' and anxious about his girls: after an unsatisfactory visit one Sunday night (he would probably have been preaching there), he wrote:

I hope all is going well with our unhappy young people. I assure you Sunday night's experience has made a most distressing impression upon my mind. I have longed to take each of these children into my arms and try to love her back to goodness and graciousness, and I cannot but feel that if there was a larger amount of real loving godliness in the Village Home among the dear mothers who are my colleagues, the necessity for punishment would be immensely diminished. But oh, how are we to get that very spirit developed which is truly the spirit of Christ and which alone will flood our Village with a tide of gracious influence and holy feeling?

I am almost heartbroken as I look out on things as they are now. There may be, and no doubt is, here and there, some one of the older girls who are out of the cottage life, responding to the invitation and claims of the Gospel and for all such cases I thank God from my heart; but I cannot hide from myself that there is in the cottages such a sense of injustice, of unwisdom, of even harshness – I do not mean harshness which exhibits itself in physical chastisement but in the constant pressure upon the spirits of these young girls, as awakens in many of them the dormant passions which are in all our hearts, arouses the very devil in their natures, makes them despair of good, and reckless of the consequences and causes them to throw to the wind restraint.[12]

Barnardo's comments in 1893 reflect, almost prophetically, the feelings of some of the girls who grew up in the Village forty years later in the 1930s, long after his death. The atmosphere in each cottage varied greatly depending on the individual 'mother'. Some devoted 'mothers' brought up 'their' children with great tenderness, sacrificed their small savings to buy birthday presents and kept in touch all their lives. But in a few of the cottages the girls felt that very sense of injustice, of harshness that Barnardo described so vividly. That was the dark side of the dream.

Agnes Bowley recalled her life in Syndal Cottage with uncomfortable clarity. She went to Barnardo's in 1934 when she was twelve years old: 'Life in the Village had barely changed since Barnardo's day. To look at, the grounds were lovely, the lawns, the flowerbeds and the almond trees. But there was a high fence and wrought iron gates and once they clanged behind you you were shut in and you didn't feel free.'

When Agnes first arrived at her cottage, 'mother' cut her long auburn hair to above her ears without explanation and put a big white bow on the back of her head. Agnes cried.

Miss D. [the mother] always opened our letters and read them. (We were allowed a stamp to write home once a month.) I remember my sister sent me half a crown. 'Mother' took it, but once a month she let me have twopence or threepence for the tuck shop. When she went out she would shop for us. I'd say: 'Please, mother, will you buy me a bar of Palmolive soap?' But she never gave it to you personally. It was left on the hall table.

The children lived in total ignorance of the outside world, without newspapers or radio. In memory, only royal events touched their lives. King George V died and the Village flag flew at half mast; 'mother' came down looking sad. Princess Marina got married and on Founder's Day the children were given a souvenir mug. That year Agnes' father came on a visit. 'My father and I were cuddling and kissing and Father cried. I said: "Can I show him round the Village," and 'mother' said: "Yes, for half an hour." '

About thirty girls lived at Syndal Cottage and every day was the same. The big girls rose at six and got a big pot of oatmeal porridge. At six thirty they washed and dressed the little ones. They had to fold blankets and sheets and hump up the mattresses. One of the house girls (older girls who had left school) woke 'mother' with a cup of hot water.

After prayers 'mother' would say, 'Anything to report?' She encouraged girls to tell tales on each other and if you'd done anything wrong you got a slap around the face or go without jam for tea. Friendships weren't encouraged, you weren't encouraged to have little gossips. We did play games, but not the running around sort.

At first I was afraid to tell her when I had my periods. When I did she said to me: 'One day God might call upon you to be a mother.' Later when I was leaving I went to the Governors' House [the Village at the time was ruled by two benevolent autocrats, the Honourable Miss Macnaghten and Miss Picton-Turbervill known as 'the Governors']. Miss Macnaghten gave me a Bible and a prayer book and asked: 'Do you know where babies come from?' I said, 'No.' She looked down at her desk and said: 'The man lets the fluid into the woman.'

Once you left school you always wore an apron and cap and had training to go into service. You weren't asked what you wanted to do; you were just told. I was the kitchen maid and that was it. There were loads and loads of cockroaches in the kitchen so I had to put down Keating's powder.

Agnes went into service in the Baldwin household after leaving Barnardo's. There was a 'family' connection since Baldwin was an ardent supporter of Barnardo's and became first President of the homes in 1938, the year after Agnes joined his household. 'Workwise it was worse than Barnardo's,' is her memory. She slept in a cold attic room, crept downstairs at six in the morning to light fires and scrub long stone passages and flights of stone stairs. Then cook would come down to inspect her work. 'My hands were raw with scrubbing all the time. You were the drab, the lowest of the low.'[13]

Of all the Barnardo homes, the Village retains the most personal memories of the founder. He chose to be buried there and later a monument to him was placed in the grounds, so that Village girls felt his power and his pervasive presence.

Arthur Runcie, a Barnardo old boy who has been disabled all his life, is now a widower in his eighties and was married to a girl from the Village Home; his wife Emily served as a model for one of the little girls in the Barnardo monument. In his comfortable room in the Village, in Scotch House, hangs a large portrait of the founder. 'Emily used to say, "Goodnight, Dad," every time she went to bed,' he recalled.[14]

Barnardo lived to see the Children's Church in the Village dedicated in 1894, the school's building opened in 1896 and a sanatorium for consumptives built in 1904. By the time he died the Village had grown to giant proportions with sixty-five cottages and 1,250 girls.

Through emigration and widespread publicity, the Village, always known as the most beautiful and pleasing aspect of the work, won popularity and appeal throughout the Empire. In 1919, the Australasian Hospital was built from donations received from thousands of Australians and New Zealanders. From Barnardo's death until the Second World War, the grip of tradition on the Village Home hindered any attempt to keep pace with changing times and changing attitudes.

However, during the First World War the quiet of the rural Village, set amidst the Essex cornfields, was disturbed by Zeppelin raids in 1916. When a shell exploded in the middle of the village green, fortunately not one life was lost. Despite soaring taxes and rising prices, the girls grew up in what the 1917 Annual Report described as 'God's plan for Family Life', still exclusively female.

Funds were short, income and legacies down and salaries so low that even long-serving staff were considering leaving. Generous food gifts from the Empire, in particular frozen carcases of sheep from New Zealand, helped to feed the children. Despite the war the demand for servants remained insatiable so that the homes could select suitable situations for their old girls.

The first significant change for fifty years in the Village way of life came in a confrontation over the management. The Governor of the Village, J. W. Godfrey, and his wife retired from Barnardo's after thirty-five years' service. In his stead two single ladies, the Hon. Miss Macnaghten and Miss Picton-Turbervill were appointed as joint Governors. Both had come out as debutantes before they took up Christian social work. During the First World War they had worked together, supervising munition hostels for young women in Coventry. They came from wealthy and influential families, outside the rather narrow circles from which most Barnardo workers were drawn.

The ladies knew Lord Sudeley, a member of Council, and were invited to view the Village; shortly afterwards the Council offered Miss Macnaghten a post as Superintendent at a salary of £400 a year; Miss Picton-Turbervill was invited to deal with the business side of the work at a salary of £2 5s. a week but was soon promoted to become joint Governor. In December 1920, the two ladies with their maids, Clay and Harris, and their furniture arrived to take up residence in the Village. Both Miss Picton-Turbervill, tall and imposing with a lorgnette, and Miss Macnaghten, dumpy and smiling, commanded respect and the girls soon learnt to drop a curtsey when they passed.

The timing of their appointment was significant. Miss Macnaghten and Miss Picton-Turbervill became Governors of the Village in December 1920 at the same time that Rear-Admiral Sir Harry Stileman was appointed Director of all the Barnardo homes. The Council's only experience of a paid Director in the past had been with Dr Barnardo himself who, in 1883, was forced to ask the homes for remuneration because of personal financial difficulties. As founder, and for many years unpaid Director of the work, Barnardo had remained possessive and intensely committed. On his death, the Chairman of the Council, William Baker, took on the role of Honorary Director. A successful barrister and former member of the Executive Committee, William Baker could be relied upon not to run the charity into debt. After fifteen years in that office, Mr Baker died in November 1920.

In appointing a paid executive, the Council chose Rear-Admiral Sir Harry Stileman, a fervent Evangelical who before the First World War had served Barnardo's faithfully as head of Watts Naval Training School in Norfolk. Despite their hopes, the appointment proved contentious. Admiral Stileman insisted on taking up residence at Mossford Lodge in the Village, given to Barnardo on his wedding and, therefore, in the Admiral's mind, the Director's residence. The Council (with some justification as it turned out) felt uneasy that the Director of all the Barnardo homes should live in one of them. Stileman did not settle in the Village until May 1921, when the ladies were already well established.

As senior staff, the two ladies held a novel position in Barnardo's at the time; they were confident of their ability and their authority was not easily overthrown. They came to the work fresh, unencumbered by the memory of the legend of the founder, and felt free to make changes.

Used to the bustle and hubbub of girls' hostels in the Midlands, they were surprised to find the large Village so quiet, tidy and orderly. They decided at once that, since it was impossible to get to know all 1,200 children, they must first get to know their fellow staff. 'As far as it can be said that we had any method, it was to know our fellow workers . . . as we moved in and out amongst them we became very conscious that the cottages were all isolated units.'[15] They felt straightaway that the girls needed outside stimulus and they decided to introduce the Girl Guide Movement into the Village.

At this distance of time, that hardly seems a revolutionary innovation but in 1920 when the Girl Guides were barely ten years old the movement sounded new-fangled and disturbing to the Village 'mothers' who were 'oddly apprehensive', Miss Picton-Turbervill wrote. 'What would it lead to? Would the girls get uppish?' Their task was a little difficult, she confessed, 'as our object was to widen the children's interest away from cottage life'. Nevertheless, the Governors breezed through the difficulties and, within a month, the first Guides were enrolled in the school hall and within a year 500 Guides and Brownies joined their own Village Barkingside Division with Miss Picton-Turbervill at their head as District Commissioner.

The Governors also decided to encourage the Village girls to seek promotion as domestics, to 'look upon service more as a profession, with future possibilities of obtaining really good posts, such as Head Housemaid in a big house or Head Parlourmaid or even Housekeeper and, perhaps highest of all, anyhow more exciting, work under a butler'.[16] In the past, after leaving the Village school at fourteen, the girls had stayed in their cottages for six months to a year, helping 'mother' and learning to become maids-of-all-work. They were usually found jobs as 'generals' in small local households where they often felt lonely after the community life they had led. ·

Under the Governors' regime, the most promising girls went to work in the Governors' house, under the close supervision of their own maids. The ladies would then find posts for them with households where they knew not only family members but also the 'tone' of the staff. Within a month of settling into the Village, the Governors had also encouraged sporting activities and set up clubs for singing, drilling and handicraft for the older girls who had left school. A dressmaking cottage and a mattress-making and upholstering hut widened the training possibilities for school-leavers. These modest reforms, introduced by ladies from a background with a worldly tinge, produced a crisis in the management of the homes which has implications on the running of the charity to this day.

Before Sir Harry Stileman took up residence in the Village, he had demanded an assurance in writing that he would be in complete command of the girls as well as the boys. He mistrusted the reforms the Governors had made and as soon as he came to live in the Village he made plain his disapproval, before he had even met them. Miss Macnaghten received a letter saying that the Director had heard the ladies had engaged an unmarried mother on the Village staff. In it the Admiral reminded the ladies of the sanctity of marriage and the necessity of 'keeping the home life pure'. Miss Picton-Turbervill remembered Miss Macnaghten gave the letter to the new Chairman of Council, William McCall, and told him that she did not propose to answer it since they had engaged no such person!

Conscious of his new position, Admiral Stileman resented the ladies' easy access to members of Council. He next took them to task for dismissing three laundry workers without consulting him. The disgruntled staff members appealed to the Admiral. 'We received a letter from the Director, a sort of liaison officer between the Council and the various homes,' snorted Miss Picton-Turbervill. 'We realised that he had expected us to consult him before dismissing any member of the staff. It had never occurred to us for a fleeting moment to consult him as to the suitability of matrons, laundry or otherwise.'

The Admiral was anxious to make his mark. The ladies were confident and autocratic and went their own way. At the Barnardo Naval School he had run a tight ship and his lady wife had played her part. She was anxious to become involved in the life of the Village.

In the autumn of 1921, some friends of the Stilemans, members of the Officers' Christian Union, were staying with them at Mossford Lodge. The Admiral was anxious to interest them in the work and no doubt eager to show them the Village. They strolled across the manicured lawns to the elementary school, where Stileman was annoyed to find the girls paraded in their Guide uniform. 'They were evidently in a state of considerable excitement,' he wrote later, 'and on the tip-toe of expectancy. I asked the headmistress why the girls had fallen-in and she said: "The Princess is coming." "Oh, what Princess is coming?" I asked and she replied, "The Princess Helena Victoria."' Not surprisingly, the Director was furious at not being informed about a royal visit and thought the ladies had slighted him deliberately. He had to learn of the occasion from 'the Head Mistress of the School of which bye the bye I am a Manager', he wrote.[17] The Princess was, in fact, a personal friend of Miss Macnaghten who had probably overlooked the Admiral.

The ladies' connections, their values, their outlook, made the Admiral uneasy. He himself had been a naval captain when he joined Barnardo's and was knighted during the First World War for his services as senior naval officer in charge of the port of Liverpool. He felt that the Governors were introducing too worldly a tone to the Village. The Girl Guide Movement, for example, in his view had been 'overdone'. Although he praised the spirit of comradeship, the thought for others encouraged by the Girl Guides, 'it took the girls away from home and transferred the seat of authority to the Parade Ground'. 'A Girl Guide does not think of asking the Mother's permission to attend a rally . . . she does not say, "Mother, may I go," but "Mother, I must go" and off she goes.'[18]

He suggested that the lady Governors neglected the girls' spiritual welfare for their material well-being by setting 'far greater value on girls being placed in situations commanding high wages than upon the atmosphere of the household to which they have been admitted'. He accused them of engaging workers who were not strict Evangelicals and, worst of all, alleged that the ladies did not attend the Village prayer meeting and 'changed it to make room for secular entertainments'.

What Admiral Stileman had failed to grasp was that with the growing popularity of Barnardo's Young Helpers' League, and the increasing links with society and royalty, Barnardo's had become increasingly a part of the Establishment. Support came not only from influential Evangelical families but also from the mainstream Church of England. The appointment of the lady Governors was a reflection of the changing status of the charity. It was the Admiral, not the ladies, who was out of step.

A stickler for the rules, Admiral Stileman also made himself unpopular by complaining of Council members' behaviour. Five members were required to retire annually but for years that practice had been ignored. As a result, the phrase requiring annual re-election was deleted from the rules at a special meeting. In addition, one Council member, T. J. Garnett, the honorary financial comptroller of the homes and a JP, had been unlawfully obtaining board and lodgings from the charity, the Admiral claimed. Formerly Honorary Governor of the Boys' Home at Stepney, Mr Garnett had offered his services as Honorary Governor of the new branch home at Hertford, the William Baker Technical School, where although he received no salary, he was allowed free board and lodging. On his own initiative, Admiral Stileman obtained Council's opinion on the question and Mr Garnett voluntarily refunded the cost of his board and lodging. Technically, Admiral Stileman was shown to be right but the victory proved costly.

During 1922 he was again in open dispute with the lady Governors. That summer Miss Macnaghten, dutifully following Council's instructions, applied to Admiral Stileman for permission to dismiss one of the cottage 'mothers' she considered slack. The Admiral agreed but changed his mind after interviewing the 'mother' himself. Miss Macnaghten wrote to him again, explaining that the 'mother' was extremely unsatisfactory; the Admiral remained adamant. A few weeks later the girls in that 'mother's' cottage were discovered to have dirty heads; the Village matron had to be sent for to disinfect them. This time Miss Macnaghten spoke a private word to a friend on the Council and the 'mother' was dismissed.

At a Special Meeting of the Executive Committee held at the end of November 1922, the ladies read a paper 'practically indicting' the Director and he replied to them. So acrimonious was the feeling between the parties that a sub-committee comprised of the Chairman and Deputy Chairman of the Council, the Governors and Stileman himself was appointed to guide the work of the Girls' Village Home.

By the end of that year, barely eighteen months after Admiral Stileman had settled in the Village, the Council felt that it would be better for Barnardo's if he transferred to another residence. Although Village affairs were managed by a sub-committee consisting of Council members, the ladies and the Admiral, neither the ladies nor the Council could get on with Stileman. The Council professed every confidence in the lady Governors; only the Admiral condemned them. He was again invited to move but refused. A small war followed. Admiral Stileman tried to institute first an investigation into the running of the Girls' Village Home, then in inquiry into the administration of Dr Barnardo's Homes. He published a pamphlet critical of the running of the Village and the conduct of members of Council and threatened to go to the press. In the end the Admiral, who, according to the Chairman of Council, 'claimed a far more absolute personal authority than Dr Barnardo himself ever claimed', was prevailed upon to leave. 'The Council are grieved to announce that owing to fundamental divergencies of opinion . . . between the Director and the Council . . . Rear-Admiral Sir Harry H. Stileman, KBE, has ceased to be Director of the Homes . . . They gladly bear testimony to his high Christian character and deplore the fact that it was found impossible to avoid a deadlock.'[19]

'We had no further trouble with the Director, he was found generally unacceptable and took his activities elsewhere,'[20] wrote Miss Picton-Turbervill dismissively. The outcome of the dispute gave the lady Governors even more authority in the Village.

In 1923 Queen Mary paid her first visit and the Village became even more of a favourite with the public. A tradition of visits and loyal gifts and messages was carefully nurtured. The Village school was taken over by the Board of Education and by 1926 a kindergarten, continuation classes for girls who had left school, as well as remedial classes for backward girls were developed. Between fifty and sixty abler older girls enrolled in classes, later known as the Meadow High School, and some even took public examinations. The Guides and Brownies flourished and in summer the children went to camp with other companies. By 1929, the Village had its own library and in 1933 the long-awaited swimming bath, built by local unemployed men, was opened.

Yet, despite the Governors' innovations, the Village was still very much a world of its own, extraordinarily cut off. The girls scarcely knew the world outside. The sexes were rigidly separated, brothers and sisters parted and tradesmen escorted round the Village. When the post boy called in the morning all the girls turned out to stare.

The age of the motor car had arrived. Women had taken their place in Parliament and the following year they would be fully enfranchised. But in 1927 the Girls' Village Home remained substantially as Dr Barnardo had wanted it. If he had come back, he would have found little to disturb him. According to the rules in 1927, girls had to be in their cottages by 8 p.m. on summer evenings and by 6 p.m. in the winter. No girl was allowed outside the Village alone at any time; girls who had left school (the fourteen- and fifteen-year-olds) had to obtain a pass to go into nearby Barkingside village in pairs. The day started at 6 a.m. for the older girls, 6.30 to 7 a.m. for the schoolchildren, with prayers at tea-time and bedtime from 6 to 9 p.m.[21] At night the iron gates were locked; the grounds were protected by a high fence.

The Protestant work ethic was drilled into the children at a very young age and Sundays were strict, as Mrs Vera Osborne who lived in John Sands cottage from 1923 onwards remembers:

From the age of five every child had a set job to do before we went to school. Five-year-olds picked up pieces off the front door mat. Next in age polished the door handles, which were all of brass. The knives, forks and spoons were cleaned each day. The saucepan lids and big baking tins were done with emery paper until you could see your face in them ... At twelve years old you were promoted to bedroom cleaning ... as there was no furniture except the beds, this was quite an easy job until Saturday when all the floors were polished. The older schoolgirls cleaned the dining-room with its three tables and twenty odd chairs.

'Mother' (Miss F.) was Irish. She was the first person I ever called 'Mother'. She really was all that a good mother should be, fair and just and very kind and we loved her ... unlike some 'mothers' she didn't have a favourite or 'pug' as we called it. It wasn't always fun to be 'mother's pug' even though you did get the best of everything. The other girls could make it very unpleasant for you if they wished ...

there was never any fear of me being a 'pug'. I was tall and skinny with dead straight hair.

For every girl in the Village prayers were a natural part of the daily round; with a short service after breakfast and a slightly longer time for prayers after tea. 'We used the Sankey hymnbook and took it in turns to choose a hymn. One of them caught our imagination. It went like this:

> The drunkard reached his cheerless home,
> The storm without was dark and wild,
> He forced his weeping wife to roam
> A wanderer, friendless with her child.
> As through the falling snow she pressed,
> The babe was sleeping on her breast.'

On Sunday mornings the Village went to church:

'Mother' took us and left the house girls (older girls who had left school) to see to the midday meal, which was cold. It was quite something to see over a thousand children coming from all directions. The church had a peal of bells which were fastened to the wall and one person could play a hymn tune on them. Each cottage had their own pews, and I was quite glad that ours were near the front . . .

In the afternoon the older girls went to Bible class, the young ones to Sunday School, but the in-betweens stayed at home. We were allowed to read books like *Sunday at Home* but no toys were allowed on Sunday . . . If 'Mother' was going to evening service we always knew as she didn't remove her hat. It sat straight on top of her head, fastened on with hat pins, which I thought must have been quite painful. Sometimes 'Mother' took us a short walk round the cornfields after evening service. We liked this as we were allowed to get 'out of order', that meant break the crocodile.[22]

Mrs Osborne had particular reason to be grateful to Barnardo's. When she joined the Village she was suffering from TB which had affected the bones in her hands and feet; she had ten operations in Barnardo's Village Hospital and remained a patient until she was four and went into her cottage.

The medical care in Barnardo's was always good, in advance of anything poor children were likely to receive in the world outside. The children were also well fed and materially better off than most working-class families.

Before the Second World War, the merits of domestic service were emphasised and the numbers of Village girls who managed to make a life for themselves beyond the kitchen sink were very small indeed. Undoubtedly the girls who settled best were those who came very young, without any memories of family life of their own. Mrs Dorothy Watt came to the Village in 1934 with her two sisters. She describes herself as 'one of the lucky ones':

> When I look back I feel that this was in almost every way possible a true home life for us. I see the advantage of being brought up in Barnardo's; it was like a very good boarding school. They were distanced. We were extremely happy and I don't think we could feel any more secure. The staff were wonderful, decent, honest, clean-living people, what better example could you have?
>
> Mum B. was a real mum to us. We got our cuddles and we got our spanks. She really loved us all. When my father wanted to take us back I didn't want to go. On my twenty-first birthday she bought me a gold watch. I brought my own children up with the same standards of honesty, self-discipline and religion that I learnt.
>
> I used to love dressing up on Founder's Day [the anniversary of Barnardo's birthday in July] when hordes of visitors would throng to the village on a special 'Barnardo' train; then at Easter time we gathered on the green where Easter eggs were broken and distributed to our eager outstretched hands.

Mrs Watt also looks back with pleasure on the Young Helpers' League celebrations in the Albert Hall, when Barnardo children would perform to an admiring crowd. And there were practical benefits from growing up in Barnardo's.

> I've always been able to live frugally after living in Barnardo's; when we were younger we used to share clothes. We were made to feel that people have to work for things . . . Of course I would like to have had a background, a home town where people knew me. I think growing up in a home makes you a little unsure of yourself. You're always frightened of doing the wrong things.

Mrs Watt left the Village at the outbreak of war, aged six, and went to Shropshire with her beloved 'mum' but when she was ten she won a scholarship to the grammar school at Ripon. Fortunately her younger sister remained with 'mum' and Mrs Watt kept in touch. She became a State Registered Nurse, a certified midwife and a missionary worker and is now married with two daughters. 'I owe everything to Barnardo's,' she admits. 'I really thought it was a family.'[23]

For almost sixty-five years life in the Village Home revolved round a ritual inspired by the founder himself. Any break in the pattern was such a novelty that Barnardo children's memories were intensely detailed and precise. They remembered their nicknames, their songs, their games and their menus. And they kept a communal memory of Village stories, like the time Miss Picton-Turbervill, who took evening service on Sundays, said to the children: 'If you want to korff, korff now.' And, of course, they remembered the high days and holidays in the Barnardo calendar.

First, came the January Fête organised by the Young Helpers' League, the Albert Hall day for song, dance and prayer put on by the little ones to enchant and disarm their supporters. Choir practice started months beforehand but all the children played their part: the Baby Drillers, the Brownie Band with bells, triangles, sledger cymbals and drums. One year, a scene of cottage life from morning to night was staged with the children eating their midday meal out of doors. 'I remember holding on high a plum pudding, while another girl held a joint of roast beef and the choir sang, "The roast beef of old England",' Mrs Osborne recalled. The scene ended with the lights of the cottages dimmed, the 'mothers' retiring for the night and a fairy child flitting through the Village.

Next came Easter, with Good Friday a solemn day when no toys were allowed and the children were forbidden to bounce a ball. Then Empire Day (when children from some of the nearby homes came to celebrate) and Founder's Day, Barnardo's birthday, when the children performed on the village green and grand ladies and gentlemen came to take tea and cakes in the cottages. The children always 'hoped the visitors would leave just a few cakes', as they were given the left-overs.

Guide camps for some girls broke the summer and in certain cottages 'mother' gave a Hallowe'en party. At Christmas, children and 'mothers' decorated their cottages for weeks beforehand. In many cottages Christmas Eve was the one night in the year when the girls were allowed to take a toy or a book up to their bedroom, as they went to bed very early in preparation for the great day. Stockings were hung up, the Salvation Army band played carols and, on Christmas morning, the children sang outside 'mother's' bedroom and squeezed inside to show her their goodies. After church the children ran home to greet Father Christmas who, accompanied by the lady Governors, office staff and the Salvation Army band, arrived in the storekeeper's horse and cart to deliver sacks of toys to each cottage. Children who had received parcels from their own families were given less than the others.

Village life with all its rituals held an inevitability safe but constricting.

Miss Chavasse, over one hundred years old and still sprightly and forthright, joined Barnardo's as a fund-raiser in 1924 after taking a social science degree. She was fascinated by the Village but found it 'very old-fashioned'. She was appalled at the separation of brothers and sisters and fought to change the system: 'In those days we had to count every penny. First the boys and then the girls asked Council if they could have a sausage for breakfast on Sunday. I also had to fight to get them jelly for tea on the day they left.'[24]

When war broke out the lady Governors retired and Miss Chavasse took charge of the Village. 'Most of the "mothers" were very good,' she remembered, 'but they were too strict and there were one or two I didn't approve of. There was too much smacking with wooden spoons. The elder girls didn't get enough freedom and they used to sneak out of their cottages at night and climb over the fence.'

In sixty-five years of existence, Dr Barnardo's dream had liberated many children from degradation, disease and poverty. In changing times, certain children found the class confines inherent in its structure cramping, even oppressive. Yet the spell Barnardo cast held the Village in its grip until the 1960s.

Just before the war, in 1938, 600 elementary school children from the Village were hurriedly evacuated with their 'mothers' and teachers to a safer part of the countryside. By June 1939, all the children were back in the Village and that summer hundreds of little girls in bright cotton dresses, dancing round the maypole, celebrated Founder's Day on the village green. A few weeks later, they were evacuated for the duration of the war and the Village was never quite the same again.

5

A New Heaven and A New Earth

'I conceive that London has got too full of children.'
Robert Joseph Chambers to the Select
Committee on Emigration, 1826

Will you climb that broken staircase
Will you look through that shattered door
Oh, can there be children sleeping
On that filthy and crowded floor?

Yet smiles thro' our tears are dawning,
When we think of the hope that lies
In the children's land of promise
'Neath the clear Canadian skies.

' "Where do the Children Sleep?"
A plea for the Emigration of Hundreds of Homeless
Children, now starving in London', *Night and Day*,
December 1883

In over eighty years, from 1882 until 1967, a total of 30,000 Barnardo boys and girls crossed the seas to the colonies as part of a nationwide emigration programme to resettle poor children. For the first forty years nearly all Barnardo's little emigrants were shipped to Canada, destined to become farm labourers or domestic servants.

Each spring, parties of children from toddlers to adolescents left in their hundreds from the port of Liverpool to the accompaniment of band-playing, hymn singing, banner waving and cheers. They crossed the Atlantic, steerage class, in a fever of excitement and sea-sickness. Each child bore a name tag and a Barnardo number tied to a coat, usually far too big. They felt an unusual sense of self-importance with their new wooden trunk made in Stepney, and packed with a Bible, a Sankey hymn book, a copy of *Pilgrim's Progress* and a new set of clothing. Dazed from the journey, they landed on Canadian soil buoyed up by hope and expectation. Within a few days they were sent off aboard a 'Barnardo Special' train to their distributing homes, with a box lunch and their belongings. After a long journey across the Canadian prairies, they arrived at an unknown destination to be driven off by strangers in a horse and buggy to a remote farm, boys and girls from city slums, most of whom had never seen a farm animal before. Compared with Canadian children they were undersized and many boys were sent back to the home after their long journey as 'too small'. The lucky ones were welcomed and treated as members of the family, the less fortunate became virtually slave labour. Despite an annual visit from a Barnardo Inspector and correspondence with the homes, they were marooned in the vastness of the landscape, vulnerable and profoundly alone.

To ship off boatloads of already deprived children to a different continent where they would be cut off from former human contact and every known experience seems, by today's standards, barbaric. This form of deportation of children was practised only by the British. Yet, at the time, all the child rescue agencies considered the uprooting to be the child's salvation. Snatched from the slime and vice of the slums and transported to the healthy fresh air and wholesome hard work of a new country, the children would surely flourish: that was the ethos of their work.

Although, by the close of the nineteenth century, Barnardo's had become the largest and best known of the rescue agencies engaged in emigration, Barnardo came late to the programme.

In 1870, when he was fully occupied in setting up his first home in Stepney, two strong-minded single ladies barely forty, Miss Maria Rye, a social reformer, and Miss Annie Macpherson, an Evangelical missionary, separately pioneered the work. Whilst Barnardo was preaching in his newly acquired Edinburgh Castle, establishing the Girls' Village Home and fending off the embarrassment of the arbitration, other rescue agencies turned to emigration as the best hope of saving the children. Occasionally, if a child was delicate and would benefit from a different climate, or if interference from what he termed 'vicious or criminal parents' threatened his reclamation work, Barnardo would take the drastic step of sending a child abroad. A few delicate children went to Natal; usually, he sent his boys to Canada under Miss Macpherson's escort. His very first street arab, Jim Jarvis, travelled to Canada with Miss Macpherson; as early as 1871 Barnardo's accounts reveal that he had set up a fund for the emigration of children to Christian homes in Canada. But in the early days he did not entirely approve of the work; he also admitted later that he did not like to follow in 'another man's line'!

His misgivings were entirely understandable. Motives for child emigration had always been mixed. As early as the seventeenth century, unwanted vagabond children had been shipped out to the American colonies, so the idea of emigration as a solution was not new. Later, in the eighteenth century, women prisoners and their children, as well as child convicts, had been sent to the colonies by successive British governments. 'Transportation', as it was called, served as a useful means of getting rid of undesirable elements as well as a punishment. Philanthropists, too, had seen opportunities for the child refuse of the streets in the wide open countryside in the fresh air, the clean start in a new country. Arguments about the desirability of the system surged to and fro but the advantages of sending pauper children to the colonies were rediscovered by penologists and philanthropists alike at times of economic depression.

In 1850, legislation had been passed permitting Boards of Guardians to send children from the workhouses to Canada. Until 1866, the year Barnardo came to London, the economy had been relatively buoyant, but that year a cholera outbreak followed by a failed harvest and an unusually harsh winter during a time of economic slump, focused public attention on the abject poverty, the homelessness, the hordes of unemployed in the streets. By 1869, emigration again seemed a useful option. Miss Maria Rye, who had earlier taken parties of women to North America to find employment, now appealed for £1,000 for child emigration in a letter to *The Times* on 29 March 1869: 'What treatment will they receive from the cold, the starvation, the temptation they meet within our gutters; what justice will they receive at our hands when the police, the gaol, the hospital and the Magdalen receive them? Can anything I introduce them to in Canada or America be worse than that to which they are doomed, if we leave them where they are now?'

Miss Rye's forceful, if questionable, arguments did not silence all her critics. Nevertheless, on 28 October 1869 she set sail from Liverpool with the first large party of seventy-six workhouse girls, nearly all under eleven years old. The following year Miss Annie Macpherson sailed for Canada with one hundred boys; she made three more journeys with children that year. Soon, other child rescue agencies followed suit and by 1874 over 900 children had been shipped to Canada from the workhouses and hundreds more from charity organisations.

The ratepayers were only concerned with the wards of state. They were sent abroad at public expense and as numbers grew local Boards of Guardians responsible for children began to become anxious. A question was asked in Parliament about the fate of the children in Canada.

In consequence, a senior local government Board Inspector, Andrew Doyle, with long experience of the workhouse system, was sent to Canada in 1874 to report on the children. He returned after three months convinced that although some English children, usually the smaller ones, were treated as family and warmly received, generally speaking the young immigrants were overworked and lacked both caring friends and protection in a strange land. 'To send them as emigrants can be regarded not as a way of improving their position, but simply of getting rid of them at a cheap rate,' he reported. He recommended that very young children should be sent overseas only if they could be properly protected by independent inspectors as they were in Britain.[1] As a result of his report, the emigration of workhouse children was suspended from 1875 to 1883, although more than 500 charity children were sent to Canada in those years.

Barnardo studied trends in child welfare at home and abroad and was, no doubt, worried by the adverse criticism of the work in Canada. Not until economic depression in England increased unemployment and homelessness did he start his own emigration programme. By 1879, cheap grain from the American prairies had produced a severe slump in agriculture; at the same time, cheap imports from Germany and America threatened Britain's industrial supremacy. With unrest in Europe, and the cities crowded with hordes of men thrown out of work, the authorities feared a breakdown of law and order. Like his fellow Evangelicals, Barnardo was concerned to garner souls for salvation rather than seek to eradicate social ills. He was also quick to sense the public's mood and turn it to his own advantage. Barnardo pleaded for support in an article entitled 'The Dangerous Classes'. In it he pointed to the recent assassination attempt on the Tsar's life, to Nihilism in Russia and Socialism in Germany as evidence of the menacing forces in society which threatened property, family life and religion. Has London been preserved from the terrible plague? he asked rhetorically. If so the instruments of salvation have been the great army of Christian workers. 'Every boy rescued from the gutter is one dangerous man the less; each girl saved from a criminal course is a present to the next generation of a virtuous woman and a valuable servant.'[2] In another article that year he emphasised the need to contain the children, one way or the other. In a favourite argument, he warned the public that they must choose between spending their money 'in the shape of rates and taxes for the support of police, magistrates, justices, houses of detention, convict prisons . . . or in the form of donations in encouragement of institutions like ours . . . Every convict costs England upwards of £80 per head per annum. Every boy or girl taken from the streets costs but £16 a year.'[3]

As the depression deepened, the debate on child emigration took an increasingly political tone. Confused with genuine sympathy for the suffering masses was a growing concern for public safety. In the circumstances, Barnardo pressed forward his rescue work. He had been anxious to open a Labour House for Destitute Youths over sixteen. 'Help or we Perish' he headed his appeal in his magazine.[4] Now, in London, there were 'thousands of poor, unemployed, characterless lads, slowly impelled to crime in the midst of a Christian people', he wrote. He had found an old house in Stepney and pledged himself to house and train the drifters: 'debt or no debt, money or no money'. His daring commitment must have made his committee wince. Emigration on a large scale would prove a blessing for the boys, he prophesied, once they had been rescued and trained.

By January 1882, Barnardo was about to open the new home formally. His accounts were, as usual, in a parlous state. At one time during the year, the donations had dropped so low that the work was only carried on 'with the greatest difficulty'. Yet he insisted on expansion: 'aggressiveness in such matters means healthy life'.[5]

Emigration must have seemed to him not only a solution to the gross overcrowding in the streets, but also a way of increasing his capacity to help, of expanding his work. By sending the children abroad he could reduce costs, free beds and thus take in more waifs.

Samuel Smith, the wealthy merchant and Member of Parliament for Liverpool who had once before intervened in Barnardo's work, now promised the homes a large donation to be used solely for emigration of which he was an ardent advocate. He wrote in emotive language of the need to dispose of the masses, 'foul sewage stagnating beneath the social fabric'.[6]

By 1882 Barnardo was committed to an emigration programme. He started this department of his work in uncharacteristic haste. At the Annual Meeting in June it was barely mentioned, but by July he asked the Governor of the Boys' Home in Stepney, Frederick Fielder, to get a party of fifty boys, ready outfitted, and with passage booked, to leave in a fortnight. By August his first party of fifty-one lads, aged between fourteen and seventeen, set off to sail the Atlantic, late for the emigration season, since the Canadian harvest, when farmers needed hands, was almost over. The Barnardo party was promised the use of the Reverend Bowman Stephenson's home in Ontario for those boys who did not find work on landing.

Mr Fielder arrived safely with his party in Canada and soon sent back glowing reports. All but sixteen of the boys were placed in farmers' homes at wages from 50 dollars to 90 dollars a year, plus board and lodging. One lad was adopted by a Member of Parliament, another by a well-to-do farmer who wanted a companion for his three little girls.

Canada, according to Mr Fielder, was indeed the promised land, for there boys might find 'a beautiful healthy climate and an immunity from the vices and want which imperil their lives in the old country . . . mansion after mansion was pointed out as being occupied by people who entered Canada as poor and friendless as any of the boys we have taken out'.[7]

Six months later Barnardo himself reported that Canadian employers had found his lads 'far and away superior both as to physique and training and general deportment to any they had hitherto seen'.

The next party of one hundred boys left late in June 1883. The girls' turn came in July, seventy-two girls dressed in stout ulsters and travelling jackets with red hoods. On board SS *Sardinia* in Liverpool docks, they formed a circle round Dr Barnardo and sang their favourite hymns:

> I know not what lies before me,
> God kindly veils my eyes . . .[8]

The final warning bell rang, the portly figure of the Doctor boarded the tender and the little girls with their older 'sisters' ran to the railings and waved their handkerchiefs until the departing figure of Dr Barnardo vanished out of sight. The youngest of the party was four years old.

On landing the party heard the news that they had acquired a reception home in Canada. George Cox, once an orphan himself and now a railway magnate and mayor of the town of Peterborough, offered Barnardo rent free a three-storey brick mansion, Hazelbrae, which had already been prepared for the use of the children. Overjoyed, Barnardo took this as a sign of divine approval of his work of emigration.

More good news met them at Toronto. Applications had come in from all over the province, asking for domestic servants or requesting to 'adopt' a small child informally, as one of the family.

Barnardo tried to safeguard his children as best he could. Applicants for a child had to supply a reference from a clergyman or magistrate and give full information about their personal, financial and religious circumstances. In the early days, he arranged that very little boys and quite young girls should have some provision made for them by their new 'parents', a sum of money in the bank for a boy and an 'Outfit and all that is needed in the event of her marriage', for a girl.[9] Boys and girls between thirteen and sixteen were to be hired out as servants with wages from 30 to 200 dollars a year plus keep. They were all encouraged to write regularly to the head of the Canadian homes and were to be visited at least once a year.

However, the huge distances involved and the severe Canadian winters meant that roads might be impassable and children isolated for a year or more in lonely farmhouses amongst strangers. Records of the children were more fully kept than in England and certainly more carefully than by any other rescue agency. But, despite all the safeguards, the young Barnardo emigrant proved to be excessively vulnerable.

At home a rosy picture of the promised land prevailed. Although he had been slow to start the emigration of the children, once committed to it, inevitably, Barnardo became its most eloquent and persuasive propagandist. The New World had become the New Jerusalem and the echoes of the excitement reached even the tiny children in the Village Home.

'Please may I go to Canada? is the most popular sentence just now on the lips of our girls – it comes even from tiny ones of four or five ... To go to Canada is the great ambition just now.'[10]

Miss Millie Sanderson, a teacher, the new Secretary of the Girls' Home in Peterborough, Canada, was sent to England for several months to learn Barnardo methods and to train and bring back a party of girls; she worked as a holiday 'mother' at the Girls' Village Home in Ilford. Miss Sanderson felt bound to reveal the 'dark tintings of the emigration picture' in the charity's magazine.

> I told them of short summers and weary winters when the poetry of life seems to be either parched with heat or shrivelled by cold ... I spoke to them of work ... Good, hard work is the order of the day and commands good wages ... but the vicious and idle are just as sure to lose all that may be left to lose ... Canadian sunshine is bright and Canadian air is pure, but I never yet have heard that they have power to renovate corrupt hearts or reform evil lives.[11]

The same issue printed a long poem, 'Canada's Plea for the Waifs and Strays'. The poem voiced Canada's filial concern for 'the babes' of 'London's moral slime' and offered them a colonial welcome:

> Overcrowded! mother England, if the homestead's grown too small
> And the servants' little children are too many for the hall,
> We have acres, broad and fruitful stretching westward to the sun
> Prairie-lands and sunny hillsides from the forests to be won.

Barnardo's imagination was fired by the opportunities in the rugged North-West and, on his first visit in 1884, he began to plan a large industrial farm where his older lads could learn to become pioneer homesteaders. Part by grant from the Manitoba Government and from the North-West Railway and part by purchase, he acquired a farm of some 10,000 acres. Here his older lads from the Labour House would train for a year on the farm. Lads over eighteen who had proved reliable workers would be eligible for the Canadian Government grant of 160 acres and, on payment of 150 dollars, a house, a small stable, oxen and plough and farm stock. By now Barnardo excelled in organising large numbers of children and staff and dealing with officialdom. He had assembled a small team of workers in Canada led by an English clergyman's son, Alfred de Brissac Owen, also an Advisory Committee headed by Samuel Blake, QC, a former judge.

For Barnardo, as for other heads of rescue missions, the advantage of Canada was largely geographical, it was the colony nearest to the old country. On his visit in 1884, he was pleased with 'the kindly, religious feeling of the great body of working people' and also approved of their sobriety: 'There is a powerful sentiment in favour of temperance,' and added, rather naïvely, 'I have been a guest in many families but I have never once been offered beer or wine and I never once saw it on the table in any private house where I called.'[12]

When he came home Barnardo wrote with his usual uninhibited enthusiasm of 'the almost incalculable advantages conferred upon the children themselves by emigration'.[13] They would be introduced to 'pure healthy surroundings where vice, drunkenness and harsh treatment are unknown. Homes too, where family life and religious life are a blessed reality situated in a fair, garden-like country.'

The reality was not always so blessed and Barnardo, who read all the children's records from Canada, must have realised it. Yet, his emigration, like all his work, depended on the goodwill, the support and donations from the public. In the case of the emigration, press and public both in England and in Canada were more likely to seize on any weakness in the work and magnify it. Canadian critics feared that their country would be 'contaminated' by dumping thousands of slum children on their fair soil. Emotive labels which Barnardo and other child-rescuers had applied to poor children, 'street arabs', slum children, waifs, guttersnipes, stuck to the children and smeared their image. To counter this criticism, Barnardo had promised, in 1884, to send only the 'flower of the flock' to Canada: children who were morally, physically and mentally sound, properly trained both in industry and moral and religious character. He also undertook to see that the children would be received by qualified people and supervised for as long as necessary. If any children should become 'definitely immoral or criminal', he guaranteed that they would be shipped back to the old country.

Canadian labour leaders were long-term critics of child immigration;

they feared that the children's cheap labour was undercutting their wage structure. Some Canadian doctors considered the children a health hazard and law officers in some areas disapproved. Certain English critics, too, had misgivings about the morality of the operation while others felt that it was a shame to send the 'flower of the flock' overseas when they found it so hard to get good domestic servants or willing farm-workers at home.

Barnardo had to counteract all that potentially damaging criticism. In a letter to one of his Canadian visitors, he frankly asked for great attention to detail and 'local colouring' in reports. 'I can never tell under what great public crisis here I may suddenly be compelled ... to supply information ... I must be able to show that if I have deliberately thrust one influence aside, I have supplanted it with another, infinitely more careful, more minute, more full of human interest.'[14]

From the time that he opened his Girls' Village Home in England, Barnardo had maintained a special and personal interest in his 'daughters', mentioning individual girls in letters to his wife. He believed, with obvious emotional involvement, that it was his duty to rescue them from evil influences. In 1886, he had opened a small rescue home in London with a secret address for the saving of young girls 'from conditions of very grave, often very imminent peril'. Presumably it was financial need that prompted him to send so many adolescent girls overseas, although some other Christian agencies considered them too vulnerable at that age. In the first five years of their lives in Canada, girls moved household on average four times, almost once a year.

Barnardo was certainly alive to the dangers and difficulties that faced them so far away from home. In 1889, six years after he had started sending girls to Canada, he sent Miss Stent, the Honorary Secretary of the Girls' Village Home, to the Girls' Home in Canada to try to devise safeguards for his wards. As a result Canadian employers were warned sternly to make sure that a respectable woman was on hand to chaperone the home girl if the mistress was away for the night; locks on doors and windows were to be made secure and girls were not to be left alone with male farm hands.

The following year, Barnardo travelled to Canada to see the work for himself. Conditions in the Girls' Home in Canada had improved under a new matron. 'No doubt,' he mused, 'the staff here see a great deal of the seamy or dark side of Canadian life.' But he himself was spared it. Forty of his old girls accepted an invitation to visit him at Hazelbrae and, as he shrewdly observed, 'occasions of this sort bring to us not those who have done ill but those who have done well and the visits were most encouraging and comforting to us'.[15]

About that time he came to realise that 'adoption' into a family did not always afford the child the love and security he had envisaged. (''doption, Sir, is when folks gets a girl to work without wages.')[16] From the 1890s, Barnardo paid foster-parents a fee of 5 dollars a month to care for his wards and stipulated that they must be allowed time off to go to school. With the vast distances involved, the sparsity of schools in rural areas, the differing demands of the farmers, it was a requirement that could not always be enforced.

In spite of his efforts, the children's lives in Canada were, even by the standards of the day, excessively harsh. The home child had to face an extreme climate, loneliness and boredom in the long, dark winters and the physically gruelling work in the hot summers.

Yet, year after year, Barnardo told stories of miraculous transformations, of homeless waifs transformed into sturdy servants. 'The letters received from these children,' said the Marquis of Lorne, a former Governor-General of Canada who had become President of Barnardo's Homes, speaking at Barnardo's Annual Meeting in 1890, 'all speak of their welfare, of their happiness, of the circumstances in which they are placed and their gratitude to the Founder of these Homes.'

Many churchmen, politicians and leaders of opinion in England held that optimistic view of emigration. As the acknowledged leader of child emigration, Barnardo's status and financial support for the homes soared.

In many ways, Barnardo's took more care of their children overseas than other agencies. They did pay to board the younger children out, visit at least once a year and try to help and guide them during their apprenticeship. They kept very careful records and yet even a cursory glance at the children's confidential records is sobering. Professor Parr's careful sample reveals that at least 9 per cent of boys and 15 per cent of girls were so badly treated by employers that they had to be taken away or their employers reprimanded – which was not done lightly.[17] Barnardo himself admitted that, despite careful screening, many employers were 'far from desirable guardians or associates of young children'. Given the numbers, it is difficult to see how it could have been otherwise.

Records reveal that some children were subject to severe maltreatment: sexual assault, fierce beatings and whippings; accidents occurred with pitchforks, impalement on fenceposts, a number committed suicide by drowning or hanging. Above all, the records reflect the immense loneliness of children brought up in crowded cities, or in the homes where there was always children's company, cut off in a remote homestead, neither a member of the family, nor a hired hand: simply a 'home' child.

Living in the Canadian wilderness, not surprisingly, home girls did become pregnant, despite all the safeguards; but probably not in any significantly larger numbers than other girls in similar circumstances. In 1905, Barnardo's opened a shelter in Richmond Street, Toronto, known euphemistically as a Rest Home for Girls. They were not encouraged to marry but to have their babies and return to work. The homes' policy of banking a girl's accumulated wages for her until she was twenty-one may possibly have increased illegitimacy, since many girls preferred to wait to marry until they had their money.

Some of the children did well. William Arthur Hughes, for example, born in Islington in 1886 was one of five children. His mother died of paralysis of the brain when William was seven, his father, a french polisher, of dropsy a year later. The insurance money of £3 8s. did not even cover the cost of the funeral.

A grandmother looked after the family on the wages of the eldest boy Richard, aged thirteen, who earned eight shillings a week working for a cabinet maker. That was the family's total income. The smaller children were half-starved and rather than send them to the workhouse they applied to Barnardo's where all four were admitted. William went to Canada with his younger brother Henry in the following year, 1896, and both were boarded out with a Mr Faulkner at Falkenberg. A year later Mr Owen reported that 'both boys attended school unfailingly', and were 'bright, diligent little scholars'. They were fortunate in having each other's company and in going to school regularly. On 20 December 1897, Mr Owen wrote that William was 'growing and thriving under the excellent care of his worthy foster parents . . . Mr Faulkner has undertaken to support William for the present year without payment. He is giving every possible satisfaction and is the object of kindly affection to both the old people.' After four happy years, twelve-year-old William was placed in work. He had been 'charged with dishonesty' by his foster-parents, Mr Owen reported, but did not dwell on that aspect. 'He has earned an excellent character in his present situation. Very comfortable, home and health good.'

By 1900, Mr Owen recorded that William's health was good and he was bright, intelligent and 'spoken of in the highest terms and doing well'. By the age of twenty, William was growing into an 'excellent hand with the machines'. The half-starved little boy who had weighed fifty-six pounds on admission was now a strapping young man of 165 pounds, set up in life. His apprenticeship ended the next month. He was one of the success stories.[18]

Wilfred Lofft, who came to Canada in 1895 at the age of twelve, had a very different record. He was employed as an apprentice farm boy, but 'the farmer had to whip the boy four times for telling lies. Wets his bed and is lazy and will not work unless watched.' Barnardo's advised Mr

Shepperd, Wilfred's employer, that a 'reasonable application of corporal punishment might have the desired effect'. Obviously it did not. Mr Shepperd wrote again, complaining that 'Wilfred was the biggest shirk' he had ever seen. In February 1896, Wilfred was sent to another farm. The record states starkly: 'still whipped and wet bed'. A month later, Wilfred was returned to the home. He complained that he had had to work from 5 a.m. to 9 p.m.

In November 1896, Wilfred was placed out with another employer and pronounced satisfactory. Then came a report stating that the boy had left his situation for no reason and applied for his box with his good suit. (This was lodged with the employer when a boy arrived and only returned to him with the home's sanction.)

The next news came in a letter from Wilfred, now aged seventeen, dated December 1899, justifying his conduct: 'I have not been wandering round the country. I have been working all the time. I am settled down now, until I get enough money to take me to England to my mother. She wants me to come home so badly.' He sent a dollar to join the Guild (the Old Boys' League) and was at last given his clothes.[19]

Robert Tunbridge was sent out at the age of eight in 1895 and boarded with a Mr Morgan. He was visited regularly. When his mother in England wrote to Stepney complaining that she had had no reply to letters to her son, Barnardo's in Stepney wrote to Barnardo's in Toronto who contacted Robert's employer to see that 'the boy writes to his mother'. The farmer and his wife both wrote to the Toronto home with the reassuring news that Robert was 'quite well and hearty'.

When Robert was ten, a neighbour who lived a quarter of a mile away wrote to the homes with disquieting news: 'The other night he had seen the employer give Robert a good thrashing', and 'his skin was cut with a whip and the blood was shining through. Another neighbour saw him kick the boy with big, heavy boots.' The home visitor paid a special visit and Robert was found another place. The new employer wrote complaining that the boy was not getting along well: 'he lies so that they cannot believe one word he says and is addicted to anything eatable he may come across'. His report added: 'he is however goodnatured and good company and pleased to see a visitor from the home'. Then Robert stole a jack-knife from a nearby store, some money and a ring from his employer's wife. For this the farmer thrashed him and Robert ran off.

Again, Robert was apprenticed to a new master. The homes asked 100 dollars for four years' apprenticeship but the employer bargained and got Robert cheap for 90 dollars since he was 'scarcely first class'. The new employer wrote optimistically that Robert was improving and he 'hoped to make a man of him'. But again Robert ran away and a letter shortly after carried the alarming news that he held a revolver and threatened to shoot anyone who attempted to take him back to his employer. The employer explained that he had caught Robert a few Sundays ago 'in the commission of an unnatural offence with a mare; the same evening he indecently assaulted his employer's little girl. He was thrashed the next morning and ran away.'[20]

Reports of cruelty to animals appear sporadically in the files, although cases of assault were not common. In their isolation, the boys wrought their frustration on the stock, the only living creatures accessible to them, usually better cared for than the hired boy.

Foster-parents often complained of physical shortcomings in the children, of 'dirty habits', presumably masturbation and bed-wetting, for which the homes sent medicine. Even the children's sufferings caused complaint. John, aged nine, was sent back to the homes with a letter grumbling about the difficulty that the farmer's wife had had on account of the 'breakings out on his feet which appear to have been caused by frostbite'.

Because of their prominence, press and public were quick to pillory Barnardo's when tragedy struck. In November 1895, George Everitt Greene, a sixteen-year-old Barnardo boy, was found dead in a lonely farmhouse, brutally beaten and emaciated with his body covered with excrement. His employer, a spinster, Miss Helen Findlay, was placed on trial for manslaughter. Miss Findlay's defence maintained that George Greene who had come into Canada 'with some inherent disease' was a half-wit, an imbecile, with poor sight. Home children were frequently rumoured to have syphilis, although there was no medical evidence to corroborate the theory. The defence had the body exhumed to prove their case. Despite the evidence of the doctor who had examined George and attributed his death to neglect and external injuries, and neighbours' testimony that Miss Findlay had laid about the boy with axes and pitchforks, the defence played successfully on the public's fear and prejudice. The jury could not reach a verdict and Miss Findlay was acquitted.

Public indignation and press comment centred on bringing children 'with tainted blood' into Canada and Barnardo vigorously defended himself against that charge,[21] urging the Canadian Government to introduce a system of rigorous medical examinations for each new immigrant. George excited as little sympathy in death as he had in his short life.

However, Barnardo's proposals were adopted by the Ontario province and in 1897 an Act was passed requiring child immigrants to be screened for physical, mental and vicious tendencies. Inspectors were required to visit the children every year and return those who became a burden on the state. Barnardo could justly claim that he had adopted all those measures; his active campaign to defend the child immigrants from prejudice benefited all the smaller rescue agencies.

Intensely jealous of his reputation in Canada, Barnardo always claimed that only 2 per cent of his children came before the courts or 'failed', a percentage that even the Superintendent of Neglected and Dependent Children for Ontario Province, J. J. Kelso, a great admirer of Barnardo, considered far too partial, since not all the wrongdoers reached the courts. Outside authorities had no means of checking Barnardo's figures, as his records were jealously guarded.[22]

With the Canadian press only too ready to tarnish the home children and their leaders, Barnardo's was constantly on the alert.

In 1898 John, a thirteen-year-old home boy, was left in charge of the farmer's four-year-old daughter, while he and his wife drove out for the day. When the parents returned, they found the two young bodies lying on the ground, shot. 'Murder and Suicide' screamed the headlines, whilst Barnardo's own paper in Canada, *Ups and Downs* (1898), explained soothingly that it must have been an accident whilst Johnny was playing with an old revolver, since he was used to shooting gophers and squirrels.[23] The truth of the tragedy will never be known. The overriding impression gained from scanning the confidential records is of the hit-and-miss nature of emigration, the risks taken with children and the lack of any of the warmth of family life. In Barnardo's lifetime few of the emigrants grew up to fulfil his extravagant expectations for them. Although, in fairness, by the 1930s, child emigrants to Canada were materially better off than if they had stayed in England.

These bleak impressions are confirmed by a living witness, Mr Barker, now back in England. He was born in 1907: 'My father died in 1913, leaving my mother with five young children. Her only income was two shillings a day, doing washing for some élite family. She could not afford to keep us all, so my eldest brother and I were taken into Barnardo's in 1914. I was seven then and conditions were very austere. They would not be tolerated nowadays.'

A year later Mr Barker was sent with his brother to Canada to board with a Mrs Moore who lived near Port Ronan, Ontario. She was a middle-aged widow who kept home boys. 'She got five dollars a month for each of us, so it was her living. Life was strict, she was very religious and all our evenings were spent in Bible reading and prayer.'[24]

After eighteen months, Mr Barker's brother was taken away and he was left with the widow. Two years later in 1917, Mr Barker was transferred as an apprentice to a family named Goodwin at Mount

Albert. The household consisted of Mrs Goodwin, aged eighty, and her son, forty-nine, her niece and the new apprentice. His salary for five years was 125 dollars, that is 25 dollars a year, or £5 a year at the rate of exchange of those days. After five years' apprenticeship, Mr Barker received his first money, 25 dollars to clothe himself. Barnardo's kept the remaining 100 dollars for him until he was twenty-one.

> It was in the five years with those people that I realised that we were just chattels for Canadian farmers. We were never allowed to forget that we were lucky to be alive; you were really a nobody. There were no laws in those days about education and when I was eleven they took me out of school. Their attitude was I was there to work, not sit around in school, so I was doomed to be just a labourer.

Mr Barker tried to better himself by serving an apprenticeship as a fitter on the Canadian National Railways but he could not afford to live on the wages. He returned to the farm and after a year went west to Winnipeg, Manitoba.

> There I met my darling wife. She came from an orphanage so we had a lot in common.
> When I was fifteen I had nothing more to do with Barnardo's. As far as affection was concerned, all those years I never knew what sympathy or affection was. If I had an accident or hurt myself it was always, 'Serve you right, you shouldn't have done it,' but as I look back over those years I hold no bitterness. Barnardo's done me no harm and maybe a lot of good . . . I thank them for what they did for me, it taught me not to expect too much in life and to stand on my own two feet.

Whatever the children had suffered, they nearly all feel a deep sense of thankfulness to Barnardo's. They appreciate that standards were different years ago and that left to the mercies of the state or the public, they might have fared worse. If they have regrets, it is usually for the breaking up of family ties, the wrench from home. In his fierce crusade to rescue the children, Barnardo was very hard on their parents. Those he considered worthless or degraded were far more likely to have their children sent away to Canada than 'respectable' parents. Indeed, parents he disapproved of were not even sent the homes' printed 'Notice of Departure' form until after sailing. By 1908, 8 per cent of the girls and 6 per cent of the boys were sent to Canada illegally, without parental consent.

These early portraits of Thomas Barnardo's youth (*left to right: aged eleven, fourteen and twenty-one, the one aged eleven is probably taken from a painting*) hint at the complexities of his character.

The remarkable young man who became a philanthropist in his early twenties, was born at 4 Dame Street, Dublin, in one of the houses on the right. His father, a furrier, catered for the carriage trade; Thomas John grew up 'over the shop'.

In Hope Place, a small back street in Stepney, Barnardo rented two cottages where he taught and converted the children of the streets.

His pioneering use of photography contributed to his sensational success but held pitfalls. The two girls (below) Florence and Eliza Holder, were sent to him by their widowed mother, poorly but respectably dressed. Barnardo had Florence, the elder, photographed barefoot, in tattered clothes, selling newspapers; Eliza's portrait was pasted on to a collecting box, captioned 'a little waif from the streets'. He was censured during the 1870s for his use of 'artistic fiction' but commended for his work with destitute children.

In 1870 he opened a residential home at 18 Stepney Causeway, the headquarters of the charity for almost a century. His home was open all night and 'no destitute child ever refused' (below right).

Barnardo sold packets of twenty photographs at five shillings to contrast the past and present of his wards.

In 1873 he raised funds to buy a large gin palace and music hall in the East End, the Edinburgh Castle. He transformed the 'satanic stronghold' into a coffee palace and mission centre. His bold gesture brought him the support of wealthy and influential Evangelicals who backed his work with children.

Top left: Barnardo illustrated his 1874–5 report of the mission entitled 'Rescue the Perishing' with ten wood engravings and two photographs from 'life'. The report contained a comprehensive account of his achievements as well as a list of nearly 8,000 donations, most of them under a pound.

Top right: Crippled boys were taught sedentary trades, tailoring and shoemaking; they made uniforms and repaired the clothes for the homes. The able-bodied boys made crutches and surgical appliances.

In his Girls' Village Home, established at Barkingside in 1873, the children lived in cottages surrounding an ornamental garden. They went to school and learnt domestic skills in the self-contained community. By the 1890s when this photograph was taken, the girls had their own Children's Church.

From 1882 until the 1930s, Barnardo's sent parties of children to settle in Canada. In 1912, the widowed Mrs Barnardo (centre) was present to bid the girls farewell as they travelled in special carriages to Liverpool where they would board ship.

This 1914 photograph shows their Barnardo 'brothers' in Canada on their way to work as farm apprentices or to meet their new foster-parents.

Mr. A. de Brissac Owen,
Superintendent of Boys' Branch, Toronto.

By the turn of the century Barnardo's sent more than a thousand children a year to Canada. With such vast numbers it was inevitable that there would be casualties. Laura Cummings, a restless teenager, ran away from her post as domestic in Toronto to the glamour of the theatre. She was retrieved but later smuggled illegally across the border to Buffalo. A US immigration official, a Mr de Barry, demanded that she be taken back to Barnardo's, Toronto. Laura wrote to Mr Owen begging him not to reveal the true story to Dr Barnardo (top left).

Barnardo's kept detailed records of the progress of each child. Robert Dixon Tunbridge was eight years old in 1895 when he went to Canada. He ran away from his foster home. 'Lad is very poorly clad and Mr P. will keep the boy until he hears from the home as to his disposal,' the register notes.

By the 1890s, Dr Barnardo figured prominently in the sphere of child welfare. At home he instituted an excellent system of boarding-out children, anticipating nearly all of the safeguards demanded in present-day fostering. Royalty patronised his work and he filled the Albert Hall regularly with his displays of 'the largest family in the world' at work and play.

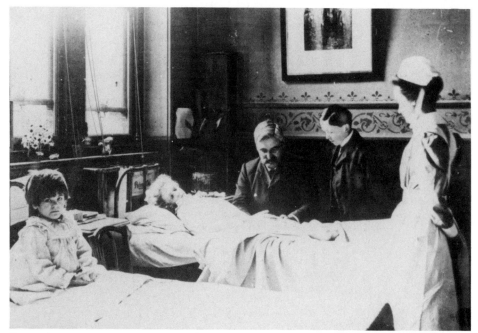

Barnardo commissioned Her Majesty's Hospital for Sick Children, the largest children's hospital in London at the time, to celebrate Queen Victoria's Jubilee. The hospital was well equipped and staffed. The doctor, Robert Milne, was the first in a family dynasty to care for Barnardo children.

Barnardo was particularly attached to his Girls' Village Home and at his own request his ashes were buried there in 1905. By 1924, when Queen Mary came to the Village, the Girl Guides were active, despite early opposition from cottage mothers.

In his publicity, Barnardo emphasised the need to rescue children in moral danger; in reality more Barnardo children were sent to Canada through loss of a parent and poverty than through immorality or cruelty.[25] Barnardo's England was, however, a fearful place for poor children. Child prostitution was rife and a poor child's life and labour were held cheap. Until 1889 the power of parents was absolute; they could do what they pleased with their children. Barnardo was criticised in some quarters for encouraging fecklessness by taking in children whose parents were living.

At the time, no benevolent institution held legal rights to guardianship. Even if parents had asked the homes to take their children and signed a form of agreement, they could take them back whenever they wished. Neglected or ill-treated children enjoyed very little protection from the law.

Barnardo showed a remarkable contempt for laws he disliked. He even boasted of his 'highhanded fashion of dealing with parents and guardians'. When he thought children were in need of protection from their parents, he did not hesitate to kidnap them or, as he perhaps rightly termed it, to 'philanthropically abduct' them. According to one journalist, by 1896 he had appeared in court eighty-eight times for similar actions.

He was still very much the Protestant missionary, frequently in conflict with Catholic authorities over the Catholic children brought into his homes. The Ever-Open-Doors of his homes took in all children, regardless of creed, but before he admitted children into the homes permanently, he insisted that he first inquired whether co-religionists were prepared to shelter them. Once they were admitted, however, the children were brought up as Protestants.

By the 1890s, the Catholic authorities were beginning to realise the need to co-ordinate their work for the large numbers of children in the big cities, rather than leave it to local parishes. Priests began to prompt parents to try to wrest Catholic children from Barnardo's clutches and frequently the cases came to court.

His most sensational case concerned the fate of an eleven-year-old boy, Harry Gossage. In the spring of 1888, Harry's mother, Mary Gossage, a widow, had sold her son to two organ grinders she met over a drink in a public house. These men trailed Harry around the streets like a pet monkey, frequently beat him up and finally abandoned him to wander the streets of Folkestone. The police arrested the boy and put him in the workhouse for shelter. Soon afterwards the local vicar, the Reverend Edward Husband, intervened, appealing to Barnardo personally to take the lad in. He was admitted at once and Barnardo's staff traced Harry's mother to obtain her consent. She duly made her mark on the agreement which did not, however, include the 'Canada' clause, giving consent to the child's emigration. She was sent the form with the 'Canada' clause on 9 November 1888 but did not return it.

On 10 November, a surprise visitor, a Mr William Norton from Canada, called at Barnardo's office in Stepney and asked to adopt a boy. The 'thoroughly well-to-do gentleman' presented a letter from a clergyman in Canada and a letter of introduction to a statesman in England. Barnardo was impressed with the stranger's manner and delighted with his offer; he brought down five or six boys for Mr Norton to inspect. Mr Norton picked out little Harry Gossage and, explaining that he wanted to bring up the boy as his own son, stipulated that he would not reveal his address in Canada in order to avoid any future trouble with 'begging or vicious' relatives. Barnardo accepted the condition and agreed to surrender Harry Gossage to the stranger. Within a week Harry was on a ship bound for Canada.

In the meantime, a Mr Newdigate wrote to Barnardo's on Mrs Gossage's behalf, enclosing a ten-shilling donation, asking that Harry be transferred to St Vincent's, a Catholic home. (Harry's mother was a Catholic, his late father had been a Protestant.) The donation was acknowledged but not until the end of the year did the Secretary reply saying that the rules of the homes forbade them to transfer a child on religious grounds. No mention was made in that letter of Harry's whereabouts.

When a letter arrived on 8 January 1889 threatening legal action if Harry was not returned, Barnardo at last revealed that the boy had left the country and his care. After two further fruitless applications on behalf of Harry's mother a writ of habeas corpus was issued in November 1889 and Barnardo was given three months to produce Harry Gossage. The case was widely reported and Barnardo was severely criticised by the Lord Chancellor. Always quick to defend his position, he called a public meeting of sympathisers at Exeter Hall. His powerful friends rallied and at the end of the meeting those present tabled a resolution calling for a change in the law of custody to give institutions such as Dr Barnardo's legal rights as guardians.

In January 1890 Barnardo appeared before the Court of Appeal conducting his own case. That appeal and a further appeal in the House of Lords in 1892 both failed and Harry Gossage was never found or returned to England.

At the same time that Mrs Gossage was seeking to get back her son, another Catholic mother, Margaret Ward, was trying to retrieve another child, Martha Ann Tye, from Barnardo's Homes. Like Harry's mother, Margaret Ward emerged as a callous, cruel person. In the spring of

1888, Martha Ann, a girl of fourteen, was found begging outside Muller's Orphanage in Bristol. An official of that institution applied to Barnardo to take the girl in. When he learnt that her mother's former lover, Francis Ward, had sexually assaulted Martha and been sent to prison for the offence, Barnardo agreed to admit her. Margaret Ward had married her lover when he was released from prison and had sent her daughter to beg in the streets. After Martha Ann was admitted to the homes, her mother signed an agreement surrendering Martha to Barnardo's care for two years. On 14 December Margaret changed her mind and sent a letter to Stepney asking that her daughter be returned. When a woman friend called at the homes with a letter of authorisation four days later, she was informed that Martha would be returned only to her mother.

Martha's case was remarkably similar to the Gossage affair. Only after three letters asking for Martha's return, the third threatening legal action, did Barnardo admit that she had left the country. Two months earlier, it transpired, a widow from Canada, Madame Gertrude Romande, had visited Barnardo's Homes and offered to take any two or three girls back with her, to educate them and eventually place them in service. The mysterious Canadian widow had taken Martha, but she could never be traced. Barnardo said that he knew her as a Christian lady, a friend who called in at the institution, but he did not know the name or address of any of her friends. Once again, despite litigation, the child was never found or restored to her mother. In court it emerged that Martha, like Harry Gossage, was intended for a Catholic institution. The court concluded that Barnardo had sent Martha away to avoid returning her to her mother.

Barnardo's intense prejudice against Roman Catholics clouded the real issue of those cases. However, the widespread press coverage of the Barnardo 'kidnapping' resulted in the public becoming more aware of the wanton neglect and cruelty, the chaos in which children like Harry and Martha grew up. A call to curtail 'the divine right of vicious and brutal parents to make their children brutal and vicious' came from Dr Anderson, Assistant Commissioner of Police for London. In 1891, the Custody of Children, known as the Barnardo Act, was passed. The Act gave protection for children in the care of the great rescue organisations like Barnardo's and restricted the rights of cruel or neglectful parents. Courts were empowered to refuse to restore children to their parents; to require parents to repay the cost of bringing up a child and, most importantly, to consult the wishes of the child. Once again, as in the earlier arbitration case, Barnardo had turned potential disaster into triumph.

The thoughtful Victorian might have felt some misgivings about the apparently haphazard way in which children found a home and the dangerous confidence shown by Barnardo in entrusting defenceless children to wealthy strangers, even co-religionists, thousands of miles away. Nevertheless, no one could doubt that out of all the detail of the lives of the downtrodden, a new concern for poor children was growing.

By the beginning of the twentieth century, Barnardo's were sending over 1,000 children a year to Canada. With the huge numbers arriving each year, and no sizeable increase in the staff, supervision over vast distances became increasingly difficult. In such a large and sensitive operation as Barnardo's Canadian emigration programme, some stains on the record seem almost inevitable. Barnardo's reputation, his funds, his survival, rested on his own assessment of his work. He defended the confidentiality of his records fiercely, both to protect the children's reputation and his own. What he revealed of the work was highly selective. In Canada he himself was apparently given only a selective account of the story.

In the autumn of 1897, Laura Cummings, a rather wild, stage-struck girl of twelve, was sent from the Girls' Village Home in England to Canada. She clearly had no intention of settling and allowing herself to be buried in the dull respectability of a Canadian household and soon showed a talent for getting herself into trouble. In November 1899, she suddenly left her employer and found herself a job as an actress with the Empire Theatre Company in Toronto. After the Christmas season, Laura was retrieved by an indignant home visitor and placed out again with another mistress. Within a fortnight she flitted.

Miss J. Loveday, writing from the Girls' Home in Peterborough in 1900, was fearful that she might have returned to the theatre. She wrote to Mr Owen pointing out Laura's 'remarkable and varied career' in her short time in Canada and suggesting, rather wearily, that she supposed Laura ought to be found and removed from the city at once. Perhaps a detective should be hired . . .[26]

No reply exists on the file, but by April 1900 Laura, just turned fifteen, had crossed the border into Buffalo, USA, and was seen hanging around 'concert and singing saloons and houses of ill-fame'. A letter from a Mr Ingram, of 'Ingram and Hebblewhite Gas Fixtures Company', suggests that 'Dear friend Owen' knew of Laura's lapse: 'There was a lady in my store by the name of Edna H. Chase whose business it is to pick up unfortunate girls and try to secure for them a home. Some way or other Miss Cummings has gotten into her arms . . . Inspector De Barry [an official of the Treasury Department of the US Immigration Service] has been informed about her and has threatened to send her back to Canada. Now you had better use your own discretion . . .'[27]

An undated letter from Laura herself to Mr Owen asked for a reference to help her to get a job and promised, 'I will keep truly the secret of your coming out to Buffalo or giving me the consent to do so on one condition, that is that if this gets to Dr Barnardo's ears you will pretend to know nothing about it.'[28]

On receiving that letter, Mr Owen instructed Mr Hodgins of the Canadian Detective Agency in Toronto to go to Buffalo and bring Laura back. He found her in police custody: she had been arrested in Gussie Watson's brothel two nights earlier.

Despite two letters from Inspector De Barry warning Mr Owen that it was illegal to smuggle charity children into the United States, and accusing him of immoral behaviour, the Superintendent managed to smother any repercussions from the affair. Laura was shipped back to England and safely out of the way before Dr Barnardo arrived in 1900 on a visit to his old boys and girls; he was unaware of the whole incident.

The general programme was flourishing and a new distributing home for boys was opened in Winnipeg in the West. Emigration reached its peak in 1905, the year that Dr Barnardo died, with 1,300 children sent out. Despite shortage of funds (the industrial training farm in Manitoba closed for that reason in 1908) between 600 and 1,000 boys and girls were sent to Canada every year until 1915, when enemy submarine action made the crossing too dangerous.

However, according to the Governor of the Village, Mr Godfrey, for some years before the war the girls disliked the prospect of going to Canada. He tried to put their case to the Executive Committee. The minutes record that Mr Godfrey attached considerable importance to the 'amount of respect paid to objections to emigration from a) relations b) guardians and c) children'.[29]

The Council for their part felt that objections from 'respectable parents' should be met by trying to explain to them the advantages of Canadian life but their 'objections should not be disregarded'. As to the children, whilst a little girl of eight or nine could not really judge what was best for her, a girl of thirteen or fourteen ought to be allowed some opinion on the subject.

By 1913 there were misgivings on the Council about Barnardo's administration in Canada. One member felt that the children were being sent out too young and that more control was needed over the work. The Council wrote to Mr Owen to ask him to make sure that the children were properly inspected and not overworked. A tour of the country by the Reverend Mayers and the 'musical boys' had not proved as successful as they had hoped.

The Council had good reason to be worried. Their reforms were interrupted by the First World War which broke out in August 1914. In the course of it, over 6,000 Barnardo boys in Canada flocked to the colours and the wave of patriotic fervour tended to engulf everything else.

However, at least one senior member of staff in Canada harboured serious misgivings about Mr Owen's rule. In 1910, Mr C. H. Black, a former stenographic reporter with the courts in Toronto, was appointed Secretary of the Canadian headquarters, deputising for Mr Owen when he was on his annual journeys to England. At first all went well until Mr Black stumbled on a scandal. In September 1912, while Mr Owen was in England, Mr Black had occasion to question a young woman who applied to Barnardo's shelter for fallen girls: 'Her story seemed to implicate Mr Owen in a serious offence. I was slow to attach much weight to it as Mr Owen had told me that misrepresentations as to his character had been made by certain Barnardo girls and that he had ignored them, treating the misguided young women ... with magnanimity and forbearance.' However, he was accustomed to sifting evidence and fresh information convinced Mr Black that Mr Owen was indeed implicated in the affair.

Once his superior realised that Mr Black knew too much his attitude changed: 'trivial tasks were assigned to me that might as well have been performed by a clerk receiving two pounds a week'. In 1915, Mr Black had once again incurred his superior's displeasure. Whilst Mr Owen was in England, preparing the last parties for emigration, Mr Black discovered that Mr Owen had been encouraging boys of fourteen or fifteen to enlist as privates in the Canadian Overseas Forces.

By 1916, relations had become very strained in Barnardo's headquarters in Toronto. According to Mr Black, Mr Owen tried to prompt him to resign. In September, Mr Black did indeed retire and wrote to the Chairman of the Executive, Mr William McCall, explaining that he 'would not and could not condone or countenance offences and irregularities in connection with the management and conduct of the work of the homes'.

He listed the affair with the pregnant girl, enclosed a letter to a boy 'not quite the form of letter ... that should have been written ... counselling, as it does, the making of untruthful representations by this boy (Alfred Camp) persuaded by Owen to join the Forces', and the letter alleged that thousands of dollars were paid to Mr Owen by 'men who have caused the moral downfall of Barnardo girls'; he also asked the homes to conduct a strict inquiry into the use of that money.[30]

Mr Black's letter listed a number of other serious criticisms. That year Barnardo's home for fallen girls was closed by the Canadian authorities because of its inadequate bedding and poor equipment. A Canadian Inspector had ordered improvements but, according to Mr Black, the Superintendent had ignored the warning.

The work in Canada, wrote Mr Black, was 'under a cloud' since the public knew of Barnardo's only through the reports of trials of Barnardo boys and girls in the newspapers and not of the better side of the work. Failure to interest philanthropic and Christian people had meant that the children, particularly the girls, suffered from a lack of protection. If the girls had been given proper protection 'there would not have been the lamentably large number of cases of moral fall'.

The following day he wrote to the chaplain, the Reverend W. J. Mayers, who had recently visited Canada, suggesting that the Council should summon Mrs Leslie, matron of the Richmond Street shelter, to England since she was determined to speak frankly about 'the serious matters connected with young Barnardo girls'. Mr Black disclosed that Mr Owen lived for six months of the year in Denison Avenue, in apartments for foreigners, whilst Mrs Owen was in Bala: 'one or more Barnardo girls occupy these quarters with him. I need not enlarge on this subject . . . enough can be proven and proven conclusively to show how false Mr Owen has been to the trust reposed in him.'[31]

Presumably Mr Owen had, as usual, covered his tracks carefully. Certainly the replies from Barnardo's seem excessively bland. Much agitated, Mr Black wrote to Mr McCall, who replied: 'It is felt that at this time with everyone greatly strained as to time and effort by the war, it would be impossible to send out a sufficiently competent person to conduct such an enquiry as you suggest. Possibly later on something of the sort may be done.'[32] That from Mr McCall, Chairman of the Executive.

The Reverend W. J. Mayers replied that although he was surprised and pained by Mr Black's letter he could not pass an opinion without hearing from other people involved. 'I can only hope and pray that the dark clouds may, in God's providence, soon be rolled away . . . Please, don't interpret my silence as indifference, but I feel I must wait for developments.'[33]

He did not have long to wait. Whatever the rights and wrongs of the accusations against Mr Owen, in the spring of 1919 he was arrested by the Canadian police and placed on bail on his own surety of 2,000 dollars. They accused him of the criminal offence of co-habiting at the time with a ward of Barnardo's, Maisie Skelton, 'in the guise of his housekeeper'. She had recently had a child by him. His wife was in Muskoka where she had lived for some time. Mr Owen made a written confession of guilt but for reasons unknown was never brought to trial.

The crisis forced Barnardo's Council to move swiftly. Mr John Hobday and his wife Rose, who had a good record with the YMCA in England, were sent to Toronto to investigate charges relating to Mr Alfred B. Owen and to take over the Canadian emigration work.

John Hobday started in his new post quietly without arousing public speculation or allowing the press to gain an inkling of the scandal. Members of the staff were 'greatly shocked . . . I found that suspicions had been entertained in some quarters', he wrote in his confidential report.[34]

By 1920, the first party of child emigrants since the war sailed to Canada. 'The organisation for placing them out in this new land and for the periodical inspection of the homes into which they go, has been tested and perfected during the past thirty-eight years,' the Annual Report stated confidently.

In reality, staff and Council were reviewing their emigration policy; by January 1921 the Executive Committee had decreed that girls going to Canada should be offered more protection. They were not to be sent out under the age of thirteen; they were to be placed on farms if possible and that only until they were old enough to be employed in domestic service. Most important of all, a 'lady of position and character' was to act as a local 'mother' and keep an eye on the children.[35]

However, by the 1920s in Britain and in Canada the tide of opinion was turning against child emigration. By now the public was more sensitive to press reports of the children's suffering. With the appalling loss of life in the war, the argument of overcrowding in Britain had lost its edge. Canadian social workers were also asking for more stringent supervision in placing young children in foster-homes. Early in 1924, Ramsay MacDonald's Government sent out to Canada a delegation headed by Margaret Bondfield, MP, to investigate the child emigration question. After two months of intensive inquiries, the delegation returned home convinced that emigration for children of school age was undesirable. Broadly speaking, they approved the work and believed that the children had better chances for making good in Canada than they would have had in England, but they argued that since children were sent to Canada to find work, they should come when they were of working age (that was, over fourteen).

They commented specifically on the boarded-out Barnardo children who were supposedly gaining an education in the summer months as well as the winter. They felt that sometimes those children were overburdened with chores in the household or on the farm.

By 1925, the Canadian Government barred children of under fourteen and without parents from entry to Canada for three years. Canadian child welfare experts now felt convinced that children from England were being placed without sufficient care or supervision. The ban was made permanent in 1928 and that effectively dammed up the flood of young immigrants from England.

Barnardo boys and girls over fourteen continued to go to Canada in smaller numbers but the depression in the 'thirties brought numbers down. In 1939 the last party of twenty-eight boys and girls sailed to Canada in July and arrived safely in Toronto before war broke out.

Barnardo the 'Imperialist' had seen himself landscaping the colonies by planting out his children throughout the Empire. He spoke and wrote of his desire to see Barnardo children in Australia, New Zealand and South Africa as well as Canada. Small groups of his children did emigrate to other colonies in the nineteenth century, usually under the care of future employers. However, the cost and difficulty of the operation prevented him from doing more. Exact figures of children sent out before he began his large programme in 1882 are almost impossible to find. In Australia he already had favourable soil for his work. By 1896 the Western Australian Parliament even debated the question of whether they should communicate with Dr Barnardo 'with a view of his sending young people to this colony'. On balance, the Western Australian Government decided that at that time, with immigrants flocking into the country, they did not need an increase in the population. A quarter of a century later, when Australia was suffering from a shortage of manpower due to heavy wartime losses, the prospect seemed decidedly more attractive.

In the headquarters at home, funds were short as usual and the charity had been further pressed by the 1918 Education Act which raised the school-leaving age to fourteen. Salaries, though still modest, were rising to keep pace with the cost of living. The Government was offering to war orphans free passage plus £20 to outfit each child, and a grant of £37 to children not born of ex-Servicemen.

In 1920, a Barnardo representative sent to raise funds and explore emigration possibilities met an unexpected enthusiasm for Barnardo's immigrants in a Sydney real estate magnate, Arthur (later Sir Arthur) Rickard. Founder of the Millions Club, with the slogan 'a million immigrant farmers on a million Australian farms', Sir Arthur was keen to bolster his Government's White Australia policy. More white immigrants would help to keep out the Japanese and Chinese, clamouring to settle.

Sir Arthur Rickard was the first President of Barnardo's New South Wales Committee and early fund-raising efforts in Australia reflect his attitudes. 'The necessity of increased population if we are to remain a WHITE AUSTRALIA, is becoming stronger and the best population we can bring to this country is the young lads of the British Empire and our own blood.' The motive was against all the principles of Barnardo's organisation from that day to this; nevertheless, enthusiastic press comment on Barnardo parties arriving in the early days carried overtones of racism.

Emigration started at a time when Barnardo's in Australia enjoyed a high reputation, largely due to one man, a former Barnardo boy, James Page, one of the most popular and respected politicians in the country. A member for Maranoa (Queensland) in the House of Representatives, and Chief Whip when Labour was in office, James Page (Big Jim as he was known affectionately) made it known that he gave £10 every year to Barnardo's. He died in June 1921 and was given the unusual honour of a state funeral.

Fittingly enough, SS *Berrima*, the P & O liner which took the first party of forty-seven Barnardo boys to Australia in 1921, was the first ship which had transported Australian troops to Europe in the First World War. The boat docked at Cape Town where the party was fêted and given a 'thousand delicious oranges' as a parting gift; at Melbourne another exciting reception with a visit to the Zoo awaited them but for the first two days the boys returned to the ship to sleep since their new hostel was not ready. At first the boys suffered from the climate and from mosquitoes but Australia soon became 'opportunity land' in the Annual Reports.

By January 1922, an organisational hiccup almost choked the new branch of Dr Barnardo's. New South Wales had set up its Committee in great haste and drafted its Articles of Association independently. They had become, in effect, an autonomous body. Under their management anyone could join the Association by paying ten shillings. The Council in England were alarmed: 'The Association might be run by Politicians, Roman Catholics or even Mormons,' they feared. A cablegram was sent to New South Wales saying that the Council 'strongly objected to the use of the name Dr Barnardo's Homes in New South Wales'.[36] Fortunately, a representative was on hand to smooth ruffled feelings and a new committee was set up headed by Sir Arthur Rickard, and A. W. Green, a senior official of the Australian Government Welfare Department, was made Superintendent of Children.

By 1923, the first party of Barnardo girls arrived in response to the great demand for domestic servants in Australia. Barnardo's had learnt from experience that placing girls in another country 'needed the utmost caution'. Rules were strict: No girls to be placed in isolated spots. They were to be settled in groups. No girl was to receive less than fourteen shillings a week at the age of fourteen. A ladies committee was formed to keep in touch with the girls and a lady visitor appointed to visit the girls once a month and report regularly. Local supervision committees were also formed in the districts where the girls were situated.

The first party of Barnardo girls, all Guides, with their Guide Officer were invited to Buckingham Palace for a royal send-off: 'Remember that life is made up of loyalty,' said Queen Mary as she bade farewell to the Barnardo girls, 'loyalty to your friends, loyalty to things beautiful and good, loyalty to the country in which you live, loyalty to your King and, above all, for that holds all loyalties together, loyalty to God.'[37]

In Australia, although life was hard, long hours of milking and ploughing for boys, scrubbing, washing and cleaning for girls, drudgery and monotony, the young immigrants rarely suffered the stigma or the callousness shown to the home children in earlier times in Canada.

They settled in New South Wales, some on individual farms and in homes; others near Perth at Pinjarra in Western Australia on the Fairbridge farm school, a model farm for training younger under-privileged children. On the farm the children lived in cottages; the founder, Kingsley Fairbridge, had based his community on the Girls' Village Home, 'the quiet life of a settler "way out back" '. By 1929, Barnardo's had opened their own model farm school at Mowbray Park, Picton.

Annual Reports on the Australian work stress the children's optimism, pluck and hard work. Some typical (unsigned) letters were always included: 'I am getting on splendidly with my work. I can plough now with three horses and three furrow plough . . . I am having a splendid time out here . . . they say I am a good stock rider. There is plenty of work out here for those who will work, but it is no place for loafers. I learnt to pick wool in one day and wool rollers' wages are good . . . You can tell the boys that the bush is the place for colonial experience, also to save money.'

By the 1930s, the effect of the economic depression had begun to dampen Australia's enthusiasm for child immigrants, since even in rural areas jobs were threatened. The Barnardo representative in Sydney wrote a personal letter to all boys that year 'warning them that difficult times were ahead and that they were to be careful to hold on to their work, even if it should mean a temporary reduction in wages'. By 1931, the Australian Government banned the immigration of boys over school age. The boys' letters home quoted in the Annual Report of 1931 showed the spirit of true grit:

Australia is a wonderful country, full of sunshine and pleasant hours. We don't want miserable people in Australia, although we have plenty of them now. Life is what we make it . . . Well, sir, I am still in the same place which will be four years next April ... I have a good, genuine boss and mistress, who have been like a father and mother to me ... I get good meals and a good bed to sleep on, my clothes, washed, ironed and sewn, anything to save my money. I even sit at the same table for meals as they do.

For the girls, emigration to Australia appeared to be less popular. In July 1931 the Chairman of the Executive Committee emphasised the importance of gaining the 'sympathy of cottage mothers for emigration'. Steps were to be taken, 'to counteract any tendency on the part of cottage mothers to oppose emigration'. Obviously children returning home had doused some of the enthusiasm for the Imperial Adventure. In future, the Council ordered, children returned from Canada or Australia through misconduct or misfortune should be placed in larger homes so that they did not stand so much chance of influencing other children.[38]

Marjorie Bicker who now lives in Sussex, came to the Girls' Village Home in May 1936 at the age of twelve. It was a difficult age and Marjorie had had a difficult childhood: 'My so-called mum died and my father remarried and my stepmother had a miscarriage.' She was placed in Larchfield cottage and felt an immediate antipathy towards her new 'mother'. 'We hated each other on sight. She was very Victorian, very strict. There was no welcome, the cottage was dark, it was an oppressive atmosphere.' She was transferred to Pink Clover where she had 'a lovely cottage "mother", kind and sweet'. Later she went home because circumstances had eased but when her stepmother became pregnant again, she was sent back to Barnardo's.

Through a misunderstanding Marjorie was placed with the 'mother' she had disliked so much and greeted with the words, 'Oh, so we have got you back again.' Her life settled down to a routine she found irksome: corned beef and potatoes on Monday; hair washing with carbolic soap on Friday, and a 'very mournful' Sunday, when the children were not allowed to play with their toys or knit but had to sit in silence between church services, reading or writing letters.

Then came an interruption to her routine. One afternoon Marjorie was told to report to the Governor's office where the girls were gathered in a buzz of excitement. When Miss Macnaghten came in she asked, 'How would you like to go to Australia?'

'All the girls were agog, trying to whisper. Did they speak English in Australia? What money did they use?'

Like the others, Marjorie had not the remotest idea about life in Australia and dared not ask questions. During the following week she was measured for clothes, given an intelligence test and a medical examination. By now she was desperately keen to leave the Village.

'Every night I used to say to God, "Please, God, let me pass for Australia." I blackmailed him into it.'

Suddenly she realised that if she went to Australia she might never see her father again. She knew of two girls who had been sent there against their parents' wishes, and became as desperate to stay in the Village as she had been so recently to leave. She wrote an urgent letter to her father asking him to stop her emigration but her letter was censored, and Marjorie was sent for by the Governor, who asked her what she meant by writing such a letter.

'You are a most ungrateful child,' the Governor exclaimed and told her that since all her clothes were ready it was too late to cancel the plans.

'She said to me, "You are going because there is nothing to stop you. I don't want to hear any more about it . . . You are to write a letter to your father and you are to tell him that you are most anxious to go and you are to ask for his blessing." '

Back in her cottage Marjorie was handed pen and paper and made to write the letter. Her father replied, 'If you're most anxious to go, I can't stop you.'

She joined a party of girls going to Australia in a cottage set aside for them. They made the most of their new status. One day when they were singing a rude song about Marjorie's former cottage 'mother', the latter, who was next door, overheard her. She came and shook Marjorie. ' "You think you're going to Australia," she shouted, "but Australia don't want the likes of you. I'll have you stopped." And there I was sobbing my heart out again.'

Three weeks before the party left there were lessons on the flora, fauna and climate of Australia in Australia Cottage. Marjorie's hated housemother gave her a diamanté brooch as a farewell present and told her to be a good girl and not let the name of Barnardo's down.

Marjorie managed to explain to her father what had happened and he promised to try to send her the fare back to England when she was twenty-one.

The days before the emigrants left were happy, the girls were free from school and singing all the time. A party was held for them and on 20 November 1937, the entire Village turned out to wave them goodbye as the eighteen girls in their brown coats and hats marched in pairs into the coach and to Tilbury Docks.

On board ship they met thirty-six Barnardo boys bound for Australia. 'It was a great shock,' Marjorie remembers. 'We never saw boys in the Village.' The children had a marvellous time although they were kept in check and obliged to attend morning service. On arrival in Sydney the sexes were segregated again. Marjorie moved on to Mowbray Park Farm School. From the beginning she enjoyed the openness of the life and the lack of restrictions. 'There was a good lot of church but the church was friendlier there and we were encouraged to make friends outside. Australia was beautiful, there were wide open spaces and we weren't cooped up. The happiest years in my life were in Australia.'

She spent two years in service, with a very approachable Barnardo office always ready to help. When she was eighteen she asked permission to join the Armed Forces. 'My first thought was, "I'm free!" I just lived to be twenty-one, free of Barnardo's claim and free to do what I wanted. I spent four years in the Forces, then I said to Dr Barnardo's office in Sydney, "I'm going home." They said, "You can't, you were meant to be an Australian citizen. We'll stop you." '[39]

Presumably Barnardo's were concerned to protect Marjorie from moral danger since her mother was unmarried and the man she called her father was, in fact, her informal guardian. She was never legally adopted by him. He was, however, the only loving person in her past. When she was twenty-one in 1945, Marjorie sailed for England and married her husband on board ship.

Today she feels that she has 'a lot to thank Barnardo's for'. 'I know,' she adds, 'that Barnardo's must have done an awful lot of good to an awful lot of people, but for me those years at the Village were the most frightening time of my life.'

Fortunately in Australia, Marjorie went to a much more homely and easy-going community, the 170-acre farm school at Mowbray Park, Picton. The school had just become co-educational (fifteen years before Barnardo's Homes in England introduced mixed homes for boys and girls). A journalist who visited the Australian school in 1939 while Marjorie was there described it as: 'a practical and successful demonstration of a feasible, sensible and humane system of migration of children from the Motherland ... There is no hint of any institutional spirit; it is in very truth a real home ... this can be sensed by the prevailing and universal spirit of contentment and happiness.'[40]

The last pre-war Barnardo party of thirty-six boys and eighteen girls sailed to Australia in December 1938. The total number of young emigrants sent since 1921 was 2,340, far short of the 'millions' envisaged in ambitious early schemes, and of the many thousands of Barnardo children sent to Canada. After the war, the Barnardo children continued to be sent to Australia on a diminished scale for twenty years, until 1967. The homes in Australia had begun to care for Australian-born children in need. By then the tide of public opinion in England had turned against children emigrating without their parents and Barnardo's were one of the last welfare organisations to send children overseas.

6

Any Beggar's Bairn

'Unquestionably the best conceived and the most successful of all the activities connected with the name of Dr Barnardo is the boarding-out of children.'

Annual Report, 1919

When he took in Jim Jarvis, his first homeless boy, barefoot and in rags, and gave him hot coffee, food and a bed for the night, Tom Barnardo became briefly a foster-father. Significantly it was the year after he started his emigration programme, 1883, that he began to consider boarding-out children at home.

For fifty years, from the 1880s until the 1930s, stories of their children overseas dominated Barnardo's publicity. As they explained, 'Transformations which come . . . to our lads and girls shipped across the seas are more dramatic and striking than the more modest successes which await our protégés placed out in England.'[1]

In the early years, boarding-out was seen as a preparation for emigration. Yet, had it been possible to apply the kind of preparation and safeguards used for boarding-out children in England, the lives of Barnardo's child emigrants in Canada would have indeed been transformed.

Since the sixteenth century it had been the practice in Scotland to place 'any beggar's bairn' with a respectable family so that the child would grow up into a sober, industrious citizen. By the nineteenth century, the Scots placed orphan or pauper children away from their own parish with small crofters or farmers in the country.

By the 1860s, with the English cities overpopulated and unemployment and poverty concentrating the misery in the slums, Local Government Boards began to take an interest in the Scottish system of redistributing the child pauper population. Most importantly, from the authorities' point of view, boarding-out destitute children cut down the number of adult paupers dependent on public relief; it usually also provided a more kindly upbringing for the child. By 1887, the Lord Provost of Glasgow was able to point out that pauperism had declined in his city from 4 per cent to 2 per cent; one reason for the decline was, in his view, the boarding-out system. Barnardo quoted with approval these results in his magazine and also included an account of the outcome of workhouse education.[2] In England, over an average of ten years, at least 14 per cent of the boys and 26 per cent of the girls speedily returned to the workhouse as adult paupers. No serious child philanthropist could ignore the signs.

For some years he had been studying boarding-out in Europe as well as in Britain and had placed a few children in carefully selected homes. They thrived and, encouraged, he decided on a well-organised scheme. In 1887, he sent 330 of his boys to 'good country homes', as far away as possible from the pollution and temptation of factories and railway stations. He chose boys between the ages of five and nine because he believed that it was young children who suffered most from institutional life. From his foster-parents he demanded high standards. They should be cottagers and working-class people, living in homes that 'promised satisfactory sanitary conditions, pure moral surroundings and a loving and Christian influence'. Foster-parents must have enough accommodation and be well intentioned. They received five shillings a week for each child, but they must not, he stipulated, be motivated merely by 'the greed of gain', nor should widows be solely dependent on foster fees for their living.

He stated clearly that only orphan children were suitable for transplanting, but the case histories he quoted indicate that he used the term 'orphan' to mean a child with both parents dead, with one parent dead or with both parents unsuitable. For example, of sixteen case histories cited, only three of the children have both parents dead. Others, like little 'street waif S. F.', aged four, had 'no mother and worse than no father'. E. J., aged nine, was a little girl of whom it was said, 'If left on the mother's hand, she is certain to become a prostitute.' The girls he seems to have chosen for boarding-out (and they were a very small number at first) were those he considered to be 'in moral danger'.[3]

By appointing a woman physician, Jane Walker, MD, as early as 1887, he set the work on a firm and progressive footing. Dr Walker visited the foster-homes at irregular intervals at first but at least every three months, and reported carefully on the child's welfare and the home conditions. Barnardo obviously respected Dr Walker's opinions: 'her reports are . . . of professional value,' he noted. Determined that no harm should come to his children, he also organised village committees headed by local worthies (generally the vicar, a non-conformist minister, or a prominent lady of the village). The Local Government Board also insisted on a supervising committee for their children. By Act of Parliament, 1870, Parish Unions had been empowered to place pauper children outside their own parishes although they were slow to avail themselves of the opportunity.

Much of the protection Barnardo devised for foster-children anticipated the 1948 Children Act by over sixty years. His first consideration,
however, was that foster-parents should not be irreligious, no matter
how respectable they might otherwise be. His organisation was excellent,
his style caring and careful. Foster-parents were required to sign a
lengthy agreement:

1.   To bring up the said child carefully, kindly and in all respects as
     one of my family.
2.   To provide the said child with proper food, clothing, washing,
     lodging and school fees.
3.   To endeavour to train the said child in habits of truthfulness,
     obedience, personal cleanliness and industry.
4.   To take care that the said child shall attend duly at church or
     chapel, and shall be taught the habit of daily prayer.
5.   To take care that the said child, when of suitable age, shall attend
     regularly at a public elementary school.
6.   To communicate with the lady or gentleman who has charge of
     the children in the district upon all matters affecting the welfare
     of the said child; and in case of . . . illness to report it immediately
     . . . and if necessary at once to call in the assistance of a medical
     man.
7.   To forward to the Director for inspection all letters which may
     be received from relatives or friends of the said child, before
     allowing the same to be opened . . . and not to enter into any
     correspondence myself with any person who may claim relation-
     ship.
8.   At all times, to permit the said child to be visited by any person
     appointed by the Director and to permit no visit from relatives or
     friends of the child without the Director's authorisation.
9.   To restore the said child to any person sent by the Director to
     receive it, on getting one fortnight's notice of removal or equivalent
     payment.[4]

Dr Walker's report, after fifteen months, was brisk and comprehensive.
She paid 'strictly surprise visits'. Only in eight cases did she have the
children moved from unsatisfactory homes. On clothing she wrote: 'I
have usually found this satisfactory but I have frequently found stockings
in holes. In one home from which the boys were moved, the stockings
were practically footless . . . I have certainly come across no instance of
the clothes having been pawned.' At Woodbridge, Ongar and Brighton,
Dr Walker discovered that the shilling a week clothing allowance was

retained by the local committee who bought the clothes themselves and supplied foster-mothers with clothing when the children needed it. In most other districts, the foster-mothers themselves bought the children's clothing which was a better plan, Dr Walker felt, since it tended to encourage mothers to be more careful and economical, more inclined to mend and patch. And there was another drawback to the local committees' well-intentioned activities: although their members usually bought better quality clothing 'they had a tendency to buy things which are more or less alike so that the boarded-out children are known in the village by their distinctive clothing'. This rather defeated the object of boarding-out by turning the Barnardo children into a clearly differentiated group.

Dr Walker discovered that most of the children slept two in a double bed and although she conceded 'for obvious moral considerations it would be better for each child to sleep in a separate single bed', that was difficult in an ordinary cottage home since 'in most homes of the agricultural classes a single bed is quite unknown'. In several cottages children were sleeping three to a bed. That, she considered, was too crowded and the foster-mother usually agreed to put up another bed or, in extremity, Dr Walker sent for a single bed from Stepney.

She wrote that she had seen the children at dinner, tea and supper and had been impressed by the abundance of the meals; they were plentiful and of good quality. She was often told by mothers that they made a cake every week 'because the boys are fond of cake' and she had tasted the cakes herself.

As to cleanliness, she found most of the children clean, nearly all of them had a bath every week. She sometimes saw children with dirty heads but pointed out that since the boys and girls were going to school, mixing with dirty children, it was difficult to keep them quite clean.

Fairness and objectivity shine out in Dr Walker's report. Of religious and moral training she remarked: 'I have found it very difficult to obtain reliable direct evidence of the children's religious and moral training, beyond the fact that they had been regularly to church or chapel and Sunday school . . . I have in many instances, been able to obtain further indirect evidence of a perfectly satisfactory character.'

No children had complained of their foster-parents, nor did Dr Walker expect them to, although she often took them out walking by themselves. 'Their fearless manner of talking and laughing showed me that they were not cowed or repressed at home.' Only children who had been boarded-out for a very short time ever said that they wanted to go back to London. Often they cried when she came, thinking they were to be taken away. The foster-parents sometimes complained of the children but only of minor matters.

In education, too, boarding-out seemed beneficial. Although many children were very backward when they arrived 'a fair proportion of them have worked up and are now quite on a par with the village children of their age'. All the schoolmasters she visited spoke of the children's behaviour as 'fairly good' (except in the case of three boys) and of 'the tidiness and punctuality with which they are sent to school'.

Among the 426 children she inspected during her first fifteen months' work, she reported only one death. Since most of the children were below standard, mentally and physically, when they arrived, it was an excellent result. A third of the fostered children suffered from rickets, some to a marked degree 'being stunted in growth of body and mind with very much bowed legs and pigeon breasts'. A great many had bad teeth and twenty-one had ringworm. Dr Walker described one boy as an idiot: 'he is also deaf and dumb and can do nothing for himself . . . On each of my visits he has been in very good condition. The foster-mother takes every care of him and is evidently very fond of him.' For her care that foster-mother was paid ten shillings a week, double the amount paid for the standard child.

The 'mental improvement' in the children struck Dr Walker forcibly. 'Boys that I have looked at anxiously and entered in my note-book as "mentally deficient" . . . have . . . so altered as to get up to the average standard.'

In her general conclusions, Dr Walker considered that boarding-out was the 'best means of disposing of very poor children especially of boys': it was the most economical, costing five to six shillings a week per child or £13 or £14 a year (a saving of at least £2 a year on the cost of keeping a child in an institution); it gave the child an individual home and family life and was healthier, she believed, than living in a city and 'certainly much better for their morals'. The villages benefited from the presence of the children; farm labourers could live more comfortably because of the extra income; it brought more money to the landlords and made it easier for cottage-owners to get their rent. Finally, it thinned out the population in the denser parts of London.

But Dr Walker, too, felt that to make the system successful certain conditions should be fulfilled. She did not consider that more than fourteen Barnardo children should be boarded-out in any one village; no more than four in a family, preferably two, if boarding-out was to be 'a means of giving to the children what they most lack, viz., a home and real family life'.

Foster-parents, besides being of good moral character, should be total abstainers. Fairly young people, agricultural labourers without children, were ideal.

She also remarked that 'parents should never be above the children socially and should always have their meals with them and treat them in every respect as their own family'.[5] In Barnardo's terms this idea was almost revolutionary. In the Village Home Barnardo had deliberately recruited ladies to refine and educate the girls, who were expected to know their place; boys too grew up in the homes with a strict sense of rank. Not until the Second World War did the staff eat with the children in the large homes.

The boarded-out children, by contrast, lived with respectable working-class families in the country and escaped the label of charity child and the burden of gratitude it often imposed. Ideally, they were indistinguishable from the other children in the village and they gained an individual sense of identity and self-respect. The poor were helping their own.

That Barnardo allowed Dr Walker to put forward that view, indicates how flexible he was in responding to the needs of the time and also the benefits that the homes gained from employing professional people so early. By the 1890s, Barnardo was to have three women doctors inspecting the boarded-out children. Under the Barnardo boarding-out system, the children were sent back to the homes when they left school to learn a trade and this often proved a wrench.

Individual cases of boarded-out children rarely featured in Barnardo publicity nor, fortunately, did scandals of maltreatment make headlines in the British press. The system was too well managed for that, as a well-placed, independent witness testified.

Miss Mason was appointed by the Local Government Board in 1885 to visit all the children boarded-out in parishes other than their own and to advise local boarding-out committees. She was impressed by the scrupulousness of Barnardo's inspector. Local people, she observed, could often be unaware of the treatment of boarded-out children, if they did not make surprise visits and examine the children carefully.

> I do not myself completely undress each child as does the lady who inspects for Dr Barnardo, although I think her precautions are on the safe side because dirt and neglect do not always show where the body is well protected by the clothing. The feet are a better guide than anything else to the treatment of the child, for it is in the hollows of the ankles that strata of dirt accumulate most visibly . . . I am generally able, by taking off one stocking, to tell the date of the last bath to a week . . . Beating is generally begun on the upper parts of the arms.

I sometimes find bruises there, evidently made by sticks and where this is the case, I undress the child as much further as necessary.[6]

Thorough examination of the children was, in Miss Mason's view, the best safeguard against ill-treatment by foster-parents. Since Barnardo's boarded-out children were seen at least every three months by a doctor, as well as by local ladies, the chances of prolonged ill-treatment were slight. The work grew and expanded. By the close of 1892, Barnardo had over 2,000 children living with foster-parents in rural areas but he was faced with a severe financial crisis and the homes were overdrawn by no less than £23,000 and, as one trustee wrote in a disturbing letter to the Chairman, 'there seems absolutely no limit to the increasing size of the work, hundreds of children, enough for a separate society, being added every year.'

The Committee, now seriously worried by the galloping debt, asked Dr Barnardo in March 1893 to limit his intake of children and endeavoured to impose conditions upon him: no new case was to be admitted which had not the element of 'extreme urgency'; he was to reduce the number of boarded-out children until it fell below 500; to pay off an average of £1,000 a month of his old debts; to ask tradesmen and others accepting orders to sign a form agreeing that the funds of the institutions alone were liable, and that creditors had no claim against any individual except Dr Barnardo. Finally they asked that his life be insured for £20,000 in favour of the trustees.[7]

Barnardo made economies in his publications, reduced his adult relief work, and agreed to insure his life, but to close his doors to a single homeless child seemed intolerable to him. He cut down on the number of children boarded-out but it never fell below 1,500 (more than a thousand over his limit!). After the homes became incorporated in 1899, which reduced the personal liability of the trustees, the numbers of boarded-out children again soared. In 1905, the year Barnardo died, over 4,000 children were boarded-out.

Boarding-out work held no instant appeal. There were no bricks and mortar, no children to display, no focus for public sympathy. It did not attract the big donations raised by more popular schemes; for example, in 1896, donations for the Village Home reached over £1,000, for emigration £1,800 but for boarding-out, only £35.[8] Yet, in the eyes of those concerned with the national welfare of poor children, Barnardo's work with foster-children was his most impressive achievement.

Speaking at a large public meeting at the Queen's Hall in 1897, A. J. Mundella, MP, a leading authority on juvenile problems and Chairman of a recent inquiry into the Poor Law schools, had lavish praise for

Barnardo, his institutions and, most particularly, his boarding-out work:

> We found ... that Dr Barnardo was often boarding-out ... more children than the whole of the local authorities of this kingdom ... He had the advantage ... due to his own good sense, to select trained ladies [by now Barnardo had three women doctors as inspectors] ... and as a result, not only did they report that these children are comfortably tended in their homes, often most affectionately tended but also the sanitary condition of all the children under Dr Barnardo's care is something that is marvellous, in contrast with those under our local and our State system.[9]

With great courage in 1889 Barnardo introduced a scheme to board out illegitimate babies close to their mothers, provided the girl led an industrious and respectable life after her one lapse. The unmarried mother was to go into domestic service with an approved employer and board her baby close by. On her half-day she would visit her baby. The employer would receive part of the fostering fee from Barnardo's and her maid would have to find the rest out of her wages. Should the girl lapse or fail to pay her part of the fee, her mistress would report to Barnardo's who would stop payment and take the baby into a home. At the time society condemned the unmarried mother outright and most charities refused to 'encourage immorality' by offering her any help. As a result most unmarried mothers without means faced the prospect of the workhouse, the lunatic asylum even, or placing their babies in the dubious hands of a baby farmer. Barnardo offered the single mother a limited independence and a chance to keep her baby. He felt compassion, not condemnation, for the unmarried mother and especially for her child.

> Young unmarried women, in most instances of decent parentage ... and of industrious habits, have become the mothers of children whom they find themselves often unable to maintain. In the majority of instances these young women are either domestic servants or are engaged in workrooms. After being led astray (often under the promise of marriage) a young woman of this class ... is plunged into a terrible struggle ... every door of employment is closed ... as soon as their story is known ... of late years, a more merciful view has prevailed and there are now to be found ladies – good, benevolent, right-minded women who, if convinced that such girls are honestly desirous of regaining a position of respectability, are willing to give them employ-

ment. But the question that stares the mother in the face is, 'What is to become of my baby?'[10]

Barnardo hedged his plan with careful safeguards. The mother had to apply for an affiliation order against the father of the child; she must sign an agreement guaranteeing to pay the specified amount of the foster-mother's fee. Before Barnardo's contribution to the baby's upkeep was paid, the charity had to be satisfied 'that the mother is still in service, pleasing her mistress and going on respectably'. They also inspected the foster-mother's home, from time to time, to ensure that the child was decently cared for. In this way Barnardo exercised some control over the girl and, in his words, prevented her from living a 'careless, extravagant or vicious life and moreover, we accompany our contribution with this distinct warning that, if at any time she relapses into a vicious or immoral life, we will at once cease our payments'. Barnardo implied that he had solved the problem and, although the conditions he imposed upon those single mothers sound harsh to modern ears, he was years ahead of the punitive attitudes of his day.

However, employing servants with young babies living close by did not please all employers. And Barnardo sprang fiercely to the aid of a young servant whose mistress wanted to have her maid's bastard child admitted to the homes, rather than boarded-out. In a letter about the case to Dr Sinclair, the Archdeacon of London in January 1903, he defended his scheme and condemned the mistress as entirely selfish. She believes that 'if this servant has to pay 1s. 6d. per week and have some of the care of her child upon her shoulders, she will be less well-dressed and less fully devoted to her mistress's interests'.

'Now, Mr Archdeacon,' Barnardo admonished the cleric, 'I have already assisted nearly two thousand unmarried mothers who were domestic servants and who sought my aid for their infants. Out of these, only three are known to have failed morally and thus rendered it necessary that we should lay the burden of their children wholly upon their own shoulders.' Never given to false modesty, he emphasised that his proposals for assisting the unmarried mother and child were 'careful, well considered and I think eminently wise'.[11]

Eminently wise he may have been but he had to be canny as well. Not until 1902, thirteen years after he had started his Auxiliary Boarding-Out Scheme, did Dr Barnardo mention it to his supporters. (Usually, he would write about intended projects in his magazine a year or two beforehand, so that he could arouse sympathy and raise funds.) His widow also omitted any account of the delicate subject although she included a chapter on boarding-out in her biography of Dr Barnardo published shortly after his death in 1905.

By the close of his life Barnardo was convinced that, provided the right kind of home could be found, boarding-out was the best method of upbringing for his younger children. 'I believe my Institutions are as good as any on earth,' he told a gathering in his last At Home held in Stepney in 1904, 'but there is something better and that is boarding-out if it is well done.' Boarding-out, he explained, had proved better for the children's health, more economical, and he had come to realise that it was a more natural means of bringing up deprived children. In his Girls' Village Home, twenty 'daughters' lived in one cottage, twenty sisters without a brother. Their life was ordered, smooth, routine, with rarely a hitch. Boarded-out children, by contrast, enjoyed the ordinary ups and downs of family life: they took part in household tasks such as shopping; above all, they enjoyed the 'deep interest which one individual life takes in another individual life . . . which makes that individual feel that she is the object of interest, sympathy and love.'[12] That Barnardo could distance himself from his dream and see its flaws indicates his breadth of mind and his flexibility.

Possibly if Barnardo had lived longer, his institutions, too, would have become more flexible in response to changing times and more children would have been boarded-out. By the time of his death in 1905 over 4,000 children were sent to foster-homes, about three-quarters in Britain and a quarter in Canada. The numbers increased to over 5,500 in 1911 and the number of illegitimate children helped under Barnardo's Auxiliary Boarding-Out Scheme crept up too. In the pre-war years, the charity either omitted to mention that work in their publicity or referred to it rather gingerly, making clear their misgivings: 'We have before us many cases where, but for our aid the mother would have sunk to the line of habitual vice and the children would have fared very hardly.'[13]

The rate of illegitimacy increased sufficiently in the First World War to give the unmarried mother a token acceptance in society, and new agencies were founded to help the single mother with a child; they usually consulted Barnardo's, as a pioneer in the work.[14] The Annual Report of 1920 could not avoid a note of complacency: 'The world has been very hard on the unmarried mother and her child; but during the past few years things have improved somewhat.' Certainly numbers increased. That year Barnardo's helped some 800 unmarried mothers and their babies, almost double the number they had assisted before the First World War.

The war also brought them a new type of case. Married women who had had illegitimate children whilst their husbands were away in the

Forces asked Barnardo's to take their 'love babies' in order to prevent the family from breaking up. These wartime babies were included in the post-war Auxiliary Boarding-Out Scheme.

Apart from the introduction of those cases, the work with unmarried mothers continued almost unchanged for fifty years. Over those years, the charity did gradually withdraw control and power from the girls' employers, as they came to realise that a mistress who wanted to keep her maid might not be a disinterested monitor of her servant's morals and behaviour. A moral welfare worker in the district was usually asked to administer the grant and keep in touch. Until the mid-1930s, the young unmarried mothers whom Barnardo's agreed to help were expected to go into domestic service with an approved mistress and a strict watch was kept on their morals and manners. Any unmarried mother who had a second child after Barnardo's had helped her with the first was refused until after the Second World War. There was also a means test which barred any unmarried mother who had a balance of six shillings and sixpence a week after she had paid the foster-mother and incidentals.

By 1937, the charity had 1,200 unmarried mothers on their books. Changing times made them reluctantly change their policy over the mother's occupation, for with new opportunities for employment in shops, offices and factories, girls were loath to go into domestic service. Barnardo's stipulated that they should live in some approved home or under approved conditions.[15]

Thanks to the excellent groundwork, the health of the boarded-out children remained remarkably good; only one child per thousand died on average between 1927 and 1937, a figure well below the national average. Yet the social climate in the 1930s had changed for the children as well as for the women. Many factors had contributed to make the child's prospect of survival and development brighter than it had been years earlier: restriction of child employment, widows and war pensions and the new legislation to protect the child from parental abuse; restricted drinking hours and successive Education Acts had all made their contribution. School meals, a school medical service for primary school children and school welfare services all helped to safeguard the children. By 1941 Barnardo's were considering whether a nurse's training was too specialised for the work of a boarding-out inspector. As their Medical Officer, Dr McCullough, pointed out, there were no women with social work training in Dr Barnardo's day. By 1942 they had appointed a psychiatric social worker as head of the Boarding-Out Department.

The very strength, the genius of the founder had its drawbacks. To its credit, Barnardo's has always attracted long-serving dedicated people whether on Council, staff or in a voluntary capacity, but their chain of human memory and their sense of reverence for the past make change painful.

To alter any scheme of 'the Doctor' went against the grain. The foster-mothers of the 1930s would have been instantly recognisable to Barnardo: 'motherly women, owning modest, well-regulated homes'. What was perhaps less acceptable was that so would the children. They remained relegated to the founder's own idea of a suitable place in society. The vast majority of the girls still became domestic servants and the vast majority of the boys became tradesmen. Yet boarded-out children won a far higher proportion of scholarships each year than the children in the large homes.[16] The children still lived in country villages although, with the growth of public transport and the wireless, they were less cut off from contemporary living than originally planned. Between three and four thousand Barnardo boys and girls could be found living in English villages as boarders throughout the 'thirties; they made up almost half of the 'largest family in the world'. The children still had to leave their foster-homes towards their fourteenth birthday to return for training to the large branch homes.

As early as 1896, Dr Walker (the medical inspector) remarked on the generosity of foster-parents. She believed that 'the children receive in actual food and clothing (not to speak of toys) more than the value of their weekly payments' (five shillings per child at the time).

Over thirty years later, payment had gone up to twelve shillings a week for small children. Help for unmarried mothers remained conditional on the mother staying respectable and paying her share of her baby's upkeep. If she failed with her contribution, the result could be distressing. Mr Webb was a thirteen-year-old schoolboy when in 1929 his mother fostered two Barnardo's toddlers, George, who was eighteen months old and Simon, who was fourteen months: 'My mother's understanding was that they would remain until they were grown up – or at least until they left school,' he recalled, 'there was no written agreement.' (Mr Webb's aunt was a travelling matron in Barnardo's so the family was known.)

All my mother got was twelve shillings a week for each child, for their food, everything. Dr Barnardo's provided some clothes. It was a labour of love. There was no profit in it . . . The boys stayed for five and a half years and came to regard it as their own home. Suddenly out of the blue, a bureaucratic type called and said: 'You have two of our boys here. We take them away when they are seven years old. Please have them ready by next Wednesday.' Just like that. The boys were very upset. Years later George called on me after my mother had died.

He remembered the awful journey, travelling by night and crying all the way!

According to Mr Webb the reason the boys were taken away and put into the homes was because their mothers did not want to continue to pay towards their upkeep. They were both maids in a doctor's household.

George Lamb was moved to a home too far away to visit and my mother never saw him again. But Simon Hunt went to Woodford Bridge in Essex . . . After my mother died I was able to make contact by writing to Barnardo's and I was also able to put him in contact with his real mother. During the war Simon Hunt joined the Navy and George Lamb joined the Army. Both boys are married now with sons of their own. My mother never took in any more children from Dr Barnardo's because of the way they treated her. One of the problems of fostering is that you can get fond of children and miss them when they go.[17]

In retrospect, former staff who worked on the administrative side of the boarding-out work realise how hard it was, particularly on the children, to wrench them away from what they had been encouraged to think of as their own home and family. The shock in adolescence was traumatic.

Mrs Porter worked first in the general office in 1937, then as a matron in the Girls' Village Home and then, in 1939, in child care:

Bringing back those children at fourteen from boarding-out was very cruel but it didn't appear cruel at the time. They had to leave their cottage and their foster-parents and their homes, the only home they'd ever known. They were so distraught. I'd say to them: 'It's being done for your good.' Later on, when the girls came to get married they would be so pleased that they were able to cook and clean. You didn't get much trouble with those girls.[18]

Miss Poole-Connor was taken on as a boarding-out clerical assistant in 1928 at £2 10s. a week. She remembers the care taken over health by the inspectors:

They weren't like social workers, they had very little experience of real life. They mainly weighed and measured the children. The children were visited about every three months and if anything untoward happened we were on to it immediately if we had a good local correspondent. [The correspondents were vicars or doctors' wives.] One day we had a telephone call from a vicar who said he was convinced that two of our boys were being beaten. The Boarding-Out Officer was sent out to investigate immediately. She took the boys home from school and undressed them in front of the foster-mother. When she saw marks of a strap on their bodies, she packed their things and they were back in Stepney having tea the same day. They were frightened of the foster-mother, she was uncontrollable.[19]

When the Second World War broke out boarded-out children suffered far less disturbance than the home children. They could usually stay on where they were, although the blackout and petrol shortages made visiting and inspection more difficult.

Between the wars, the homes' boarding-out programme had, overall, a good name and a good record. Fifty years on, the street arab, pitiful and unprotected when championed by Barnardo in the early days, had given place to the deprived child, an individual with a number of rights embodied in legislation and a frail dignity. That Barnardo helped to bring about the change by his fierce campaigning, his progressive methods, his flamboyant publicity, is undeniable.

7

The Little Sufferers

'I will never decline a boy or girl who is really destitute merely on the grounds that he or she is likely to become a burden on the funds.

'I always ask myself when I have to deal with children committed to my care, what would I do in such a case if the child were my own daughter.'

Barnardo

Throughout the nineteenth century child life was cheap. When Barnardo began his work in 1870, one infant in every seven died in England and Wales and infant mortality remained at the same high rate until the twentieth century.[1] In the 'good old days' early in the century, before Acts of Parliament prohibited child labour, little bodies twisted and maimed by machines, or climbing boys badly burned by chimney sweeping, were a common sight in city streets. Very badly deformed children with large labels tied round their necks were sent into the streets to beg or exhibited at sideshows.

The children of the poor suffered from rickets, respiratory diseases, curved spines, hernia, poor eyesight, diarrhoea, infections, inherited syphilis and a variety of other deformities and weaknesses. Much of the ill-health among the poor could be traced to their living conditions, dank, overcrowded, insanitary houses where whole families slept, ate an impoverished diet, huddled in a single room, cold in winter and stuffy in summer. They lived in rat-infested courts, and smoky, un-sewered streets. Gradually, towards the end of the century, sanitary reforms improved living conditions and reduced the mortality rate of all but very young children.

From the beginning, Barnardo accepted children handicapped by ill-health or deformity into his community. They were doubly welcome; he stated, as an article of faith, that the lame, the blind, the deaf were to be sheltered. Moreover, his careful wording gave them a dignity. 'We receive cripples into our homes, not because they are cripples but because they are destitute. Given the destitution and when accompanied by disease, deformity or ill-health . . . we will render assistance,' he wrote in February 1877, the year of the arbitration. He had already provided a thirty-bed infirmary for his 'little wounded soldiers' at the headquarters in Stepney Causeway. In due course, he was to build more specialised homes for the sick and the handicapped. His vision and his brilliant planning undoubtedly helped to introduce the public to the doubly handicapped children and the funds he raised and the provision he made helped to set standards for their care.

He worked, as always, in the limelight, with an eye to the cases which would attract the maximum publicity. Early in 1883, John Kinsman, a sixteen-year-old boy paralysed in 'hands, legs and tongue', came up before Westminster Magistrates Court charged with begging at Victoria Station. The magistrate tried to place John in the Cripples' Home but he was refused admission because he was too handicapped; he could not move his hands or mutter more than a few words. The School Board Officer, Mr Lawrence, reported that he could find no suitable school for the lad. The case was remanded so that the chief clerk of the court, Mr Safford, could try to get John Kinsman admitted to the Home for Idiots at Earlswood in Surrey. Even there, John was rejected, since he was not technically regarded as 'an idiot'. At the second hearing, the magistrate, Mr D'Eyncourt, remanded the lad again and commented that it was a great pity that a home could not be found for him, since he could not be brought up to a trade and seemed deficient in mental powers.

At that point Barnardo, who had been following the case carefully and had had the boy's circumstances investigated, intervened and offered to take John Kinsman in temporarily. Industrial or reformatory schools for destitute children would only take in healthy children; the sick were left on the streets. At the third hearing Barnardo's offer was accepted and John Kinsman went to a Barnardo home by the sea. The intervention was reported in the national press and Barnardo wrote about it in his own magazine.[2]

Barnardo was always drawn towards the most vulnerable children, afflicted, maimed or diseased. They aroused his medical curiosity and his instinct for a human story as well as his generous compassion. As early as 1875, he announced plans to establish a special home for the many crippled children, suffering from deformity of the limbs and spine, but for two years the expense and the discomfiture of the arbitration took up all his energy and he was constrained to delay his plans.

He returned to the subject of a cripples' home for chronically sick children in 1877, but it was ten years before he was able to open such a home. On the whole he disapproved of a segregated life for handicapped children for reasons which are often advanced today by professionals in the field. Both able-bodied and physically handicapped children benefit from mixing, he argued. 'Unkindness to these little unfortunates from the other boys or girls is a thing quite unknown among us. It seems as though the presence of a child maimed for life or marked by some serious deformity draws out only kind deeds and gentle thoughts from the roughest boys and wildest girls.'[3] He noted touching instances of strong young boys carrying the lame and helpless to their beds.

He was soon made aware of the need for an infirmary, for the type of children he took in were particularly prone to sickness and disease. After he had opened a Home for Destitute Boys, he opened a small infirmary for sick children in a dingy little brick house at 19 Stepney Causeway, close to the homes. In 1887, despite straitened funds, a larger hospital became a necessity and Barnardo bought up the houses close to the infirmary, numbers thirteen, fifteen and seventeen, and converted them to accommodate his large new hospital. In Queen Victoria's Golden Jubilee Year, Barnardo pegged his appeal for an enlarged infirmary for Stepney to the royal jubilee, an event which eclipsed all his other fund-raising efforts. Her Majesty's Hospital for Sick Children was opened in Stepney in January 1888, a solid brick building, three and a half storeys high with cots for seventy children. The hospital, connected to the Boys' Home opposite by a subway, was exceptionally well equipped with a dispensary, an operating ward, playrooms for boys and girls, linen rooms (clean and soiled), a food lift the height of the building, nurses' rooms, an apartment for a resident physician and a large flat open-air exercise area on the roof for convalescents. The building was as fireproof as possible and walls, staircases and corridors were heated by hot water pipes. All the wards and apartments had open fireplaces. Nothing was forgotten, including a mortuary. Many of the children he took in were dying already.

At the time, Poor Law Institutions, or isolation hospitals, were the only public hospitals for the poor. Charitable foundations supported the other hospitals for the 'sick poor' and admission was gained by a 'letter' from a donor or subscriber which ensured free treatment. Only a handful of hospitals designed for children existed. Barnardo frequently appealed for 'letters' for hospital admission for his children in the columns of his magazine, *Night and Day*.

Of all the work he undertook, Barnardo perhaps fulfilled himself most completely in his work for sick or maimed children. It was a lifelong interest. 'His studies,' wrote Dr Milne (the first physician to his homes and the first in a dynasty of Milnes who became physicians to Barnardo's), 'lay specially along the lines whereby the children could be benefited ... The most recent books and journals were ever by his table ... He was at home in diagnosis and treatment of disease and in Hospital construction.'

He was unwilling to cut costs in his hospitals and his efforts on behalf of sick children won the approval of the medical profession. 'His face beamed with joy as the Chief Surgeon for children in the London Hospital said, after inspecting 170 cripples of his, "Oh . . . I never saw such a sight as this. All I can say is, everything has been done for them that surgery can do." '4

His Ever-Open-Doors brought in many incurables. And in the year he built the hospital he also built the imaginatively named 'Children's Fold' for one hundred lame, crippled and deformed children, so badly maimed that they needed special surgical and medical care.

The Children's Fold, too, was built like a hospital, with seven dormitories or wards, all with nurses' rooms attached. At the time, he explained that he had a number of crippled children living in the branches of the homes. For most, that was a desirable arrangement. But for one class of crippled children, different care was needed: those who had to lie flat; those unable to move about; those with weak general health who also suffered from abscesses, sinus problems and open wounds. Before the home opened, he appealed ('Something Attempted') directly to the readers' sympathy for funds: 'What mother or father, having healthy, straight-limbed children, can look with dry eyes upon the darlings they love . . . and will not feel that they ought to manifest their debt of gratitude by aiding, as best they can, the little wounded soldiers in the fight of life who hobble along its painful highways with nothing to cheer or alleviate their case?'

And to stir the heartstrings further, Barnardo painted some of his saddest cases:

U. Y. (thirteen). Not only hopelessly crippled, but sadly deformed, the result of angular curvature of the spine. Admitted, with his sister, aged eleven from a northern town . . . Fatherless. A drunken mother, who is broken down in health, and earning a precarious livelihood by hawking; for home, two miserable underground rooms, dimly lighted by a window half underneath the street pavement. This is the sum and story of the poor boy's life. Has sold newspapers and begged on the streets late at night.

R. F. B. (ten). Fatherless, motherless, and a cripple. Through hip dislocation and angular curvature of the spine disabled for life. Mother died two years ago of lock-jaw. Father, as the result of fits of depression, committed suicide. Nine children left orphans, only three of them earning a little. No home for this bright little fellow, who, afflicted as he is, could not have obtained employment.[5]

What really happened to the Children's Fold has never been satisfactorily explained. Barnardo announced its opening in his lengthy report for the year 1887–8. A year later, in his Annual Report of 1889, he stated blithely that crippled or deformed children were not to be segregated unless so ill as to be confined to bed and to need constant surgical care.

The Children's Fold was transformed into a nursery home for 'little boys of a tender age . . . managed chiefly by women'. Perhaps Barnardo overreached himself in attempting to take in such severely disabled children; perhaps the Children's Fold was a fund-raising venture at a time when Barnardo was hard-pressed.

To support his humane work for sick children Barnardo became even more ambitious in his fund-raising. In 1890, he held his first Annual Meeting in the Royal Albert Hall, the largest public building of its kind in London. An audience approaching 7,000, respectable supporters in bonnets and top hats, glowing with charitable impulses, beamed down upon Barnardo's waif children going through their paces. In his role as ringmaster, Barnardo proudly presented his cripple boys. These boys, nearly all on crutches, limped on to the platform, paraded up and down and performed a few simple exercises to a ripple of sympathy from the crowd.

'Some people,' he suggested, 'might think that it is scarcely kind to ask the boys to come here.' Barnardo took a more robust view. 'These are very jolly boys,' he explained to the crowd reassuringly, 'and they would not like to have missed the meeting.' Then he drew attention to an even more handicapped group, the helpless children. Barnardo described them as his saddest cases, since their existence was so 'compassed round by ill that all the music of their lives is dumb'. He introduced a group, one blind, one deaf and dumb, two or three wheeling themselves on go-carts, many on crutches or in nurses' arms and, again, a sympathetic murmur travelled through the crowd. And, again, Barnardo tried to dispel any misgivings his audience might have felt at the display of the handicapped: 'Even these have all been delighted with the prospect of coming here tonight.'

Such a parade would not be tolerated today and even at that time the Waifs and Strays (Church of England Children's Society) would not permit their children to take part in public fêtes.[6] On the other hand, Barnardo was encouraging acceptance of handicapped children through his public relations; he often put on cricket matches with legless boys batting and stomping round the field on crutches.

However, his public championship of handicapped children was not always consistent. By law parents or guardians were forbidden to exhibit handicapped children in the street for begging purposes and a number of these unfortunate children came into Barnardo's care. In his magazine he outlined the sad case of twelve-year-old Rosie. 'Her hands resembled the claws of a lobster and her feet are also very much deformed,' he wrote. Rosie's mother had sent her into the streets to beg with a card tied round her neck calling attention to her deformity. A police constable took pity on her and took her into custody. At Westminster Police Court she was charged with begging and sent to the workhouse. The newly-formed Society for the Prevention of Cruelty to Children prosecuted the mother and Rosie was committed to Barnardo's care by the magistrate. 'Let me show my readers a portrait,' Barnardo wrote and exhibited an engraving of 'Poor little Rosie Hilton' with her claw hands.[7] He evidently gave her real name since he mentioned that her case had been featured in the press.

Barnardo certainly wanted to admit every destitute child but he began to realise, in later years, that there were some children he simply could not care for. At the end of the century he confessed that the single exception was, 'Children who are idiots or who have insane tendencies.' Even then, he explained, he never abandoned them but tried to bring them to the notice of the Poor Law authorities. 'There is no other exception,' he added firmly. Five years later, however, he reluctantly added another category, epileptics. 'As a rule,' he wrote with unusual candour, 'I have tried to shunt these cases wherever I could.'[8] If that were not possible, he took in a few epileptic children. In explanation he announced that he was considering founding two special homes for epileptics, one for girls and one for boys, but he died two years later and those homes were never built. In 1907, two years after Barnardo's death, the homes declared that the only destitute children who could not be admitted were those suffering from epilepsy or mental deficiency.

Barnardo himself was far more concerned and courageous with mental affliction than were his successors in the homes for almost sixty years. Early on in the Girls' Village Home, 'feeble-minded' girls had been specially trained, taught to embroider fine linen and lawn handkerchiefs. Towards the end of the nineteenth century more mentally handicapped children were surviving; gradually their existence and their needs were acknowledged and institutions set up to cater for them.

In 1894, an appeal for £1,000 was launched in *The Times* to found a home for feeble-minded boys, so that they could be segregated, trained 'so that such lads may not, as they grow older, exercise the ordinary liberty of the subject'. Barnardo, always alert, wrote to *The Times* opposing the foundation in print, arguing cogently that a voluntary organisation ought not to have the power to control the liberty and procreation of the feeble-minded, as that was the state's responsibility. He put forward a far more radical proposal, suggesting that feeble-minded children would do far better boarded-out, 'under the care of a good woman, living an ordinary, healthy, industrious life in the country'. (In his own magazine, dated 1893, Barnardo displayed a photograph of ten of his own feeble-minded girls who were doing well, working hard in the homes and gardens of their foster-parents. Had they been boarded-out from the beginning, he asserted, they would have done even better.)

Barnardo neatly turned his letter in *The Times* into an appeal for support for his own work. His plan was much less expensive, he argued; it cost only £18 a year to maintain a boy (£16 for a girl). Wouldn't *The Times* readers like to help?[9]

Barnardo's ebullient claims of success in boarding-out mentally deficient children were backed by rather more sober evidence from a woman doctor, Miss Jean F. Robertson, LRCPSE, one of his boarding-out inspectors: 'I have observed,' she writes in the Annual Report of 1894, 'that those children whom I knew to be very backward and dull, if not even mentally deficient . . . have, in an incredibly short time, mentally developed and improved most wonderfully when placed in the free and quiet home-life of a cottage.'

The dates of Barnardo's particular interest in the feeble-minded are significant. In 1890 his wife, Syrie, who was then forty-three, gave birth to their seventh child, Marjorie Elaine, who was born mentally handicapped. Her very existence was glossed over for years. She was described as 'delicate' by her mother and, apart from Tom who had died as a baby of a few weeks old, Marjorie was the only child omitted from the page of family photographs in her biography of her husband.[10] So Barnardo had had to face the problem of mental handicap at home in a very personal way. According to his widow, he was devoted to his youngest daughter. Certainly his attitude to the care of mentally handicapped children was far-sighted and compassionate.

Eighty years later, when the organisation he founded launched a 'pioneer' scheme to find new families to foster or adopt mentally handicapped children, it was welcomed and emulated by local authorities throughout the country. There are, of course, no means of measuring the differences between what were regarded as mentally deficient children in the 1890s and mentally handicapped children in the 1970s. But it is fair to assume that then and now the children look and behave in a way which marks them out as different.

By the 1890s, Barnardo was jealous of his reputation as champion of all the children. However, it is clear from this brisk communication to the Governor of the Girls' Village Home at Ilford that in 1904 the chain of command was still not as clear as the founder about the new category:

15 November 1904

To Mr J. W. Godfrey
The Governor's House

Dear Godfrey,

With reference to communication from the Association for the Feeble-Minded and to your note to me on the subject. I do not quite understand your saying that we have no category of feeble-minded girls. If you have blind girls don't you keep a list of them? If you have crippled girls don't you keep a list of them? And surely you should do the same with feeble-minded girls. And is there any note made of such cases at Stepney? No doubt we have a note and careful record at Stepney. But the majority of cases of feeble-minded girls you have had in the Village were not apparent as such, or at any rate were not noted on their admission, but could only be detected at Ilford as the girls grew and developed, as they were tested in school and found defective in this respect . . .

It would be a very serious reflection upon an Institution such as ours if we could not answer such simple questions as they have asked . . . No doubt you will send papers back for me with all the information you can get over the last three years, from January 1901 and send them back to me with all the information you can get in the course of the next few days . . .[11]

No reply exists but it is fair to assume that a category of feeble-minded girls was created forthwith at the Village. It was a category that was to cause trouble for many years after Barnardo's death.

In his encouragement of integration and acceptance for both physically and mentally handicapped, Barnardo must have seemed embarrassingly progressive to his successors. He was keenly interested in medical matters, kept abreast of professional journals and practised preventive medicine in his homes. He insisted on rigorous cleanliness, a sensible precaution when children were coming in with head lice and body sores, and he enforced his rules in military style. To a word of command at

Stepney, a gang of twenty boys scrubbed the floors every day until no stain showed. The children (both boys and girls) had a programme of drill and exercise, a diet which was plain and nourishing and plenty of sleep, a programme which he hoped would transform the 'raw material' to physical health.

Barnardo insisted on employing reputable physicians and nurses and his medical knowledge enabled him to select the most up-to-date treatment and equipment for his children. Over sixty years before a National Health Service was introduced, his homes provided the 'family' with spectacles, surgical boots, crutches and other special equipment for the disabled.

He vacillated on the question of segregated homes for severely disabled (it was, presumably, a matter of funds). However, by 1895 he began to assert again that he needed specially designed and adapted homes to care for bedridden or severely disabled children. He opened his first Home for Incurables in Birkdale near Southport, the year before. As usual, his eye for detail was impressive. He insisted that the cots had springs and movable sides and, in this home, he did allow boys and girls to be nursed together. His older brother, Dr A. E. Barnardo, 'Fred', was the honorary physician. 'Nothing so interferes with the training of children as lumping all ages and classes together,' he wrote.[12]

In matters of safety, too, the homes showed Barnardo's ingenious and inventive mind. A cry of 'Fire! Fire!' disturbed the solemnity of an Annual Meeting in Stepney in August 1898. Bugle and bell rang out the alarm as flames and smoke belched in volume from the second floor of the huge building. From one of the top floors a canvas fire escape was flung out of the window and dozens of boys in night-shirts slid to safety inside the chute, whilst scores of others trooped down the iron staircase. When the meeting heard that all the lads were safe, the company cheered loudly. They obviously enjoyed the novel and interesting experiment of a mock fire drill carried out with all Barnardo's sense of the theatrical.

In 1899 Barnardo took over a crèche in Stepney Causeway founded by Mrs Marie Hilton, one of his neighbours who had introduced the system into England in 1871, the year after Barnardo founded his Boys' Home. On her deathbed, Mrs Hilton expressed the wish that Barnardo would take over her crèche and in 1899 the formal transfer was made at a prayer meeting in the chapel of the Stepney Boys' Home. The crèche served the working mothers of the East End for forty years until the Second World War. In the early days they paid twopence a day to leave their babies or toddlers up to five. When the mothers returned from work at six thirty or seven in the evening they would find the children fed, rested, and content after a day's play, dressed in clothes which had been freshly washed. Later, the homes opened two more crèches.

Towards the end of his life, Barnardo was constantly adding new homes for physically handicapped children, including three homes for incurable children in Birkdale, Bradford and Tunbridge Wells, a quarantine house in the Girls' Village Home and an isolation house in the East End.

He was particularly proud of his art school for deaf, dumb, blind or physically disabled girls at Hackney. There, the girls wove Persian pile carpets and rugs, fine pile Gobelins tapestry, made perambulator sets, hand-painted lace, Honiton lace and marqueterie to order. 'It is quite wonderful what these have been able in a short time to accomplish,' he wrote in 1902.[13] He promised a full article on this 'very interesting and attractive branch' but Barnardo died in September 1905 and not for almost sixty years did workers in his homes display such understanding and enthusiasm for the care of the profoundly handicapped.

On his death, of the 8,000 children in his care, more than 1,300 were handicapped, about one in six of his family. The homes were also in debt for more than a quarter of a million pounds.

Barnardo had always insisted that he would not allow the financial burden on the funds to prevent him from admitting handicapped children. He was an autocrat with the confidence and the conviction to overrule those critics on the Council who looked to the budget with dismay as Barnardo built more and more specialised homes for more and more children in need.

At the time of the arbitration, the legal responsibility for Barnardo's work had been placed in the hands of trustees and a Committee; they were empowered to appoint a new Director after Barnardo's death. William Baker, a distinguished Irish barrister, who had served on the Management Committee and supported the work for years, was appointed Honorary Director to succeed Barnardo. A devout and kindly man, he gave up a flourishing legal practice to work for the charity. He was, however, a lawyer, not a doctor, naturally concerned to reduce the huge debt and lacking in Barnardo's medical understanding.

Anxious to find a way to economise, the Council reconsidered first the question of the feeble-minded. An article in the January 1906 edition of *Night and Day* paved the way. It concerned 'the weaklings of the nation', feeble-minded children, and continued in a pseudo-scientific vein that Barnardo would surely have deplored. 'The question of alleged degeneration or race deterioration is being studied in all countries and from many points of view ...'

The homes, it went on, had always taken in children who were 'below the average bodily or mentally', but added that those children (whom Barnardo had called doubly welcome) imposed great difficulties in terms of management, education and 'subsequent disposal'. Then the writer attempted to categorise Barnardo children who were feeble-minded. They included the deaf and dumb, a number of children backward at school because of poor feeding; girls with a very limited capacity for school work but 'they develop intelligence for good hard work', and could be placed out with careful mistresses; a third class not as a rule capable of living away from institutional care, who could be taught needlework or even fancy needlework in the embroidery school at the Village; other children who were almost hopeless and could only occasionally be induced to work. The last classes were those 'who are clearly deteriorating into imbeciles, or who have already deteriorated. The only possible course with such is to have them certified as insane and passed on to the Guardians.' (That Barnardo had always done although he phrased his rejection with more compassion.) The categories described were based not on the degree of handicap, but on the earning potential of the child.

Feeble-minded girls were apparently a more numerous and more worrying category to the Council than the boys and the article commented on their care in the Village and at the Hackney home. The writer saw the presence of two or three 'more or less feeble-minded girls in a cottage of eighteen to twenty' as valuable provided they were educable. The ineducable were a disturbing factor. No doubt Barnardo's attached immense importance to simple teaching and added, 'many of the girls acquire wonderfully clear religious views'.

Barnardo's were dismayed by the prospect of an ever-increasing number of dependent girls whom they would have to support for all their lives.

Feeble-minded girls and boys continued to come into the homes for some years but after Barnardo's death the attitude to them changed markedly. Barnardo had written of his special children with pride and compassion; now they were termed mentally deficient in line with the language and legislation of the day, judged to be not only mentally afflicted but morally degenerate.[14] If an occasional account of an awkward member of the 'family' crept in, it was with a new and long-suffering note:

Lizzie was thirteen last year. She has been ... knocked about from pillar to post all her life. Latterly, she stayed with an aunt who allowed her to run the streets. She never passed the first standard at school, is an exceedingly difficult child to manage and, because of her precocity and vile talk, is not fit to mix with pure-minded children . . . She has already been in a small home which could not keep her. She is regarded as mentally deficient. Is not such a girl one of the most difficult problems in this world?[15]

By 1913, Barnardo's cared for 300 mentally deficient girls out of their 8,000 children, a problem which increasingly concerned them. New legislation was passed and a central association for the care of the mentally deficient was set up to co-ordinate the work of voluntary societies and state and municipal agencies. 'The Mentally Deficient child is now dealt with by Act of Parliament,' the Annual Report for 1914 commented with relief.

Since the local authorities were made responsible for providing for backward children under the 1913 Mental Deficiency Act, Barnardo's hoped that the burden of these difficult cases (many now in their thirties) would be taken off their hands. The Board of Control was horrified at the prospect and informed the homes that 'it would be disastrous' if they did not keep on their long-term residents. Provision took time and delayed the execution of the Act. However, from 1912, the homes officially excluded mentally deficient children, although it took almost nine years to formulate a policy on the delicate question.

This was achieved in 1922 by the new Medical Director, Mr Albert Carless. Wherever possible, the homes would exclude mentally deficient children; borderline cases were to be admitted on probation. When they reached the age of sixteen or eighteen, every effort was to be made to dispose of the mentally deficient: some were to be restored to their parents, some of the worst cases were to be handed over to local authorities. A considerable number of women, however, lived on in the Village, employed in the laundry and other working departments. 'They do,' commented Mr Carless, 'choke up our machinery to some extent.'

The fate of the girls disturbed the Council more than that of the boys. A number of the older mentally deficient men were employed as sweepers in Stepney Yard or at the home at Woodford Bridge. But the girls, alas, 'are liable to go under, becoming the victims of unscrupulous men and possibly swelling the sad sisterhood'.[16]

By 1922, eight cottages in the Village had been set aside for girls who were found to be backward and the Village school had a special class for them. For the first time a mental specialist, 'a lady of keen intelligence, genuine sympathy and real Christian sentiment', was employed.

However, the children, handicapped either mentally or physically, cost the homes almost twice as much as normal children. In the years after Barnardo's death, the numbers of handicapped children admitted to the homes dropped. By 1925, twenty years after the founder's death, 371 'afflicted' children, out of a total of 7,415, lived in the homes (about one in twenty, compared with one in six at the time of his death).

Very gradually, by the early 'thirties, an understanding of the development problems of disadvantaged children was growing in society. 'Mental powers . . . cannot be assessed nearly so easily or accurately as physical characteristics and the task is particularly difficult when the children concerned have had . . . early experiences . . . to make them frightened, secretive and distrustful of those around them.'[17] Barnardo's set up three homes for 'special children' in the late 'twenties and early 'thirties. As the physique of children improved, more effort was concentrated on their mental and emotional problems.

Howard Home, in Bedford, catered for 'children who want to catch up'. Many were left-handed. Some would probably be labelled dyslexic today. The boys and girls in the home in 1928 were described as having great difficulty in writing. 'They show a tendency to write backwards . . . and we had one boy who not only wrote backwards but upside down as well! Many of the children had speech difficulties. A number progressed so well that they were able to join ordinary schools.'

At Tunbridge Wells, formerly a home for crippled children, boys and girls with 'severe temperamental difficulties' often did well thanks to a sympathetic matron.

The Hackney home, formerly used for deaf, dumb and blind children, was converted in 1932 to an admission home for 'some of the most backward and neglected little folk'. Here, the children learnt 'right behaviour and good conduct in a family setting'. This home was regarded as a sieve for borderline cases, apparently mentally defective children, possibly retarded through early social deprivation, for example. 'One little girl aged seven had never known what it was to sleep in a bed. She had been tramped round the country and had never been to school.' Another eleven-year-old girl had lived all her life on a barge: 'She refused absolutely to conform to any order and kicked and screamed at the slightest provocation.' Gradually, however, she began to understand that these things simply were 'not done in well regulated families'. Most of the children passed the test of mental soundness by conforming.

At Boys' Garden City, in Essex in the 'thirties, Barnardo's maintained two small private schools to coach up to thirty boys who were backward through illness or lack of education. Despite the extra coaching, the City included a large number of boys of low, dull, or undeveloped mentality. To cater for them the Essex Education Authority organised a special curriculum based on handwork. Yet, despite the increased understanding and help for backward children, an attitude of unease surrounded the work for mentally deficient children.

Warlies, a stately home in Waltham Abbey, was opened in May 1928 as a home for fifty-three girls between the ages of fifteen to thirty–plus who had lived in the Village since childhood and had been certified as mentally defective. The girls were transplanted because they were judged 'unfit on account of their mentality to take up normal life and work'.[18] Staying in the Village tended to make them more keenly conscious of their disabilities, an explanatory article revealed. They realised they were 'inferior to their younger "sisters" although they were kept occupied with laundry work, dress-making, handicrafts'. In addition, the ever-increasing numbers caused congestion, especially in the Village.[19]

Miss Picton-Turbervill, the brisk and efficient Governor of the Village, was placed in charge of the home for mental deficients and apparently took a practical and optimistic view of their future. The 'senior' girls would do the washing for the London branch homes at a 'very consider-able reduction' in the splendidly equipped laundry, and the crippled inmates would dressmake and embroider. A motto placed at the far end of the lofty hall of the stately home set the tone: 'Cheer up and go on' it encouraged.

The girls 'are happy in the beautiful house and grounds and leave more space for younger children in the Village', the Annual Report for 1928 confirmed. A photograph of the house and grounds were shown un-peopled. After that, silence fell over Warlies. The home did not feature in Annual Reports or publicity for the twelve years the 'MD' girls lived there.

If Miss Picton-Turbervill sounded confident in public, in private she confessed that she found the Warlies girls difficult. Trouble dogged the home. Miss Picton-Turbervill could not at first find the right matron, although she appealed to the Board of Control for help. Eventually she did make an appointment but the matron soon proved unsatisfactory. One by one, the cottage 'mothers', who had transferred with the girls from the Village, began to resign. Then Mr Tetley, a member of the Council, 'told us that he had heard disturbing rumours about Matron and he thought we ought to know that it was said she had been very unkind, in fact, almost cruel to her girls'. Naturally, Miss Picton-Turbervill found the situation upsetting and she began to drive to Waltham Abbey frequently. But, although she came away uneasy, she could never locate the trouble. Some weeks later, another member of the Warlies staff burst into Miss Picton-Turbervill's office in the Village, covered her face and burst out: 'I can't stay there another minute. I will never go back.' When the 'mother' had calmed herself she explained that Matron 'crept about the house and stood staring at people'.

Miss Picton-Turbervill took decisive action. She drove over to Warlies with her co-Governor, confronted the matron with yet another staff resignation, and asked her to leave at once. She had had the foresight to bring the matron's salary for the month and in less than an hour the matron was *en route* for the station in the Governor's car. Miss Picton-Turbervill next called the staff together and explained the situation, promising to send someone from the Village to help next day.

'I think that there is little doubt that Miss F. was a drug addict,' Miss Picton-Turbervill wrote later. 'I never knew what she did beyond "creeping about the house" but I am certain she had a guilty conscience. The staff contented themselves by saying, whenever I tried to get actual facts from them: "She was a very odd woman" and we were content to leave it at that feeling very thankful that she had moved off so quickly and quietly.'[20] Until well after the Second World War, the power of the superior in Barnardo's was a formidable force, imbued with a majesty and authority that junior staff rarely dared to question.

Unfortunately, Warlies seems to have remained an unhappy home. Barnardo's were criticised by Board of Control Inspectors for the strict regime of the home in 1935.[21] The Inspectors disapproved of the silence at dinner-time and of the practice of sending girls to bed as punishment. Warlies was to be the last venture in caring for the mentally subnormal for almost twenty years. By 1940, the home was converted into an up-to-date domestic training school where Barnardo girls came to finish their training.

The care of the mentally deficient was, however, little understood and generally neglected at the time. Barnardo's successors could not perhaps have been expected to match his progress, although it was saddening that they slipped so far behind.

However, the physical care of children in the Barnardo homes continued to be remarkable. In health and hygiene the children were educated out of their class. Before the First World War very few working-class people owned a toothbrush.[22] By 1907, the dentist visited the Stepney homes three times a week and by 1909 he also visited the girls in the Village. At Stepney a bugle call would summon the boys to parade for tooth inspection. This novel form of seeing the dentist was 'found of much value in educating the boys to attain greater dental cleanliness' wrote Barnardo's dentist, Evelyn C. Sprawson in 1913.

Although no doctor's certificate was needed for admission, the Barnardo child admitted to an Ever-Open-Door or a branch was first given a complete overhaul by the doctor and the state of eyes, hair, head, teeth, glands and general development noted on the child's health dossier. New children were also photographed and placed in quarantine before they were finally assigned to a branch home. That first overhaul and the encouragement by the Medical Officer to treat even minor ailments in hospital quickly helped to account for the low death rate. A table of admission in 1914 gives an idea of the state of health of children admitted that year. One in eight was verminous, one in seven delicate; many suffered from eye disease and poor sight, scars and sores, scabies, ringworm and rickets, whilst a handful had amputated limbs and one little girl was deaf and dumb.

In the years before the First World War 'the white scourge' of TB was a killer and Barnardo's, as well as health authorities, were trying to find the answer to a disease which, in 1913, caused the death of sixteen out of forty-one of the homes' fatalities that year.

By 1918, tuberculosis was still Barnardo's 'chief enemy' and the Council was already planning to open a home for boys and girls requiring surgical treatment. Before the home was opened, TB was treated at the hospital in the Girls' Village Home in Barkingside, opened in 1912, or in the hospital at Stepney. Both hospitals possessed the new X-ray equipment and first-class medical staff.

In 1919, Mrs Vera Osborne was just over a year old, suffering badly from abscesses on the joints of her hands and feet caused by TB. Every day the district nurse called to treat her but she did not seem to be making any progress and her mother was waiting for a bed for her in a state hospital in Scarborough. Through a friend of the family, she was taken to Barnardo's. She went straight to the Australasian Hospital in the Girls' Village Home and was saved from permanent disablement.

At the time I arrived, there was a young doctor called Gushie Taylor, a medical missionary who was extremely interested in my case. He performed ten operations, five on my hands and five on my feet. They were a complete success. Since I was such a baby, I was made a pet of and I stayed there till I was four years old.

Later Mrs Osborne returned to hospital from time to time.

The hospital was formed in the letter 'E', the three horizontal strokes being the wards, the upright one contained the theatre, staff quarters, dispensary and outpatients. It was very capably run by Matron, whose word was law. She would come down the ward like a battleship in full rig, and everyone would be rather quiet. Under Matron was Sister Noakes, a very sweet person who flitted about like a little robin . . .

Then there was Nurse Robson from outpatients. For some reason she took a liking to me and used to take me out on her days off and buy me presents at Easter and Christmas. At the end of each ward was a verandah – glass at the back and sides but open to all weather at the front. This held four beds and whenever I was in hospital I occupied one of those beds. The curious thing about the wards was that they were built on a dry concrete moat. You could scramble down one side, crawl right underneath the ward and come up the other side. When I was older I used to feel very brave if I did this. I always had a feeling that the hospital floor would sink and squash me flat.[23]

Apart from being the loving centre of her world, Barnardo's hospital gave little Vera the use of her right hand. By 1923 a new hospital at Woodford Bridge in Essex replaced the old one in Stepney. The 'Light Department' opened in 1925 helped to counteract the ravages of rickets and TB by the new artificial ray treatment used at the two hospitals and at convalescent homes at Folkestone and Harrogate. By 1929, the Barnardo Chief Medical Officer reported the beneficial effects of psychotherapy in nervous cases.

In the 'twenties, the after-effects of a poor wartime diet due to shortages of sugar and fat, according to medical opinion of the day, the soaring cost of food in the war years, inflicted scars on the health of the nation. Barnardo's Medical Officer noted the deterioration in the children's condition and in 1926 the children's milk ration was doubled to a pint and a half a day.

Rising unemployment and poverty continued to show up in the nation's health record. By 1930, four out of six recruits to the Army were rejected on physical grounds. That year, of the child 'raw material' admitted to Barnardo's, only 2 per cent were graded A1. The rest were underweight, undernourished, with bad teeth, with tonsils needing attention, with weak hearts, flat feet and paralysed limbs.

In the 'thirties during a time of high unemployment and trade recession, Barnardo's made an outstanding contribution to the health of poor children. By 1937 the homes had two 100-bed hospitals with outpatient and massage departments and four convalescent homes. They employed five full-time doctors and used the latest electrical and ultraviolet ray equipment to restore the children to health. Lord Horder, who spoke at an Annual Meeting in 1937, described it as 'a unique work, a national work; it can't attract too much support'.

But personal life, even in the homes for crippled or sick children, depended on the quality of the staff. Birkdale home for crippled children, near Southport, was described in the Annual Report for 1932 as a 'very varied and happy family. It numbers about seventy members and includes girls of all ages and boys up to the age of about nine or ten ... good food, loving care and the bracing sea air usually bring about such a recovery that the majority of the kiddies of school age are able to attend outside school and make friends with other children in the town.' That was the official version.

Miss Mollie Wearne, who worked for Barnardo's for almost forty years, found the atmosphere in Birkdale in 1931 very different. She was a young assistant at the time:

It was very hard there. The house was cold, warmed by a furnace in the cellars. If the children were naughty they were taken down to the cellars and told 'if you're very bad, you'll be put on the fire'. The children didn't go hungry, but every day they had semolina pudding. They didn't have many outings, and very few pleasures and if they were naughty, the pleasures were taken away. There were no Guides or Scouts or concerts at Birkdale. Matron was a Plymouth Brother and very strict. There was one child called Yvonne about eleven years old. She used to talk to me and I was very interested in this girl. When I went on holiday I said to Yvonne, 'I'll see you in two weeks.' When I came back she'd been moved. The staff said to me, 'We knew she would be moved because you took an interest in her,' so I went to Matron and asked why Yvonne had been moved and she said, 'It's not for me to discuss it with you.'[24]

As a last resort Miss Wearne wrote to the General Superintendent of the homes at headquarters to ask permission to write to Yvonne on her birthday. He consented gladly but the staff at Birkdale warned her that Matron would intervene. They were right. Miss Wearne soon discovered that her letters to Yvonne in her new home were never delivered. The matron there had been given instructions not to pass them on.

Years later she did meet Yvonne who had grasped the position. 'She said, "I know what happened, this is what some matrons do ..."'

Miss Wearne was working a ten-hour day at the time for a wage of £16 a year. But it was the atmosphere in the home she could not tolerate. 'The money never came in and you accepted that. I was there for three years and I never spoke about it. It was like being in prison.'

Christmas came as a welcome relief. 'It was quite a happy day. We used to fill the children's stockings, we worked till 2 a.m. on Christmas morning. Then on Christmas Day the Doctor came in and the Mayor.

Coming in like that they didn't see what it was really like. It was a closed book.'

Miss Wearne never spoke of that experience. She moved to another branch and stayed on happily at Barnardo's for thirty-five years, caring for adolescent girls and helping to create a free and friendly atmosphere for them.

Poverty had been the main cause which brought children into Barnardo's care between the wars and the effects of poverty were reflected in the stunted bodies, the rickets and TB of the 'twenties and early 'thirties. By 1938, the public health services, the pre-natal services and clinics, the day nurseries, cheap school milk and school meals had begun to build up the health of all the nation's children. Barnardo's noted the difference in the condition of the children admitted to their homes. 'We gratefully record that the physical condition of the children we admit today shows a noticeable improvement upon that of children a generation ago. Today we can pick out from among the children we admit about 6 or 7 per cent who are of A1 standard. About ten years ago we received only 2 per cent who were in this grade.'

The following year, when war broke out, the large Barnardo communities in the Girls' Village Homes and the Boys' Garden City were evacuated and their hospitals used for the war effort. The homes had to call on local GPs and general hospitals as well as school medical and dental services to look after the health of their scattered children.

With all its shortcomings and the inevitable personal failures, Barnardo's had brought about a magnificent new deal for the handicapped child and anticipated a new spirit of practical compassion. Their children had benefited from positive discrimination to counteract a heritage of poor health. By 1948, a National Health Service Act would guarantee every child the right to health care and hospital treatment, a right Barnardo had battled to win.

8

A Start in Life

'While I value much the result of schoolwork, I prize even more the training imparted in the Trades Shops, in the Kitchen and in the Laundry.'

Barnardo, Annual Report, 1889

Three outstanding qualities raised Barnardo above the other missionaries and clergymen striving to save the children in the East End of London: his personal dynamism, his flair for writing and his organising ability. A self-made man himself in an age of expansion, he harnessed the children's need to the opportunity for development for both skilled and unskilled labour in mid-Victorian England. For the children of the gutter, he became the voicepiece, the entrepreneur, the trainer, the rescuer, the employment agency. In Barnardo's homes, children were transported to a new station in life, a new vision, a new future. Despite inevitable disappointments and failures in individual cases, under Barnardo's guidance the work held a mesmeric quality that captivated the public and held them spellbound.

No question that he did transform the lives of thousands of boys and girls. He turned young tramps and beggars into labourers, wild girls of the street into docile, domestic servants, townees into country dwellers and generations of the 'submerged tenth' into respectable working- or lower-middle-class citizens.

The transformation was wrought, Barnardo would have claimed, by faith and prayer but he would not have denied the detailed and careful planning and organisation that went into it. Barnardo believed in method. He always had great faith in the value of work; no one embraced the Protestant work ethic with more ardour. Even in the early days as a missionary, he started a vocational training programme. While he was preaching and teaching the Gospel, he initiated sewing classes for Bryant and May match girls; encouraged thrift among his young people by opening a Penny Savings Bank; and promoted the notion of self-help, by explaining that his mission endeavoured to supply every necessity by 'making the necessitous their own helpers'.

He operated in the climate of his time and none of his ideas was new. It was his persuasive selling technique, his business acumen, his feel for the right approach to the public and his selection of employees that guaranteed his success. Within ten years, he had taken over the Limehouse Shoeblack Brigade with its debts and its small lodging house for twenty boys, and put in his own lads. He dressed his East End Juvenile Mission Boys, as they were called in the early days, in sailor suits and named them the Union Jack Brigade.[1]

At the same time as he opened his first home in Stepney for working and destitute lads, he also founded a City Messenger Brigade from a group of trusted boys who came from very poor families and lived in their own homes. To drum up custom, he visited the proprietors of local businesses personally and also sent out a series of pamphlets which lent a sense of authority and importance to his enterprise. 'The accurate and careful delivery of TRADE CIRCULARS and other PUBLIC NOTICES cannot be achieved in a more economical or satisfactory way than by the systematic employment of the Boy Commissionaire Corps.' All the boys, Barnardo asserted, were literate and of good character, chosen from the 'better class attending our free day and Sunday schools'. Dressed to look sober and smart in black tunic, piped with red, matching trousers and peak cap, with the initials EEJM on their buttons, the lads, ranging in age from twelve to seventeen, were posted in key positions throughout the City. They stood like cabbies and plied for hire for threepence for an hour or ten shillings and sixpence for a week. The boys, who each had a guarantor, not only delivered messages and parcels but were also an excellent advertisement for the mission.

By 1874, the boys of the City Messenger Brigade had earned £1,650 13s. 8d. After the brigade inspector's salary and the cost of uniforms, printing and other expenses had been paid, the boys took home £1,409 11s. 1d.[2] For years the boys earned about nine shillings a week and some of them were given permanent jobs by City firms.

Barnardo's second and most profitable brigade was the woodchoppers, 'the most hopeful and encouraging'. The boys sawed and chopped up firewood into bundles in a large yard and sent them out to private families. Customers living within a mile of the East End had their wood delivered free by cart; those who lived beyond that distance could only have carriage-free wood if they ordered 1,000 bundles or more. But in his advertisement, Barnardo suggested, with his usual common sense, that 'two or three families in any neighbourhood should combine their orders'. His little woodchoppers proved so popular that they were soon selling hundreds of pounds' worth of wood. In the 1880s, Barnardo the timber merchant was importing wood from the Baltic and hiring barges, horses and vans to deliver his firewood. By 1888 the earnings of the three brigades, woodchoppers, the messengers and the shoeblacks, totalled over £4,400.[3]

The shoeblacks, the only resident boys, came from the poorest families. They lived in lodgings rented from Barnardo, 'Jack's Happy Homes', and earned the least. They were drawn from his Sunday school and, with other Sunday school children, had an outing once a year on a steamer, a picnic and a game of tug o' war; they also visited Wimbledon Common to pick up waste-paper. (They later added picking up rags and waste-paper to their shoeblacking skills and became known as the Union Jack Rag Brigade.) Barnardo's ability to introduce sound business practice into his philanthropic ventures and to colour them with playful and appealing sentiment captivated the public.

His Annual Reports, in the early days, always carried announcements which advertised his boys' origins, their wares and their worth. In 1870–1 (the first year of the Boys' Home) he announced that his 'destitute arabs' made brushes of all kinds and his 'little rescued gutter lads make good and serviceable shoes'. Evidently the tone of the advertisements and the quality of the goods produced impressed the public for the following year he made a modest profit from the sale of shoes and brushes.

In the beginning nearly all the boys in the home helped to contribute to the common good. He introduced the halftime system in his first home for destitute boys. The boys spent half of the day learning the rudiments of a basic education and half in mastering a trade. The system was used similarly for training children on the kibbutz in Israel at first, although a good education was always considered important.

In Barnardo's home, a skilled workman instructed the apprentices in each workshop. 'Primarily of course,' Barnardo explained, 'these shops exist for the benefit of the boys; by equipping them for the future.' But he also saw moral significance in the system: 'in mastering his tools a boy always . . . to a certain extent, masters himself and thus our shops teach him not merely to be a thorough tradesman, but also to be a good man.'

Increasingly he acknowledged that, by using the boys as bootmakers and carpenters, he saved the home a great deal of money. Gradually the number and variety of the trade shops increased. By 1872, a tailoring department was opened, sedentary work which particularly suited his many crippled boys. The young tailors made uniforms for the City Messenger Brigade and for the boys resident in the home. Later, bakers, blacksmiths, brushmakers, harness-makers, mat-makers, printers, tin-smiths, upholsterers and wheelwrights all helped to service the growing establishments. Like the girls in the Village Homes, the boys did their

147

own cleaning, waiting at table and housework. To induce work-shy boys to join the trade workshops in the early days Barnardo used a wily psychology.

In 1874, Henry, an independent lad from Whitechapel, evaded Barnardo's attempts to persuade him to come and live in the home, where he would have a comfortable bed, plenty of food and learn to read and write and master a trade. At last, Henry gave in and agreed to go into the Stepney home but on his own terms. 'All right, mister,' he conceded, 'I'll go with yer; but mind I AIN'T TO DO NO WORK. I wants the learning but I ain't going to kill myself for no one.'

Once in the home, the bargain was kept. The other boys either went to school in the morning or worked, according to their timetable. Henry was left to go his own way. After a few days he began to feel bored and left out. He ventured into the brushmakers' workshop where thirty-five boys were making house-brooms, putting bristles into the holes in the wood. Henry was ignored and not allowed near the work. Then he wandered into the shoemakers' boot shop and the tailors' room and the same thing happened. Everyone was busy and left Henry to his own devices but he was not allowed to touch anything or to interfere. Disconsolate, Henry wandered through the home to the dormitories; there, he discovered that working boys slept on real beds with iron bedsteads, sheets, pillows and blankets, while he had to make do with a canvas hammock with rugs; at meals he noticed that working boys were allowed butter instead of dry bread and tea. But the real shock came one Saturday (a half-holiday). Henry saw one of his friends, a working boy, buy sweets from a stall. The boy treated him to a few sweets and explained that working boys were given a penny for every shilling they earned. (Half of that money went into the boys' pockets and half into the bank. When the boy left the home, Barnardo doubled the sum he had saved to help the youth start an independent working life.) When he heard all that, Henry decided he wanted to leave. Then, he changed his mind and asked to become a 'snob' (slang for a bootmaker). 'At the end of a fortnight's trial,' Barnardo said, 'the idle, lazy and thriftless boy was transformed into the diligent and aspiring workman.'[4] The homes encouraged industry and thrift in all their young charges and rewarded those who saved their money for many years.

For lads coming into the teeming, noisy city Barnardo provided a Young Workmen's Hotel in the East End in 1881, a place, he announced, where youth could live in reasonable comfort for a modest price under the influence of a Christian couple: 'A type of house mother and father who would not, however, impose the strict discipline of a home on the youths.' For some time he had campaigned for a Labour House, a home to train lads between seventeen and twenty who had drifted into the capital and now found themselves without home, job or friends. His President, Lord Cairns, opposed the extension of Barnardo's considerable range of responsibility and wrote to him saying: 'By chance in *The Christian* I saw the announcement of your intention to aid destitute cases beyond the age of boyhood and I think it better to write at once and say that if an organisation of this kind is added to your present homes, I must cease to be President.'[5] Not, Lord Cairns added, that he was casting doubt on the need to help homeless youths or the possibility of meeting that need, but he felt that Barnardo had already over-extended himself. The Lord Chancellor had proved a powerful friend in Barnardo's time of trial and he might have expected Barnardo to heed his warning, but the record reveals that his objections were swept aside in the tide of Barnardo's enthusiasm. The Labour House was opened in 1882 with Cairns remaining as President.

The fifty lads in the home were, Barnardo insisted, in the Labour House for testing their ability, not for training. They were introduced to a habit of work (a kind of early Youth Training Scheme). Their day was gruelling, starting at five thirty with morning prayers. For long hours the boys chopped wood, made packing-cases and later attended evening classes with intervals for meals and military drill. The day ended with evening prayers at 9.15 p.m. and lights out at ten. To boost funds, in 1882 Barnardo introduced a mineral water factory in the Labour House where the youths made seltzers, soda water, fruit champagne and his own patent tonic, Fizzo-Done.[6] He announced in 1886 that the work supported a 'large and growing outside trade ... though it is much to be desired that the public would employ my young workmen more freely'.

Many of the lads from the Labour House emigrated to Canada; others went to work on Yarmouth fishing smacks and steamers. Life at sea had always held a romantic attraction for Barnardo. He dressed his own sons, and some of the lads in the homes, in sailor suits. Almost from the time he began the work, he yearned to run a training ship for boys, like Lord Shaftesbury's *Arethusa*. He appealed to Shaftesbury, but in vain as the older man felt that Barnardo lacked the experience and financial solidity to manage such a scheme. Barnardo, however, was irrepressible. He managed to send some of his 'family' to sea by opening two small shipping agencies in Yarmouth and Cardiff with an experienced skipper in charge. By 1888, he announced that he had put sixty-four boys to sea.

From his earliest days, much of Barnardo's success was due to his ability to persuade wealthy Evangelical supporters of the worth of his cause and, towards the end of his life, it helped him to fulfil even his maritime ambitions for his boys. In 1883, however, he was enabled to train boys for farm life and eventual emigration through the offer of Richard Phipps, Esq, a gentleman farmer from Bromyard, near Hereford. Mr Phipps built an extension to his large house on his estate so that he could train Barnardo boys between the ages of eleven and thirteen. Each year, he came to London to pick out about forty boys himself to train for farm-work on his land. Barnardo considered that the home, run and financed by Mr Phipps with 'minute and constant supervision', was a valuable addition to his work. Because of the small numbers involved 'the boys enjoyed a freedom denied to those in larger establishments', he wrote. The boys did not wear uniform and Barnardo felt that the 'standard of comfort and of attainment is probably higher than in any other branch of my work'.[7] When they set off for Canada, Mr Phipps provided his lads with a 'very superior outfit'. The home closed in 1896 when the Phippses decided to travel abroad.

For Barnardo boys, training in the homes offered opportunities in a variety of trades or for life on a farm, or at sea. For his girls, from the 1870s until the 1940s, domestic service was virtually the only outlet. Barnardo considered that household work helped to give girls from a rough background a framework of family life and a refining influence. He worked to transform female factory hands into respectable domestic servants. Factory work, he argued, gave the girls work 'at the expense of those gentle and nameless womanly graces which made wise mothers and happy homes'.[8]

Young girls from the factories turned up at his mission tea parties and Barnardo winced at their style of dressing, 'with at least four of the primary colours in most inartistic conjunction'. He deplored the way they wore their hair cut in a fringe, evidently regarded as a most immodest hair style. As an earnest Evangelical, he believed that growing up in a Christian family, and the dependence and obedience that imposed, conferred both spiritual and moral benefit on a child. He mistrusted the 'spirit of precocious independence which weakens family ties'. He was also somewhat contemptuous of the girls' natural families who were, he wrote, 'always poor and frequently not very reputable'. As ever, he wanted to reclaim those young girls by providing them with a model family. Working as servants, in a respectable middle-class religious household, seemed to him an ideal substitute for girls who lacked parents (or at any rate suitable parents) of their own.

In 1883, with the generous help of a supporter, George Sturge, he opened a training home and free registry for young servants. This training, Barnardo claimed, saved hundreds of girls from certain ruin. With an estimated 80,000 prostitutes on the streets of London at the time, the possibilities of exploitation were real and alternative employment hard to find.

At Sturge House, the former factory hands spent three to four months learning the rudiments of domestic work as well as a smattering of general education. The home could train forty girls in the 'arts of the hearth'. They spent successive fortnights learning the routine of work in a scullery, a kitchen, a laundry, a dormitory, a bedroom and a parlour. When the girls were considered proficient, they started a day job in a nearby household. The servants' registry on the premises suited a girl to her mistress. After their day job, the girls had to be back in the home for the night by 6 or 7 p.m. Once they were considered ready to live out and take up permanent posts, suitable Christian households were found. The mistress of the household had to promise that Barnardo girls would not be sent out in the evenings on errands and that they would *never* be asked to enter a public house.

In 1888, Barnardo opened a small quarantine house opposite Sturge House for older girls freshly rescued from the streets. This served as a temporary shelter until the girls were considered fit to be admitted to Sturge House or another Barnardo branch home.

Everything the children learnt in the homes was to be of practical help to them in adult life, with one exception, the use of music. In the school, in church, at drill and at play, Barnardo saw the value of the bugle call, the organ, the band. In this he gave rein to the imaginative side of his nature. At Leopold House, boys from ten to thirteen studied music. The most promising joined his band of 'musical boys'.

He used music, he once wrote,

as a means of culture. It is to the undeveloped or half developed higher natures of these little people of ours what bread is to their bodies . . .

Secondly it is invaluable as a means of drill . . . Again and again we have found that some irregular and eccentric boy, who could never be got to respond to ordinary methods, has been attracted by music, which has found in his chaotic nature some responsive chord.

Thirdly we use music because of the pleasure it gives. Their little lives have been all too dull and grey of hue under sombre skies . . .

Fourthly we use music because of its pre-eminent value as a handmaid of religion . . . Our children's worship is full of singing and no one who has heard their fresh young voices will deny its heartiness and earnestness . . .

Fifthly and most conclusively, we use music because we cannot do without it. Children will sing, and the only question is, how shall they sing and what shall they sing?[9]

At Stepney, half an hour was set aside every day for compulsory band practice and by the 1880s Barnardo had appointed a musical director, Joseph Proudman, a retired military bandmaster, to instruct the children in instrumental music and singing. Boys with a good ear were encouraged to join the band and once or twice a week 400 boys in uniform, headed by their band, marched through the East End. For years, 'musical boys' travelled the country to play at fund-raising meetings. Some of the boys joined military bands when they left Stepney and one lad, Walter Reynolds, who learnt to play the cornet in the home, was invited by Sir Henry Wood to join his Queen's Hall orchestra as solo euphonium, tuba and contra-bass trombone and became a soloist at the Promenade concerts at the Queen's Hall, London. Before the First World War, Walter Reynolds was appointed Musical Director of the LCC. He left to the homes a Walter Reynolds scholarship for talented Barnardo boys.

Because of the nature of the homes and the huge numbers of children involved, such encouragement of individual talent was rare. The children were required to become model workmen, farm labourers, domestic servants and latterly, sailors.

At about the turn of the century, Barnardo noticed that the old Norfolk County School at North Elham, on the river Wensum, suitable for a sea school, had come on to the market. He was offered the property at a very reduced price but could not afford it. An estate agent from the south coast volunteered to appeal to moneyed supporters and Barnardo let it be known that he wanted to build a 'ship on land' run by 'good men of prayer and of Christian character, also total abstainers'.[10] As usual his imagination warmed to the prospect of building a community shaped to his mould. The pale cheeks of his East End boys 'would be suffused with colour, their eyes would sparkle with delight'.

Barnardo's dreams for a naval training school, so detailed and wellplanned, were blueprints and his supporters were dazzled by them. In June 1901, the 'miracle' happened. E. H. Watts, senior partner of the City shipping firm of Watts, Watts and Co., presented the deeds of the school to Barnardo's Council.

He spent much of the last five years of his life making plans and alterations to equip the school for his scheme. He installed heating, hot water and gas lighting and, since the inside staircases were wooden, he insisted on building fire escapes to all the dormitories. A hot water bath was built in the basement 'so that the inmates may be tubbed in all weathers', the outside swimming bath was deepened and improved, dressing sheds were erected, the fives court and cricket ground repaired, the laundry fitted up and the little private chapel restored. The dining hall seating 400 boys and great hall were repaired, as well as ten other rooms. The building and repairs cost over £10,000 and there were endless delays before the work was completed. Barnardo had hoped to open the new branch in September 1902. By April 1903, ninety boys moved into Watts Naval Training School and the ship's bell was going up in the central hall but the school was far from finished.

Barnardo was delighted with the 'pleasant place ... where sailor laddies live, where they are shielded from all harm and where they are taught "Keep ye the law – be swift in obedience". They meet as a family,' he mused, 'morning by morning and night by night in their new Norfolk home. But in ten years, where will they not be scattered?'

Never was isle so little, never was sea so lone,
But over the scud and the palm trees an English flag has flown.

He did not live to see the official opening of his cherished sea school. Watts Naval Training School opened officially in April 1906, six months after his death, now equipped to accommodate 320 boys aged from ten to fourteen. A fully rigged ship, the *Cholmondeley*, was lent to the school by the Mission to Deep Sea Fishermen so that the boys could sail round the east coast.

Watts masters were skilled seamen appointed by the Admiralty and the school was officially recognised. Eleven years after Barnardo wrote the couplet musing on his boys' destination, the First World War broke out and the sailor boys from Watts Naval Training School merited their tag as 'bulwarks of Britain'. Watts boys took part in all the naval engagements of the First World War. One boy in the attack at Zeebrugge asked for a Watts ribbon before the action and wore it on his hat all through the war. By the time the Armistice came in 1918, forty-four Watts boys out of 566 who had served in the Armed Forces had been killed. Earlier another Watts boy, Frederick Humby, a steward on the *Titanic*, died when the great liner went down.

Throughout the 'twenties and 'thirties, the school reflected the close link between the Barnardo homes and the patriotic Establishment. Perhaps it is not without significance that from 1903 to 1946 (with the exception of four years) the child on Barnardo's Annual Report was always a wistful sailor boy, bearing a Union Jack with the inscription 'For God and Country'.

Barnardo's fostered a sense of pride in the school, in the traditions of the Navy and in the boys with evident success. Throughout the years between the wars, the Admirality carried out a formal annual inspection. In a typical report in 1925, Admiral Sir Hugh Tothill, KCB, KCMG, commented: 'The boys are very alert and keen and take an obvious pride

in themselves and their establishment. They are happy and cheerful . . .
I was again very favourably impressed by the tone of this school.'[11] That
tone was maintained only by rigorous control of the boys' lives. A Council
Minute in July 1924 noted, with disapproval, that boys from Watts
visiting their relatives 'often returned with a different spirit and spread
Bolshevik and Communistic ideas'.[12] To discourage these rebellious
notions, the Executive unanimously passed a resolution on 29 October
1924, banning children in all homes from going home at Christmas 'as
full and sufficient provision is made at all the Homes for proper cel-
ebration of Christmas'.

The school was winning praise from the Admiralty in 1928 when
Bertram Busby, a Barnardo boy since babyhood, joined. He was eleven
and at first found the life hard and the food 'awful'. He couldn't face
the breakfast: 'two pongy rounds off a full loaf stuck together with
dripping: on most days it tasted like candle grease'. (According to a
booklet on Watts written by Guy N. Pocock, a member of Council,
'pongy rounds' were replaced by 1936 by fresh herrings, eggs, sausages,
'all sorts of good things at breakfast'.) 'I couldn't stick the "cocoa" served
in tin basins in the morning or the tea in the evening . . . I used to come
off the messdeck after nibbling at the bread and go straight to the
drinking fountain.' Fortunately, the fountain was underneath the window
of Busby's kindly dormitory matron who noticed his antics and told him
to come up to her for a drink of milk at playtime, without telling anyone.
Busby found the soup, served three times a week in tin basins, another
ordeal:

> On the bottom of the basin was a thick, muddy mixture of lentils,
> bones and chunks of meat with plenty of fat and gristle on it. The
> middle section was clearer, while on top, for a good quarter of an inch
> was green grease . . . When I first joined Watts, this soup nearly made
> me sick, just to look at it. And I must have gone without dinner three
> times a week for a month. For the second course on soup days, 'niggers
> in the snow' or boiled rice with a few currants added to sweeten it
> were served. However, if you didn't eat your soup, you got no niggers
> in the snow. After a few weeks I became used to it and ate it as quickly,
> and eagerly as the other lads.[13]

In Busby's days, from March to October boys went barefoot, without
shoes, socks or slippers. They ran across a coke cinder path and even
played football (except for the school team) with bare feet. A Council
member, Guy Pocock, visited the school and reported that the boys'
boots wore out within a fortnight unless they were patched all over with

iron-protectors. A Minute of the Executive in January 1929 records the decision not to issue the boys with shoes or slippers since the system had worked 'very well for the past twenty-five years'.

The routine of the school was well established and Busby retains a vivid memory of a day which began at 5.45 a.m. when nautical officers would wake the boys to get up at the double, strip their beds, dress and then make their beds. Fourteen minutes later, at 5.59 a.m. precisely, the 'Still' on the bugle signalled the boys to kneel by their beds for a minute's silent prayer. At 6 o'clock a different note on the bugle would sound the 'Carry on'. The boys then had to attend to their 'clean ship' duties, sweeping, scrubbing, polishing, skirmishing (picking up paper). At 6.45 a.m. 'Cooks' was sounded and two boys from each mess laid the tables with tin basins. Sometimes the boys would be sent for a brief cross-country run to give them an appetite for their 'pongy rounds'. After grace, the boys ate in silence. Later, after more 'clean ship' jobs the boys would assemble on the parade ground, under the mast, for an inspection of their clothes and boots in winter. If a boy's suit was torn or his boots in need of repair, it was his responsibility to see to them. If any lad let his boots wear down so far that they were difficult to repair, the 'cobbler's strap flew left, right and centre', Bert Busby remembers.

After the inspection, the parade stood to attention, the ten buglers sounded the 'Alert', the band struck up 'God Save the King' as the ensign and school flags were hoisted. The parade marched on to the quarter deck for prayers, the central hymn sheet would be lowered and the staff would file in to the order of 'Toll the bell'.

While most of the 300 boys in the school studied lessons in schoolwork or seamanship, certain boys would be detailed for special duty in the kitchens, in the laundry, in the linen room, the stores or the bakehouse.

Corporal punishment, like the rest of the school routine, was carried out with due discipline and ceremony. A boy found breaking school rules was hauled up in front of a defaulter's parade. His punishment, according to the severity of the offence, would vary from standing on deck for half an hour, to six cuts of the cane on the bare backside. 'Just prior to my arrival,' Bert Busby mentioned, 'such punishment was carried out in the Drill Hall. The general assembly was sounded and every boy watched the execution of the punishment.' Boys' letters, both incoming and outgoing, were censored.

They worked at their lessons or nautical classes from ten in the morning to five in the evening. On Wednesday, a boiled egg was served. 'These were seldom fresh eggs but eggs preserved in isinglass . . . some of them were really foul . . . If a boy had a bad egg he was permitted to take it up to the Mess Deck officer and have it changed for a good – or better one . . . the offending egg was judged by the Mess Deck officer – at arm's length. "Smells all right to me, son," he would say, "so you try taking it back to your mess and having another taste." ' After tea the boys scurried out to the playing fields in summer or played conkers, tip, cat, rounders, marbles in the winter: some attended voluntary bugle, band or PT practice. They had chess, draughts, halma, snap and other games, but playing cards was banned. 'Books and periodicals were donated or on loan,' says Busby, 'I cannot remember seeing a newspaper at all.' Perhaps the newspapers were considered a dangerous influence, although, in some of the Barnardo homes in the 'thirties, the *Children's Newspaper* brought in a breath of the outside world.

Supper, at 7 p.m., consisted of a mug of cocoa and a handful of broken biscuits, 'always Gunwheels', hard thick biscuits some five inches in diameter, 'quite capable, when whole, of supporting the corner of a piano'. They were eaten eagerly and some bits stuffed in pockets to be savoured later in the dormitories. Before bed the boys trooped to the shower room for their ritual teeth-cleaning. A senior boy stood at the door holding a large earthenware jar of cooking salt. Each boy was given a dessertspoonful of salt in his cupped hand, as one by one the 300 boys went to the troughs with cold water taps, to clean their teeth with salt and gargle with salt water. Then, the boys lined up for inspection, baring their teeth in front of the duty officer. On bath nights, the Watts boys were numbered off in their hundreds as they ran to the bathroom. They stripped off by the showers, then the duty officer turned on the overhead watering cans and the boys soaped and rinsed with fresh water three times. They lined up naked, with their hands above their heads, for the duty officer's inspection. 'The duty officer could learn a lot from that inspection,' said Busby. 'For example, if you had just had six cuts and had the Union Jack on your backside.'

Boys went to sleep, as they had woken, to a series of orders from the bugle. At 8.45 p.m. the bugler on the bridge sounded the 'Last Post' and three minutes later, at the 'Still', all 300 boys got out of their beds to kneel for one minute in silent prayer. At a minute to nine the 'Carry on' call signalled the boys back to bed; and at nine o'clock precisely the duty officer would blow a long blast on his whistle and bellow 'Pipe down' as he turned out the master switch. The great house soon slept but one boy on watch, a sentry, nightshirt tucked into his trousers, walked up and down on the 'bridge', a central balcony overlooking the quarter deck. Each hour, the sentry changed with his relief, until 'Reveille' sounded at last and the school sprang to life again.

When Bertram Busby left Watts in 1932 to join the naval training ship, HMS *Ganges*, he was fifteen and a half. 'The other recruits on the ship cried themselves to sleep for a month,' he recalls, 'but the Watts boys thought it was great. Many ex-Barnardo boys who joined the Forces in wartime had a similar response to service life. The food was better, the organisation was better and we knew most of the preparatory work. Although I didn't like it at first, Watts taught me a lot,' Busby added. 'It made me self-reliant. You could sew, you could clean and look after yourself.'

The school was grant-aided, by the Board of Education, both as an elementary school and as a further education school of nautical training. In 1935, the Board of Education carried out a full inspection and were on the whole favourably impressed. They found the working week for both boys and staff too long (the boys spent approximately thirty hours a week at their studies); the classroom temperature (a chilly 40 degrees) too low and provision for the 40 per cent of boys not destined for life at sea unsatisfactory. Watts concentrated their efforts on the abler boys, those who would do well in the Navy or in a services' band. Only the best nautical boys learnt any science; the boys destined to become landlubbers received a more limited training. The contrast was to be found in the classrooms. The Inspectors found the seamanship room 'a model of what such a room should be' but were not impressed with the ordinary classrooms which, in their view, were 'somewhat drab . . . very little attempt has been made to make the surroundings attractive'.

The report generally approved of the staff, particularly the Chief Officer, a retired Naval Warrant Officer, 'a man of outstanding ability who maintains a discipline which is remarkably free from harshness and yet is firm . . . He is devoted to the boys and, judging by their affection for him, this devotion appears to be well repaid.'

They praised the leisure activities but regretted that instructors, rather than schoolmasters, supervised them. 'The danger . . . is that a deck, rather than a home atmosphere, may prevail.'

They made one perceptive comment upon Watts staff which was applicable to almost all of the Barnardo homes at the time: 'It is unfortunate that the teachers appointed to this school generally remain. Occasional changes are good, both for the school and the teachers and young teachers should be encouraged, after a few years, to seek positions elsewhere.'[14] The danger of institutionalism in a highly organised and ritualised community was very real.

Russell-Cotes Nautical School for Merchant Seamen, another Barnardo home founded in 1919, just after the First World War, was not so highly disciplined or traditional as Watts. The home was named after the donors, Sir Merton and Lady Russell-Cotes, who presented their estate of thirty-four acres at Parkstone in Dorset to Barnardo's Homes.

The blockades during the First World War had shown up the need for trained seamen in the Merchant Navy. With Watts' wartime record in mind, a plan to train Barnardo boys for the Mercantile Marine was designed with the blessing of Admiral Lord Jellicoe. During the 'twenties and 'thirties many former Russell-Cotes boys served as stewards on Union Castle liners.

In an elaborate publicity pamphlet published in 1919, Barnardo's described the new venture as 'philanthropic patriotism'. 'Surely nothing could be further from the old and hateful system of "charity doles" than this new scheme for making the poorest child a self-respecting and honourable citizen, a credit to his country and part of the bulwark of England.' Their publicity reflected a new language of respect for the indigent child.

The position of the school, three and a half miles west of Bournemouth, encouraged contact with the town and the boys joined in local fêtes and sporting events. The new school was small, less than half the size of Watts; boys lived in cottages in a more informal community. Punishments, for example, were treated as corrections. When a boy robbed a bird's nest at Russell-Cotes, the Captain Superintendent accompanied the boy to his dormitory locker and confiscated his most prized possession for a time . . . 'The psychological training of the mind requires more care and study than the mere castigation of the body.' A far cry from the ritualised six cuts on the bare bottom witnessed by the whole school at Watts.

For over fifty years, until 1922, the dingy houses at Stepney had served to train generations of older boys. After the First World War, Barnardo's were anxious to send children out of the East End. Barnardo himself had often written longingly of the clean, fresh air, the benefits of country living. From his early experiences of seeking out children in miserable haunts and lodging-houses, he harboured a profound mistrust of the influence of the city upon the child. The smoke, grime, the pollution in the air at Stepney must have been appalling. But, at the time also, there was a romantic idea that the countryside, with its pure and natural air, fostered pure and healthy living. Barnardo had gone further; he had been convinced that the farmer was a sound man 'seldom a Socialist, a Communist or an Anarchist and he is slow to lend himself to any of the crazy fads and theories for the reorganisation of society'.[15]

To give their boys the benefit of the rural surroundings and small homes enjoyed by the girls in their Village Home, in 1909 the Council acquired a thirty-nine-acre estate in Woodford Bridge, Essex, only three miles from the sister institution. Plans were drawn up to create a complete community, a Boys' Garden City which, in the course of time, would accommodate 900 boys living in thirty cottages (although they never quite attained that number). The first thirty-four 'pioneers and pick-nickers' came from the Labour House for Destitute Youths in Stepney, which was subsequently closed.

By December 1909 those first boys camped in the old manor house until the new school homes were built. They worked hard, clearing the overgrown land, breaking up the surface of the ground, trenching, lining and making roads. They soon had enough land under cultivation to produce potatoes, cabbages and greens (the Superintendent was very keen on greens) for their own needs. The young labourers were mainly boys considered ineligible for emigration or training at the naval school because of some mental or physical defect. Those unable to tackle outdoor work repaired shoes, made baskets or recaned chairs. By 1912 when Boys' Garden City was officially opened by Her Royal Highness the Duchess of Albany, over 300 boys, from four to fourteen, lived in cottages with a cottage 'mother'. As they were moved out of the East End, other Barnardo homes in the city were closed. At the Annual Meeting that year older boys 'sported smock frocks and looked country-men, every inch of them'.[16]

Of the communal buildings, a swimming bath was one of the first additions, a gift from a philanthropist; then came Canada Hall, a huge building with vast kitchens able to cater for 750 boys in the 1930s. After the First World War, a steam bakery was built where a dozen boys learnt to bake the thousands of loaves needed for the nearby homes.

In 1923 a new hospital was built to replace the old one at Stepney, complete with a nurses' hostel in the grounds. Most of the children went to school outside but there was a special house for crippled boys who were taught tailoring and bootmaking. Backward children also received special education. They were taught along Montessori lines and trained in outdoor work, gardening, carpentry and the care of pets, so successfully that some boys were able to take up places in ordinary elementary schools.

In the early days, Garden City boys were easily distinguishable by their sailor suits and closecropped heads when they went out to church or school. In 1928, however, the Council decided to permit boys over eleven to grow their hair longer so that they would not feel a sense of inferiority at school.[17]

The majority of Garden City boys left to take up work in the cabinet-making or tailoring trades. Practised in domestic work, some became house boys and graduated to positions as footmen, butlers and chauffeur-gardeners. One Garden City boy became the first in Barnardo homes in the UK to gain a BSc degree in 1931.

Five years later, in 1936, Peter Lott, now a social worker living in

Poole, went to Garden City as a five-year-old. He was lucky, since a cinema projector was installed in the new gym that year and he enjoyed the weekly cinema show, a big picture, an educational film and the news. Peter remembers the home as a 'totally enclosed institution with all the trimmings, rather like a small Vatican state'. He settled in as one of a group, with no possessions of his own and little sense of his own identity. Overall his memories are pleasant: 'It was a good, secure, safe experience. You had a feeling of orderliness, of things being done for you. I remember the joy of going to the tuck shop.'[18]

Peter stayed at the Garden City until war broke out when he was evacuated and boarded out. He enjoyed the spaciousness of the grounds and the 'sense of Empire'. The names of the boys' houses, King Edward VII, Union Jack, Empire, New Zealand, Britannia, as well as Canada Hall, their vast dining room, reflected Barnardo's patriotic traditions.

One incident stands out. As a small boy, Peter was scrubbing the floor in his stockinged feet when he got an enormous splinter in his big toe. He missed his dinner that day and still remembers it.

By 1922 the Council was able to announce that they had a 'new Stepney' in the country. They bought Goldings, formerly the home of a wealthy banker, a pseudo-Elizabethan pile standing in fifty acres of ground near Hertford, as a country home for 300 boys. The new William Baker Technical School was to replace Stepney Causeway shops where from 1870 onwards generations of Barnardo boys had learnt a trade.

Although Barnardo, the founder, had been dead for almost twenty years, when the boys made the 'great trek' they departed in a manner he would have approved: 'On the 19th of April 1922, two hundred and sixty of the lads from Stepney mustered for the last time in the stony playground. They saluted the portrait of Dr Barnardo which had been placed in full view of them, and then with tuck of drum and following their bandsmen, they marched out at the front gate and along Commercial Road to begin their lives in a new environment.'[19] Admiral Stileman, the Director of Barnardo's, as well as Mrs Barnardo and other dignitaries, awaited them as they marched through the entrance gates and on to the lawn facing their imposing new home, Goldings, known as the William Baker Technical School after the former Director.

'We have brought you here,' said the present Director, William McCall, 'to breathe in God's fresh air and to build you up, not only in health but in character ... This school will be a tremendous help in fitting you to go out in the world, strong and worthy lads and God-fearing citizens.'

At the official opening ceremony that November, the youthful Prince of Wales addressed the boys:

At Goldings you are being taught to play the game. You can play the game in your workshops much better in these surroundings and much better on your playing fields here than in the small courts at Stepney ... I hope that all of you will get all you can out of your allotments and that every single boy will have pegged out his claim to one. By doing this you get a sense of proprietorship, and when you get a sense of proprietorship you realise and learn to respect the rights of others.[20]

By 1926, homegrown self-sufficiency was in full swing. The gardeners had evidently taken the Prince's advice. They harvested thirty tons of potatoes and large quantities of other vegetables. Four new cottages erected on the Goldings estates were wired and plumbed by young engineers; the young carpenters took on all the carpentry and joinery including roofs, doors and window frames, the tinsmiths made kettles and saucepans and the modernised printing shop and bootmaking department improved the supply of publicity and footwear supplied to the homes.

In 1927, Goldings made a break with Barnardo's tradition of a military style of schooling at Stepney. Instead of calling senior boys NCOs, the school now sported prefects and was divided into houses and house masters and a house captain in public-school style. Military parades ceased and senior boys took on much of the responsibility for discipline and good behaviour.

By 1939, the blacksmiths, brushmakers, harness-makers and wheel-wrights of Dr Barnardo's day were training as motor mechanics and electricians. Barnardo's little rescued gutter lads were young artisans and craftsmen in training; many of them worked in aircraft and munition factories during the war. But the principle of self-help established in 1870 by Barnardo himself was upheld. The boys dug for victory in the vast gardens of Goldings and, by their trades, helped to contribute to the homes and keep down costs. The considerable savings that Barnardo had envisaged were effected.

Had he been alive in the 1930s, it seems certain that Barnardo would have stayed ahead of the times in his care for children. When he began his work, it was eminently sensible to concentrate on 'the rudiments of a very plain English education' for his wards. As he explained, he had no time 'to attend to the ornamental adjuncts of advanced education'. The three R's, a little grammar, geography and history as well, of course, as Scripture and music and singing served them well enough. To get his homes recognised by the Privy Council for Education was a struggle. He needed official approval so that he could obtain the education grant, have the schools inspected by the Government and give their pupils the right to sit public examinations.

But between 1870 and 1939, educational opportunities began to offer poor children social mobility and a way out of dead-end jobs and second-class status. The cry went up for real educational opportunities and secondary schooling for all. Yet Barnardo's before the war was slow to seize those opportunities. Until the 1944 Education Act, their children were expected to attend elementary schools and to know their place. By and large, children in the branch homes were not encouraged to develop academically. As late as 1940, the Council passed a resolution disapproving of the suggestion that boys at Goldings should be encouraged to matriculate.[21] Significantly, among the small number of Barnardo children who did obtain scholarships and places in secondary schools before the war, those in boarded-out homes formed the majority.

As late as 1942, 139 out of 195, almost three-quarters of Barnardo girls, graduated to a life below stairs. By the end of the war, about half of the girls who left the homes took up a variety of occupations: book-binding, librarianship; shorthand, typing; hairdressing; kennelmaid and even factory work. The other half went 'naturally' into service. Due to wartime demand factory work, the occupation of which the founder had disapproved so fiercely, had, at last, become respectable. As to the boys, the majority became skilled tradesmen, entered the Armed Forces or worked on the land.[22]

Before the war, founder worship gripped the homes; like many great men, Barnardo's legacy was taken too literally for too long. In the optimistic post-war world, Barnardo's Homes began actively to encourage their brighter children to attend grammar or secondary schools. An Education Adviser was appointed who commented on the relatively low number of children obtaining free places at grammar and technical schools and adolescents were, at last, counselled to seek higher education and to avoid 'anything which looks like a dead-end occupation'.[23]

9

Passport for Life

'Over the front of the House in Stepney Causeway is a board bearing the welcome words: "No destitute boy ever refused admission".'

Annual Report, 1874

Barnardo kept open house for destitute children; his Ever-Open-Door policy meant that the home in Stepney Causeway was always crowded in the early years. Sometimes he put up 150 boys in a house with 140 beds. His difficulty, a limited number of beds and an unlimited invitation, was deliberately compounded by his nightly search through the streets for homeless children. As a young student, he had seen the waifs, cold, neglected and starving, and the sight left an indelible impression.

His lively accounts of his midnight excursions suggest that he also revelled in the drama of the slums. He used sporting metaphors, netting the children, catching the children, angling for them – and there was always the prize. 'Catch your hooligan before he is made,' he would say, 'and in nine cases out of ten you will turn him into a self-respecting, useful man.'

As a young man, Barnardo would change into old clothes, stuff his pockets with cake and halfpennies and walk briskly through the deserted streets, slowing up beside the quays and wharves, in the deserted markets and under the archways of courts and tenement buildings, peering down into doorways and up into the guttering. He usually took a companion, either a rescued boy who knew the haunts, or a boys' beadle.

He seems an unlikely racegoer yet, every year, he would visit the Derby, an unfailing attraction for the street boys of the East End. Barnardo travelled by cab to Epsom Downs, arriving about three or four in the morning on the eve of the races; he was soon surrounded by a crowd of boys munching the fish and chips he had bought for them from a nearby stall. Whilst they ate, he spoke to them of his home, his mission, of the grand new future that awaited them, with plenty of food, real beds and money to earn. His ardour and his easy manner made him a magnetic force to the boys. The attraction must have been mutual for it seems clear that the vitality of low life held a fascination for him; when he travelled abroad in America and Canada, he visited not only philanthropic institutions which cared for destitute children but the dives and low haunts of New York and Chicago, with an American detective as his guide. The endless tales he told of child rescue reveal that he entered into the lives of the street children with great empathy.

In the early years, Barnardo himself acted as field worker, office worker, fund-raiser and social work Director. He left a vivid picture of the human refuse from the streets who filled his waiting hall every afternoon: 'rough young desperadoes, fresh from the streets, who have come to the end of all their resources, who cannot get work, dare not beg and who, if not helped, must steal. Younger children are also there, boys and girls pitiful in their wretchedness, sometimes brought by an equally poor relative or occasionally introduced by a letter or visiting card from some friend who knows of their case and has sent them on to me.'[1] On a Friday, he would interview all the new 'intake' in his office: 'little boys, big boys, fat boys, thin boys, ragged boys, tidy boys, merry boys, sad boys, fair boys, dark boys'. A few years later, he employed ten beadles in all, usually retired police constables, to search out the boys and girls, visit their parents or guardians and check their stories with magistrates, police, parsons and other respectable local figures.

Not all the candidates were genuine and Barnardo found that many youngsters 'apply with a lie in their mouths'. Some were children on the run from home after being punished, others out for a childish prank to taste a life which they thought consisted mainly of 'eating, playing and sleeping'. Barnardo and his beadles soon sorted out the impostors: 'While Charity hopeth all things, she dares not believe all things concerning these varied applicants at our gates; and it is only by cultivating a spirit of healthy and persevering scepticism, that I am able to maintain the advantages of the Institutions unimpaired for those who are deservedly in need of them.'[2]

Once Barnardo had satisfied himself as to the real condition of the child and his family, a history would be written up on the basis of which the child was either admitted or turned away from the home. That numbered early record, with a photograph attached, was the child's passport to Barnardo life and, expanded and extended, would follow the child until 'his or her life is again merged in the outside world'. In those early days, Barnardo expected (in normal circumstances) to keep a child from babyhood to adolescence. The record became a symbol, almost a substitute for the child.

In 1888, he admitted 1,768 children on a permanent basis and helped seventy-seven others who were needy but not totally destitute. Once admitted, each child would be given a thorough medical examination, either by Barnardo himself, who was keenly interested in the children's health, or by the homes' Medical Officer. Next, he would be photo-graphed in street clothes: sometimes Barnardo would take the photo-graphs. As the homes grew, decisions had to be taken about allocating the children, and age, health and sex would all be taken into account as well as 'moral depravity' or the need to hide children from cruel or depraved parents.

Barnardo painted a picture of the way a boy over thirteen would be received in the Stepney home in the 1880s. After having his photograph taken, the lad was 'thoroughly bathed and washed, has his hair cut and is then inducted into his uniform and a bed and locker in one of the dormitories are assigned to him'.[3]

Then the recruit would be launched briskly into the military style of Barnardo life by a bugle call at five thirty in the morning and a half-hour's 'sharp set up drill in the yard' followed by breakfast, school, a session in the trade shop, all punctuated by prayer, drill, lessons, work, with lights out at 9 p.m.

So powerful was Barnardo's personal influence that for many years after his death his successors followed without question his methods, his military style, his pattern of admission. By the 1920s, women officers, as well as men, were employed as inquiry officers, a recognition that a woman might pour out her story with freedom to another woman, but little else had changed. Inquiries still involved 'mazes of detail' and boys and girls were received at Stepney much as they had been in Dr Barnardo's day: cleansed, fed, numbered, clad and sent to the studio for a photograph. Personal histories and religious denomination were as important as ever in classifying, checking and monitoring the children. Now, medical inspection took place at a more leisurely pace, presumably because the general health of the children had improved. However, if a child needed medical treatment, red tape was slashed: 'All rules of procedure, all formalities ... are regarded as naught, compared with the needs of that one tiny, suffering little bundle of humanity.' And, according to a senior administrator in 1928, all the cases were approached in the Barnardo tradition: 'a desire to help, if at all possible, rather than to decline'.[4]

In the early days, Dr Barnardo himself would decide whether or not a child should be admitted to the homes. Later, he delegated some of the responsibility; the Medical Officer's report always carried a great deal of weight. By 1937, two senior clerks in the general office at Stepney had taken over the decision-making. If the case was complicated, they referred it to one of the two principals: either the General Superinten-dent in charge of the children, or the Secretary to the Managers, the Chief Administrator. Barnardo's spirit of scepticism still prevailed and applicants deemed unworthy were turned away. Barnardo's, the General Superintendent explained at a staff conference, was not intended to be used 'either for shelving of legal responsibilities or for making it easy for unmarried mothers to get rid of unwanted children'. (Unmarried mothers were helped through the scheme started by Barnardo himself. If they lapsed more than once, however, they were turned away.)[5] Nor did Barnardo's indulge adoptive parents who merely wanted a respite from their new responsibilities. If two healthy parents had 'an enormous family' they were not allowed to off-load one or two of the children on to the charity. Only in circumstances of great hardship or disability were boys or girls from single-parent families admitted. Above all, parents with even a very modest income were barred from admitting their children. Destitution was the key word and families above subsistence level stood no chance.

Since Barnardo's death, mental deficiency and epilepsy had become formal barriers to admission. The religion of a child's parents did not bar entry, although Roman Catholic and Jewish children were always referred to their own ecclesiastical authorities. If they refused to help, which was very rare, Barnardo's brought up the child as a Protestant.

Just before the Second World War, admission procedure became somewhat more sophisticated, although still based on Barnardo's own practice. Now boys and girls in the provinces were sent to London accompanied by a travelling matron; lodged in one of the new receiving houses and medically examined. The doctor and the clerical staff still decided the child's future, with scant personal knowledge of the boy or girl, their interests, inclinations or potential. By 1943 an Observation Centre was introduced at the Boys' Garden City, where children received a routine 'mental test' with a psychiatrist and two educational psychologists in charge.

In Barnardo's, as in other children's homes in the 'thirties, there was no question of the institution adapting to accommodate the child. Traditionally in Barnardo's the 'normal bright healthy child would be boarded out . . . a boy of a suitable age sent to one of the two Naval Schools, a girl to the Village'.[6] Once a child's destination was decided Transfer and Statistics departments made the arrangement, the child's papers were written up as a history and a uniformed 'travelling matron', especially employed for escort work, would accompany the boy or girl to the branch home and make sure that the child's history was safely deposited.

In Barnardo's day, babies were sometimes left overnight on Stepney's scrubbed white doorstep, with a note pinned to their swaddling clothes, a reminder, if one was necessary, of the human content of the records.

At first, Barnardo had housed the babies in a cottage in the Girls' Village Home. In his broad vision of a 'natural' family for the girls, he regarded a baby in the cottage as a 'blessing in the home life of a little family'. As his work became more prominent, too many babies were placed in his care to accommodate in the Village. Again, he was faced with overcrowding for his smallest wards. As so often happened with his work, his persuasive tongue and pen influenced his growing personal following. In 1883, a Mr Theodore Moillet gave him two villas standing back from the road, with a pleasant garden and shrubbery and nearly an acre of meadow land in the village of Hawkhurst, Kent, to provide a home for babies. The following year, twenty-six babies were housed in the Kent home. Once he had publicised his work with babies, more and more applications for places for neglected infants poured in. Local people named the villa 'Babies' Castle'.[7]

The home was barely a year old when Barnardo began to plan an extension. By now, the homes owned a considerable number of properties and Barnardo juggled with his space. He converted Church House, a three-storey, red-brick semi-detached house in Bow, originally used as a quarantine house for girls from the streets, into 'Tinies' House', a reception home for the 'unshielded weaklings of the City slums'. The home in Bow served as an adjunct to Babies' Castle.

By the summer of 1886, the new enlarged Babies' Castle, 'one of the most organised of our Institutions', was ready for the pomp and circumstance of a royal opening. On a fine August afternoon, Princess Mary Adelaide, Duchess of Teck, her daughter, the Princess Victoria, and her sons, Prince Adolphus and Prince George of Teck, arrived by royal train at the little station of Etchingham, near Hawkhurst. Crowds of cheering Kent villagers, fluttering flags and banners, greeted the royal party as they drove in open carriage to Babies' Castle. The Director and dignatories of the home met the party, while men from the West Kent Yeomanry and the Hawkhurst Volunteers formed a guard of honour. To the strains of the National Anthem, played by the boys' band, the party entered a specially erected marquee. After loyal addresses and prayers, a number of ladies, bearing purses containing not less than £10 for Babies' Castle, were presented to Her Royal Highness whilst Barnardo's 'little hand-bell ringers' played suitable selections of music.

The inmates, toddlers and babies in their nurses' arms, made a small procession and the Duchess formally declared the building open. The enlarged Babies' Castle was equipped with nurseries, dormitories, play-rooms, a dispensary and doctor's room as well as 'the most modern ideas as to sanitation'. The original building sixty yards away was turned into an infirmary for infectious cases.

The Castle, according to Barnardo, proved invaluable in saving the most neglected babies who came from wretched hovels, even prison cells, to Babies' Castle. By 1888, Barnardo employed a woman doctor as resident physician and careful records were kept of the ailments from which the babies suffered, principally rickets, ophthalmia and roxola. In his Annual Report that year, Barnardo, in his inimitable style, highlighted some of the saddest histories:

> J. C. (seven months). Born in a prison. Daughter of a wretched and thoroughly abandoned girl, who was undergoing imprisonment for theft – who is still living a dishonest, and, it is feared, an immoral life, and who declared that she would 'drown the little beast' if they brought it to her.
>
> T. R. (two months). Mother died of starvation and anxiety four days after giving birth to this child. Father aged; afflicted with heart disease; utterly broken down in health, and unable to work. Another child at home and all three actually starving. No relatives able to assist.
>
> S. G. (two months). A tiny female child with a withered, weird face, smaller than the palm of a hand. Mother lying, incurably afflicted with dropsy, at her mother's house, and cruelly deserted by her worthless and drunken husband, who cannot be traced. Four children of whom she cannot support one . . . Relatives all miserably poor.[8]

Like all Barnardo's homes, Babies' Castle was kept scrupulously clean and hygienic. A competent matron, Barnardo described her as 'the Commander-in-Chief', supervised the home and ensured that floors and furniture of each room were daily scrubbed and polished until they shone. From April until an autumn chill, the little ones went barefoot and Barnardo boasted that they had 'no croup, no fits and no chilblains'. Considering the numbers, their life was as informal as possible. The little children took their meals out of doors in fine weather. In their kindergarten school, the toddlers learnt about gardening and natural history with a collection of pets, a tortoise, tadpoles, frogs, goldfish and silkworms, to liven up the lessons. Barnardo was aware of the drawbacks of bringing up babies in hordes but felt that the kindergarten system tended 'to develop their individuality and to replace, to some extent, the knowledge they would gain in home and family life'.

He was particularly progressive in his care of mentally handicapped children at Babies' Castle. 'We have had some most interesting cases of feeble-minded children making marked mental progress; the start being given by thyroid treatment and kept up by individual petting and attention.'[9]

Despite devoted and meticulous care, small babies, particularly bottle-fed babies, suffered from internal disorders. Sister Alice, a former matron of Babies' Castle, described the lengths to which she went to protect them. They were 'fed on the most scientific methods, bottles were kept scrupulously clean, food was measured out as a prescription and given at regular intervals. Every infant was made a special study.' Yet, in spite of all, the babies still suffered from relaxed bowels, they became emaciated, some even contracted enteritis and a few died. At last, they decided to try boarding-out the babies: 'We did it at first knowing the trouble we took over bottles and feeding and yet our comparative failure.' The first few boarded-out babies were visited anxiously every two or three days.

Within a week their bowels had become normal and they rapidly gained weight. 'We brought them back to the Castle, only to begin our troubles again.'[10] The individual love and attention a foster-mother was able to give to the baby, as well as the diminished risk of infection weighted the scales. Sister Alice, who had transferred from Babies' Castle to supervise boarding-out babies, concluded, with her colleagues, that it was undesirable to care for babies *en masse*. By October 1897, Barnardo had decided that all infants under three should be boarded-out.

That rule was not so easy to apply in practice. Very delicate babies who needed a special diet or skilled medical or surgical treatment fared better at Babies' Castle, where expert attention was on hand, so the Castle came to house the most vulnerable infants. Six years after Barnardo's death, the Castle had ninety cots occupied by sixty-seven boys and twenty-three girls. Of the babies and small children there, many were delicate, needing special care; others, less afflicted, suffered from rickets, defective vision, deafness, lupus, eczema or hernia. One or two were mentally deficient, one boy had deformed legs and feet, another suffered from hip-joint disease and two from infantile paralysis. One baby had only one leg. Yet the photographs from Babies' Castle always showed bonny babies. 'King Baby' was, as Barnardo had always recognised, a great favourite with the public.

From the beginning older Barnardo girls had trained in domestic service at Babies' Castle and later worked there; sometimes they were girls suffering from handicaps; perhaps it was felt that those disabled girls benefited from the protected environment.

For over forty years, the enlarged Babies' Castle, designed by Barnardo himself, remained virtually unchanged. In 1922 an outdoor playground with a covered way was donated by girls' colleges and schools; three years later, in 1925, some twenty-five years after electricity came into general use, the lights were switched on at Babies' Castle to replace the old-fashioned oil lamps 'which had been a source of much anxiety'.[11]

In the Village babies were cared for at Queen Victoria House, a tall, rather grim building with lofty rooms, flights of stairs and long passageways. In 1926 modern accommodation was built, a bungalow to house a dozen babies, and two blocks for toddlers and children. They were a part of Cherry Court, the new reception home in the Village.

Soon after modernisation, Barnardo's began to train staff in baby care. In 1930 a training course for the Nursery Nursing Certificate awarded by the National Society of Children's Nurseries was introduced. Students came from both the UK and overseas and paid twenty guineas a term for tuition, board and lodging. They studied nursing, first-aid, cookery as well as infant welfare. At Babies' Castle, too, students trained for the examination and by 1933 three nurses who were trained at the Castle came back as staff members.

By 1937, Babies' Castle was caring for sixty-five children from a few weeks to five years old. The shadow of war cast a chill over the staff and the young children were presented with some 'funny noses' to try on. The Home Office had asked permission to test gas-masks on the babies and the older children: in the Girls' Village Home six months later, Miss Picton-Turbervill, Governor of the Village, wearing a gas-mask, marched into a van with a gas-filled chamber to inspire confidence in the new apparatus.[12] When the public got wind of the unusual event, letters of criticism were sent to Barnardo's Council. But, as Council members pointed out fairly, gas-masks were not mentioned to the children and the knowledge of suitable head measurements and the most effective masks for young children was for 'the benefit not only of Barnardo children but for the whole child life of the nation'.[13]

By March 1938, with war only eighteen months away, shelters were built to protect the infants of Babies' Castle. In the early days of the war, the Council wrestled with the difficult question of whether to leave their babies undisturbed during night alarms or take the risk of their catching cold by transferring them to the shelter. The bombing and the blitz increased the need for refuge.

Since Barnardo had found a child frozen to death because he had to wait for admission, the principle of never turning away a destitute child held sway. From 1874 to the Second World War, wretched children, wandering the streets, found refuge and food at Stepney Causeway. Often they found their way by lantern (later, electricity) to the sign blazoning the words, 'Children's Shelter, Open All Night'.[14]

The accommodation was for the night only, with a hot bath, a comfortable bed and breakfast for the straggler. The following morning the child would be turned over to the home next door and inquiries started, the child's history noted and health investigated thoroughly. The first Ever-Open-Door in Stepney was fitted with a grille so that the Superintendent in charge could peer out to see who his night-caller might be before opening the door.

In his own account of the all night refuge, Barnardo listed two typical girl applicants for the year 1888:

> L. and B. Y. – nine and six. Homeless in the streets of London and cruelly deserted by a drunken and immoral mother, these two girls knocked at the door of the All Night Refuge and begged admission. Father died three years ago. Family altogether bad, & these little ones in grave moral peril . . . Paternal grandmother utterly disreputable. An elder brother already a thief. No redeeming point about the mother, who is wholly abandoned and on the streets.

Barnardo admitted the little girls to the homes after careful inquiry.

He travelled extensively, both in the cities of the United Kingdom and abroad, and by 1892 he had decided that the street children of some of the provincial cities were as badly in need of a children's refuge. He had always argued that his was not merely a London charity but cosmopolitan: children came to him, not only from every part of the United Kingdom, but from all over the world, from Alexandria, Brisbane, Hamburg, New Jersey, Paris and St Lucia.[15]

Despite misgivings by his Committee, Barnardo opened Ever-Open-Doors, each consisting of a single house which could take up to fifteen children in seven large provincial cities: Bath, Cardiff, Edinburgh, Leeds, Liverpool, Newcastle and Plymouth. Overwhelmed, as usual, by his powerful arguments, the Committee resigned themselves to yet more expansion and more expense and merely stipulated that the refuges should not cost more than £250 a year each. Beadles from Stepney and their wives staffed the Ever-Open-Doors. The beadle was expected to hunt the streets for stray children as well as to shelter those who turned up at the doors and he also had to sift the children's stories and communicate his findings to Stepney. A bell and a speaking tube from the entrance to the beadle's bedroom kept him in constant touch with the street.

Opposition in Edinburgh from two local newspapers, 'notoriously subject to Romish influence', during the time when Barnardo was exceedingly unpopular with Catholics due to the notoriety of an abduction case, forced him to close the Edinburgh branch in 1894 and it never re-opened. Within eight years, he had opened Ever-Open-Doors in Bristol, Belfast, Brighton, Hull, Portsmouth and Southampton, now fourteen in all, including the chief Ever-Open-Doors at Stepney. After Barnardo's death the Ever-Open-Doors continued to take in children until, in 1947, they were officially named Reception Centres to conform to the new attitude to the destitute child and the legislation to provide shelter.

By opening provincial centres, his homes came to be regarded as a truly national charity. Barnardo claimed, in 1898, that his was the only charity in the world which sought out poor children night and day in lodging houses, tramps' kitchens and in the low haunts of the cities. Perhaps the most valuable service the Ever-Open-Doors rendered to the nation was to take in what Barnardo described as the 'flotsam and jetsam', the crippled, the handicapped, the rejected, turned away at other doors.

However the children reached Barnardo's, once accepted they became automatically lifelong members of the largest family in the world. Since the original aim was to reclaim and convert the children, monitoring their progress was of paramount importance, and Barnardo cherished the ideal of sending children out to employers who were 'profoundly Christian'.

He initiated an ingenious system of prizes to encourage his protégés to remain steady in their places of work.[16] Awarded out of the Committee's personal pocket, the prizes were graded according to the length of service: boys and girls who had kept their situation for a year 'with a perfectly good character' received a prize to the value of ten shillings; the value went up to a guinea for those who stayed in their positions for two years; and star workers who remained in posts for four years received a silver watch.

The prize-giving ceremony, held at Annual Meetings, was a visible demonstration that the homes had 'saved' the children, body and soul. 'My boys and girls,' wrote Barnardo, 'are encouraged to correspond with me, to bring their joys and sorrows and difficulties before myself or my co-workers.' In Canada, too, visitors were employed to keep the family together. In the beginning of this century, Barnardo founded the Guild of the Grateful Life for his former wards. Through reunions, Annual Meetings, services of thanksgiving, sports days, a quarterly magazine and schemes to support cots and beds in the homes, old boys and girls were held together. Nowadays, Barnardo ties, scarves, badges and blazer crests are on sale to old alumni.

For the girls particularly, elaborate schemes were worked out to keep them in touch. By the 1930s, Barnardo girls in service were given the names and addresses of others working as maids in their district; their mistresses had to agree to allow the girls to visit each other. A fortnight's holiday at the Village and three weekends were offered free to Barnardo girls who had just left. Contact and control went hand-in-hand. The girls were not allowed to leave their situation for two years without Barnardo's approval.[17] Old boys, too, were visited and, in some areas, hostels were provided or boys invited back for a day or weekend but the restriction of leaving jobs did not apply to them.

The family illusion was carefully fostered, with Barnardo referring to his 'children' and his 'grandchildren'. Before the Second World War, snapshots captioned from the 'Family Album' appeared in Annual Reports; they pictured Barnardo children at the seaside, at school desks, on the playing field or at their devotions. Many old boys and girls were photographed proudly in uniform and wedding photographs frequently appeared. Nor was it entirely an illusion. The children did have a strong sense of their 'Barnardo' identity. For some, Barnardo's was the only home they had ever known. A Christmas letter goes out to every known old boy and girl to this day.

In such a huge operation as Barnardo's, it is almost impossible to gauge whether the children fulfilled the earnest aspirations of the founder. From 1870 to 1939, close to 125,000 children passed through Barnardo's Homes. Countless lost touch with the homes; they may have been the very men and women who prospered in life; of the many who stayed faithful to the 'family', the charity obviously chose to highlight the good news.

Every issue of the pre-war Annual Reports contained letters from the children, expressing gratitude: 'I am writing this letter in lodgings that Barnardo's found for me, wearing clothes that Barnardo's provided for me, even the pen I am using I received through the Homes. My poor vocabulary cannot possibly express my deep gratitude for everything that has been done for me,' wrote an unnamed young man in his first job. Barnardo's, he continued, had made him into a skilled tradesman and proficient athlete and gymnast. 'All this and more Barnardo's gave me. Now I am out in the world, earning my own living . . . I shall ever remember the Homes and when I am able, may I try and return a little in exchange.'[18]

In 1939, a gunner waiting to go to France wrote: 'When the time comes that I must go to do my duty for this Motherland, I shall go with the thought that not only do I go to fight for my country but, as so many old boys in the last war went, to uphold the honour of a great and noble cause, Dr Barnardo's Homes, and to bring additional honour to that institution.'

In describing old boys and girls, the word 'gratitude' crops up again and again in Barnardo literature. 'Pages of this report would be needed to give anything like a comprehensive survey of former wards' gratitude,' the Annual Report of 1944 remarked. And, indeed, the 'gratitude' may be seen in the small subscriptions and donations of a few shillings noted in the old girls' magazine and the homely little letters accompanying them. 'Thank you for your letter and the receipt for 2s. 6d. I will try to make it up to £1,' wrote Lucy Fleming, a cook-general in Eastbourne in the *Guild Messenger* in March 1933. 'I do thank you all very much for your kindness to both of us. I am quite strong and well.'

From Canada, and later Australia, reports, letters and photographs showing upstanding young colonials, leading a healthy outdoor life, figured prominently in the success stories.

In 1936, an official visitor to Canada, W. W. Hind-Smith, a highly respected member of Barnardo's Council, returned home delighted with his findings: 'During the whole of this tour I never met one discontented boy or girl, no one that wished to come back to England. Although only some of these have risen high up, they are all doing well and are men and women of whom we may be justly proud . . . during the course of our visits we saw several who are occupying important positions, some owning their own farms.'

Inevitably, the official overall view cannot accurately reflect the complex and varied picture. Like children from any family, Barnardo children usually wanted to please, even if they had mixed feelings about their upbringing. All their lives, the stamp of gratitude had been impressed upon them.

Ed Cousins, who always visits Barnardo's on his rare journeys to England, still feels a debt of gratitude. Born in 1916, Ed was six years old when his father, a professional soldier, died, leaving his mother with three children. His sister was privately adopted and Ed and his brother, Herbert, six years his senior, were taken to Barnardo's.

'Mother took us to Stepney early one morning, turned her back and walked up the street. I clung to the railings and screamed and they had to take me inside.' The two boys were placed in Boys' Garden City and, two years later, Herbert went off to Canada, leaving Ed feeling very alone:

I thought I was going with him but he went off . . . By then I had accepted the way of life in Barnardo's. We weren't physically abused. But not once can I remember any affection being shown. You had to accept a way of life so foreign, so disciplined. When we got up we had to turn the mattress; sometimes they would come and feel it, to see if it was still warm on the top side. I think I was always hungry. The only happy day I remember was Founder's Day when we went to the

Girls' Village Home . . . We had prayers morning and night. I liked the prayers, especially the hymn at night 'Now the Day is over'.

In February 1925, Ed was told he was to go to Teighmore Home, a home for delicate boys ('I believe I was slightly undernourished') in Jersey.

I felt very lonely when I went on the boat from Southampton. At the home in Jersey, the Superintendent, Captain G., assembled all the new boys in a small yard. Then he made a little speech, telling us what we had to expect. He dismissed us into the play yard, but we weren't moving fast enough, so he produced a cane and proceeded to whack us on the knees to drive us faster.

The next three years were torment. Only one boy ever ran away. When he was brought back we were all assembled in the yard in a circle and the boy (Fisher) was placed naked in the centre and his arms outstretched. The Captain whacked him as hard as he could on the buttocks. Afterwards he had to jump into a cold bath with iodine in it because he was bleeding so badly. I never thought of running away after that but I often thought of suicide . . . But our island was 100 miles away from England and there was nobody to help us or say anything.

I was happy in school, when I was out of his reach. He would appear after breakfast, after prayers, morning and evening. One day, in my lunch hour before school started, I was playing and ran out of the school field into the farmer's field, jumped into a cesspool and sank to my chest. I was covered with thick slime and I had to walk through the playing field. I had no other clothes to change into so I went to the master and he made me take my clothes off and go to bed. I had a bath and the smell was terrible. An hour later Captain G. came up and put me across his knees and hit me with the palm of his hand fifty times.[19]

For other misdemeanours boys were made to march round the yard until midnight; sometimes they were forgotten. If a boy wet his bed he was made to wear his dirty sheet over his head and clean out all the chamber pots. One main toilet served 100 boys and if they used too much toilet paper they were reprimanded. After toilet the boys were assembled and their trousers inspected. If they were at all soiled the children were thrashed. After thirty years Mr Cousins visited Jersey and met two of his schoolmasters, Leslie Gale and Dick Gale. The retired schoolmasters apologised: they had not realised the situation in the home.

Evidently someone at headquarters did get to hear of it eventually. One day in the summer of 1928 the boys were told that Captain G. was leaving the following morning and a rousing cheer went up. When the new head, Commander Pettman, arrived, 'it was like being released from captivity. He was kind but firm. If he did punish you, it was done a kindly way. He didn't cane us in public, he took one boy into his study at a time. Also everybody received payment [possibly pocket money]. Up to that time I'd never had any money in my life. I was a bugler and had to waken the boys at "Reveille" and blow my bugle until the "Last Post" at night. I was paid a shilling a month.'

At fourteen Ed was sent to headquarters at Stepney where he delivered the mail for two months. When he was asked what he wanted to do, he naturally replied that he wanted to join his brother in Canada. Kitted out with a Bible, a trunk and two suits of clothes, Ed arrived in Toronto in 1939 in high spirits. Despite his slight build (he was five feet two and weighed about 100 pounds) he was told he had to work on a farm.

For the first eighteen months I earned 100 dollars plus washing and clothing. I was never physically abused and I had plenty to eat, but the farmer cursed and swore at me; in six months I could outswear him. Much later in Canada I met my sister after thirty-four years. She didn't even know she had two brothers . . .

In spite of all that happened what was the alternative? I've always been thankful for Barnardo's Homes, for the wonderful work they've done. In spite of the hardship and suffering, we were trained to be honest and trustworthy. Being brought up military seemed to prepare me for POW Camp in Germany. I joined the Old Boys' Guild before the war. I feel I owe Barnardo's Homes a lot.

Mr Cousins, now retired, lives a quiet, pleasant life in a suburb of Toronto. His years in Barnardo's have, to this day, left him somewhat timid and lacking in self-confidence, a heritage a number of former Barnardo children seem to share. How much is due to their early experiences of rejection, how much to the homes' regime is impossible to tell. Care in all homes for deprived children before the war, when no professional training or standards were laid down and inspection was rare, depended almost entirely on the qualities of character of the staff in charge.

Nowadays, with Barnardo homes sited in towns rather than in large, inaccessible country houses, with regular, careful visits from local staff and Council, as well as from the local authority, any misconduct by the staff would soon come to light. Most of their children go home at weekends, visit the town and have friends in the community outside.

By contrast, Linda Bowley who came to Barnardo's as a baby in 1954, remembers her childhood with affection. She was put into their care in the Village at four weeks old. 'Barnardo's gave you a sense of belonging. You didn't know anything else. I had a happy life, otherwise I wouldn't bother to be associated with them.' Since her teens, Linda has worked voluntarily for Barnardo's running a stall at the Annual Fête, making cakes for coffee mornings, collecting money on Children's Day. A tiny, bustling brunette, at three feet eight inches Linda reaches to the height of a door handle; she also suffers from a deformed hip. Her disability (a form of hereditary dwarfism) barely inhibits her. She works full-time for the Gas Board, drives her own car and enjoys a hectic social life revolving around her voluntary work for Barnardo's and other charities. 'If I'd stayed with my mother,' she reasons, 'I might not have had the opportunities Barnardo's gave me, the education and the advice. They were always willing to help, to find out what I could do.'[20]

In May Cottage where Linda grew up, one of her aunties (house-mother) was a former Barnardo girl with a disability herself and the atmosphere was friendly and encouraging for the eight children. 'We all had problems so we tended to help each other.' Linda went first to a nursery school, then by coach to a special school.

When we came home, the aunties would be in the sitting-room waiting. They always had a sweet for us and they asked us what had happened at school that day. They were really interested. We had a cat and a dog and a budgie. It was a real home.

Out aunties were diamonds, the best in the Village. They brought us up as if we were their own. They'd sit and eat with us and eat what we ate. We always had tablecloths on our tables. And they'd do little personal things for you. I'm mad on meringues and they'd make meringues as a birthday treat or take us out to have eggs and chips from their own money. They used to alter the clothes we had from the store to fit us and do extra sewing. One of my aunties still does some sewing for me.

If you were naughty they'd reprimand you. You had to do a chore or the telly was switched off for the night. We were lucky. We had one of the first TV sets in the Village. Our aunties rented it themselves. Some of the 'mothers' were awful, frumpy old spinsters, but although our aunties weren't married you could talk to them about anything. They didn't try to instil beliefs into you. On a Sunday in our cottage we were expected to go to church once, then we used to play quiet games. Some of the children in other cottages just sat and read the Bible all day long.

The medical care was fantastic. Every six months we had our teeth done. I belonged to the swimming club and I used to swim in the pool.

When I left, I wondered how I would cope. I went to college and I had a Barnardo's social worker assigned to me and they helped me to find a room. Barnardo's gave you the inspiration to know that you're no different from anyone else. There are plenty worse off. I've supported myself since I was eighteen. Without Barnardo's I wouldn't have been capable of doing what I do in society.

Whether the experiences of little Ed Cousins were at all representative of life in Barnardo's in the 'twenties is hard to know; his was certainly not an isolated case. But there were many very loving staff who showed exceptional kindness to the children as Linda Bowley's story shows. Like all children's homes, Barnardo's attracted a sprinkling of sadists as well as a fair share of saints; child abuse is not confined to children's homes.

Even in a private family, one child's memory of his upbringing may differ completely from his sister's or brother's. What seems reasonably certain is that the roseate view of childhood presented year after year in testimonials of the children was a group portrait that did not seek to penetrate the shadows.

Perhaps it is unnecessary to emphasise that the Council, as well as the great majority of the staff, wanted the children to have a happy as well as a worthy childhood and tried hard to ensure it. But 'parents' of a family of between 700 and 800 children have so little control over their daily lives.

Until at least the 1970s, and beyond in some cases, Barnardo's did consider itself a family. As proud parents, Council members were enormously pleased when the children succeeded, as the rather touching entries in the Minutes record:

March 1916: Three out of four Anzacs mentioned in dispatches at Gallipoli were Barnardo Boys.

November 1921: Two good news cases read out by the Director. A girl boarded-out had been adopted by her foster-parents. She was now earning £2 a week as short-hand typist; her foster-father was a City missionary. Dorothy S. aged nineteen was another boarded-out child who had gained a scholarship to secondary school and was earning £92 p.a. as a teacher.

May 1932: Marjorie P. has taken her BA, with second class honours in Canada.

In November 1938, the Minutes record a legacy of £13,700 from a Barnardo boy made good, Thomas G. Meadows, sea captain and pilot, who left the homes this very tangible token of his gratitude. With the bequest, the first and only Barnardo home built with funds from an old boy, the Meadows Memorial Home for backward boys in Southborough, Kent, was constructed. Opened in 1939, the home is still used for remedial education.

Girls and boys getting married received wedding presents of cash, and for years wedding dresses were hung up for girls to borrow on their marriage.

There were, as with all families, other not so happy occasions: moral 'falls', misdemeanours, even an occasional case of murder by a former ward. With the huge numbers involved, it would be surprising were it not so. To their credit Barnardo's stood by the children, offered them legal aid and kept in touch. Although they naturally tell the public of their success stories, the Bruce Oldfields, the Leslie Thomases and now, Mike Hatcher, it is with their failures that Barnardo's keep fast to their promise to see a child through and never to reject it. To this day, they visit dozens of Barnardo men and women who are sick, lonely or in prison.

10

Waifs in Wartime

'The art of placing children in homes, owing to the upheaval of
evacuation, is receiving more attention today than ever before in
history.'

Annual Report, 1941

For over sixty years, the children in Barnardo homes had grown up in
the class-conscious, Victorian world of their founder, with their betters
looking over their shoulders to the past, seeking both the inspiration and
the boundaries that Barnardo had provided. Throughout the 'thirties
the upstairs, downstairs barriers were upheld. The shattering events of
the Second World War sliced through class barriers and created new
expectations for 'charity children'.

In a world at war neglected children were more prevalent and more
vulnerable than ever. Parents, mothers as well as fathers, were caught
up in the war effort and many families were broken up with the result
that more and more children needed the shelter of the homes. In 1940,
admission totalled 2,000, the highest number since 1922.[1] After a heavy
air-raid, Barnardo inquiry agents would search the streets and bring the
stray children back to safety. Many child casualties of neglect, accident
or bereavement found their way to Barnardo's doors. In wartime conditions the rate of illegitimacy quickened. In 1939, 31,000 babies were
born to single mothers in the UK; by 1945 the numbers had more than
doubled to 71,000.[2]

With increased numbers of children, staff shortages due to call-up
and the immense problems of evacuating thousands of children, the
problems of management of the homes intensified. In September 1938,
Barnardo's was urged by the Home Office to transfer their children
immediately to the West Country since they were living in areas regarded
as vulnerable to air attack. They spent an anxious week making pre-
parations to evacuate 2,000 children from their large Essex communities
in the Girls' Village Home at Barkingside and the Boys' Garden City at
Woodford Bridge. The Stepney headquarters staff spent a whole day
telephoning to Helpers' Leagues throughout the West Country pleading
for accommodation for the children. For the next two days, telegrams
and phone messages jammed the switchboards. That autumn hundreds

of Barnardo children were packed up with sacks, satchels and gas-masks as well as sandwiches for the journey and within three days over 2,000 children had been evacuated.[3]

No doubt the new President of Barnardo's, Stanley Baldwin, who had accepted the appointment shortly after the Abdication and his retirement as Prime Minister, had advised the homes of the need to evacuate and also to prepare for air-raids. In April 1939, six months before war broke out, the homes spent £2,000 on protecting their children against air-raids, digging trenches at Boys' Garden City, building shelters at Babies' Castle and erecting supports to the basement at Watts, their naval school in Norfolk. As the national conscience awakened to the plight of children in Nazi-occupied Europe, Barnardo's agreed to shelter 150 Protestant children from the Continent in their homes and to set up a fund for their maintenance. They were careful to point out that the help to the refugee child would in no way diminish the national character of the charity nor their 'ability and readiness to accord immediate admission to any British destitute child'.[4]

By 1943 Barnardo's proudly announced that their most brilliant boy of the year was a German refugee who had taken his Higher Certificate with four distinctions twelve months after taking his School Certificate.[5]

Konrad Tybus, now an established surveyor in West Berlin, was one of those bright refugee children. When he came to Britain in May 1939 with his older brother he was ten. Konrad travelled with a party of 172 children, most of whom were Jewish and not destined for Barnardo's. When he arrived at Liverpool Street Station, he remembers that:

All the Jewish children were picked up by Jewish families, but four of us were half Jews and there was nobody there to meet us. Suddenly a German boy came up to us and said: 'You're coming to our place.' We travelled in a Green Maria and when we arrived, a film camera crew took pictures of us going into a Dr Barnardo's Home, Boys' Garden City at Woodford Bridge.

We lived in a house with a matron in charge, about twenty-five boys. None of the German boys spoke English and nobody spoke German. We just did what the others did. The Vicar tried to teach us English but we really learnt the language through the other children and through *Beano* comic.

With the war coming there was a lot of animosity towards Germans. We had fights with the boys and they threw stones at us. Most of the children left us alone but one matron kept calling after us 'dirty Germans'. Children aren't hurt so much . . .

Konrad came from a comfortable home and found it hard to adjust to his new life. He felt strange sleeping in a dormitory and disliked household chores, sweeping, scrubbing and polishing the floors. He found the meals, eaten off 'bashed up' tin plates, unappetising and grumbled in letters to his parents about the quantities of greens, bread and watercress, mustard and cress dished up. 'They think we're goats,' he wrote. At that time it was still possible for his parents to send parcels of sweets and fifty pfennig stamps. In every letter home he complained of being hungry. 'It must have worried my parents. They wrote to Barnardo's asking if we were getting enough to eat. Later Barnardo's took ten of us German boys on to the lawn, gave us a huge bar of Cadbury's milk chocolate and took a photo of us with it, smiling. Then they took the bar of chocolate away.'[6]

Twelve days before war broke out, in late August, Konrad was moved as part of the general evacuation of Barnardo children in vulnerable areas. The boys from Boys' Garden City were settled in imposing stately homes scattered throughout East Anglia. For a year Konrad lived in Pampisford Hall, near Sawston. He attended Pampisford Church and pumped the church organ.

We German boys stuck together. When we got sweets we jumped into the old well in the grounds and ate them down there so that the English boys wouldn't take them from us. We were so hungry we used to chew candles. In those days they used to cook the soup in real cauldrons. One day the last boy to get his portion doled out found a rat in it. If you didn't finish your soup up, you had to sit there with your plate in front of you until it was all gone. Those things stick in your mind. One night there was a thunderstorm. I couldn't sleep and four of us were talking. 'Miss' called out 'Be Quiet.' Then she brought us down to the big dining room and made us get down on our hands and knees and Ronuk the floor in the middle of the night. I felt very lonely all the time. We were shown no affection.

Konrad's brother was transferred to Goldings, and although he himself was under age for vocational training, he was allowed to stay at Goldings and attend a school nearby. The school had a band and Konrad learnt to play the French horn. He still remembers the beauty of the park at Goldings. From a vantage point high up in the branches of a big cedar tree he saw his first German plane. One night four bombs fell in the grounds and killed the bandmaster; fortunately the boys were safely in the trenches.

One of the Executive Officers carried a walking stick and if he caught you talking or doing anything wrong he would hit you on the head. Still, I did well at school, I got along. The teacher said, 'Konrad, you should go to grammar school,' and Barnardo's gave me the chance. They said, 'If you're suitable for grammar school you must go.'

Miss Dyson, the boarding-out officer, saw Konrad and arranged for him to be boarded out.

I stayed with a lady and I didn't have to do any more chores in the house. I was friendly with the headmaster of the school, Mr Bunt. He was exceedingly kind and highly intelligent. When I was nineteen I went to the Poly and lived in a hostel. Barnardo's gave me £5 a month for my living, clothing and books. I worked in a hospital to earn a little money.

I think Barnardo's is a wonderful institution. It gets kids off the streets. But I feel that those who looked after us in my day had no knowledge of children. They just used brute force. It's true that they made respectable citizens of the boys. But they had a tendency to crush your initiative.

I have no grudge against them. They tried their best in sad times and I'm thankful for what they did.

Impossible from this distance of time to judge how typical Konrad's youthful impressions were. From contemporary accounts it seems clear that many children without families were far worse off. At that time some unfortunate children were still dumped shamefully in the workhouse, Barnardo's old bugbear. They were housed in large, gaunt-looking buildings with dark stairways and corridors, high windows and unadapted baths and lavatories.[7] In one nursery in the children's ward was an eight-year-old mentally defective girl who sat most of the day on a chair commode because the nurses said 'she was happy that way'. She could not use her arms and legs.[8] Compared with those horrors, Barnardo's in the 1940s was progressive and caring. Any harshness seems to have stemmed from individual staff failures and a Victorian attitude rather than general neglect.

Yet times had changed. Two world wars, the introduction of National Health Insurance with sickness and unemployment benefits, a school meals, milk and medical service had all helped to take the edge off child poverty. The world of private charity, battling to save waif children from starvation and to shame the state into action, had vanished. In fairness, Barnardo had helped to speed its passing.

Now the call was for the individual rights, emotional as well as physical for the deprived child. In the 1940s there was no specific training for child care, but since the beginning of the century, a social science training at a university had been the recognised avenue of approach.

Gradually university women were entering Government Departments; specialist courses for hospital almoners, probation officers and psychiatric social workers had already been set up.

In Barnardo's the principal requirement for staff was the Christian devotion that the founder had insisted upon. In the 1940s there were still members of staff and Council who had served with 'the founder'. So proud were they of their past, so sure of their worth, so awed by Barnardo's personal myth, that to challenge any decision he had made must have seemed like sacrilege. In his lifetime Barnardo had assumed the divine right of child care; he ran his charity with a fiercely independent and competitive spirit, the 'Barnardo's is best' spirit which lingers to this day.

Slowly and painfully Barnardo's did come to grips with a new world. From the 'thirties the charity had begun to co-operate rather than compete with Government Departments, local authorities and voluntary agencies. The wartime emergency increased mutual dependence. Barnardo's worked with the Ministry of Health, the newly formed Women's Voluntary Services and the Local Education Authorities to evacuate their children. Two retired senior civil servants on the Council when war broke out had an important influence on policy: Sir Malcolm Delevingne, the Chairman of the Council, was a former Under Secretary at the Home Office. He was joined in 1939 by the first woman member of Council, Hilda Martindale, who had worked briefly for Barnardo's early in her career and had gone on to become Director of Appointments at the Treasury, the most senior post a woman in the Civil Service could attain.

In 1941 Barnardo's were discussing the need for staff training in Council. Another woman on Council, Mrs (later Lady) Ogilvie, wife of Frederick Wolff Ogilvie the then Director General of the BBC, urged reform. By 1941 Dr Culverwell of the Home Office was asked to review the adequacy of the medical arrangements of the homes.

Wartime difficulties accelerated change. In March 1940 and January 1941, the Ministry of Health made two critical reports on one of the homes. In the second report the Ministry of Health proposed to withdraw their certificate from one Barnardo's home unless improvements were made. The Minutes record in staid, discreet language that there were staffing and accommodation problems and, significantly, that reforms were needed.[9]

The offending home was Dame Margaret's in Washington, County Durham, taken over by Barnardo's from another private charity in 1910. The big house with parkland and a small farm was the childhood home of Gertrude Bell, the explorer. Barnardo girls in starched white aprons stood out distinctively at the village school. Most Barnardo homes were single sexed but Dame Margaret's housed up to 120 boys and girls. Until 1939, boys at Dame Margaret's learnt to become gardeners, farm workers or shoemakers while the girls were trained traditionally in domestic service.

In August 1940, an eighteen-year-old girl at the home was found to be six months pregnant; a Dame Margaret's boy who had since left the home was alleged to be the father. The incident occurred, the Minutes record, because 'certain communicating doors in the home which were always kept locked had been left open as an emergency exit in case of an air-raid. The open door had been taken advantage of.' As a result of the incident the Council took the rather drastic step of withdrawing the girls from the home altogether and making Dame Margaret's into a home for boys.

That event had taken place six months before the Ministry's report of January 1941 threatening to withdraw their certificate from the home. Undoubtedly the Ministry's report stung the Council into action. By October 1941, a staff training school was opened at Woodford Bridge, Essex, and the first nine students enrolled. In that first year, Barnardo students studied the care and welfare of children, child psychology, hygiene, first aid and home nursing, children's hobbies, games and Bible story-telling. All subjects, commented the Annual Report of 1943 reassuringly, that every mother needs to understand. Their course included visits to children's homes and schools and a stint at the Housecraft Training Centre studying cooking, mending, account keeping and other practical skills. For the last six months the students applied their new skills by working at a branch home for a small salary. The only other voluntary home to introduce training at the time was the National Children's Home, who had founded a training college in 1933 and had from the mid-nineteenth century advocated training as a safeguard against 'pious blundering'.[10]

By 1942 Barnardo's were committed to the new professionalism. They appointed a professional social worker to take charge of boarding-out, one of the most successful areas of work which had run into difficulties in wartime. Miss Muriel Dyson, who stayed with Barnardo's for twenty-five years, was one of the first professional social workers in the organisation, well qualified and with wide experience. She had worked formerly as an assistant organiser of LCC School Care Committees and later when she had qualified as a psychiatric social worker gained experience supervising the billeting of children in wartime.

At the time Barnardo's senior staff tended to be drawn from former colonial administrators. Both Mr Kirkpatrick, in charge of child care, and his deputy, Mr Lucette, fell into this category.

> The staff of the homes had no relevant training. They had the natural skill of nannies. They stayed until they retired [Miss Dyson recalls]. They were paid a pittance and spent a lot of their pay on the children, buying them treats at birthdays and Christmas. Despite an outstanding Council there was no one who knew anything about children in care.
>
> When they went to staff training school they learnt about child psychology, the importance of personal relationships and when they came back to the homes they were no longer content to stay in the same post until retirement. They were seeking a professional structure so they either moved within Barnardo's or left the organisation. Either way the children lost the continuity of care.[11]

When they returned to work, Barnardo's staff had little opportunity to apply their newly acquired knowledge of psychology to their charges. In most of the staff a stern morality held sway. The rescue motive, the motive Barnardo himself had enshrined, coloured the 'Barnardo way of life'. The charity was still concerned with bringing up guttersnipes from vicious homes and families to become law-abiding Christian citizens, grateful for their rescue.

As a consequence Barnardo's wanted to keep parents away from their children. As an Annual Report of 1937 put it: 'our boys and girls learn to love the name Barnardo's because it signifies not institution or orphanage but home and family'. When Miss Dyson joined the homes in 1942 the emphasis was still on separation. 'The children were sent a long way from their homes and the parents were discouraged from visiting,' she remembered. 'At Stepney the instructions were that if any child wanted to know about their history they were to be referred to Mr Williams' (A. E. Williams, Barnardo's personal secretary from 1898). He would tell them: 'We are your parents. Barnardo's will look after you.'

'When I joined, a teenage boy came up to me at Stepney and said: "Say, miss, can you tell me where me Dad is?" His father was so cruel to the boy he had been imprisoned.' Not until they left the homes were the children given a censored version of their personal history. Sometimes at that stage, the children found their background too painful to acknowledge, Miss Dyson recalled, and said they wished they had never been told. But whether children came from loving homes and from parents forced by poverty or ill-health to place them in Barnardo's or from cruel or criminal backgrounds, all the children were cut off from their roots.

Even children who had been fostered by Barnardo's since babyhood were part of the possessive 'family'. According to the rules they had to return to Stepney at fourteen for vocational training regardless of the attachment they might have formed to parents. However, a new flexibility was creeping in. On 27 October 1941 a foster-mother wrote to the homes pleading to keep her foster-daughter, Elizabeth: 'I have had her since the age of four and have grown passionately fond of her, both she and her sister take a keen interest in church . . . I have just lost my father who was greatly attached to the children and this loss together with the loss of Elizabeth is more than I feel I can stand.' This moving appeal was met with leniency and Elizabeth was allowed to stay in her foster-home. She was the only exception to the rule between January and June 1942, but gradually the practice changed.[12]

Miss Dyson emphasised that most of the other voluntary agencies held similar attitudes and were lacking in trained staff. Above all, nearly all of the Barnardo staff worked devotedly for the children according to their lights.

Conditions in wartime would have taxed the most ingenious staff. The home children were, it is true, evacuated to stately homes but often to the back rooms (one lady of the manor labelled one of the two bathrooms 'For the Mistress only') and to homes totally unsuited to small children. Plumbing in those homes was often deplorable or non-existent. Children had to be washed with water drawn from wells in buckets, bathed in the kitchen sink or in tin baths in front of the fire. Many children splintered their fingers and toes when sleeping on camp beds near the floor. Boys had to fill their mattresses with straw and as a result some suffered from hay fever. Village schools could not cope with the influx of evacuees and many of the boys missed months of schooling.

Boarded-out children were put up in homes far below the required standard. Although Barnardo's stipulated before the war that each child must have its own bed, in wartime brothers and sisters were allowed to share. Some even had to drink the water from a pond. When Miss Opie, one of the new breed of psychiatric social workers called to see one little boy due to be sent away from home because he persistently soiled, she found a large spider in the garden toilet. Once she removed the spider the boy stopped dirtying his trousers.[13]

Troops, particularly Americans, showed great kindness to the children. At Little Bardfield Hall in Essex, eighty girls from babies and toddlers to teenage trainees were individually 'adopted' by Americans through the

Foster-Parents' Plan for War Children. An enterprising and sympathetic matron with her pony and trap became a popular local figure. The boys and girls received wonderful parcels of toys and clothes from their overseas 'parents'. Treats included a rare excursion to London and the children even broadcast messages to foster-parents in America over the BBC at Christmas. An American sergeant living in the village was adopted by the home, 'kidnapped' after his visit to the village church. Through their American connection the children enjoyed visits, chocolate and VIP treatment. They lived in the glow of publicity and even received a letter from Helen Keller. Those home children were encouraged to learn about the outside world and one year twenty small girls from Little Bardfield wrote to Mr Churchill to wish him a happy birthday.[14] The children had a lovely war. But for many Barnardo children the war made growing up in the homes an even more isolating experience.

The children were physically cut off by distance and in some homes the staff tried to reproduce artificially the Barnardo atmosphere by shutting out the external world.

Mary went into Barnardo's at the age of five in 1938 at a particularly vulnerable stage in her development – she had witnessed her father die of an overdose. For her, the whole experience was traumatic from the day she arrived on Barnardo's doorstep in Stepney.

> My mother gave me a brown paper bag of plain biscuits, broken bits, and they took them away from me. I asked and asked for those biscuits. I missed them more than my home and I cried for days . . .
>
> What I remember above all was the hardness of the staff. To me that was everything. I went to Exeter into a big communal home from 1938 to 1942. We all had to have pudding basin haircuts and they combed our hair for nits. We were always hungry, I remember. The food was stodge and we hardly ever had fresh fruit. During the whole of my childhood I was never linked with the outside world. Even now I find it difficult to mix with men. You just never met any men except for tradesmen. [Mary is now married with a grown-up family.] I was at the home in Exeter when a bomb fell. We were in the shelters and we were all saved.[15]

The bomb, at Feltrim, Topsham Road, Exeter, fell between the shelter and the house, mercifully missing the sixty-six children and the staff. However, it left the building an empty shell. Mary was boarded out in Suffolk, then moved to Lilleshall Hall, a large turreted country house in Shropshire, set in magnificent grounds with sunken gardens and peacocks strutting through them. Three hundred girls, most of them from the Girls' Village Home, lived in groups with their housemothers in charge and went to their own Barnardo school in the grounds. Mary found the life totally oppressive:

My housemother, Miss S., was a real martinet. She wore a tight Victorian dress, buttoned all the way down. She made you make your bed with hospital corners, rub the floor with linseed oil before you polished it. You had to darn and it had to be complete perfection. You were almost taught to be a robot, you did certain things on certain days and for long stretches of the day, you just did what you were told. We weren't allowed to mix with the other families [the other children with different housemothers] and we had a long period of silence after meals.

I was hungry all the time and some of the little ones just had to chew and chew their food. There was a lack of thought and finesse in dealing with children. You had no personal life. Everyone was known by numbers. Mine was number nine and everything I had had to be chainstitched into number nine . . .

It was a narrow world in every sense. It wasn't real life. Our Sunday was a Victorian Sunday. We weren't allowed to read a book or pick up sewing. I dreaded those Sundays. For many years it was a religion of fear for me. In Barnardo's we recited prayers every morning, prayers every evening and always grace before meals: 'Thank you for the world so sweet' . . .

For years I didn't talk to anybody about it. Life was so drab, it was always the same, no different. Except I remember we occasionally had parcels from Canada. Then we had new clothes and that was fantastic. [Normally the children wore hand-me-downs.] Otherwise every day was the same.

In the morning you stripped your bed and stood on the shiny parquet floor with no slippers or dressing-gown and queued up for a strip wash. There was no privacy for growing up. We slept fourteen or fifteen in a dorm, with the beds fairly close. You had to undress under your top garment and there were always little girls about. We were never given bras. I was always rather plump and I wore an elasticated band to keep me flat. I didn't want anything that made me different. It wasn't done. You weren't supposed to have any thoughts of your own.

At Lilleshall we were cut off from the world. We occasionally heard the radio but we never had use of the knobs. I doubt if we'd have known that the war was over except that we had to wave a Union Jack.

One or two girls used to try to get out to meet the local lads, we were so cut off we hadn't a clue about the latest songs or the cinema. Any physical contact was frowned upon; your sexuality was dormant.

I was moved nine times between the ages of five and eighteen. I never understood why we were moved so much at Barnardo's. As soon as you were settled and happy you were moved. There wasn't real physical cruelty although Miss S. wasn't averse to giving the odd whack. They were kind to children, as long as you accepted your station.

Yet, like nearly all former Barnardo children, Mary confesses herself still 'drawn to Barnardo's like a magnet'. She supports the charity to this day.

The quality of the child's life depended almost entirely on the relationship of the person closest. With the girls it was the housemother. Gladys Smith and her sisters had lived with 'Mum' Barnes in Mickleham Cottage in the Girls' Village Home and both she and her sister, Dorothy, felt 'that she had been a real mother to them, kind, fair and disciplined when necessary'. For Gladys the first experiences in wartime away from the Village were actually liberating. Loosened from the discipline of the system, she went to Tattingstone in Suffolk with 'Mum' in 1939 when Gladys had turned twelve.

We all had kitbags with our name on a card tied to them. We packed all our clothes in them but we weren't allowed to put in our toys or treasures because they would be too heavy and we had to carry them ourselves to the station. At Tattingstone, 'Mum' kept most of the sisters, the Smiths (that was us), the Perrings, the Theobalds, with her. [Other children were billeted elsewhere in the village.] We went to the big house called Tattingstone Park, the home of Lord and Lady Cobbold. We were given a whole wing of the house, stretching to the back door, long corridors leading to a scullery, kitchen, dining and playroom, mother's sitting room and a small room for storing food. When we arrived we had a meal of corned beef and spam, salad, bread and butter which we enjoyed. Then we all went upstairs, which was the same stairs as the Lord and Lady used, but we only saw them now and again.

Beds were short, so Gladys and her sister had to sleep top to tail. They peered through a locked iron gate at a beautiful garden in the grounds but were only allowed in accompanied by 'mother'. But they walked to school through the park and learnt to overcome their fear of the cows and enjoy playing in the open space there. Indoors girls over ten mended and darned for the younger ones and helped to wash up and scrub potatoes.

On Christmas morning they woke to find a stocking on the end of their beds filled with oranges, new pennies, cards and puzzles: 'We all had a gift from Lord and Lady Cobbold, mine was a long scarf, very pretty in bright colours. I still have it.'

In the New Year older girls had to share their bath water because of a shortage. They took it in turns so that every girl would have clean water on alternate bath nights.

Gladys still remembers the day 'Mum' took her and her two sisters on a bus to Ipswich to have their photographs taken to send to her relatives. (That took place about every two years in her case.) As a treat they had their tea in a shop before going home.

> We were moved to Coggeshall, in Essex, as Barnardo's decided we were too near the coast . . . We were all very sad to leave Tattingstone, it had been an ideal place, we had no sign of war and air-raids, it was like an oasis. We were free and doing lots of things we had never done before which most children take for granted, like shopping at the village shop, going to a local school, even playing and walking alone in parks and roads. I, for one, will never forget it.[16]

The Council was clearly aware of the children's cramped lives. Yet in wartime it was extremely difficult to implement change. In the 1944 Annual Report a new and more imaginative note creeps into the description of the children's homes:

> At one nurse's branch, no member of staff touches the lockers containing the children's personal possessions without the owner's permission: one of our Scottish Superintendents had found each of her children a local 'aunt and uncle' and gave a Christmas party allowing each child to invite a school friend and take responsibility for entertaining that special guest; at an Essex home 'mother' arranges a special Christmas-pudding-stirring ceremony at which each child wishes aloud for the Christmas present most desired, and she endeavours to see that each child's wish is fulfilled.

The difficulties for a large institution to acknowledge the child's individuality are illustrated in those remarks. Even in the poorest families, children usually bring their friends home more than once a year, but of course to invite 300 guests would strain a home's resources and take extra staff effort. In those conditions, it must have been extremely hard for the children to gain a sense of themselves. That account was one of the first official acknowledgments that the Barnardo children needed to have a sense of their own personal identity.

That same year the Barnardo Book was published for the guidance of staff. The book came about as a result of the report of Dr Culverwell of the Home Office. He had criticised the lack of pre-school training for the under fives, the lack of stimulating leisure for older children (so graphically described in Mary's account) and the need for staff training. The book offered guidance to staff and struck a compassionate and cautionary note. To maintain the sense of reverence for the past the book explained 'the spirit of the Founder should be embodied in the everyday life of the home in the 1940s'. The authors counselled 'that anything in the nature of harsh or repressive treatment [be] avoided, even in difficult circumstances in an organisation which boldly proclaims its Christian character and whose existence is only justified by the happiness and well-being of the children'.[17]

This confidential publication contains explicit instructions on how to behave in every conceivable situation from daily routine (children should not rise before 6.30 a.m.) to discipline in the dining room ('complete silence is not desirable and savours of Institution rather than Home'). In fact the striking feature about the book is that it seeks to curb the rigid routine in the homes and positively encourages a more relaxed attitude to the children.

Nowhere is this shown more clearly than in the chapter on the maintenance of discipline. 'The ideal home is a place where each member feels secure in the kindliness and affection of the others and willingly co-operates in the duties to be done, taking a full share in the activities and pleasures of the community . . . No community can be run completely without rules, but they should be those of courtesy and common sense.' In the section headed 'Corporal Punishment', the book rules that 'striking, cuffing, shaking and any other form of physical violence should never, in any circumstances, be inflicted on girls or threatened'. As to boys: 'A cane should only be used when all other methods have failed . . . The boy must be wearing his ordinary clothes and must not, in any circumstances, be tied down. The maximum shall not exceed six strokes for boys under fifteen or eight for boys of fifteen and over.' The Council also ruled that boys under seven, or those physically or mentally afflicted, or in a hospital or convalescent home must not be caned. Nor must caning be administered in the presence of other boys. A third person (a senior officer) must be present and a record of every case entered in the Punishment Book.

By the 1930s with the introduction of Widows' and Orphans' Pension and other benefits, the charitable public were beginning to ask if there was a need for Barnardo's Homes. But children were still grossly neglected or ill-used. The posed NSPCC official (left) has just handed over the three children to Barnardo's care.

For boys who wanted to join the Navy, Watts Naval Training School, North Elmham, Norfolk, was the best choice. In 1933 the 300 pupils lived as if they were on board ship and slept in large dormitories.

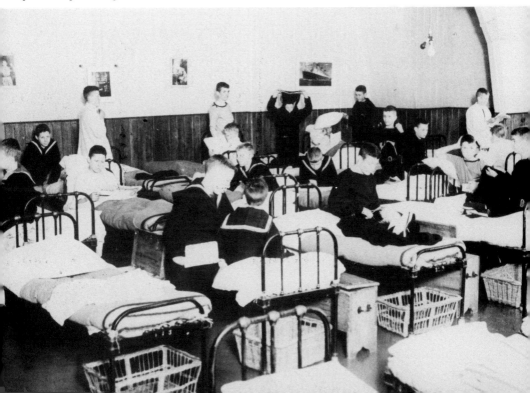

Children were taken to unknown destinations all over the country; often they were escorted by travelling matrons in uniform whom they had not met before.

Almost half of the children growing up in Barnardo's care in the 'thirties were boarded-out in villages in the south and east of England with the hope that the 'orphans' would become normal village children. Often a close bond grew up between foster-parents and their charges.

From the Doctor's day hygiene was of prime importance in the homes. Both the children and the institutions were kept spotless. A dentist visited the homes regularly before the First World War.

Over 700 boys lived in Boys' Garden City in Woodford Bridge, Essex, in the 'thirties. The boys were housed in separate cottages, but ate communally in the vast central dining room, Canada Hall.

Barnardo's co-operated with the Home Office in 1938 in air-raid precautions; their children were measured to develop and adapt junior gas-masks. To inspire confidence, the lady governors of the Village, the Honourable Miss Macnaghten and Miss Picton-Turbervill, led the staff into a gas-filled chamber.

Boys in all the homes helped to dig trenches and build shelters and, as this photograph taken at the Kingston home demonstrates, they were all familiar with the drill.

In 1939 Barnardo's agreed to take in up to 150 Protestant refugee children from Nazi Europe. This party arrived at Stepney in a Green Maria.

The children were evacuated to the country where they enjoyed the glories and inconveniences of stately-home living. Often the big houses were lent by wellwishers. About 300 girls from the Village were housed at Lilleshall Hall, Lilleshall in Shropshire.

Peggoty the pony was a favourite means of transport for the children of Little Bardfield Hall, Essex, during the war. About ninety girls, from babies to teenagers, lived in a happy community. Each child was 'adopted' by an American foster-parent overseas.

Early in 1940, at the request of the Home Office, Barnardo's opened their first Approved School, at Druid's Heath in the Midlands, for children committed by the courts. The boys were expected to work hard, and play hard.

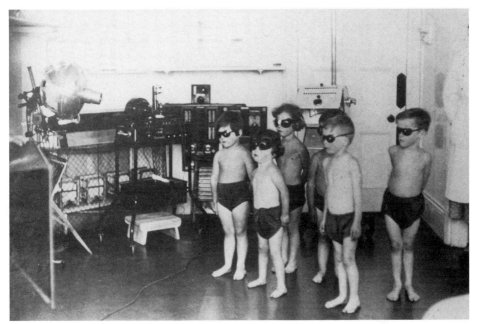

The homes were justifiably proud of their excellent health care. Children suffering from tuberculosis and rickets were given violet ray treatment and massage in the Folkestone hospital home. In the 'thirties only about one per cent of children admitted were classed A1 in health.

Fresh air and exercise supplemented the professional care of the medical staff in the Birkdale home for sick and crippled children in 1931.

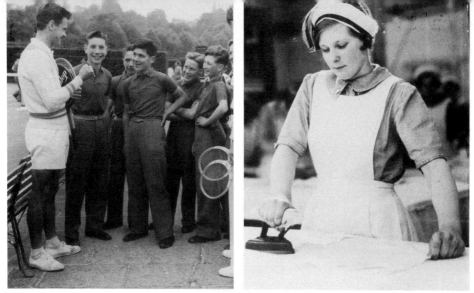

In the post-war world Barnardo boys from a home in Hertford enjoyed the two weeks of Wimbledon when they acted as ball boys on the courts. An admiring group surround Sven Davidson, a tennis star of the day.

Top right: After the Second World War there were fewer Barnardo girls willing to go into service although the homes still ran a domestic training school.

Dr Barnardo worked for thirty years to open a sea school. His charity's two naval schools, Watts in Norfolk and Russell Cotes in Parkstone, Dorset, merged in 1949 to become the Parkstone Sea Training School. By the mid-'sixties the school closed. A life at sea was no longer the favourite option.

The old taboos against masturbation were broken with courage and compassion. 'The old-fashioned practice of threatening boys with TB, insanity, heart disease, etc. if they indulge in self-stimulation is absolutely wrong ... Nothing must be said that may create fears or perpetuate fears. Nor should children be punished for bed-wetting or nail-biting.'

The book does, by inference, support the children's stories of harsh and repressive treatment in the homes as well as displaying a determination to overcome them.

Miss Chavasse, the Woman Administrator, a marvellously humane autocrat, appointed a number of Superintendents capable of introducing a more tolerant and up-to-date regime into the homes.

At one girls' home in Yorkshire, the Superintendent called her girls together and told them that she wanted to make them her family. She explained that it was her only home as well as theirs and she asked them to help her to make it a happy one. If she misjudged them, she promised, she would apologise and she expected the girls to apologise if they were in the wrong.

This lady relaxed the rules on Sunday afternoons by allowing the girls to play ball or tennis; she also managed to wheedle bikes out of headquarters so that they could go for country rides. If she considered it necessary she would even flout the rules. Like all Superintendents she was expected to open the girls' letters and read them before handing on the letter, without the envelope. In the case of one child who was very attached to her foster-mother, the Superintendent decided that it was important for the girl to have her letters uncensored. Her girls attended the local high school and she encouraged them to join in outside activities, the local choir, St John Ambulance, make outside friends and bring them home.

Whether consciously or not, that Superintendent gave her children the chance to break the charity mould. There were increasingly individual heads of homes who encouraged suitable extra-curricular activities and helped the children to a sense of their individual worth.

As early as 1943, the Staff Planning Committee was advocating keeping families closer together. As the Superintendent, Mr Kirkpatrick, pointed out, 'the keeping of children within a comparatively small area would facilitate the meeting of brothers and sisters and visits by relatives ... whereas under present conditions, brothers and sisters are often separated by hundreds of miles'. However, a veteran Council member, Mr McAndrew, objected. He remarked that he 'could not see the benefit of keeping children within a very short distance from the homes from which they were rescued, particularly as in normal times the Council endeavoured to migrate a considerable proportion of the children in their care'.

In the course of the war, the care for children had become more professional and more complex. Barnardo's, so critical of the state in the past, was now officially acting as the agency of the statutory authorities by administering two Approved Schools, for children who had come before the courts. Under the 1933 Children and Young Persons Act 'Approved Schools' had replaced the Victorian Industrial Schools, where children found begging, homeless or 'beyond control' were committed. The new Approved Schools both senior and junior were controlled by philanthropic and religious organisations as well as local authorities, under Home Office supervision. As early as 1937 the Home Office had asked Barnardo's to administer an Approved School. In wartime, with many fathers away from home, juvenile delinquency increased alarmingly and the need for places in Approved Schools grew more urgent. Since rescuing children 'in moral danger' and reclaiming them had loomed so large in Barnardo's own mission, the Council had no qualms in acceding to the request.

Their first Junior Approved School, Druid's Heath, Walsall, was opened in January 1940. Barnardo's bought the Druid's Heath building in the autumn of 1938 for approximately £23,000. The sum was repaid by the Home Office over a twenty-year period. The long, low, brick building, used as an orphanage for thirty years looked like a prison. The first eighty-four Druid's Heath boys, nicknamed the 'pioneers', slept in dormitories in long rows of beds. They were housed, fed and taught in the building. In wartime four acres of the grounds were turned into a potato field and garden and the remaining five into playing fields.

Despite the rather forbidding building, the regime was, according to a member of staff, 'boy-centred' and Home Office Inspectors were sufficiently impressed to encourage Barnardo's to enlarge the accommodation and take on a senior Approved School for thirteen to fifteen-year-old boys committed by the courts. The work was financed by the Home Office, who initially paid an allowance of twenty-eight shillings per week per boy; it was kept separate from the main body of the charity's work and the public heard little of it.

Wartime also saw Barnardo's beginning to help married women. As early as 1939 a scheme to help keep Forces' families together was started: the 'soldiers' wives' cases. Often a tommy would return from abroad to find a new baby in the home. He could sometimes be persuaded to stay with his family provided the illegitimate child was fostered. Under the Special Assistance Scheme, known as SAS, grants were given to the mothers to help pay the foster fees. Grants were also made occasionally for the legitimate children of widows or separated wives. That was the beginning of systematic work with the families.

By the end of the war Barnardo's knew of 5,598 old boys and girls serving in the Forces, including many enlisted in the Canadian and Australian contingents. There was far less flag-waving publicity for their wards' military prowess than in the First World War. Soon after the war the sailor boy bearing the Union Jack inscribed 'For God and Country' was to disappear for ever from the cover of their Annual Reports.

During the war the charity had become immensely complex and diverse. Impossible not to have a certain amount of sympathy for one Council member who remarked in a meeting in March 1946 that when he joined the Council in 1927 and up to the outbreak of war, the objects of the homes had been very simple: to rescue children from bad homes and degrading surroundings and place them in care of those who would look after both their bodies and their souls. Now, he felt, there was a tendency to ring the children round with every sort of specialist, psychiatrists, educationalists, careers officers, etc. Expenses were leaping up and he feared no better results would be achieved than with the old, simple methods.[18]

11

'Whose Children?'

'Where a child is in the care of the local authority, it shall be the duty of that authority . . . to further his best interests and to afford him opportunity for the proper development of his character and abilities.'

Children Act, 1948, Section 12

'Our aim is to give . . . children, not merely food and shelter but individual care . . . although translating this ideal into practical achievement is sometimes an almost baffling task.'

Barnardo's Annual Report, 1945

In the spring of 1956, a young Barnardo assistant was taking a group of children out for a walk when two boys of the party spotted a bird's nest in a tree. In their excitement, the children knocked the nest out of the tree and tumbled the eggs.

The assistant scolded the two boys responsible: 'How would you like to be thrown out of your nest?' she asked. 'That's just what did happen to us,' replied Keith, aged eight.

That story and others similar were told at a Barnardo Staff Conference in the 'fifties to illustrate the complexities of a child's mind, the damage of by-passing the family and the fact that Barnardo's could be wrong.[1]

For the first time in their history, Barnardo's were openly questioning their methods of care, a stance impossible to imagine before the war.

Since the 1940s, a wave of concern for deprived children had swept through the nation and changed attitudes, practices and legislation. As a result of war and evacuation, 'ordinary families' had rubbed shoulders with 'charity children'. No longer cut off from the rest of the community, girls and boys from Barnardo's and other children's societies, as well as Poor Law institutions, were billeted with families in safe areas and shared their village schools. With so many families split up by war, the public began to understand the suffering of children brought up in unfamiliar surroundings away from parents, brothers and sisters.

The disruption of war brought 'nobody's children' to the attention of officialdom, too. Inspectors were appointed to visit evacuees and they, of course, included charity children. Welfare officers appointed by the Ministry of Pensions also visited war orphans.

Soon after the war, with service families reunited, the plight of children without families touched the heart of the nation. Earlier, Lady Allen of Hurtwood, who had been visiting evacuees, gave voice to that concern in a letter to *The Times* in July 1944:

> I write of those children, who, because of their family misfortune find themselves under the guardianship of a Government Department or one of the many charitable organisations. The public are . . . unaware that many thousands of these children are being brought up under repressive conditions that are generations out of date and are unworthy of our traditional care for children. Many who are orphaned, destitute or neglected still live under the chilly stigma of 'charity'.[2]

Lady Allen went on to criticise the plight of the staff who cared for the children, 'for the most part overworked, underpaid and untrained'; the lack of a recognised system of training; the inadequate inspection and supervision and the spread of Government responsibility. She called for a public inquiry to explore 'this largely uncivilised territory'. Her letter spoke up on behalf of all neglected children and produced a torrent of replies.

Six months later, Lady Allen published a pamphlet 'Whose Children?' describing the plight of deprived children with evidence from those who had been brought up in children's homes and staff who had cared for them.[3] Her initiative produced far-reaching results but the timing of the tragic death of Dennis O'Neill, a thirteen-year-old foster-child, starved and beaten to death, helped her case. As if on cue, the inquest on Dennis O'Neill was reported in the press within days of the publication of Lady Allen's pamphlet. Dennis had been rescued from brutal parents and boarded-out by the local authority in a remote country farmhouse near Shrewsbury. The coroner's jury returned a verdict, stating that Dennis's death was due to 'acute cardiac failure, following violence applied to the front of the chest and back, while in a state of undernourishment and neglect'. They added a rider, criticising the serious lack of supervision by the local authority. The case caused profound disquiet at the time and it still has a disturbingly modern ring.

A public inquiry into the incident was followed by a far wider investigation into the care of children 'deprived of normal home life with their own parents or relatives'. The inquiry set out to discover what more should be done to 'ensure that these children are brought up under conditions best calculated to compensate for the lack of parental care'.

The wording is important for it emphasises that 'the wards of state or charity' were the nation's responsibility: that they were to be given a new status and a fair chance in life as of right.

By a curious irony, Barnardo's, the charity that had 'uncovered' the waifs and strays in the nineteenth century, that had dramatised and championed their plight and reclaimed thousands, were at a low ebb. Through no fault of their own, Barnardo's could no longer live up to their proud slogan, 'No destitute child ever refused admission'. By 1945, they had some 'pathetic cases' waiting for six to nine months. The charity was faced with the unenviable choice between refusal and overcrowding. Shortage of beds (their property, particularly the Girls' Village Home, was still requisitioned), the return of many Barnardo evacuees from foster-mothers who were content to do their bit in wartime but were now returning them, and shortage of staff, all contributed to the lowest admission figures for years. Nor was their style of charitable work suited to the egalitarian mood of the day. The Ministry of Labour would not direct domestic workers to Barnardo's because the charity was not paying wages according to the appropriate scale.[4] The new senior child care workers, with their professional status, worked not only for 'love' (although many were not short of intense dedication) but for a salary commensurate with their skill and knowledge.

Even the Barnardo 'look' did not seem to fit into the post-war world. Miss Poole-Connor, a stylish middle-aged lady who had progressed from clerical work to child care in the organisation, took a party of ten girls to Edinburgh for a holiday based on the YWCA. When she escorted her girls to a dance a sergeant-major present remarked, 'You don't look like a Barnardo worker. They all wear their hair in a bun, have prominent teeth and pull their hats down in front of their eyes.'[5]

With that old-fashioned image, and a weight of history and tradition behind them, Barnardo's was trying valiantly to change. In 1945, an effort was made to get to know each child personally before parcelling it off into a home or foster-home. In the past, the decision had been taken on the basis of written records, principally the Medical Officer's report: 'Our essential records are the boys and girls themselves,' wrote a staff member explaining the new thinking. 'They are integrated developing personalities – not cases of measles.'[6] Now, when reaching a decision, a new Placement Committee made up of other people who had actually met the girl or boy had a voice; and for the first time the effect of sending a child away from home and the consequences for the whole family were taken into account. The Placement Committee was a post-war attempt to suit the homes to the boy's or girl's need rather than press the children into a mould.

In 1946, the exhaustive survey of children 'deprived of a normal home life', which came to be known as the Curtis Report, shook up the whole child care world. The survey covered destitute children, homeless evacuees, children removed by court order, children pending adoption, the mentally disordered, ineducable, mentally defective, the physically and mentally handicapped and war orphans. They numbered almost 125,000 and Barnardo's estimated that they were responsible for one in fourteen of the children under survey. They sent the largest number of witnesses to the Committee of any voluntary group or association and whilst paying public tribute to the initiative, they privately considered that the Committee was encroaching on their preserve. Their methods had worked in the past. Why not now? The report 'can teach us little in regard to general recommendations for child care,'[7] they considered. If Barnardo's was falling short at all, they argued, it was due to shortages of staff and equipment in wartime. The report left them uneasy. The possibility of state interference by inspection of their homes and foster-homes threatened their historic 'freedom of action'. The founder would have been horrified.

The Curtis Report had a profound effect on the care of deprived children. Adoption was recommended as the best option for children without parents or a satisfactory home, with fostering as the second best. If children had to be cared for in institutions, the Curtis Report urged that the home should be small (eight children to a home, preferably, and not more than twelve), that children should be encouraged to make friends outside the home and to keep in touch with relatives; and that brothers and sisters should be brought up together. The report set the tone for the Children Act which was to follow in 1948.

One immediate effect was that in 1947 Barnardo's became a registered adoption society. Legal adoption had only become possible in 1926 and the scandalous baby farming of earlier times, the lack of legal safeguards for adopted children, had appalled Barnardo, though he had 'adopted' children himself. In the 'thirties, after the Adoption Act, adoptive parents frequently applied to Barnardo's to 'dump' children and the charity was aware of the suffering caused by failed adoptions. Besides, since the Doctor's day, Barnardo's had cultivated a family image; the emotional appeal of the Barnardo family, the largest family in the world, was powerful. As late as 1939, Alan, nearly thirteen, the 114,000th child admitted, was welcomed in the Annual Report and ensured that he would 'enjoy the full rights and privileges of a son of the household and a member of the family'. But the climate in child care had changed and the days when Barnardo's could assume 'parental responsibility' in the full knowledge of public approval had gone for ever.

The Senior Boarding-Out Officer, Miss Dyson, who came to the charity in 1941 opposed to adoption, now urged Barnardo's to change course. She had discovered that boarded-out girls and boys growing up in foster-homes under Barnardo's care had come to fear their fourteenth birthday, when they would be taken back to a home for technical or domestic training. 'It is a terrible thing that a child who has been happily settled in a foster-home for years should go white when Dr Barnardo's Homes are mentioned ... it is painful to hear of a girl of thirteen going off her food and suffering from insomnia because she fears she may be removed from the foster-home ... Many of our children ask again and again if they may not use the foster-parents' name.'[8]

At the time foster-parents were kept in ignorance of the children's background and medical history. Their files were closely guarded at Stepney. The policy had its drawbacks. In 1946, two sisters who had been fostered by Barnardo's were told that they were to go home to their parents. The girls were stunned. They were under the impression that their parents were dead!

Some foster-parents did make private arrangements to adopt 'their children' at the time and Miss Dyson argued that if Barnardo's became a registered adoption society they would be in a better position to safeguard those children. It was the children's fears that spurred Miss Dyson to press for adoption but she also referred to the Curtis Report and without that, it might have been difficult for Barnardo's to flout tradition.

In November 1947, Barnardo's became a registered adoption society. Like most other adoption societies at the time, they would only consider children under three for adoption. They started the work with extreme caution, demanding a two-year probationary period for adoptive parents.

Many of their first adoptive parents were already known to them through long-term fostering. For forty years, with increasing confidence, Barnardo's have been placing children for adoption and today their innovative schemes have led the way in finding homes for handicapped and older children.

As a result of the Curtis Report, Barnardo's decided to curtail the hours the children spent doing chores in homes. And there seems little doubt that the report spurred the drive to find a more varied working life for ex-Barnardo girls. Homes which clung to the 'old-fashioned idea that domestic service is the only outlet' were briskly criticised.

Barnardo girls had, of course, the advantage of the charity's influential connections. During the war the Prime Minister, Winston Churchill, and his wife employed home girls as housemaids and these were specially fortunate. After a year of housework, Mrs Churchill would ask her girls what they would really like to do. One Barnardo maid told her mistress that she longed to train as a hairdresser and Mrs Churchill arranged for her to be apprenticed to her own personal coiffeur.

Even after the war, Barnardo supporters continued to expect that Barnardo girls should be trained for domestic service.

In October 1947, a Lady Blackford, a regular subscriber, wrote: 'It is the most crying need of the day and one of the most desirable in the interest of girl children, well fed, looked after and with good homes and personal care ... yet because of idle nonsense, it is true to think that not half of your girls are thus prepared. I have of late tried to get a young girl from the Homes without the slightest success.'[9]

It was a complaint which Barnardo himself had had to contend with in the late nineteenth century, when subscribers reproved him for shipping all the trained girls to Canada.

The reply to Lady Blackford made it clear that Barnardo's girls preferred to train as nurses, teachers, librarians, even work in factories and workshops rather than go into service in the post-war world. However, the official diplomatically agreed 'without any reservation, that most girls would be much better off in domestic service'. He added that in 1946 Barnardo's had received 250 applicants for every girl placed.

That year, the first Wimbledon after the war, gave the home children a chance to show their paces in a popular light. The All-England Lawn Tennis Association needed ball boys to start off the post-war season. Their Chairman visited Stepney to inquire whether Barnardo's would permit their lads to go to Wimbledon. Consent was given, provided that the boys from Goldings would be transported to and from the courts each day. But the boys had no socks or rubber-soled shoes and coupons, in those days of rationing, were hard to find. Generously, the members of the Lawn Tennis Club subscribed their own coupons. 'On the very first day of their training, through some mistake, the boys took their shoes home and left them in the train. A pair of shoes was almost as precious as a bottle of gin and the whole lot were stolen.'[10] However, the resourceful club members managed to conjure up more coupons and buy more shoes for their ball boys. Each July, from 1946 to 1966 when the school closed, the Goldings boys soaped their trousers into a careful crease at night and put them under the mattress. Next day they revelled in the outing, 'the crowds, the colour, the silence, the roars, the fascinating litter (cigarette packets from all over the world), individual fruit pies, icecold drinks'.

On the journey home, with their five shillings glowing in their pockets, they munched thick Stepney doorsteps, spread with jam, and sang Barnardo songs.

That was the kind of image of Barnardo children, fleet-footed, hard-working, clean and cheerful, that both the public and Barnardo's wanted to see. The goodwill of supporters was particularly important at the time: the cost of keeping a child had almost doubled since 1939, and now the new climate, with the voluntary principle under threat, left all who supported and worked for the charity uneasy. Barnardo's stressed that they were 'an absolutely voluntary association, receiving no subsidy from the state'.[11]

For the first time, under the Children Act 1948, responsibility for the deprived child which had been split between three departments, Public Assistance, Health and Education, now rested with the Home Office. Local authority children's committees, acting through a Children's Officer, were required to act as good parents 'to further [the child's] best interests and to afford him opportunity for the proper development of his character and abilities'.[12] In the past Barnardo's and other charities had voluntarily assumed the responsibility; now it was no longer purely a charitable concern.

The Children Act also stated explicitly that whenever possible parents, relatives or friends of the child's own family should be helped to take back a child in care, a new concept in law.[13] Now Barnardo's historic method of making each child a member of their family, giving them a new Barnardo identity, was implicitly called into question. Despite objections raised in Parliament, Barnardo's, like other voluntary societies, were required to be registered and integrated into a nationwide network of child care, under the overall supervision of the Home Office Children's Department.

At the time of the Act, Barnardo's were managing a vast empire of ninety-six homes and caring for between 7,000 and 8,000 children. In territorial terms the charity had pushed out its boundaries to Scotland and west Wales. Their children had been evacuated to those areas and this led to opening homes.

New thinking, new methods, even new buildings were needed to fit into the sweeping changes in child care. Barnardo's were struggling with a Victorian system, antiquated buildings, an underpaid and largely untrained staff and an instinctive fear of the future from some staff anxious about their jobs and some members of Council uneasy about change.

Stepney itself, the large, yellowing brick barracks which had served as headquarters for over sixty years, was inconvenient, draughty and highly unsuitable for office work, with its flights of stairs and labyrinth of corridors. Barnardo had wanted the public to enjoy a personal response, a family feeling, and much of the office routine was still Victorian. Every single letter from the ninety-six homes was sent out from Stepney under the signature of either the Honorary Director or the Honorary Secretary.[14] This meant that those two gentlemen were frequently telephoned or asked questions about matters of which they knew nothing. Every cheque was drawn from Stepney; staff out in the sticks were constantly complaining of the delays and the endless paperwork.

Meanwhile the conditions grew increasingly chaotic. The work had grown up piecemeal, scattered all over the country wherever a generous donor might have a property. As each new department, each new home was added, more office space in Stepney was winkled out for more voluminous correspondence. Barnardo's filing system was highly personal to say the least. Departments might sub-divide: Emigration, for example, had two sections, one in the Village and one in Stepney. Before the war, little attempt was made to keep the members of a family together administratively. If a senior official wanted information about a family of children, he called the heads of departments together and asked them to bring their files on each child with them. After the war, several small departments were amalgamated into GA & R (General Administration and Records). But three 'parental officers' still held responsibility for three different departments: Girls and Toddlers, Boys, and Boarding-Out. That meant that a family of three children could still have three Barnardo 'parents'.

New departments, Approved Schools, Staff Training and Adoption, further complicated the administration. Each new specialist, and by now they included educational, religious, vocational and psychological advisers, had their own offices, their own clerks, their own correspondence.

At the end of the war, Barnardo's began to put their great exodus of children into reverse, close wartime homes and open permanent, peacetime ones, refurbish, decorate, improve homes, some of them seventy or eighty years old. The increasing need to co-operate with the Home Office, to conform to new Government requirements, all entailed extra work and put more strain on the system.

Yet, despite its grime and inconvenience, Stepney, steeped in sentiment and memories of Barnardo, held a fascination. The world outside might be turning to TV and plastic, but at Stepney the brass was polished, the stone steps scrubbed and the fires lit in the grates as in the Doctor's day.

In a remarkable way the building had come to replace Barnardo himself as the father figure of the charity. Children in the homes thought of Stepney as a sentient being, the ultimate authority. 'We have to ask Stepney,' housemothers would reply when boys and girls asked permission to visit a cinema or join a children's club. Occasionally the unpredictable Stepney would refuse sternly; at other times Stepney in munificent mood would despatch huge sticks of rock or bumper Easter eggs to children in the homes. Stepney would always remember your birthday, children noted, and they in turn felt curious, grateful and resentful towards the omniscient Stepney. Not only did a child have to be admitted by Stepney (provincial children were not officially admitted until they had been to Stepney, which might take months) but when they left it was to Stepney they came for a farewell service, a talk with a member of Council, a gift of a Bible or religious book and, sometimes, a suitcase. They always received a fountain pen and a stamped envelope addressed to the Chairman of Council at Stepney to remind them to keep in touch.

Staff, too, sensed the magic of Stepney, part office, part counting house, part warehouse and overworked 'parent'. The senior officers eating lunch served by an aproned maid in the boardroom and the lower orders munching sandwiches in the basement, swapped stories and folklore. For years, it was said that an extra bottle of milk and a spare copy of *The Times* was delivered to the door. Ordered by the Doctor at the beginning of the century, nobody had summoned up the courage to countermand the orders. In a sense, that probably apocryphal story summed up Barnardo's dilemma at the time. Council and staff were struggling to find ways to modernise a charity that depended for its appeal largely on history and sentiment. Staff flung themselves into the work, some with immense dedication, others coasted by. 'There was a Victorian atmosphere about Stepney,' Mr Tipple, an administrator, remembers. 'The office furniture was very poor, a washstand served as a table. There was a poverty-stricken feeling that you shouldn't expect much, yet you felt you were doing something worthwhile.'[15]

The senior Purchasing Officer, Stanley B., prowled round the dustbins at night in a fanatical drive extracting carbons that he considered not hardpressed enough. 'If the money didn't come, we didn't get paid,' Miss Poole-Connor remembers. She did not have a rise for five years. Leave was an 'act of grace' by the Council. The Barnardo spirit and the Barnardo family were much discussed. There were grand Christmas parties for the children, cheer if a child did well, an almost reckless abandon of the world outside Barnardo's. The staff and Council were drawn together by the crusade for the children, by the secrecy, the air of conspiracy that surrounded their work where even the printers were sworn to silence.

All the children's files were kept under lock and key in Stepney's jealous care and some fourteen Children's Clerks dealt with the correspondence. Although untrained in social work, the dedicated Children's Clerks played a powerful role in the children's lives. They opened the letters sent to boys or girls in foster-homes. They might withhold letters containing what they considered 'a somewhat tactless and thoughtless pouring out of a lot of family problems', or keep back 'postcards of questionable taste' (seaside postcards of fat ladies, perhaps). Their motives were well-intentioned: 'any letters we feel would not be good for the child, we send back to the parents, with a kindly explanation and a request that they re-word the letter'.[16]

They were also the first to receive requests from parents asking for a child to be sent back home. This they regarded as a 'momentous and very serious occasion' and added 'it is generally recognised in Barnardo's that difficult though it may be to squeeze a child into the homes, it is infinitely harder to get a child out, and rightly so, because it is obviously not desirable that the child should leave the security of one family until it has comparable security in another'. The handful of professional staff in Barnardo's who were keen to effect change were impatient of the Children's Clerks, many of them old-timers, who had come up through the ranks. In the eyes of their professional colleagues they wielded undue influence without the necessary knowledge or training.

For their part, the old guard were wary of the newly trained staff from university or college, were fearful for their jobs and found the desire for brisk efficiency and expertise incompatible with the all-embracing family care of the past.

Meantime none of the welfare workers had offices of their own; if they were based outside London, they worked from their own homes, bicycling to their clients and endlessly posting letters or telephoning Stepney. Because of their geographical isolation, Barnardo's could not keep in personal touch with the new Children's Officers and Children's Departments where work was beginning to prevent children coming into care.

To senior staff at least, it appeared imperative that Barnardo's must decentralise if the charity was to conform to post-war standards of child care. At a Staff Conference, an almost unanimous vote was taken to divide Barnardo's work into regions so that their Chief Executives could be more closely in touch with the children in their care and the local authority Children's Officers.

Mr Kirkpatrick, the General Superintendent in charge of children's work, wrote candidly to the Council telling them that the work had become too complex for one individual to control. He proposed that Barnardo country be divided into regions, with an administrator in each in charge of not more than twenty homes, aided by assistants from the

Finance and Works departments. The Council felt uneasy. They feared that if the work moved to the regions their influence would be diminished. Because of their two dominant past Directors, Barnardo himself and more recently Stileman, they were apprehensive of too much power in the hands of the staff.[17]

Originally, Barnardo had run the organisation single-handed without committees. After the arbitration, the trustees prevailed upon him to appoint a Committee to control and advise upon his activities, although he frequently ignored their advice.

After Barnardo's death, the Chairman of Council, William Baker, was appointed Honorary Director and apart from the brief and unhappy three-year reign with Rear-Admiral Stileman as a paid Director, the Council did not appoint a Director for over sixty years. The balance of administrative power, until well after the Second World War, rested with the Council and its Committees, with its two principal officers, the General Superintendent in charge of all the children in their care, and the General Secretary responsible for finance, fund-raising and carrying out their instructions. With the growth and complexity of the work, it became increasingly difficult for honorary officers to supervise all the work and for paid staff to function efficiently without more delegation of authority. That was the background to the power struggle that racked Barnardo's for almost forty years.

At the time, the Council were haunted by increasing Government intervention, a fear that the charity was becoming 'the appendage of a Government Department'[18] and losing its soul. In the debate about devolution, Council members spoke of the 'special flavour' of Stepney and expressed the hope that matrons and Superintendents of homes would keep in 'personal touch' with Stepney, almost as if the spirit of the Doctor would pop out at any moment from the endless desks and files.[19] The Council turned down the proposal for dividing Barnardo's into regions and agreed instead fully to regionalise Scotland and Northern Ireland, which were a great distance off. Not until five years later, in 1952, did the subject come up again for discussion and not for twenty-five years was Barnardo's to devolve completely.

Yet change had to come. In the past, Barnardo's had sent some children out of reach of their parents, out of harm's way, as they saw it; under the new directives, they were bound to take parents' wishes into consideration, to place their children as near to them as possible. Parents were beginning to be partners in the work, but it went against the grain. In 1953, Miss Coe, the Superintendent of a small home in Saltburn, Yorkshire, described how she coped with a delicate problem. She had received a letter from a mother in London, 'a very bad prostitute', saying that she wanted to visit her daughter. 'Though headquarters withheld the visit for a year or more, they could not put it off altogether,' she explained. Miss Coe was told by Stepney that she need not put that mother up in the home. She decided, however, that it would be better 'to keep her under my eye', so she called her staff together and told them that one of the mothers who would need a little extra care and attention was coming on a visit. The enterprising Superintendent put on a different programme every day to occupy her guest and the weekend passed successfully. She was astonished to find the mother weeping when she was to leave. The 'very bad prostitute' confessed that she had never been so happy in her life. 'There was no doubt she loved that girl . . . we felt no harm had come to her daughter during the visit.'[20] With tact and initiative Miss Coe had managed to bridge the uncomfortable gap between Barnardo's Victorian morality and the attitudes of the post-war world.

Barnardo's had begun to modify and adapt their homes and to build purpose-built small homes. As early as 1945, some staff had been concerned at the shortage of homes in which brothers and sisters, particularly older boys and girls, could grow up close to each other. The ideal, outlined in a Home Office Memorandum in 1952, was a small family group home for a dozen or less boys and girls. Segregating the sexes had been a first principle with Barnardo himself: even the files had remained separated and before the war only one or two mixed homes existed. Photographs of boys and girls together were a rarity. Gradually, in the post-war period, homes taking both boys and girls grew up and by 1955, Barnardo's were trying to evaluate the success of their twenty-five mixed homes. Superintendents with boys and girls were asked to report progress. Nearly all of them were favourably impressed.[21]

A fairly typical comment from the Abingdon Home remarked on: 'A happier home, a more normal environment . . . less unhealthy sex play.' Shotley Park in Durham noticed 'An improvement in both sexes: the roughneck attitude of the boys has disappeared . . . and the girls have become less gauche and timid.' At Clacton, the head remarked that 'the girls come backwards and forwards to the boys' side without the slightest sign of unpleasantness'. Birkdale approved of young children growing up together but injected a note of caution: the Superintendent reported that the introduction of a new member of the opposite sex at the age of eleven or twelve 'caused too much excitement among the girls'. At Gillingham, the Superintendent certainly liked the scheme but, in trying to create a family atmosphere, he had found it difficult to get older children to respond to younger brothers and sisters, 'almost as if they had been cast off by their parents and so adopted the same attitude'. But the most robust and unequivocal approval came from the head of a Scottish home. 'When boys first appeared the presence of a man was astonishing. If I appeared on the scene when girls were playing active games with navy blue gympants showing, they would all down skirts as fast as possible.' Life in the home now was more 'homely and normal' he added.

In practice, the atmosphere in the homes depended as it had always done on the character, the training, the maturity and experience of the head of the house. A child's experience in Barnardo's could vary from home to home, from year to year. Shirley Kendall, now married and living in California, came to Barnardo's as a six-month-old baby in December 1935 and left at the age of seventeen in 1952.

From Babies' Castle Shirley was sent, at the age of five, to a foster-home in Sussex where she was extremely happy. To this day she thinks of that foster-mother as a real parent. During the war, Shirley was transferred, with her two sisters, to another foster-home in the Midlands. There she and her sisters were made to dig the garden, do the washing, chop the wood. Food was meagre and they looked 'like Belsen kids'. The place was filthy and Shirley clearly remembers wetting the big bed with its flock mattress. Her foster-mother would hit her for it and rub her head in the sheets.

When Barnardo's discovered what conditions were like, Shirley was moved to Haughton, Shifnal, Shropshire, a home for about sixty girls. She did well at school and made friends with local children. 'I think they felt for us, they treated us with great pity and sympathy. At Christmas we had big parties and we invited the local children.' She was happy again and to her delight won a scholarship to a technical college.

Barnardo's kitted her out with a satchel and uniform when she went to Walker's Technical College. 'They even bought me a very big dictionary. My sisters were jealous. I started school for a term and loved it. In the second year we were going to learn Latin, history and geometry.' But at Christmas the blow came. The children were told they were all leaving Shropshire: the lease was up. Shirley was bitterly disappointed. 'In fairness to Barnardo's they did try to get me a transfer, but in the end I went back to a secondary modern school. Why on earth didn't they board me out with someone locally? I'd love to have learnt Latin. I could have got further in my career. I feel I was robbed of my education.'

The fault, if there was a fault, lay not in Barnardo's as such but in the fact that Shirley was the child of a system. Private arrangements were difficult to organise. She was transferred to another Barnardo home in Leamington Spa and, not surprisingly, was unhappy. She was naughty and rebellious, always running away. 'Then it was "No tea and straight to bed". I was always in bed. I really didn't like that matron. I sensed she shouldn't be around children.'

In 1949, Shirley aged fourteen was sent to live in a hostel for girls in Wembley, in a small suburban house for twelve girls, a post-war innovation. There she settled and looks back happily on those years.

'At aunties' they tried to make it up to me. I'm so grateful for what they did. Every year I was living with the aunties we always had new clothes, summer clothes and winter clothes. And we always had a holiday. They knew I was interested in music, so I had piano lessons and tried acting.' Used to living in children's homes or foster-homes deep in the country, Shirley appreciated the small freedoms of her life. She went to Pitman's Secretarial School. 'I was one privileged to go on the bus to Ealing and sit in the park,' she remembers. 'At Christmas we were taken to panto and the Military Tattoo. And we got one and six a week pocket money. We used to save up like crazy for the aunties' Christmas presents. They were so good to us, they used to spend their private money on us. At first I was very rebellious but gradually love and care got through to me.'[22]

The aunties, long-serving Barnardo staff, gave Shirley her first taste of a stable and caring relationship. She remains in touch with them and visits from her home in California. What she missed was a sense of her own past. For years, she had tried to find out about her parents but was always met with a 'wall of silence'. As far as she could gather her mother went 'from pillar to post' and her father didn't know that her mother was pregnant. 'My mother wrote to Dr Barnardo's begging them to tell her where her three children went. She tried again and again and nearly went out of her mind but they wouldn't divulge any information at all. But Blackpool knew, Blackpool Council, because they sent me money every year. I got the feeling that Barnardo's thought I was better off not knowing, not finding my mother.' Shirley was, of course, quite right. As a former psychiatric social worker writing about the 1940s noted, 'the traditional Barnardo attitude to the child's past was to blot it out . . . only when children reached school-leaving age and relatives turned up was communication allowed.' Yet neither the former social worker nor, more remarkably, Shirley doubted the very real concern for the children's welfare felt by both the Council and staff of Barnardo's.

Deleting the past meant that Shirley had almost no tangible trace of her own childhood, no photographs of herself as a small child to show her own children, not even a school report.

Rescuing the children, restoring them to physical health had taken priority before the war; only very gradually did Barnardo's accept that the only way to help a teenager sort out his problems was by 'complete honesty about his parents and early years'. Most branch homes at one time were staffed by 'kindly people with authoritarian views and some mistrust of anything to do with psychology'. The efforts of Council members and a handful of professional staff to change attitudes were not always successful. That they tried can be seen in official documents such as a new instruction in the 1955 Barnardo Book: 'Superintendents will need to use their imagination and sympathy to realise what it must feel like to a child to be separated from all it has known . . . There must be warmth in the welcome, friendliness, informality and understanding. The child should be allowed to retain his own possessions and the comfort of all possible links with home.' Not for many years, since Barnardo himself had called, in different terms, on the Village staff to soften their attitude, had Barnardo Superintendents been asked to use imagination in their work. As to links with home, that was a new idea.

Peter Taber, now a deputy manager of a workshop for the intellectually handicapped in Napier, New Zealand, came into the homes in 1939 when his parents split up. First, he was fostered with his three sisters in Chelmsford and, despite the blitz, the children lived 'a hard yet cosy life'. In 1944, at the age of ten, a change was decreed and Peter was once again heading to 'an unknown institution with an unknown person'. He was sent to Barnardo's Nautical Training School in Poole, Dorset.

There, he found himself the 'new bug', the smallest boy in a school of some 170. Learning to cope with rigorous discipline, 'lining up, parades, sir this, sir that, bedmaking and floor polishing . . . to military standard', taught him to survive, but his schoolwork suffered.

Some of the practices have overtones of *Tom Brown's Schooldays*. Peter discovered that birthdays were traditionally for 'longstanding customs of torture'. Floor polish or boot polish were ceremoniously splattered on the boy's naked parts, then he was tossed to the ceiling in a blanket. A black boy, 'Nigger Morrison', became Peter's protector and coach: he tried to build Peter up by ordering the smaller boy to piggy-back him several times a day round the parade ground.

Occasionally the boys would rebel: 'Something was wrong with the porridge. A deathly hush as everyone received the lightning call to down spoons . . . The officer in charge commanded we eat it. He broke his stick against a boy's shoulder but the boy still refused. The whole school pounded their spoons on the table.' When the officer left the room to fetch help, the boys quickly filed past the large empty drum to dump their porridge. 'Stiffy' came back with another officer and took in the empty plates and the full drum. Senior boys were made to dole out the porridge and this time they ate it. As a result many were ill. The boys heard through the grape vine that the porridge had been 'off'.

Peter missed his sisters and found the naval-style discipline difficult for a ten-year-old.

> But it wasn't all bad. There was the real enjoyment of being a sailor, complete with uniform, marching behind the school band; muckin' about in boats down on the town lake and our very own cutter, swung from its derricks . . . weekly film shows, and plenty of recreation areas . . . There was pride, too. Pride in the school band; the gymnastics team; the sportsmen who excelled . . . Sunday morning the whole school, in best uniform, marched to the chapel. Inside the stirring sound of the mass choir of 200 boys, singing from the heart, regardless of belief.

Nevertheless, Peter dreamt of 'doing a bunk'. He had lost his status as the smallest boy, and he disliked the discipline. The staff tried hard to help him. 'They somehow dug out a relation for me, living locally . . . but nothing much came of it. With good intentions, I'm sure, they called my father in.' That, too, proved a flop and Peter felt more rejected than ever.

'No wonder boys lay together in the secrecy of their dormitory beds – the only real human comfort some would ever have. There are a lot of generalisations . . . regarding sexual deviation in institutions. Plainly and simply pals would masturbate together and there was a kind of ethical code to keep the bully boys at bay.' He found at Barnardo's, as he almost certainly would have found elsewhere, a great deal of hypocrisy about the question. Inevitably there was one master 'actively involved with boys . . . never questioned, never discovered. He obviously had a good understanding of boys as he was generally well liked. Of course children can be quite mercenary and only too willing to co-operate.'

Peter remained restless throughout his life in Barnardo's. He ran away from his naval school home and was twice transferred. At the Crowborough home he applied to emigrate to Australia; when he was rejected he escaped again. After his rebellious behaviour he was sent to a psychiatrist for assessment. According to Peter the psychiatrist said to him: 'Tell the people who sent you to come themselves next time.' He did not quite understand the message but did not dare to pass it on.

The next solution was for Peter to learn a trade. He chose engineering but was informed that printing was the most suitable trade for him. He was moved again, this time to Goldings.

He was still breaking the rules:

It was so easy to get into trouble if you had any life in you: climbing the water tower; gymnastics on the haystacks; out of bounds; girls in school grounds; scrumping; soaking the parade ground overnight with fire hoses to produce an icerink in winter; nude swims after dark; smoking; missing, or late on parade; talking after lights out; midnight feasts; alcohol; were the many tempting events leading to punishment.

Despite the 1943 ruling in sex education which stipulated that every child had a right to a proper education in regard to sex development and hygiene, many Superintendents continued to deal with the sexual awakening in children by ignoring it altogether. As a teenager in the late 'forties Peter had little opportunity to mix with girls. He took dancing lessons at Goldings with other boys as partners.

Peter turned into a good boxer, joined the cadets, became a Wimbledon ball boy and an extra for the film, *The Browning Version.* He even gained prefect status but was still a rebel. 'Some of my escapades were criminal in the eyes of the law ... but ... they were carried out in the sheer challenge ... of the moment.' He managed to stay just the right side of the law.

More than thirty years later, Peter looks back on his Barnardo life somewhat ruefully. Some staff, he believes, were inexperienced, not properly trained, others authoritarian and hypocrites. 'There were also many staff I admired and respected ... I have felt indebted for their fairness, values and patience.' Now, turned fifty and happily married, Peter tries 'not to be too aware of my past'. He still wonders about the fate of his Barnardo 'brothers'.

Many have succeeded in all aspects of life. Often their background is an advantage urging them to better themselves by extra effort. Millionaires some. Sadly jails hold those who did not make it – to end life as they began – between the walls of an institution. That makes me terribly sad, for I knew them. They were not bad boys. No worse than I ... just that somewhere along the way they took the wrong turning.[23]

For boys like Peter, the homes seemed an immutable force. They were unaware that by the 1950s, Barnardo's were very self-critical and were not short of outside experts pressing advice upon them.

In 1953, Miss Glynn Jones, a senior Inspector at the Home Office, openly questioned at a Staff Conference the intense loyalty to the Barnardo family built into the system: 'I cannot help wondering whether in building up a child's loyalty to Stepney, you do not build down his ability to put down real roots in his immediate surroundings,' she remarked. Today she admires Barnardo's work but in the past she found the system inflexible:

> They moved children about like chessmen, they forgot that children have a past, a present and a future. They didn't think about them as real children, they were files, cases. A Children's Clerk would simply send a message to a home saying that a certain boy or girl was moving. That child was sent off with a travelling matron, a stranger; nobody was prepared to receive them and they were moved without any regard to the child's feelings. Their work for boys in those two big homes [the technical school, Goldings, in Hertford and the sea school in Poole] was dreadful. The boys had no sense of being wanted. It wasn't homely care, it was institutional care. There was no loving relationship with one individual who knew about what had happened in the past and cared about what would happen in the future. How would you expect them to react?'

Miss Glynn Jones's view as a senior Home Office Inspector at the time lends credence to Peter's account of his childhood in those two large homes. Miss Glynn Jones added:

> It wasn't the staff's fault. They knew they were supposed to be loving and tender and kind but they were working in a system so wrong that they couldn't be. The children were like so many units pressed into a mould ... They had this idea that a child whose home had failed was different from other children, that if you cut off the roots and put the child in a good hygienic home it would blossom ... But they had some very loving people on the staff, especially at Babies' Castle.[24]

On their side, Barnardo's staff felt that Home Office Inspectors were sometimes unfairly critical. A Chief Executive Officer remembered a call from a Home Office Inspector complaining that the Superintendent of one children's home was so indifferent to children that she had had her own newborn baby packed off to a relative. The Superintendent concerned had rung headquarters beforehand to say that she had sent her baby to her sister's for the day because she didn't want to be accused of favouritism.

In reality in one unpublicised and almost unknown area of their work Barnardo's were helping to fulfil the Home Office's desire to keep deprived families together, by giving money, help and advice to families struggling to keep their children. As early as 1947, the charity was awarding temporary grants of money to 'good families' in difficulties because the breadwinner was temporarily unable to work due to illness or accident. Married women with illegitimate children, divorced, deserted or widowed women as well as unmarried mothers, all qualified for Barnardo help.[25]

Dr Barnardo's original scheme to aid unmarried mothers had been modernised and instead of working as a resident maid, supervised by a watchful mistress, with her baby fostered nearby, the unmarried mother of the 1950s was usually looking after her own baby or employing a childminder while she went out to work. Nor was the strict morality still imposed. By 1953, one in five of the unmarried mothers helped was either a bad manager or dirty, untidy or feckless, some had several illegitimate children. They were the very women who needed the help most, Barnardo's concluded.[26]

By 1957, the 'Homes for Orphans' began in reality to take in whole families in trouble, Dad, Mum and the children. They co-operated with the LCC in a brave small-scale experiment to house two families in the Village Homes. The families, overwhelmed by debts, ill-health, wretched housing, unemployment, or petty crime were given a new start. In the course of nine months it was hoped that the man of the family would be encouraged to get a job, the wife to learn child care and housecraft and the children to acquire social habits. Then the local authority would offer them housing and Barnardo's gifts-in-kind department would help them to set up home, providing furniture, clothing and prams, books and toys. Barnardo's even offered the family a holiday later on in a house by the sea.

Even professional workers knew little about Barnardo's preventive help for families, yet by the end of the 'fifties at least a quarter of the charity's help to children went in assisting them to stay with their own parents rather than bringing them into the Barnardo 'family'. Although within the organisation people were asking for more publicity, the pamphlets for professionals were not published until 1962. Perhaps one reason for Barnardo's immense popular appeal is that it keeps in close touch with the feelings and prejudices of the general public. To this day the plight of mothers and single parents does not possess the emotional appeal of the 'poor orphans'.

Post-war developments directed the charity to another group of children who had yet to win the sympathy of the public: mentally handicapped or mentally defective children as they were called.

By the 1940s and 'fifties more newborn babies with congenital, mental and physical deformities were surviving due to modern medical techniques. The 1944 Education Act had promised every child a training but few individual local authorities could finance special schools or centres for handicapped children. Many of the hospitals for the mentally handicapped were overcrowded and bleak and beds in them so scarce that only mentally handicapped children abandoned by their parents or those who presented a threat to society could hope to find a bed. In desperation, since the 'experts' were not answering their needs, the parents themselves grouped together and formed the Association for Mentally Handicapped Children (now Mencap). Those parents began to explore ways of increasing knowledge and understanding of their children and improving standards for them. They had firsthand experience and trained themselves to become 'experts'.

At the time, Barnardo's Charter of Association excluded mentally handicapped children. The staff were not trained to care for them and the possibilities for Evangelical work amongst them were extremely limited. The Medical Officer, Dr Bloom, explained to the staff the grave need for places for those children and pleaded for more understanding: 'I know that most of you long to care for normal children; blue-eyed boys and curly headed girls, and sometimes I hear fears expressed . . . that in these days of an all-providing state, it is increasingly the abnormal, physically or mentally handicapped who will demand our care.'[27] Dr Bloom added that he sensed there was 'nostalgic longing for those good old days when orphans really were orphans and not maladjusted or introspective children.' Sometimes babies were admitted to Barnardo's who developed into mentally defective children and Dr Bloom called upon staff to do their best for those children, 'knowing that we shall find relief as soon as we can'.

Since the war the charity also had a waiting list of some ninety physically handicapped children; places for them were desperately short. Despite opening a special home in Scotland for forty-six children and converting the girls' training home, Warlies in Essex, into a home for physically handicapped, Barnardo's could only accommodate about 220 handicapped children, a number the Medical Officer described as 'pitifully small'. Parents of physically handicapped children suffering from cerebral palsy, the 'spastics', had banded together to crusade for better facilities for the treatment and care of their children. Like Mencap, they had improved standards and increased the demand for better facilities.

The change in the intake of children was changing the character of the charity. The numbers of normal children were falling and their average stay (just under three years) was less than half that of former days. Yet Barnardo's at that stage were loath to accept the new circumstances. There was the dangerous feeling, sometimes expressed in Council meetings and Committees, that Barnardo's had done so well in the past that they had no need to change. Barnardo smug, staff called it.

There were also small but encouraging signs of new attitudes. The work of restoring children to their parents went quietly forward and, despite the complications, staff were beginning to work well with the children's families. For the first time Barnardo's were erecting purpose-built, smaller, more personal children's homes. Then there was the scheme to rehabilitate families and, finally, after a gap of fifty years, Barnardo's were taking on a responsibility, however small, for what they called 'mentally ailing children'. A short-stay holiday house for twenty-five such children was opened in Derbyshire in 1957.

However, to stay effective and certainly to lead in the field, the charity recognised that some form of reorganisation to dear old Stepney was inevitable. A team of business efficiency experts was appointed which made sweeping recommendations for change: it insisted that Barnardo's must be nationalised, that fund-raising departments which operated different schemes must amalgamate; that child care work be decentralised and that Barnardo's Stepney should, quite literally, give up the spit and polish.[28]

12

With a Grateful Heart

'Remember that Barnardo himself was a wonderful beggar.'
Mr Tetley, Chairman, Finance Committee,
Staff Conference, 1957

'We have mortgaged the future I am aware; but we have done so in the interests of the children.'
T. J. Barnardo, letter to Lord Radstock

To modernise Barnardo's, to replace or redesign large, ugly, antiquated buildings with small, compact, convenient homes or offices; to create new regional offices and employ new and highly trained staff; to care for more difficult children, would mean that Barnardo's would have to draw on thousands of pounds from their hard-won financial reserve. Throughout almost all of Tom Barnardo's career the homes had been in debt, mortgaged to the buildings in which he cared for the children. Only in 1916, eleven years after the founder had died, did the homes rid themselves completely of their debt. But in the early 1960s the outlay was imperative; without it the homes would have fallen behind. Progress was always dependent on fund-raising.

In the early days Barnardo reached out to the public through his letters to the press and his friendship with R. C. Morgan, editor of *The Revival* (later *The Christian*), an important Evangelical periodical of the time. Like George Muller of Muller's Orphanages, Barnardo assumed Supreme Guidance in his fund-raising. The title of his first Annual Report, 'The First Occasional Record of the Lord's Dealings in Connexion with the East End Juvenile Mission 1867-68', makes that clear. Yet, unlike Muller who relied on faith and prayer to meet his needs, Barnardo appealed to the public with increasing confidence over the years.

In his first report, he intertwined a great deal of religious sentiment with a few well-placed remarks on the needs of his mission. 'We never beg money for the Lord's Work', was one of his early principles, but he did guide would-be donors by pointing out what their monetary gifts would supply. He appealed directly for old clothes, flannel shirts and boys' garments being particularly prized; for jewellery and for articles made by Christian ladies.

Every donor of even the smallest amount received a printed numbered receipt and he included a numbered list with the donors' initials in his Annual Report. Contributors were begged to keep receipts and to scrutinise his books at any time. He warned them that donations or subscriptions would be received by a private individual, Thomas J. Barnardo.

'We do not go into debt', was another early principle. If funds were withheld, it was a sign, he wrote, that he was commanded to 'stand still' and not go forward. 'So strongly do I feel this that I think it would be better that the whole work should cease than that it should be involved in debt.'[1] That was not a position he was able to sustain.

His early reports combine lofty passages of prayer, quotations from the Scriptures and very practical instructions: parcel sent SHOULD BEAR THE NAME AND ADDRESS OF THE DONOR WRITTEN DISTINCTLY . . . Cheques should be crossed, London and South Western Bank, and POs made payable at General Post Offices . . . Very early on, he included a form of bequest to his mission. 'I give and bequeath unto Thomas John Barnardo, or the Treasurer for the time being of the East End Juvenile Mission and Home for Working and Destitute Lads . . . the sum of . . . pounds sterling; to be paid with all convenient speed after my decease.' Many Christians disapproved of direct appeals for money and Tom Barnardo admitted that to rely on prayer was the 'highest and happier path' yet he felt that he must go his own way: 'I dare not imitate others.'

Through his writing, he managed to convey a sense of moral superiority. His first Annual Report reads like a sermon. He told three stories of sinners dying, two to be saved, repenting through his agency. In one, a tall, muscular young man looked in at the service held at Barnardo's ragged school one Sunday evening. After the service, Barnardo approached him and tried to impress upon him the need for salvation before it was too late. 'Don't fear, teacher, plenty of time, I aint a-going to die yet,' replied the stranger.

Two months later, the young man lay desperately ill; he sent for Tom Barnardo and asked him to pray for him to be forgiven. At the eleventh hour, the dying young man found salvation. 'I may add that the clocks were just striking twelve, the last hour of the old year, as leaving the body of sin and death behind, he entered into the presence of the King,' Barnardo recalled.

In the early years, Barnardo struggled hard to keep out of debt and abide by his own principles. He discovered early on that growth in the work and in his property attracted more funds and almost every year until his death he enlarged and improved his buildings.

He took on more children, more premises, more evangelistic work and more poor relief, with the inevitable result that the cost of rent, salaries, food, clothing, equipment and other expenses rose steeply. His justification, his faith, drove him on. How could he turn away a single destitute child, he argued?

At first, the public interest he generated and the enormous rise in donations seemed to warrant the risks. But in the troubled years from 1874 to 1877, when scandal surrounded his mission, the funds fell off and some of his plans had to hang fire.

In those years, when Barnardo's name was constantly in front of the public in both the local East End press and in the national newspapers, unexpected benefits accrued. The funds were depressed while .accusations of fraud, cruelty and sexual misconduct were blazoned across the headlines. However, the outcome of the arbitration vindicated Barnardo and his homes completely and the result was an astonishing turnaround of Barnardo's fortunes. The case personalised his homes and glamorised the founder. He was deluged with requests to preach and lecture, and became more hard-pressed than ever. Yet the debts remained and grew with the work.

Barnardo's great personal appeal was, paradoxically, one reason why he was forced to depart from his principles and go into debt. From the arbitration onwards, wealthy Evangelical supporters seemed eager to press the deeds of their properties into his hands, to play a part in the thrilling adventure of saving the children.

As early as 1878, 'an aged gentleman who had property in Jersey kindly offered to place at my disposal a house and grounds situated in one of the healthiest parts of the island,' he explained.[2] His Committee debated the offer for a year, aware of the cost it would incur. Eventually, as the house was offered at a nominal rent of a shilling a year, they concluded that it was an offer they could not refuse. The home was opened for boys under ten, especially those in delicate health, 'to secure for these small mites of humanity fresh air, sea breezes, abundant milk and delightful scenery'. Barnardo airily dismissed the cost of transit, saying that it would be offset by the cheaper prices on the island. Yet, with more children to feed and clothe and more staff to pay, his costs inevitably went up.

Against this background of extraordinary expansion, Barnardo's fund-raising became even more urgent. Twenty-one years after he founded the East End Juvenile Mission, he announced that he had rescued 12,500 children and housed almost 3,000 residents in his thirty-eight homes.

He had started with nothing but his faith and had opened his first home 'in defiance of all the rules of worldly prudence, without a penny in the bank nor the promise of a shilling'. His receipts had grown from £214 in 1868 to £110,478 in 1890, over half of them under £5. Yet, the homes were faced with a £23,000 overdraft. Barnardo's attitude was that he had been acquiring the freehold of property, improving it and borrowing on the security of that property. 'The whole matter is therefore simply, as book-keepers would say, one of account, which will adjust itself (DV) in a few years.' He gambled that the expenditure would benefit his charity in the years to come. As, indeed, it has.

At the time, his Committee were understandably disturbed at the amount of money needed to keep up with his vision. The Committee announced that the freeholds of all the properties were now acquired and the programme of improving and adapting the homes was completed. They had reckoned without Barnardo: nothing could restrain his urgent activities. He had always argued that his children came from all over the country and that the national character of his work ought to be recognised. He persuaded his reluctant Committee that, since so many children came to him from the provinces it would be more economical and efficient to admit children on the spot in provincial centres. He opened a chain of Ever-Open-Doors in 1892, which to Barnardo's delight, brought in more children. Two years later, he noted that well over half the children admitted now came from outside London. Although the setting up of the Ever-Open-Doors helped to establish Barnardo's as a national charity and created important bases throughout the country, the debts still multiplied.

In 1893, Barnardo's trustees and Committee, thoroughly dismayed by the enormous liabilities, held a joint meeting; as a result they endeavoured to impose financial restrictions on him. In an appeal for help in his magazine, Barnardo defended his position vigorously. To his kindly, long-suffering treasurer, Mr William Fowler, he wrote:

> I really incurred a debt of £200,000 to acquire and build property; rather more than one-half of that has been gradually paid off. I hope the remainder will melt in due time as the snows and ice of winter are melted by the advancing sun ... we have 'mortgaged the future', I am aware; but we have done so in the interests of the children ... Had the British Public ... come forward with a capital sum ... we would not have required to have touched our income or to have pushed to the background our various tradesmen's accounts.[3]

Barnardo was, of course, constantly forced to parry tradesmen's demands. To judge from this letter to his advertising agent, he dealt with them in a cavalier fashion:

> Advertising Agents are like the Horse Leach's [*sic*] daughters, you will remember he had four and they all cried 'give! give!' . . . I think I did very well to send you £150 when you expected £300. I do not think you will get any more money this week; but I think very likely some time before the end of the month we will send you another £150 . . . I am afraid until the millennium comes you must not expect that you will get a cheque on the 1st of every month . . . we will be a trifle short during the next three or four months.[4]

In the face of the crisis, Barnardo did make some economies. Despite misgivings and some resignations on the Committee, his personal popularity helped him to continue to expand. The year after his Committee had attempted to curtail his activities saw him acquiring more property. A house in Birkdale, Southport, the Jones Home, was presented to the homes *in memoriam* and Barnardo opened it for incurable children. In the Village the Children's Church, the gift of an anonymous donor, was finally completed and dedicated. That year, too, saw him defend ferociously other property in the Village. The lease of Mossford Lodge, a wedding present to Barnardo, was due to expire when, to his dismay, he learnt that a Roman Catholic sisterhood planned to acquire it. He immediately launched a £7,000 appeal to buy the lodge and the adjoining twenty-six acres of grounds, explaining that the presence of a hostile community who had hindered and harassed him would seriously damage his work. Evangelical supporters, alarmed at what Barnardo described as 'the Romish plot' rallied to his support. The tone of his appeal provoked the Catholic press to challenge his facts and the basis of his appeal and to mount a personal attack. Barnardo's Committee was eventually drawn in to the dispute and, after quizzing the Director, issued a statement to the press and supporters confirming that 'Dr Barnardo's statements as to the attempt of certain Roman Catholics to purchase Mossford Lodge and adjoining lands were well founded'.[5] Despite the adverse publicity, Barnardo reported that the funds 'so far as I could judge it had positively benefited by my unpleasant experience'. They had risen from £134,000 to £150,000. That increase of £16,000 was not maintained during the 1890s.

In the face of the increasing debts, the warnings, even the resignation of two members of his Committee, Barnardo opened more Ever-Open-Doors, more homes for children and received one more valuable gift of a large property in Norfolk. He even bought the freehold of a property without first obtaining the approval of his Committee. By the turn of the century, the homes were incorporated and the Committee and trustees relieved of their heavy burden of financial responsibility. The move was prudent, for when Barnardo died in 1905 his liabilities amounted to almost £250,000. The receipts for that year totalled £196,000, his greatest fund-raising effort.

Four years after he founded the Stepney home Barnardo omitted one of his early principles, 'We never beg money for the Lord's work', from his Annual Report. For the rest of his life he was engaged in appealing, charming, begging, cajoling the public into giving money to his poor children. Before the arbitration, Barnardo had made his work known by means of preaching and writing to the Christian press. He did not advertise or issue circulars of appeals, with the exception of an annual Christmas letter to the children of England.

After the arbitration, with a Committee guiding his work, a mortgage on his property and legal expenses to pay, he began to advertise nationally and to send out begging letters. At first, he took on the work with apparent reluctance: 'I can honestly say that I long for the day to come when . . . the Mission may once more resume its old position of quiet usefulness, avoiding as far as possible and on principle those appeals to the public which, in my mind have always been so sad a defect in the system of Christian charities.'[6]

Two years later in the same journal he was just as vigorously defending his means of collecting money to support his 'large adopted family'.[7] 'It should be remembered,' he pointed out, 'that the work of giving is spread over a very small area – the great supporters of Christian missions might almost be counted on one's fingers . . . I have always felt that a positive duty was laid upon me to stir up the minds of Christian people generally . . . not the rich or a particular class only, to a greater sense of their responsibility.'[8]

Barnardo's high profile, his business sense and his feel for publicity discomfited some of his more pious supporters from the beginning. In 1873, when he announced that he would hold a three-day sale in the Edinburgh Castle, letters of protest came in accusing him of worldliness and an unspiritual attitude. 'We earnestly hope you won't have any raffling at your bazaar,' wrote one distressed supporter. In explanation, Barnardo replied that he merely proposed to hold a big shop at the coffee palace of the Edinburgh Castle, where he would sell articles made and contributed by his supporters. 'We trust that nothing will be done throughout the sale upon which we cannot ask God's blessing,' he added reassuringly. Characteristically, he published the correspondence and turned the debate to his advantage: 'I would remind some of my lady friends that their needless ornaments, jewellery, trinkets, etc. if laid at the Master's feet may be advantageously replaced by the brighter and more seemly jewels referred to in 1 Peter 3, 3-5.'

The first year's sale brought in a profit of £188 and by the following year he had decided to move the venue to a fashionable sale room in the West End, to hold the sale just before Christmas and charge one shilling entrance fee. An extraordinary assortment of gifts arrived at his doorstep year by year: clothing and food; live animals, including dogs, pigs, cats, birds and donkeys for the children; hundreds of books; musical instruments (harmoniums, concertinas, flutes etc.); paintings and drawings; sewing machines; aspidistras; astronomical telescopes; opera glasses; old china; curios from foreign lands; clocks; furniture. Eventually, he set aside a storeroom in Stepney and the Gifts in Kind Department supplied the needs of children in the branch homes and the rest of the goods were sold.

Jewellery and precious stones were common gifts as well as watches and family plate. In the home at Stepney Causeway Barnardo had showcases installed to display the more attractive articles of jewellery and bric-à-brac which began to form an appreciable fraction of his income. The Gifts in Kind Department survived until 1981. Nowadays, gifts are collected in the different areas where the charity works and are either sold through their shops or, when suitable, given to children in need.

Throughout his life, Barnardo castigated the rich for their wealth and told them forcefully of the benefits of placing some of their worldly goods at his disposal. He rarely missed an opportunity to press home his 'mission to the stingy'.

When he read in the press that diamonds, pendants and other valuable jewellery had been found on the floor of the House of Lords, he commented pointedly: 'those ladies of rank who honoured the golden chamber with their presence do not place great value upon such meretricious aids to personal adornment, else they would have taken better care of them'. The £1,000 spent on a diamond necklace might be more usefully employed meeting the entire cost of sixty-four orphan girls for a year or it would give 4,800 hot breakfasts every morning and 2,400 hot dinners every day in the year, he claimed extravagantly.[9]

He was a natural communicator, a man who used words with skill and evident enjoyment. If he spoke as he wrote, it is not hard to see why the public flocked to hear him. 'He operated,' wrote his wife, 'with the skill of an accomplished hypnotist, the strength of one who knew the justice of his cause, and as a Christian with an audacious faith which sometimes looked like tempting Providence.'[10] At meeting after meeting, in Annual Report after Annual Report, in sermon after sermon, he repeated his stories, his warnings, his solutions. The repetition was one reason for his success. His appeal told as 'water falling upon stone'. His detailed planning and supervision of the fund-raising, down to the smallest detail was another. He sent out on average 100,000 letters a year and appealed to correspondents to enclose a twopenny stamp. 'For goodness sake do use good ink, good paper and a decent pen and above all write distinctly and clearly if you want people to pay attention to you,' he wrote in irritation to one of his staff.[11] The form of his appeals was always as attractive and thoughtful as he could make it. He included information on transport, trains and buses for his supporters or arranged to have them met.

Above all, he was a superb entertainer. He managed to make accounts of good works and lists of donations interesting, human, amusing, material which in other hands could prove unutterably dreary. His magazine *Night and Day* devoted pages each month to acknowledging donations.

A Weymouth family of children, despairing of Papa who was 'so very fond of making puns' evolved a novel solution: 'We are trying to cure him by charging him a penny for every pun and we are going to send the money to you.' A pious policeman and his wife agreed at the start of the year 'to forfeit sixpence every time we got cross with each other'. They sent five shillings to the homes. Many donors gave gifts *in memoriam*: 'My little darling has been taken away to be folded in the Saviour's arms and I should like the pocket-money she had to be used for the good of his poor little lambs.'

Rarely did Barnardo misjudge his supporters; however, one account he gave of an outing with 'poor wee mites' from a ragged school misfired badly.[12] On the way home, he related, the party passed a home for lost dogs, clean, commodious and well-built. The lads looked enviously at the place. 'Cor, think o' people givin' a grand place like that for lost dawgs. I expect they 'ave a time of it inside and plenty o' grub. I won'er why they don't think o' having a home for poor chaps like us.'

'Is it not a fact,' Barnardo mused, 'that there are numbers who will give to anti-vivisection societies and societies for the prevention of cruelty to animals for the few who will help to reclaim human waifs and strays?'

His mail was always heavy, but in the weeks after those remarks appeared the pile was huge. Then, as now, the animal lobby was vociferous. 'Some of the readers said I was wicked, others cruel; some said I was ignorant but all declared I was to blame.' Barnardo rarely apologised. He merely pointed out that he was a thorough antivivisectionist and he frequently emphasised 'the absolute duty of kindness to animals'. However, he drew a distinction between protecting dumb animals from suffering and the Christian duty of rescuing poor children, 'creatures made in the image of God, possessing immortal souls and destined for a glorious and eternal future'.[13] He never made the mistake of comparing the rival claims of lost children and lost dogs again.

Perhaps Barnardo drew on his newly acquired knowledge of the English weakness for dumb animals; the following year, his Annual Bazaar included a menagerie stall selling 'birds, beasts, fishes and reptiles, ALL ALIVE'. As usual, supporters rallied round with gifts: a hedgehog from Saffron Walden, collie puppies, white mice and white rats from Tunbridge Wells; pigeons, bantams and kittens from East London; a bevy of cats from Woolwich. The rest of the menagerie included a Blenheim spaniel, marmoset monkeys, Persian cats, parakeets, cockatoos, canaries, Java sparrows, a salamander, goldfish, eels, water tortoises and a Pomeranian goat.

Barnardo made sure they were fed and carefully tended, the cats well separated from the pigeons. 'As far as the little creatures could express by looks that they were comfortable, they did so freely, so that I can assure kind donors everywhere that our project was carried out without causing pain or suffering to the feeble animal entrusted to our care.'

The menagerie stall had, of course, made a particular appeal to the children. Barnardo always paid special attention to his little helpers, quoting from their letters. Harold from Bristol (only a little chap, six years old) recruits his mother as secretary: 'mother reabed me your letter about your little boys and girls and I went round the table in the dining-room and then to our nursie and the kitchen and I now send you the money [ten shillings] and hope some little boys and girls will be made happy . . . I want a card to klect for you.'[14] There, commented Barnardo, beneficence, ideality and actuality in one small parcel.

His magazine also served to advertise his needs: laundresses for the Village ('must be first-class washers and ironers and able to teach in all departments. Must also be total abstainers and communicants in some Evangelical body'); umbrellas and waterproof cloaks for the girls, shirts for the boys, a convalescent home for sick children.

The donations and the gifts depended heavily on Barnardo's insistent and entertaining pen and his timely reminders. His personal appearances brought in the crowds and the contributions. From the beginning he had received invitations to speak and preach from all over the British Isles. By the end of the 1880s, when he was travelling to Canada as well as attempting to supervise every detail of his vast enterprise, funds fell.

To keep the funds flowing in his absence, he decided to appoint deputies, Deputation Secretaries, to travel all over the country and speak from the pulpit and lecture in his stead. His Deputation Secretaries were given explicit and detailed instructions: they must seek out churches with large congregations and endeavour to obtain free hospitality. They should try to make a few influential friends before their arrival. They should hold no less than two or three meetings in a town or village, a 'drawing room meeting', followed by a public meeting for 'all sorts and conditions of men'. They must draw up a poster advertising sermons and lectures as well as copy for the press, and pew papers must be provided. (These would be printed in advance at Stepney.) Finally, before they left, they should make sure that local committees set up funds and spread publicity and were firmly established.

He began with two ministers and, within a few years, he had built up a network of clergymen from both the non-conformist churches and the Church of England.

By the 1890s, he was sending a small group of his 'musical boys', in specially made uniforms, little hand-bell ringers and Scotch pipers, to accompany the clergymen on their tours. The 'musical boys' delighted the public and the tours were an outstanding success at a time of deepening financial crisis. Since he received generous support from Australia and New Zealand, and many requests to visit 'down under', in 1891 Barnardo sent out a party of eight 'musical boys', led by the Reverend Walter J. Mayers, who carried with him a letter of introduction, asking for hospitality for the clergyman and the little boys, the loan of a public hall and support:

> I know that when once you hear from Mr Mayers' own lips the wonderful story of the work which God has given me to do during the past twenty-five years among homeless and destitute children in East London, your heart will be stirred ... and you will be impelled to stretch out the hand of brotherly compassion and of loving help to my large family of Orphan Waifs and Strays.
> Believe me to be
> Your very faithful Servant among the
> lost and homeless children of our
> great British Cities,
> Thos J. Barnardo[15]

The Reverend Mayers preached his message and the children played their pious, homely little tunes on the hand-bells and bagpipes and their efforts raised £10,000.

Barnardo was constantly reminded of his growing debt and yet made plans to expand, to build refuges in the provinces. To stem the debts, he devised a number of novel fund-raising schemes. The most successful, the Young Helpers' League, came to him after he had spent a busy day at Stepney admitting poor children, including two little crippled girls and a blind boy. He fell asleep sitting by the fire in his study in his Surbiton home and had a curious dream. He was out walking by a dark and rapid stream when he heard a cry for help. A boy was drowning in midstream. Barnardo could not swim in his dream although, in reality, he was a powerful swimmer. As the boy swept by, Barnardo stretched out his arms to pull him to safety, calling out for help to a group of children playing nearby. 'We will hold you, sir, don't be afraid,' the children answered. With the children behind him pulling him to firm ground, Barnardo clutched the drowning lad and hauled him to safety on the bank. 'I felt such a thrill of happiness at the thought that I awoke.'[16]

Publicly Barnardo unravelled the meaning of his dream: with the children helping him, he could continue to expand his rescue work. Barnardo's 'dreams' nowadays might be considered too ordered and logical to be other than daydreams, his semi-conscious inspirations.

In Barnardo's plan, the children of privilege were to reach out to rescue the children of the streets. His Young Helpers' League for the upper and middle classes became immensely popular with the aristocracy. Princess Mary of Cambridge, Duchess of Teck, was the first President. In the country, the county supported their local branches and half Debrett turned up at the annual parties held at the Royal Albert Hall.

Like all Barnardo's work, the Young Helpers' League was highly institutionalised with rules, badges, banners, divisions, sub-divisions, ranks and rewards. The most senior award was the DOWS (Distinguished Order of Waif Service). The children were enchanted by the novelty of it all. Initially, in 1892, the annual subscription was sixpence; it doubled in August that year to a shilling to cover expenses and for over eighty years remained the same. Within five years the Young Helpers' League had an income of over £8,000. The League had its own Advisory Council, with the Chairman usually a Church of England clergyman. More than any other single scheme, the Young Helpers' League served to raise the homes' social status and place them in the mainstream of British life.

Barnardo's aims were lofty. He set out not only to raise money but to provide an army of young supporters and to span the widening gulf between the 'classes' and the 'masses' by the 'golden bridge of sympathy'. The League's daily prayer was simple and tender: 'Our Father, bless all poor little children throughout the world and fill our hearts with loving desires to help them, for the sake of Jesus Christ, our Lord.' Boys and girls in happy homes were invited to raise money for cots in the Children's Hospital in Stepney or in Barnardo's new Home for Little Incurables. Every effort was made to involve them. If a branch had raised the £30 needed to maintain a cot for a year, then the cot was named after that branch and the children were allowed to visit a child in 'their' cot any afternoon. From the beginning, the League was a great success and Barnardo claimed he had drawn together young people all over the world.

In the *Young Helpers' League Magazine*, edited by Barnardo himself with his usual flair, a Cot Chronicle of Endowed Beds reported patients' progress. Here is a typical entry from the 1895 edition: 'Hampstead (Ellen Hughes-Hughes Ward). Catherine de Pellette has a grand name at any rate! She is a bright, intelligent child of eleven and would be very active but for a troublesome leg, that will need a great deal of attention.'

The tone was sentimental, Dickensian, with appealing pictures of 'crippled Tommy', a dear little chap only six years old, who had lost his left leg. If he had not been taken into the home he would have gone into the workhouse, the accompanying story notes. In Barnardo's time, many little Tommies were certainly given expert care beyond their parents' means.

But, rather than uniting the classes, the League cultivated the view of two nations. Pictures of Lady Margery, a child wrapped in furs, helping Elsie, dressed in rags, adorn the 1897 magazine. At Christmas 1898, there were 'boys to lend' for five days over the holiday, provided the borrowers would send the railway fare. In the same issue, free tickets were offered to view the waifs eating their free supper!

Nevertheless, Barnardo's bold venture was a financial and social success and membership of the League became fashionable and popular. As far afield as France, Switzerland, Australia, New Zealand and South Africa, the movement grew. By 1903 Barnardo decided to enlist his old boys and girls in the service branch as helpers in the YHL. The reason, he wrote, was twofold: he wanted to maintain a strong link with his 'family' and also to exercise 'a good influence over their lives after they had gone out into the world'. He felt that they ought to do something for the homes which had helped them so much. Above all, he wanted his old boys and girls to realise the 'unspeakable pleasure in service for others'. Old boys and girls were asked to enrol, pay a subscription of one shilling and to take collecting-boxes, sew for the homes and help in other ways. The boys' branch changed its name to the Barnardo Old Boys' Guild in 1907; the girls' Guild of the Grateful Life retained the title until after the Second World War. To this day thousands of Barnardo old boys and girls pay a yearly subscription to receive the magazine, the *Guild Messenger*, and help the homes.

Since the Young Helpers' League was so flourishing, Barnardo set out to enlist the man-in-the-street to his cause. He had discovered early on in his work that it was the poor who were most willing to give. We take children from the street, why not collect from the street, he reasoned? His was by no means the first street collection. The Royal National Lifeboat Institution had held street appeals in Manchester during the 1880s.

As usual he set out to organise his efforts in a thorough and business-like way. Through his magazine he drummed up volunteers and supplied each with a notice, box, arm badge, literature and an authorisation. Nevertheless, the first collectors went out fearful of their reception, shaking their wooden, two-handled boxes. Despite protests in some quarters, Barnardo would occasionally send out uniformed Barnardo boys to help the ladies. His collection for 'Waif Saturday' was held in London and a number of provincial towns and raised £203 made up almost entirely of pennies, halfpennies and farthings. The poor had responded to his appeal. Nevertheless, he was cock-a-hoop in 1898 when he noted 'the Prince of Wales' was successfully 'dunned by a young collector'.[17]

In the second year of his street collection he was more ambitious; he held collections in 184 centres and gave his volunteers detailed advice. They should choose suitable sites close to known supporters, where many persons of the most respectable classes pass; where the street was roomy and unobstructed and where shelter could be found in case of rain. In most cases, he advised, the police were only too ready to help, but should trouble arise the collector could remain undisturbed if she obtained permission to sit in the doorway of a shop, restaurant or church with her box. (The collectors were evidently all female.) By 1899 he had introduced house-to-house leafleting followed by a return call, which always did better than the street collections.

Barnardo latched on to any occasion for fund-raising and a royal event was for him a special opportunity. In the year of Queen Victoria's Golden Jubilee (1897) he was urged by many supporters to drop his street collection since there were so many appeals that year. On the contrary, he argued, her Gracious Majesty had reigned sixty years; his homes for rather more than half that time. And, since his institutions by rescuing street children had added so materially to the glory of her reign, his street collections should be more successful than ever. In the year of Edward VII's coronation in 1902, he gave his collection the title of 'Coronation Waif Saturday in aid of their Majesties' most helpless subjects'. The year he died, Waif Saturday collections were held in over 5,000 centres and raised £18,000.

By that time the interest in his work was growing among the boys and girls in schools and Bible classes. Barnardo had organised a network of speakers and lecturers to cover the social strata; talks at elementary schools for the working classes, where no appeal was made but a request for help with street collections; lectures to the grammar and private schools for the middle classes and for the public schools.

He launched Self-Denial Week, another scheme to raise funds, designed to appeal to the conscience of his staunchly Christian supporters. In 1894 clergy were urged to preach on the subject from the pulpit and Barnardo whipped up enthusiasm in his magazine with suggestions: the paterfamilias was asked to give his family good, plain food for the week which, Barnardo put in, would give the digestion a rest, often better than the physic; the businessman was asked to travel third instead of first class; the sportsman to stage a football match; the shop assistant to place a collecting-box on the counter; the servants to make small household economies and even the children to give up jam or sweets for a week.

Barnardo raised between £2,000 and £4,000 from Self-Denial Week, but his personal influence was vital. In 1899 he raised over £3,200 from the scheme; when he was absent in Canada the following year, the amount collected fell to £800.

In 1894 he also added twelve Church of England clergymen in dioceses all over the country to his Deputation Staff to urge 'the claims of neglected children upon the heart and conscience'. At the time he was meeting opposition from the Church of England Society for Waifs and Strays who were advising Anglican churchmen to boycott his homes since they were not run on Church lines. To counter this criticism Barnardo established a Church of England Auxiliary Fund, specifically for Church of England children in his homes.

Of his several appeals the legacies were always the most fruitful source of income, the only ones likely to produce donations in three figures. A bequest form first appeared in the Annual Report for 1871 and appeals for legacies recurred every year.

Founder's Day was originally a summer reunion at Stepney for some of the old boys and girls, who would renew old acquaintances, talk with each other of old times, the boys would play a game of cricket and then they would go on their way after shaking Dr Barnardo by the hand and leaving a little offering to the funds.[18] The function usually took place in July and soon came to be associated with Barnardo's birthday. By the 1890s when funds were desperately low, the occasion became a more formal fund-raising event. In 1896 the homes at Stepney were thrown open to the public for an admission fee of sixpence on Founder's Day and a number of the children repeated the display work from the Annual Meeting at the Royal Albert Hall. Two years later, Founder's Day was transferred to the Village, with drills and exhibitions, tea in the cottages, a bazaar and an evening service. A summer fête is still held there.

All his fund-raising bore his own personal style, sometimes imperious, sometimes jocular but authoritative even when he was pleading. It was Barnardo himself who commanded the respect and the cash from the public. But his almost superhuman efforts to raise funds in the 1890s, the constant speaking, writing, organising, cultivating new friends, cost him dear. He suffered an attack of angina in 1895; when he recovered he still drove himself furiously, seldom leaving his office in Stepney until midnight, living for his work, his 'family'. In 1905, shortly after his sixtieth birthday he died, worn out by years of overwork. To the end he was desperately seeking for new ways to raise more money.

His death in September 1905 released a tidal wave of sympathy and affection from the nation. In the East End his coffin lay in state for three days at the Edinburgh Castle and thousands of men and women filed past for a last look at the street child's friend. On the day of the funeral it seemed as if the whole of the East End was in mourning, with houses draped in black, flags flown at half-mast. Barnardo's empty cab followed the hearse and behind that, in procession, came the top-hatted Council members and senior staff, the veiled matrons and 1,500 boys and girls, marching slowly to the mournful music played by his boys' band.

The Times described Dr Barnardo as 'among this country's greatest benefactors' and both King Edward and Queen Alexandra sent messages of sympathy to Mrs Barnardo. The Queen's message expressed the hope that his work would go on 'as an everlasting tribute to his memory'. With the royal rallying cry in their ears, the charity launched a national memorial fund for a quarter of a million pounds to wipe out the financial liabilities of the homes.

Large funds, with large targets to wipe off debts, rarely succeeded and the fund did not achieve its object. By 1908 only £76,000 had been raised and later the fund petered out. But by strict economies, selling the farm in Manitoba, curtailing expansion and cutting down on some of the more handicapped children, the Council gradually paid off the overdraft.

For a year or two after his death, Barnardo relics became a profitable source of income. Curios and coins collected by Barnardo were advertised for sale, as well as shells, sponges, flint arrowheads, tiger claws, an edition of the *Encyclopaedia Britannica* and a picture of the Magna Carta.

Even the Annual Report for 1904, the last prepared by Barnardo himself, was offered for sale for nine penny stamps. Likenesses of the founder, from postcards at twopence each to fine mezzotint engravings at £1 10s. were also on sale (and one cannot help feeling that Barnardo would have looked benevolently on the enterprise).[19] He would also have been reassured to know that the schemes he had set up with so much care gained in momentum after his death.

For over fifty years in fund-raising, as in child care, the enterprise and personality of Barnardo pervaded the charity. The year Dr Barnardo died a young friend of his on the Council, W. W. Hind Smith, began to visit public schools and colleges to talk to sixth-form boys in schools such as Harrow, Rugby and Marlborough about the 'lost children of England'. Each year he called on more schools and many of them took on the upkeep and training of a 'protégé'. Often the schools undertook the cost of migrating the children and by 1939 well over 350 boys and girls had been emigrated to Canada or Australia through public schools' efforts. Mr Hind Smith remained a member of Council until he died in his eighties.

Effie Bentham, an ardent Christian from the north of England, was another remarkable helper who came under Barnardo's spell in 1892, when she was not yet twenty. Her two younger sisters had joined the newly formed Young Helpers' League and undertaken to organise a sale-of-work in a large hall in their home town of Spennymoor, County Durham. The event snowballed and the younger girls appealed to Effie to take charge, which she did with splendid results. Her success led to a meeting with Dr Barnardo and she soon became an active helper and trusted friend. Just before he died, Effie donated a house, Lincoln Villa, in North Ormsby which was later used as a home for twenty-five girls.

Effie worked as a factory inspector, an unusually practical occupation for a young girl of her day, but she was also given to dreaming dreams and seeing visions. Before Lincoln Villa was officially opened, Effie had a strange dream, three times. In her dream, she was inspecting a local works when she came upon a crowd of workmen surrounding a group of twelve children, black and white, all chained together and screaming for help. Unable to free them herself, she appealed to the workmen who quickly set the children free. Effie's dream bore a remarkable resemblance to Dr Barnardo's when he rescued a drowning boy from the river, helped by nearby children.

She herself was convinced that her dream was a call from God to raise funds, with the aid of the workers. When William Baker, Barnardo's successor, arrived to open the home she had donated, Effie suggested that she should start a fund for the homes, based on a subscription of a farthing a week from working people. The idea appealed to Baker, a religious man himself; he asked Effie to give up a year to organising the scheme. She worked for Barnardo's for over fifty years.

'For many years all Farthing League speakers and office staff were honorary workers,' Effie wrote in her ninety-fourth year. 'I'm sure God led me to found the Farthing League because the first sub Dr Barnardo received was twenty-seven farthings.'[20] Effie's dedication drove her to work with an eccentric fanaticism reminiscent of Barnardo himself. She cajoled, exhorted, prayed for help from management, workers and helpers, her own patent commitment an almost irresistible force. She grudged the merest expense, using scrap paper in the office and old envelopes, even lavatory paper, for her official correspondence, which was lavishly sprinkled with quotations from the Scriptures. Later, a picture of two little mites with the caption 'Two Mites Make a Farthing' was the National Farthing League's emblem. Effie pressed all her contacts into service and expected from them a devotion similar to her own. Bank managers became her honorary treasurers; almost without exception they donated the accumulated interest on monies deposited and forwarded them to her without charge. She saw her Farthing League as a mission from the greatest number of workers to the greatest number of children and could claim, almost literally, that all the money raised went to the children.

Barnardo had encouraged competition between his various funds, printing league tables and charts and encouraging the successful. Before long her National Farthing League had outstripped both the popular Barnardo's Helpers' League and the Barnardo Waif Fund. Like Barnardo, Effie was highly individualistic in her methods. A lady who brooked no interference, she ran her department almost independently of the rest of the organisation. 'God called a man, not a committee,' she would say.

In the beginning, individual agreements from the workers were re-quired. Later, when 'contracting out' became union law, she would still address mass meetings of workers, inspiring them with her fervour. After she spoke to a work force, a motion to join the National Farthing League was proposed and seconded, with an option to 'contract out'. But such was the respect for Barnardo's reputation and the power of Effie's oratory that very few held out.

Not surprisingly, Effie attracted helpers who shared her commitment. Her first assistant, a Mr Williamson, was a railway engineer who had previously worked in Central Africa. After a fearful night in the bush when lions prowled round his frail leaf hut, Mr Williamson resolved to devote his life to good works and as a result joined Effie Bentham's National Farthing League. After the First World War, Effie followed

Barnardo's example by sending a member of staff to Australia to raise funds. The following year, 1920, she called the Empire to service, founding the Australian Penny League. In 1921, with another devoted assistant, Jack Stephen, who subsequently became her deputy, Effie Bentham travelled through Newfoundland, Canada, the USA and Jamaica on a three-year tour, without Barnardo's paying a penny in expenses! The Canadians in particular responded generously in recognition of Barnardo's work in Canada (10,000 workers from the Canadian National Railway gave a dollar each) and the income of the League soared from £33,000 in 1919 to over £46,000 in 1922.

At home, Effie and her workers visited steelworks, dockyards and shipyards, collieries and quarries. At a well-known coachworks in Bucks in 1937, a mass meeting was held in the main road to the accompaniment of passing traffic and itinerant musicians singing to a piano accordion. Every single employee of the factory elected to join the League![21] Through shop stewards, trades unions, works councils and committees, Effie and her helpers pressed their cause, speaking with fervour and ending with a simple heartfelt prayer. Jack Stephen remembered addressing no less than thirty meetings of the different departments of a large engineering works in twenty-four hours.

In 1925, Effie Bentham decided to restore Dr Barnardo's Prayer Union, and to raise money for the homes by winning influential friends and pressing them to become contributors. Her target was to raise £50,000 a year through her Farthing League and £50,000 through bankers' orders from her better-off friends. By 1930, despite unemployment, her Farthing League had reached its target but the new Sunshine Fund supported by influential people never raised more than £3,000 to £4,000.

By the Second World War, when the income of the National Farthing League was threatened by the closure of many inessential firms and factories, factory workers agreed to increase their donation fourfold to one penny a week and the income of the League actually rose from £66,000 in 1939 to £89,000 in 1940, a handsome feat in wartime. Effie finally retired in 1956 at the age of eighty-three and her deputy carried on the League until his retirement in 1963 when it came under the jurisdiction of the General Secretary. By then the League had raised over six and a quarter million pounds in farthings, halfpennies and pennies.

In the 'seventies and 'eighties, decimalisation, takeovers, unemployment and more sophisticated means of paying workers have complicated the work. Nowadays the weekly wage packet is more likely to arrive at the bank in the form of a monthly pay cheque, paid at the dictate of the computer. The miners' strike, redundancies and a shorter working week in many firms made canvassing more difficult for the Industrial Appeals staff. In addition, since the beginning of the decade, a disagreement with NALGO over the recognition of a NALGO branch of Barnardo's and deduction of union dues has led to loss of support from some local authority and hospital workers (Barnardo staff may belong to individual unions but, after a ballot of staff, Barnardo's has declined to be unionised).

Effie Bentham's National Farthing League now deals in millions and the name has been changed to the more accurate and prosaic title of 'The Industrial Fund'. The Industrial Fund is one of the few that permits of forward planning for child care work, with fixed amounts of money promised. Barnardo Appeals staff today are highly trained with their own training courses giving instructions in such subjects as letter writing, efficiency, skills with people and improving management performance. Those were skills that Barnardo himself and Effie Bentham had to learn on the job. They would, no doubt, applaud the energy and initiative of the fund-raisers who today canvass no less than 14,000. In 1986, the Industrial Fund raised two million pounds for Barnardo's.

Effie Bentham's inspiration clearly came from Dr Barnardo. In 1920 his brother-in-law, Harry Elmslie, for many years Chief Steward of the homes, invented another popular fund-raising device. He pioneered the notion of using book matches to promote charity. In the first year over two million 'Barnardo' book matches, produced by Bryant and May, were ordered, a quarter of them by the Young Helpers' League. The booklets contained before and after photographs of the children on the covers (reminiscent of Barnardo's early publicity). Inside, the public were asked to tear off a small sheet and send a donation to the homes. One well-remembered donor sent over £1,000 but, in general, the booklets made only a small profit. The value to the charity in making the name Barnardo known nationwide was, however, incalculable. In the early years, little information was given about the work. From 1922 to 1933, the exhortation appeared on the front cover, 'Is it nothing to all ye that pass by?', accompanied by an appealing 'waif' photograph. Millions of Barnardo matches were produced and, as the founder might have said, millions of lights struck for Barnardo's.

In 1938, when matches had become scarce, the 5,000 booklets available bore a more lighthearted message on the back:

> 'In my life,' Father William replied, with a smile,
> 'I've burnt matches all day with bravado
> And the coins that I gave for the booklet I took
> Helped the children of Dr Barnardo.'

235

Those were the last Barnardo book matches produced until after the war when an order for five million booklets was placed. After the war the moral imperative implicit in the brief earlier messages was tempered somewhat and by the end of the 'forties the words 'Please' and 'Thank You' appeared with brief information about the work of the homes. In 1967 the last photograph of a real Barnardo child appeared on the booklet and that year the Barnardo logo (two children, hand-in-hand, protected by a ring of safety) replaced it. After fifty-six years, the book matches project was reluctantly abandoned in 1976 since production had become too costly.

Barnardo and his followers divided society into rich and poor, into upper and lower classes, for fund-raising purposes and the fund and their helpers took on quite separate identities. The system worked well in the early days but produced difficulties later as society itself changed. Like the National Farthing League, his street collectors were originally intended to draw on the generosity of the working man.

After Barnardo's death, his annual 'Waif Saturday' was renamed 'Barnardo Saturday' to strengthen the connection with the great man. The goodwill and the sound organisation he had built up kept the momentum going and, by 1916, the street collection had overtaken the annual target of £30,000 that Barnardo himself had set. By that time Barnardo's street collections had become flower and flag days (the first was not Barnardo's, it was Alexandra Rose Day, introduced in 1912). Characteristically, Barnardo's used a two-tier system for donors, one for silver, another for coppers; these were either a pansy, symbol of thought (presumably for top-class givers) and a flimsy Union Jack. Eventually, during the war, the system of rank was abolished and the emblem standardised into a flower with a picture of a Barnardo boy in the centre.

Despite the years of depression and growing competition, Barnardo's raised between £40,000 and £50,000 annually in the years between the wars. By 1936, however, the public were beginning to complain about the endless flag days and house-to-house collections and Scotland Yard advised charities with similar aims to combine their street collections. Barnardo's disliked giving up their independence but they joined forces with the principal children's charities, the NSPCC, the National Children's Homes, the Church of England's Children's Society and the Crusade of Rescue, to hold a joint Children's Day. None of the charities lost income from the combination and in 1941, when the King and Queen gave their consent for the fund to be titled 'Princess Elizabeth Day' after their daughter (the present Queen), the royal connection brought an extra £17,000 to the children's charities. (The joint flag day for children is still held twice a year.) By 1961 the Barnardo Day Fund had merged with other Barnardo funds and their staff became known as General Organisers. In sixty-six years the annual income had grown from £203 in 1894 to almost £200,000 in 1960.

To avoid clashing with other charities, Barnardo's decided in 1970 to concentrate their fund-raising efforts into a Barnardo Fortnight, the first two weeks in March. At first the notion was highly successful. In recent years, however, inflation, recession, rising costs and emergency funds, notably for the Ethiopian disaster, have made it more of a struggle for the house-to-house and street collectors to hold their own. In 1981 Appeals Director, Nicholas Lowe, reported: 'For the first time our house-to-house collectors have met with the response that it is quite inappropriate to be soliciting gifts "in times like these".'[22]

The charity has, however, always tried to appeal for money through a dazzling variety of means. From the very beginning Barnardo projected the name and the image of his work upon the public with a clarion confidence. Within a year of starting work he invested his East End Juvenile Mission with a 'history' and his shoeblack brigade with the promise of a mission uniform, badges and a distinctive name. Within three he was selling 'before' and 'after' photographs of his charges and within six he was employing a photographer and assistant in his own Photography Department.

For almost 120 years, through drawings, engravings, sepia photographs, magic lantern slides, silent films, black and white 'talkies' and, today, attractive colour films, magazines, leaflets, books, Barnardo's have presented their story, their history, their personalities. No other children's charity, indeed few other charities, possesses such a wealth of visual, as well as written records, which can be used for education, information and fund-raising. A Barnardo's stand or fund-raising meeting nearly always includes displays, films and videos. Barnardo left a gigantic debt to the charity but he also left an unparalleled legacy. Even today, his own blend of enthusiasm and inspired ambition can infuse a fairly mundane fund-raising gathering with the atmosphere of a revivalist meeting.

In the years between the wars, the Deputation Secretaries helped to drum up volunteers to sell flags in the street to raise money. The 'musical boys', ever popular, gave concerts and in 1936 the senior clergyman in charge of the work introduced mayoral meetings, a useful gathering of local dignitaries which still takes place fifty years on. After the war the teenage 'musical boys' were forced by the raising of the school-leaving age to give up their missionary journeys and to stay on at school.

By the 'sixties, the Deputation Secretaries no longer wielded the same influence and the Department was disbanded.

The link with the churches, however, has never been lost and in recent years thanksgiving services in cathedrals and churches, hymn sing-ins and, above all, the continuing patronage of the dignatories of the Church of England and the Free Churches assure Barnardo's of continuing ecclesiastical patronage.

Barnardo regarded his missionary work with children as a branch of the Christian Church, reproved those in the churches who did not help him as much as he would have liked and yet drew most of his support for funds and fund-raising from them.

Despite all the immense effort and enthusiasm that goes into fund-raising events, over the years the income from legacies has proved most valuable. In 1986 Barnardo's received well over ten million pounds in cash and investments from this source, more than half of all the other money received. The legacies must be a tribute to Barnardo's intensive work over many years to keep their name and reputation in front of the public.

In terms of actual fund-raising, the Trust Department plays a relatively small, although painstaking, public relations role. They keep in close touch with the legal profession and attend Annual Conferences of the Law Society, with a suitably attractive Barnardo stand; they mail Annual Reports and special calendars to prominent legal and church luminaries as well as the trustee departments of all the major banks. In 1934, they also invited solicitors to become honorary members of Barnardo's Association.

The work of the Trust Department involves the stewardship of estates, the handling of wills (the Probate Registry supplies Barnardo's with an extract of any will in which their name is mentioned). They also administer some seventy trusts. Every sort of goods and chattels comes their way from a motor boat, motor cars, paintings, manuscripts, clothes, to the complete contents of houses.

The Trust Officer, Hector Mullens, and his deputy, Martin Runciman, keep black ties in the office, since they are frequently asked to act as Executors, arrange and attend funerals and supervise the upkeep of graves. (In 1983 they sprinkled the ashes of a lady from Tasmania, Australia in Richmond Park, Surrey!) The work of their department rarely gains much publicity. However, in 1986 the Annual Review pictured them with a story about a teenage girl who had enjoyed a holiday thanks to a holiday trust set up through their department. The charity, it adds, prefers trusts designated 'for general purposes'.

Barnardo's also keeps a keen eye on grant making trusts to find funds and bursaries. In 1982 they launched a corporate appeal through personal high level contact with top companies. This has brought in large donations and treats, such as transatlantic flights for some lucky children. (A similar approach was made to wealthy individuals and firms in the 1920s.)

Barnardo himself counted the citizens of the world as his subscribers. 'Many a pound comes quietly and unobtrusively from sheep farms in New Zealand,' he mused in 1885. Correspondents from the Empire and from New Zealand, in particular, sent frequent gifts and their generosity continued long after his death. Year after year, New Zealand would head the legacy list from overseas with Australian bequests coming second. More British than the British, New Zealand had supported Barnardo's since the 1860s. A collection-box for 'Mr Barnardo's Boys' was kept at Fernside Sunday school, Canterbury from 1867 to 1945. When Barnardo founded the Young Helpers' League in 1892 New Zealand ladies all over the islands banded together and gave strong support.

Encouraged by the donations from New Zealand, four intrepid lady workers of the Young Helpers' League set sail from London aboard the SS *Ruahine* on 11 August 1914 after war had started to establish a fund-raising office in New Zealand. A French warship commanded them to stop and a German battleship chased them off Tenerife but fortunately the ladies landed safely in Auckland. In 1915, they established a Young Helpers' League appeals organisation with the Countess of Liverpool, the Governor General's wife, as patron. For fifty years, Barnardo's New Zealand organisation supported the Young Helpers' League. As a result of their efforts, New Zealand sent handsome donations and food parcels to the mother country during the Second World War. In 1918, a number of diligent New Zealand ladies joined the Stitchwell Union and pledged to make four garments a year for Barnardo's and pay a shilling a year in subscription. This modest international scheme produced much goodwill and many useful garments.

By 1967, New Zealand was facing its own economies and social problems and Barnardo's UK was asked to help develop services for children in the dominion. As a way of saying 'thank you' to the hundreds of New Zealanders who had supported the charity for more than fifty-five years, Barnardo's planned and paid for a family care centre in Auckland. The centre, which opened in 1972, comprises a large day unit, emergency overnight accommodation for a family and five flatlets for unmarried mothers. Today, Barnardo's, New Zealand have twelve care centres and provide family support, a foster-care programme and adoption advice.

The scale and vision of Barnardo's work today must owe much to the grandiose plans of the young Barnardo so long ago. However, to achieve his ends he was ruthless and used everyone who came within his ken including the children, to raise funds.

Barnardo had set up his funds and enlisted fund-raisers through appealing to class consciousness. The divide between the education, expenses and social milieu of staff engaged in raising money led to misunderstanding and friction. The county ladies of Barnardo's Helpers' League (fêtes and garden parties) moved in different worlds from the street collectors, the fervent, tub-thumping fund-raisers of the Farthing League. Although they all worked nominally for the same organisation, Effie Bentham and her followers fiercely resisted any interference from any other Barnardo person, even members of Council! When, in the 1930s, two bold lady wardens from the Middlesex Young Helpers' League discovered the names and addresses of the male counterparts in the Barnardo Day Fund (street collectors) and invited them to tea they met with a chilling rebuke. The sexes were segregated and the fund-raisers did not fraternise. Barnardo supporters in the 'thirties and 'forties often discovered that Barnardo functions had different names and different collecting-boxes. They might even be approached to support two different Barnardo events on the same day.

Competition between the funds, used as a spur to success, raged fiercely: 'High pressure persuasion upon the public to help a particular department was beginning to cloud the real issue . . . service to the children,' wrote a correspondent to the staff journal.[23] 'Members of one department "sheep stole" helpers of another department.'

A Co-ordination Committee formed during the Second World War gradually began to heal the rift. By the 'fifties collecting-boxes were standardised, forthcoming events synchronised and subsistence allowances levelled out. By 1961 an Appeals Department absorbed all the fund-raising departments of Barnardo's; as the principals of each department retired, the funds were renamed and revamped.

Barnardo Helpers' League had had its own Advisory Council from the beginning, to share ideas between the different geographical branches and encourage and advise the Young Helpers on ethical questions. Today, the modern Appeals Department has an Advisory Board with similar responsibilities.

In 1973, a hundred years after Barnardo organised his first big shop in the form of a three-day sale at the Edinburgh Castle and invited the public to donate goods, the idea of a Barnardo gift shop was first mooted. No doubt the founder would have applauded the speed and efficiency with which the idea was developed from one rather poky shop selling jumble to the 250 well-lit 'boutique' type High Street shops throughout the United Kingdom that the charity now owns or leases. Barnardo's prefer to buy up freeholds where possible; their architects and building inspectors then convert and improve the properties. However, some of their shops are leasehold and others temporary. Highly organised and rationalised, the Shops Appeal has its own shops' officers and award certificates for good performance. Staff and some 4,000 volunteers are given training in selling, display techniques, operating electronic cash registers and putting across the Barnardo message.

Since Barnardo first bought an East End pub and converted it into a missionary centre, their charity has dealt in property. Throughout his life, Barnardo raised funds to build or convert schools, homes, hospitals, chapels for the children. From 1925 onwards, Barnardo's have had their own Architect's Department. (Today the charity focuses on buying shops rather than homes, since increasingly they help children living with their parents in their own homes.) This year Barnardo's raised over a million through their shops, the latest and fastest-growing appeal. Next year, they expect to double the figure in an operation conducted with a drive and verve worthy of Barnardo himself.

Nothing perhaps has done so much to raise Barnardo's image in the eyes of the public as the royal connection. Barnardo himself fostered the connection with care and named his Children's Hospital in honour of Queen Victoria's Jubilee. The Young Helpers' League enjoyed royal patronage from 1892, when Her Royal Highness Princess Mary of Cambridge, Duchess of Teck, became President, until 1944, when the fourteen-year-old Princess Margaret became President. In 1947, Princess Margaret also became President of the parent body, Dr Barnardo's Homes. After forty years' service, she retired in 1984 but remains a patron: the current President is Her Royal Highness the Princess of Wales. In the space of two years, the Princess has brought a new air of glamour and excitement to Barnardo's.

The contrast of rags to riches, the Princess and the under-privileged child, has the magic of a fairy-tale. Three ex-Barnardo boys have contributed to that Barnardo magic. One is Leslie Thomas, best-selling author, who frequently appeals on behalf of Barnardo's. In 1951, when he was a young reporter, Leslie Thomas described in the Homes' Annual Review the 'rich vein of family friendship' he had found in Barnardo's Homes 'in spite of inevitable knocks'. To this day, Leslie Thomas frequently appeals on behalf of his old 'family'.

Perhaps the most famous Barnardo old boy of all, Bruce Oldfield was abandoned at birth in 1951 and fostered by Barnardo's. Fortunately, Bruce's foster-mother was a dressmaker in Durham who taught him to sew and encouraged his interest in fashion. Barnardo's supported him through art school and in 1974, when he was beginning to make his name as a fashion designer, the charity lent him £500, interest free. He has paid back the loan handsomely. Just over ten years later, Bruce Oldfield staged a fashion show at London's Grosvenor House Hotel in aid of Barnardo's. Over 800 guests sat down at a banquet in the presence of the Princess of Wales and watched a glittering fashion show. The association of Barnardo's President and an extraordinarily talented Barnardo's old boy together with the kind of aristocratic patronage that Barnardo's has always enjoyed produced £106,000. Even more importantly it encircled Barnardo's name in an aura of fashionable glamour and success. In 1986, a third spectacularly successful Barnardo old boy came to the surface bearing splendid prizes. Captain Mike Hatcher, the man who led the discovery and salvage of the Nanking china, auctioned his treasure for record prices and announced his intention of setting up a trust for Barnardo children. In almost 120 years, Barnardo's have produced many worthy citizens and a handful who have made a name for themselves in different callings. None perhaps has caught the public imagination or invoked more generosity and goodwill than Bruce Oldfield and Mike Hatcher.

Like other charities, Barnardo's uses more conventional methods to raise money. They make a vast postal appeal and also sell Christmas cards and gifts through mail order catalogues. When they began selling cards in 1959, their selection showed a markedly religious character: a picture of the Child Jesus; the globe surmounted by the cross; children kneeling together. Today, the cards are the mix of most charities; art reproductions of the Mother and Child as well as seasonal scenes.

Over the years, they have raised money through an inventive variety of schemes: auctions and appeals; flag days and rag days; grand balls and bike rides; carol parties and purses; soccer matches and spell-ins; church services and covenants; food bill funds and festivals.

Although the work has changed profoundly, the public remember with affection the old style Barnardo's occasions like Founder's Day, still celebrated at the Village, and Christmas. In the recent past, Barnardo units and centres throughout the country were swamped with sacks of toys: expensive dolls and legless teddies; cuddly toys and broken games. As Barnardo's no longer care for very small children in homes, their appeals for toys have ceased but the toys still arrive at headquarters. The charity will give a new toy to a needy family or sell the secondhand toys through their shops.

Since the major reorganisation in 1969-70, the Appeals staff work in the regions for regional appeals, close to child care colleagues. They keep abreast with the work either through visits or videos and are able to act as ambassadors as well as fund-raisers for Barnardo's. For, although it is true that the huge sums come from legacies, shops and star-studded events, in the end Barnardo's score because of the immense goodwill from the ordinary man or woman in the street.

At headquarters, staff work hard to ensure that public support. In recent years, they have sponsored a Champion Children competition, mailing 33,000 schools in the country to nominate their children (free of charge) for dance and drama, sports and music or outstanding personal qualities. A prestige luncheon when awards are distributed brings in the funds and the publicity but the goodwill springs from the grassroots. That, and the staff's genuine enthusiasm for their cause are, perhaps, Barnardo's greatest invisible assets.

13

The Years of Flux

'The Barnardo family is not just the children, it is every one of us as well.'

V. L. Cornish, General Superintendent
addressing a Staff Conference, 1965

'Barnardo's has changed from offering a service to everyone, i.e. a service of quantity . . . to a service of quality.'

A Review of Dr Barnardo's Child Care Services, 1968

For the adults who worked for Barnardo's, the 1960s were years of radical change and upheaval. The crisis culminated, at the end of the decade, with homes closing, offices moving, senior staff leaving and a new style of urban social work rising from the debris. Each child who came into the homes, however, saw Barnardo's from the perspective of his own experience.

'You were living in an island of Victorian values,' is how Janet, a dignified black woman in her early thirties, describes her childhood. She was sent to Barnardo's as a baby of three months old and left as a teenager in 1969. Soon after that time, Barnardo's ceased to rear their wards from 'helplessness to independence'. Indeed, 'ordinary children' like Janet, unlucky enough to come from a broken home, seldom spent their childhood in Barnardo's Homes in the 'seventies, as the charity gradually moved to care increasingly for physically, mentally or socially disadvantaged children.

Janet grew up in the Garden City, Woodford Bridge, Essex. Before the war, the Boys' Garden City had housed generations of Barnardo boys in the large community, with its own hospital and school. By the time Janet moved in, the home housed both boys and girls in small family groups of children growing up with houseparents to look after them.

I always loved the Garden City. In the spring, the cherry trees were beautiful. I seem to recall being quite content there. But when other children were visited, I can remember feeling very jealous. When I grew up, there were a lot of children in Barnardo's who stayed only for a short time because their parents were in hospital; they were visited and taken out. We weren't. The long term children were scattered in different houses and baby houses.

One of the myths is that home children were terribly deprived. As children, we had more toys than we could cope with. We had our own swimming pool in the Garden City, our own cinema, films every week and we usually had plenty of crisps and sweets. I remember one of the kids at school making various attempts to pity me and I retaliated by telling her what we had. She was green.[1]

On birthdays the children were allowed to invite up to twenty guests for tea. At Christmas their pillowcases were overflowing with presents. That was one of the few days in the year when rules were relaxed. Janet found the regime very rigid, more like a boarding school than a private home. Although houseparents were called 'auntie' and 'uncle' by the children, she felt no family atmosphere since the home was so large and the population, both staff and children, constantly changing. She felt at the same time both privileged and underprivileged. She realised that Barnardo's was an important charity:

They were intensely religious and very middle class. They were concerned to produce the sort of children who would be models of virtue; they'd kit you out with all the social graces. I don't think Barnardo's ever blamed children; they started from a different assumption. If children were naughty, the staff would assume it was because you had bad blood. They thought of the children as little victims.

They never punished without good cause, but the punishments were very much as God punishes, the wrath was swift, unexpected, not explained. You could be punished for not brushing your teeth, or not cleaning your shoes.

If you said bad words you had to eat carbolic soap. You weren't allowed to waste food and various forms of torture were meted out if you did. If you couldn't eat gristle, for example, you had to stand in the pig bin with your plate in your hand.

Still I was very attached to the place, it was my kingdom, my domain. I'm grateful to Barnardo's for treating children as well as they knew how.

All the long term children in our home were black. People didn't want to foster black children. All the staff were white and I grew up with all-white authority figures.

Barnardo children were intensely aware of not living in a local authority children's home. They felt convinced that their home was superior to Government-run children's homes, that Barnardo children came into the homes because of difficult circumstances, whereas Council children were sent to homes because they were stupid or wicked. Janet's attitude was expressed by a number of Barnardo children who grew up in the post-war years; they may reflect the intense competition between statutory and voluntary bodies at the time. By the end of the 'sixties half of the children in Barnardo's care were referred by 'the Council'.

Until I was eleven, I had no idea about my parents. I just thought some children had parents and some didn't. One day, when I was cleaning my shoes, I was called into the office. I remember they sat me down and proceeded to tell me, quite sensitively, how I came to be there. They told me my mother was married. From then on, it became more and more confusing.

Janet had two brief spells in foster care; both broke down.

I've never really missed a family because staff came and went so rapidly you never had time to develop a close relationship. But I've missed being close to people. Children can sense if they're important to the people who are looking after them. I find it difficult to visualise a close relationship and nowadays I never expect automatic affection.

The day after I left, I went back. They'd let me go on holiday with them that summer (1969) although I should have left at the end of the summer term. I was terrified they'd forget all about me. They had social workers who kept in touch. They didn't prepare one for leaving. The only time I'd cooked was at school occasionally. We had everything done for us.

Janet left the homes in 1969 with two O-levels. She wanted to go on to college, 'I remember being told I wasn't college material.' She took a clerical job and at the age of thirty decided to try to go to university. She is now at London University reading for a degree.

By the 'sixties, it had dawned on Barnardo's, gradually and painfully, that in the eyes of the state they were offering their home children 'second best' beds. Only when it was not practicable or desirable to make arrangements for adoption or boarding-out of deprived children (1948 Children Act) were Children's Officers enjoined to place a child in a home. Barnardo's larger homes, the Garden City (where Janet grew up) and the Village, came in for particular criticism from the Home Office who considered that large complexes encouraged staff and children to be inward-looking. Barnardo's still considered that to break their large homes into smaller units would destroy their community spirit.

From the post-war period onwards, emphasis in child care had increasingly moved from rescuing the deprived or delinquent child from a harmful family or environment, to working to improve family life so that children could remain at home with their own parents. The Children and Young Persons Act, 1963, imposed a duty on Children's Departments to reduce the need to take children into care by giving advice, help and, in exceptional cases, cash to problem families. Unfortunately, the Act did not make any mention of extra resources needed to carry out these duties and many local authorities failed to take up the challenge of the new and demanding approach.

In the early 'sixties the mood was optimistic. For children who could not be satisfactorily adopted or fostered, many Children's Departments set up their own children's homes. The new local authority Child Care Officers were imbued with a crusading spirit, albeit secular; they were eager to rescue the children from institutions. Only one child in five was sent to a voluntary home and institutional care; even an institution with Barnardo's reputation was unpopular. By the 'sixties most local authority children's homes could be found on busy council estates.

At Barnardo's, by contrast, the children lived mainly in large, rambling old-fashioned homes, many of them fifty to one hundred years old. The majority of the staff who cared for them, often with great dedication, were loyal men and women who had come up through the ranks, steeped in Barnardo practice, remote from changing ideas.

With the care of the deprived child now a matter of Government policy, a new urgency was injected into the question. Barnardo's realised that they, too, had to turn aside from their past as the business efficiency experts had recommended. Their report had made it uncomfortably clear that change was inescapable. But any change in Barnardo's was suspect: a challenge to the proud traditions of the past.

Margaret Granowski, now a psychotherapist and social work consultant, joined the staff of Barnardo's as a qualified social worker in 1961; she remembers her induction vividly: 'On my first day at Stepney I was taken to be introduced to the "Doctor". Keys were taken out of a cupboard and a door unlocked with ceremony (and a few giggles). There sat Dr Barnardo at his desk with his ear trumpet.'[2] The waxwork figure of the doctor was still a powerful presence, exerting his influence.

Perhaps that was one of the reasons why change took so long. As early as 1952 the Home Office had proposed a new departure to Barnardo's Chairman, Sir Alfred Owen. He was asked whether he would consider releasing staff to teach child care in underdeveloped countries since Child Care Officers were taking over so much of Barnardo's traditional work. The Council indicated, understandably, that they would prefer foreign trainees to come to Stepney.[3]

Throughout the 'fifties the question of Barnardo's overseas work recurred. (At that stage emigration to Canada had stopped altogether and the numbers of children sent to Australia were dwindling.) Reports from Kenya of hordes of orphan boys roaming wild (and the breakdown of the tribal system) as a result of the Mau Mau uprising called forth Barnardo's sympathy. In Britain they had always been quick to take in stranded children after air-raids or pit accidents.

In 1954, the Colonial Office asked the Save the Children Fund to set up a Kenyan branch and that charity developed a camp for lost boys in a youth park. Late in 1955 a delegation of the Africa Inland Mission called at Stepney to urge Barnardo's help. As a result T. F. Tucker, second-in-command of Child Care, was sent to Kenya to investigate. 'It came as something of a surprise,' Mr Tucker reported, 'to discover that no Mau Mau orphan problem existed.'[4] By the time Mr Tucker arrived the 'lost' boys had either found shelter in the city or remembered kinsmen or tribal chiefs prepared to take them back to their villages.

Mr Tucker did identify the plight of one small group of children rejected by both the African and the Asian communities. These were illegitimate half-castes badly in need of refuge, truly waifs and strays. Under its charter, Barnardo's were and are committed to caring for children of any race or colour. Yet in Kenya, at the time, an unofficial colour bar kept half-caste children out of many schools. Politically and racially the issue was complex.

In London, the Council debated the question carefully. One or two members urged caution, believing, as did some of the staff, that the charity would do better to study new methods and uncover new needs for deprived children at home 'keeping our light ahead of local authorities'. Then came the question of the effect on fund-raising. How would supporters feel, knowing that most of the mothers of the half-caste children were prostitutes and that the 'excesses of the white settlers' had caused the problem? In the end, the spirit of Barnardo himself was invoked and the Council's strong sense of duty prevailed. Despite complex political and racial tensions, Barnardo's decided to help.[5] A married couple, the Reverend and Mrs Lemon, was seconded to work with the Kenya Child Welfare Society 'on our Barnardo principles and doing the work in the spirit of the work in the United Kingdom'. In 1958, after two years in Kenya, the Lemons recommended that Barnardo's should build a multi-racial home where European children could be brought up with normal European standards and 'coloured children on lower European standards so that there can be a process of levelling up'.

Finally, in 1961 Sir Alfred Owen, the Council's Chairman, flew to Nairobi to open Thomas Barnardo House, a small home for thirty children.

The following year, Barnardo's instituted a training course for African students in residential and welfare work with children. Their aim had always been to raise standards of child care. In 1963, the year of Kenyan independence, they also added a nursery wing where students could take a nursery nursing course, recognised by the London-based Nursery Nurses Examination Board. Unfortunately, by then criticisms reached Stepney suggesting that the home was an 'ivory tower largely irrelevant to the needs of large numbers of starving children'.[6]

Thomas Barnardo House, regarded as the most luxurious children's home in Kenya, stood in isolation on the brow of a hill in eight acres of grounds, surrounded by institutions: a prison, an airport and an Army barracks. The only African-style building was the cottage for lower paid residential staff, workmen and gardeners. Standards in the home were 'higher than anywhere else', according to a visiting Barnardo official. Other children's homes in Kenya had floors made of concrete and the staff cooked with charcoal (the cheapest local fuel); in Barnardo's the children walked on lino, tiled or woodblock floors and the staff cooked by electricity. In the new nursery wing, electric floor polishers shone the parquet flooring to a high gloss but the African house boys did not understand the machinery and kept the motors running too long.[7] This kind of problem was symptomatic of the difficulties of imposing Western standards on a Third World country, a mistake made by many planners.

In Britain, Barnardo's were keen to replace their Victorian image in child care circles, and had begun to erect modern purpose-built homes, taking care to ensure that the individual boy or girl had space for privacy and play. In Kenya, they were criticised for just such consideration. At home too, Barnardo's had drastically reduced the household chores expected of the children in post-war years. In Kenya, after independence, when increasingly the children admitted were black and most of them came from villages hundreds of miles from Nairobi, to free the children from household duties was to make it more difficult for them to return home where they would be expected to work in the fields and look after younger brothers and sisters.

Kenyan independence, rapidly changing political conditions, the departure of the Europeans and the Asians, the population explosion and, above all, the new status of the Africans, complicated Barnardo's conscientious and well-intentioned work.

The Chief Medical Officer, Dr Bywaters, visited the home in 1970 and wrote a refreshingly candid report. She found the care of the little ones in the nursery unit too impersonal and inflexible. The staff fed the children but did not eat with them, and spent too much time on tasks such as washing, ironing and cooking which kept them away from the children. Dr Bywaters discovered that all of the seventy-four children were institutionalised and hungry for affection.[8]

She also thought that the children were too isolated from local life; they went to school by Barnardo van instead of public transport, attended the more expensive ex-European schools and were befriended by European adults (many on contract and due to leave shortly).

In the early years children were referred by relatives, the police and other welfare agencies and some curious cases had crept in. 'Some of the older children appear to have relatives who could easily support them,' Dr Bywaters commented briskly. 'It is an anomaly that they remain in the care of a children's charitable organisation.'

Of the seven children who had left Thomas Barnardo House in its nine years of existence, three boys had jobs, although one in the Kenyan Army was waiting for his discharge, one lad was in England living with relatives, two boys' lives were described variously as 'chaotic and very disorganised' and one girl left the home to sing in a night club.

The aim of the small home in Kenya had been to set a standard of child care, but the training of nurses had proved disappointing. More than half of the 120 students had left training without taking their exams and only fifteen had passed them. Employment prospects for trainees were poor since the Asian and European families had moved out and the girls did not want to work for African families.

Dr Bywaters made some radical recommendations. She advocated closing down the nursery nurse training, replacing students with staff and putting the babies in small family groups of mixed-age children. (At home, Barnardo's were closing down residential nurseries, opening day centres instead, since they were convinced that a baby needed the constant care of one person.) Dr Bywaters wanted to see far more flexible and homely care for all the children, and advised that they should mix more with local people and be asked to take on small chores in the home. She recommended appointing a social worker experienced in adoption procedures, and taking in whole families of children wherever possible. She also considered that a plan should be worked out for each child admitted to the home, twice yearly reviews held and fuller and more personal records kept. Her recommendations naturally reflected Barnardo's practices at home.

With all its shortcomings, however, Barnardo's was one of only three organisations taking in orphaned babies in Kenya. In her candid report, Dr Bywaters concluded by paying tribute to the 'very loving care of the staff for the children at Thomas Barnardo House' and added, 'there is a foundation here on which it is possible to build work of real quality'.

Despite its local reputation as a 'luxury home', at £17,000 Thomas Barnardo House had been relatively inexpensive to build. However, running costs were high and local support difficult to attract and the expense of sending staff out frequently (which Dr Bywaters considered necessary) was considerable at a time when Barnardo's were reorganising and changing so greatly at home.

When Barnardo's began their work in Kenya in 1961, the country was still a colony under British sovereignty. With independence, the existence of a children's home built with different standards for European and non-European children and run by a British charity became more complex and anomalous. Discussions on a transfer began in 1970; by 1973, the home was finally handed over to the Child Welfare Department of the Kenyan Government, with a Barnardo subsidy guaranteed for fifteen years.

In Britain, too, changing social conditions in the swinging 'sixties had intensified the need to change. Eager to replace the old 'charity' image, Barnardo's had built modern children's homes 'on stilts' and of glass which aroused sarcasm and suspicion in the old-timers. 'Should Barnardo's seek to purchase Brighton Pavilion as a branch home?' asked one wag at a Staff Conference in 1965. Another Superintendent recounted the story of a boy just returned from holiday with relatives who said he was glad to be back in Barnardo's because it had a bigger television screen. Raising material standards in the homes might make for unfortunate comparisons with homes of private families, some felt.[9]

Now that children were placed near their own homes and relatives encouraged to visit, the clash of standards and of culture complicated the work. Diet, religious observance, material standards and patterns of behaviour differed. In the past, when relatives were kept at a distance and their visits strictly regulated, Barnardo's could uphold absolute standards to the children. Now that was no longer possible.

But it was the question of race and colour, so complex and taxing in Kenya, that could no longer be ignored in Britain. Before the war, the numbers of 'coloured children' (as they were called in those days) were negligible. After the war, Barnardo's began increasingly to admit the babies of English mothers and black American servicemen stationed in this country. The matter was delicately mentioned in the Annual Report of 1951 in the caption to a portrait of a charming little girl: 'When Dr Barnardo was named "the Father of Nobody's Children" the title was never more appropriate than for those little ones in our care of mixed parentage. The bringing up, and more particularly, the launching into life of coloured boys and girls growing up in the homes is a special problem.'

The problem was not, of course, unique to Barnardo's. Other children's homes all over the country were experiencing similar difficulties and for a time during the 'fifties all the welfare agencies seemed only too happy to cover up. Although the 'intractable and unhappy problem' was discussed in Council, no official count was taken until 1955, and no mention of the considerable numbers of new immigrants coming into Barnardo's care appeared in either the staff magazine or the Annual Reviews for years. Only indirectly did the question arise. For example, a Council Minute in May 1959 records the 'considerable surprise' shown by the Townswomen's Guild at the large number of coloured children at Babies' Castle in Hawkhurst, Kent. Unless they were assured that no white child was being deprived of admission, the Guild threatened to withdraw support.[10] About this time, the Superintendent of a branch home with a large proportion of coloured children asked the General Superintendent not to send any more coloured children to her, a request he found 'reasonable'.

When the business efficiency experts questioned staff about the reasons for photographing the children on admission, one answer given was that the photographs would show 'whether a child is coloured and whether its hair is straight or fuzzy or curly'.[11]

By the 'sixties, the numbers of coloured children in the homes could no longer be ignored. They rose from 1,049 (15 per cent) in 1961 to 1,486 (just over 20 per cent) in 1965 and that at a time when the coloured population in the country comprised only 2 per cent of the whole.[12]

Prejudice against the black children, lack of understanding of their background, was predictable, given the rural character of many Barnardo homes and the strict mores of their inmates. 'Staff tended to be less than understanding of the number of children of West Indian origin brought up in the homes,' a former senior member commented carefully. 'They were critical of the high proportion of children born out of wedlock.'[13]

Black children in the homes suffered from the conflict of cultures. One boy was afraid of all black grown-ups, including his own mother, when he left. A black girl disliked going to her mother's house because she couldn't eat the food.

Against this background of prejudice and misunderstanding, Barnardo's set up a high-powered working party to consider the question of racial integration. For an old-fashioned charity, with a strict Victorian code of morality, to make the effort to adapt its standards and outlook to the ideals of a multi-racial society showed courage and vision. Barnardo's has a corporate sense of responsibility which may lie dormant for a time but always reasserts itself with surprising vigour.

In 1965, a hand-picked working party of senior staff, which included two members of the National Children's Home, met to consider the 'care of children of non-European descent'.

For a year the working party interviewed its witnesses: Child Care Officers, representatives of the relevant High Commissions, academics, employers and clerics as well as many of their own staff and children. They wrestled with basic problems: Ought they to take in the children of immigrant mothers living in wretched housing conditions or would it be better for the child to stay with its mother? Was it practicable to bring up children in Barnardo branch homes on the West Indian, African or Asian pattern? Should there be a quota in branch homes (in a nursery home in Derbyshire over 80 per cent of the small children were coloured)? Was repatriation an option? How could fostering and adoption be encouraged? (At the time Barnardo's had arranged for some coloured children to be adopted by white parents.) Would white donors be put off by Barnardo's assistance to so many coloured children?

Underlying the report was the intention of identifying the needs and problems of coloured children and creating a climate of understanding and acceptance. Some of the evidence assembled was disquieting: many foster-parents refused to accept coloured children and those who did were paid an extra five shillings a week for the 'special difficulty'. Extra payment was made for bed-wetters and children with behaviour problems as well. Since foster-parents for coloured children were hard to find Barnardo welfare workers sometimes placed them in foster-homes below standard. Superintendents of branch homes sometimes found visits by coloured parents trying. Certain parents disappointed their children by breaking a promise to visit. Others visited their children 'with a car-load of friends and regard it as a jolly outing for the adults'. Some Superintendents remarked that coloured parents were fault-finding, truculent and obstructive with the staff, encouraging the children to be naughty. Parents were criticised for bringing food which they wanted staff to cook for them and for bringing back their children very late at night and disturbing children already asleep.

In the employment field, the working party discovered that their coloured school-leavers' prospects were bleaker than those of their white children. A few white boys had done outstandingly well in the professions or in business. (At that stage no coloured boy from Barnardo's had achieved prominence or even higher education.) The majority was unskilled and a number ran into difficulties. A sample check of coloured boys who went out to work in 1960 revealed that thirteen out of thirty-nine (one in three) had subsequent convictions. Their difficulties with the law were only slightly greater than the white boys, with sixty-one out of 256 (just over one in four) with convictions.

The report concentrates mainly on the boys who for some reason numbered twice as many as the girls. The only specific reference to girls concerned their hairstyles. 'We heard of cases where coloured girls experienced deep distress and a sense of unacceptability until their hair was straightened.' So strongly did Barnardo's feel on this subject that they recommended that local coloured ladies with successful experience in hair straightening be invited as friends of branch homes to 'come and demonstrate to our girls how this is done'. Superintendents should be authorised to buy the necessary combs and rollers, they advised. It was all part of their effort to integrate the child and seek her happiness, although today that recommendation might be viewed differently.

The report as a whole, the first to consider the needs of deprived black children, was an impressive document and received acclaim in the press and in social work circles. Significantly, it was titled 'Racial Integration'. Barnardo's took the lead in recommending wholeheartedly that their homes should be multi-racial, that more black staff should be employed on an equal basis in their homes and that more education and information be given to their white staff about the children's country of origin, their habits and culture: 'Some of our staff . . . do not make adequate allowances for the fact that until the nineteenth century slaves in the West Indies were legally prohibited from marriage but were, nevertheless, encouraged by their owners to have as many children as possible.'

The working party tried hard to keep a balance: 'We think it desirable that a child should be given the opportunity to learn something about his parents' country . . . but we do not wish him to feel an unrealistic yearning for another land . . . we are emphatic that we should . . . do everything in our power to make these children feel that they belong to British society, which is historically multi-racial.' They resolved that no quota of coloured children should be fixed to any branch (with the Council's proviso that the matter must be kept under constant review). Repatriation 'must never be a way out of our difficulties', they pronounced and they also resolved that their policy should not be influenced by racially prejudiced donors.

Parents were not to be discouraged from visiting branch homes, even if Superintendents found their behaviour inconsiderate. In future, Barnardo's would foster all children, black and white, at the same rate of pay and in the same standard of home; they would encourage coloured families to foster and would look into the question of adoption.

To help coloured children in Barnardo's to face up to prejudice, the subject was to be openly discussed with them. More than half of the coloured youngsters they consulted were 'anti-church and anti-religion', a fact that disturbed them deeply. 'All our children should be brought up in an atmosphere in which they have personal experience of Christian love and come to know of God's acceptance,' the report remarked and included a list of relevant passages from the New Testament.[14] For Barnado's, racial integration was a moral question. Inevitably, the changing of attitudes and of practice, particularly the recruitment of black staff, took a very long time.

However, by 1968 pictures of children in the Kenyan home featured on the front and back cover of the Annual Review. And a significant caption beneath a small black boy's photograph states that 'children of all nationalities belong in the Barnardo family'.

This sense of belonging was one of the most important features of Barnardo home life. That is why those who grew up in them feel so passionately about the homes, with the tangled emotions that all children in all families share. Only, with a corporate identity, there were added layers of feeling, orchestrated by the organisation. Former children retain a sense of gratitude for things done, resentment for missed opportunities, injustice at being in the homes at all and a deep desire to be wanted, appreciated.

Geary, who lives in Edinburgh, came into Barnardo's care as a baby in March 1961 and remained with them until he was eighteen in 1980. 'Barnardo's are my parents,' Geary says today. He was in hospital recovering from a minor illness. A tall, articulate young man, he launched straight into his main grudge:

I wasn't adopted. I should have been, but on the boarding-out form they asked for physical defects. Barnardo's put down 'coloured'. [That process was stopped by the recommendation in the 'Racial Integration' Report.]

My colour was the barrier. I became more dependent on Barnardo's, that's why I became so insecure. I used to break down when families came. I heard the words 'mum' and 'dad' and I was physically pulled towards those people. I would leech on. My nickname was leech. If we ever saw a coloured woman in the street I used to ask if she was my mum. I was always on the eye for sweets being passed round, always asking for money. I pestered them to tell me about my mum, but they never finished the story. My mother was young, still at school when she had me; she was a mere fourteen-year-old. In my imagination she was going to come back when she'd got the money. When I found out my dad was an American airman, I said he was a pilot.

Geary grew up in Scotland in a small mixed home for twenty-six children. He disliked the regimentation of the home with life punctuated with bells and gongs. He remembers being given an orange by the Boys' Brigade. So rare was it for a child to have something of his own that he was immediately suspected of stealing: 'If they thought you'd done wrong they'd clout you and knock you about. If you broke a plate you'd have the money deducted from pocket money and they'd belt you. The social workers would see the bruises on the children.'

In 1974, Geary was transferred to Glasclune, a larger children's home. At Glasclune each member of staff was allocated one child and became that child's 'special person'.

My special person was Eric, the Superintendent. He taught me to drive, brought me out of my shell. I started smoking and skiving when I was quite young. If you got into trouble with the police you knew you were going to get off, 'cause your special person would cover up. I wouldn't allow any close affection. I couldn't accept it. To some people all the staff were mum and dad. I've seen hundreds of people leave Barnardo's and everyone cried. I said 'Thank You' and walked out.

Geary acknowledges the value of Barnardo's after-care. At sixteen after leaving school he lived in a unit outside the main building and received an allowance. He learned to budget for himself and to do his own laundry. At group meetings youngsters were encouraged to discuss their problems, but he was still defiant.

I became such a rebel for a year, I was homeless and skint. Still, where would I be without Barnardo's? If I won the pools I'd give them half the money. They are my parents. I regard myself as Geary Barnardo.

When I was growing up, we were three black children and we stuck together. My aim in life is to have a family, a new generation. I like to think that my own mother is at home round the fire with her children.[15]

Post-war attitudes to child care effectively curtailed the hours of housework children in homes were expected to work. Until the late 'forties, boys as well as girls spent hours polishing, scrubbing and keeping their rooms shipshape.

Though obviously posed, this photograph of the new cottages in Hallow Park, Worcester, shows the more homely atmosphere introduced in the mid-'fifties.

Barnardo fund-raising was always effective, with loyal helpers like these ladies in the 'twenties, a vital ingredient.

Today volunteers are still highly valued but a large professional Appeals Department organises all the work. Even Dr B. was pressed into service recently, looking every inch a showman.

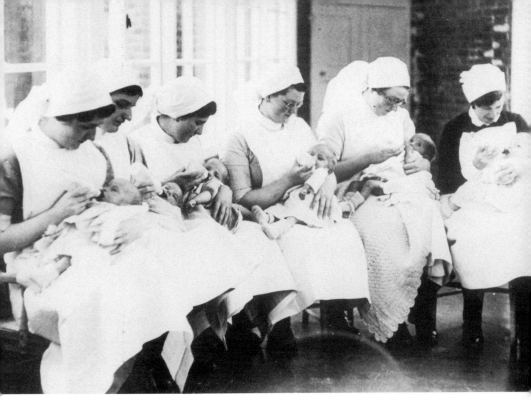

In the 1930s, eighty babies and toddlers under three were nurtured with a careful regime at Babies' Castle in Hawkhurst, Kent. Today the emphasis is on the individual baby and parents who need extra help; Barnardo day centres and support units like this one in Bathgate, Scotland, offer expert advice in a sympathetic setting.

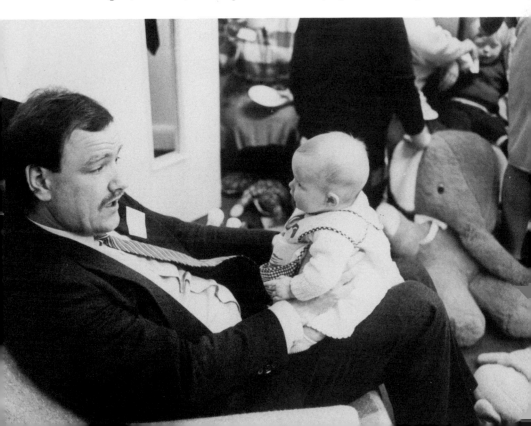

Tea in the garden. Although the little girl on the right is catalogued as Barnardo's grandchild, her appearance suggests that she might have been the Doctor's handicapped youngest daughter, Marjorie Elaine, who was a special favourite with her father. Barnardo treated mentally handicapped children in his care with an enlightened compassion much ahead of his time.

In Liverpool, Barnardo's pioneered a means of caring for severely mentally handicapped children from longstay hospitals in pleasant suburban homes, with a view to restoring them to their parents or arranging fostering.

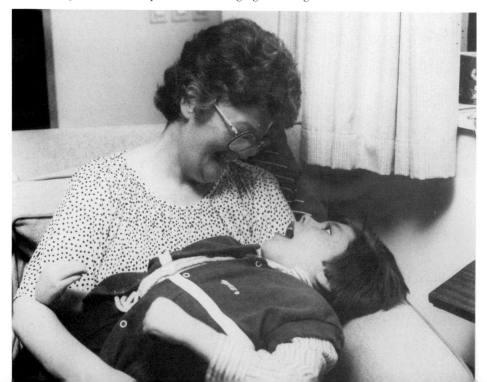

This 1956 photograph of boys and girls growing up side by side in a Barnardo home in Yalding, Kent, represented an innovation at the time. The children lived in a self-contained world; their pocket money ranged from sixpence for the under fives to six shillings and sixpence for the over fifteens.

Today at least two-thirds of Barnardo children come into centres from their own homes. This Intermediate Treatment Centre in Cardiff provides schooling, advice and recreation for troubled teenagers.

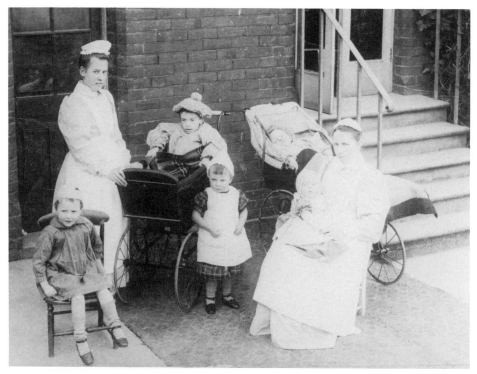

Barnardo children a hundred years ago were far better off than the children of the slums but their care was confined to an institutional environment.

Today holiday play schemes, like this one held near Cardiff, stimulate the children, allow parents a welcome respite and brighten up the cities.

Settling children in new families
is a skilled occupation. Barnardo
social workers help and
encourage prospective 'parents'
for many months before handing
over a child.

In Belfast, Barnardo's works
across the religious divide,
providing care for children and
families from both communities.

Barnardo's today operates from eight divisions throughout the country. Projects and personnel differ from city to city and from family to family. Yet all would agree that, for disadvantaged families, learning to play is an important part of the help provided.

Royal encouragement from Barnardo's President, H.R.H. The Princess of Wales, to an aspiring young cook at The Princess Margaret School for Physically Handicapped Children, Taunton.

Despite his difficulties, Geary now holds down a job as a cab driver for the disabled, and keeps in touch with Barnardo's, a tribute both to the charity and to their charge.

In Scotland, Barnardo's had specialised in the care of disturbed children. By the mid-'sixties, they were increasingly concerned about the number of boys and girls whose families had been allowed to disappear completely. In 1966, senior staff began to look into the home background of all 210 children in Barnardo homes, schools, and nurseries in Scotland, tracing and contacting parents.[16]

A happy ending was by no means inevitable. After years of absence parents often felt guilty and children disillusioned but the Scottish staff clung courageously to their belief that it was 'deception and not reality that does irreparable damage to children'. Some reunions were difficult, even harrowing. After careful preparation on both sides, the teenage daughters of a man in prison for murdering his wife were taken to see their father. (He was a physically small man who, for years, had been dominated and provoked by the girls' mother.) That was no fairy-tale reunion, but the girls were given the chance to come to terms with their real situation and to reveal their true feelings about their parents. The girls continued to visit their father with a social worker and gradually a fragile bond was formed. Scotland was working in the best traditions of Barnardo's. It was their creed that the charity should never give up on a child, no matter how difficult, and in the 'sixties that philosophy began to include the child's family.

For many Barnardo children, the 'homes', loved or hated, represent a constant in their fragmented lives and any form of change in buildings or methods of care is regarded with suspicion. Throughout the 'sixties, Barnardo's at Stepney were battling with desires to preserve the past and move with the times.

Most of the Council and many staff suspected change. At the close of 1959, S. J. Noel-Brown, the company appointed to survey the organis-ation and methods of headquarters, had presented their report. Broadly speaking the business consultants advocated uniting the different sections of the Appeals Department and devolving the Child Care side. The Council was concerned that the Christian work with children might suffer as a result of reorganisation and was also determined to protect staff from redundancy. In November 1959, members resolved not 'to make any major change affecting the principles of our work before January 1961'. That was the date when E. H. Lucette (General Superin-tendent of Barnardo's for twenty-two years) retired. He was replaced by his second-in-command T. F. Tucker, another stalwart who had served the charity for eighteen years.

The matter of long service and of long memory was of some importance. On the Council at the time one senior member had served for over fifty years, two others for more than thirty years and all three were members of the influential Committees of Management and of Finance. A 'kindly muddle' was how one former staff member described Barnardo's of the 'sixties.

The logic of the situation, however, demanded radical change. There was less need for Barnardo's traditional care for children. Many local authorities had now built their own children's homes for 'normal children' and the emphasis in professional circles was increasingly to help families and so prevent children from coming into care, or to take them in for short periods. Even in Barnardo's, the average length of a child's stay, which twenty years earlier had been seven years, was now reduced to just under three years. The numbers of boys and girls in their homes were gradually decreasing as also were those referred privately by parents, guardians or moral welfare agencies. The kind of children that local authorities referred to homes or schools were often emotionally disturbed or severely handicapped (they had three thalidomide babies in 1963) and needed special care, a special environment and specially trained staff.

At the time, Barnardo's were short of specialised care and reluctant to undertake it. Any development of experimental work (with severely handicapped and disturbed children) could only succeed if 'we maintain the structure of normal work', Mr Tucker declared in 1961. Normal, in Barnardo terms, meant bringing up boys and girls in Christian homes, just as they had done for almost a century. Their principal care in the early 'sixties was the spiritual work, and taking in unfortunate ineducable (mentally subnormal) children would mean a considerable outlay on new homes with special facilities. Although the Council agreed in principle upon the need, they were slow to act.

The Council was, however, concerned to give the homes a face-lift. Many of the buildings were fifty to one hundred years old and badly in need of rebuilding or refurbishing. The centenary was to be held in 1966, with the date hallowed in Barnardo folklore. With this in view, the Council had agreed on an ambitious and expensive building programme. Twenty Barnardo homes were to be rebuilt on new sites from Eastbourne in the south to Balerno in Scotland at an estimated cost of £600,000.[17]

'No longer will our children live in lovely mansions that bear no sort of resemblance to the kind of places in which they will live when going out to work, but in modern type houses or flats – perhaps some ultra modern types that will fit them for contemporary living,' the Annual Report pointed out. Despite the optimism, the buildings were planned for 'normal' children and did not allow for the fact that Barnardo's would be working with a different type of child and needing a different type of home. By 1972, only four of the original homes were in use. Bricks and mortar alone were not the changes needed to revitalise Barnardo's.

By 1963, staff and offices did move into three regions and a further division of the work was implemented. The three existing regions, North and East, West and Wales and Southern Region, were subdivided into three and Area Offices were set up in Exeter, Guildford, Liverpool, Tunbridge Wells, York and Worcester. Scotland and Northern Ireland had been more or less autonomous since 1947 and had their own offices in Edinburgh and Belfast. The new structure meant that senior staff were more closely in touch with the children in homes and foster-homes and with those responsible for their welfare, as well as the local authorities. Barnardo welfare workers still worked from their own homes. They were sent a filing cabinet and a table and they collected the children's files from the Area Office. The social workers looked after the children's after-care, helping them to get jobs and lodgings and introducing them to the local vicar. But to be admitted all new children had to come to Stepney where the mysterious black folder containing their history would be numbered. Officers at Stepney still took charge of the Village and of special homes and schools all over the country, as well as the migration and adoption. Despite attempts to streamline, Barnardo's administration remained extremely complicated.

Barnardo's had always been a law unto itself, engrossed in its own myth and given to pronouncing on moral questions (the standard of television programmes particularly concerned them in the 'sixties). The Council was very wary of any sort of Government intervention. Gradually, however, with new Council members joining Barnardo's, and a new man in charge of Child Care, in 1964 the charity began to face up to some of the drawbacks of their Victorian heritage. A regime now out-of-step, antiquated buildings and increasingly difficult children, bedevilled Barnardo's in the homes.

At Parkstone Sea School in Bournemouth, a naval training school since 1919, with a lieutenant-commander in charge, numbers of pupils were falling, and only half of the boys went on to a life at sea. Parkstone lacked modern educational facilities and in the summer of 1964 the school was closed.

Goldings in Hertford, the technical school founded in 1922 to replace the Stepney workshops, illustrates another of Barnardo's difficulties at the time. Although two new wings were opened by Princess Margaret in 1961, and another by Sir John Hunt in 1965, the school closed in the spring of 1967. The official release gave the reason as declining numbers, principally because Barnardo's aimed to keep boys close to their own

families. The recently retired headmaster, R. F. Wheatley, took issue
with that statement in the final edition of the school magazine, *The
Goldonian*. He suggested that a more likely reason was the high cost
of running Goldings and the 'inadequate state of the buildings'. A
nineteenth-century mock Tudor mansion, Goldings stood in beautiful
parkland but the 'dining arrangements for boys have never been such as
to prepare them for taking meals in a private house'. In the 'sixties,
according to Mr Wheatley, the type of boys admitted to Goldings had
been emotionally disturbed youths from broken homes; it was not until
the spring of 1966 that houseparents and teachers qualified to care for
difficult boys had been appointed.[18]

When, despite staff protest, Goldings closed, the Council decided to
honour the commitment to the twenty-three apprentices and to keep on
the printing school. Barnardo's printing school in Hertford still exists
and many of Barnardo's publications are printed there.

The public had little idea of the realities of Barnardo life. In 1965
less than half of the 8,000 children advertised as being in Barnardo's
care actually lived in Barnardo homes; the majority lived with their own
mothers or with relatives or foster-parents, with the support of Barnardo
social workers. That work received little prominence in Barnardo publicity. Annual Reports gave the impression that the main purpose of Dr
Barnardo's Homes was to bring children up – in a home.

The new Superintendent, V. L. Cornish, was, however, not content
to trade on past glories: 'Nobody owes Barnardo's a living,' he was prone
to say. Perhaps no loyal long term employee, steeped in tradition,
could have steered Barnardo's on a new course. Like many senior staff
members, Mr Cornish came to Barnardo's in 1963 from a background
of colonial administration. Crisp, clear, kindly, he was concerned from
the outset to set Barnardo's work against the national background of
care for deprived children, certain that Barnardo's should not merely
duplicate the work of local authority Children's Departments but find a
new means of caring for deprived children.

Some of the charity's time-honoured nostalgia was swept away with
the new broom. To correct the impression that Barnardo's were only
concerned with children in residential homes, the title was changed on
1 January 1966 from Dr Barnardo's Homes to Dr Barnardo's. Up to
1966, the telegraphic address had remained the splendidly emotive
'Waifdom, Ever Open Door'; that, too, was sobered down.

As soon as he became General Superintendent in 1964, Mr Cornish
had set about reviewing Barnardo's position in order to set a course for
the future, with committees and working parties on procedure, race,
boarding-out. A tremendous flurry of paper memoranda, minutes,

memos flew around headquarters and the regions. From the beginning Barnardo's had conducted its affairs in an atmosphere of intense secrecy. (The very first Executive Committee resolved on procuring a locked Minute Book and cabinet file or chest of drawers with a good lock and seven keys.)[19] Now, in 1964, the Minutes carried an extra warning against breach of confidentiality. Senior staff and Council members met separately and together in privileged seclusion as change and rumour of change infected Barnardo's. In the lower echelons, staff sensed the new mood and pondered anxiously on its implications.

In the spring of 1965, a year after his appointment as head of Child Care, Mr Cornish issued a courageous policy statement. In it he praised the work of the local authority Children's Departments who had opened many children's homes and questioned the need for Barnardo's to overlap or merely fill in gaps. Should not Barnardo's, he asked, 'concentrate an increasing proportion of its resources on meeting new and hitherto unmet needs?'

To disarm his critics, he demolished two favourite arguments against change: firstly, that Barnardo's had had longer experience in residential work than the new Children's Departments and, secondly, that they had a stronger Christian basis to their work.

Mr Cornish asserted that the work of Children's Departments was 'improving and is in some cases better than ours'.[20] To compare Barnardo's unfavourably with any other child care agency had been up to that point almost an act of lese-majesty in the charity. But Mr Cornish went further. He pointed out that Barnardo's lagged behind local authorities in the employment of trained staff. As to the Christian influence, 'it must be accepted that a great deal of sound Christian training does go on in many local authority homes and foster-homes'. After all, he argued, Barnardo's now employed staff from local authorities and they had demonstrated their Christian convictions and support of Barnardo principles. He proposed, therefore, that Barnardo's should run down the branch homes and pioneer new work for children with the help of a new Department of Research and Development. The Council approved the paper and the charity was committed to change course. Indeed, at the Staff Conference of 1965, the Chairman, Sir Alfred Owen, stated publicly that the mantle of leadership now fell upon Mr Cornish, with the Council supporting him whenever they could. The following year, the Annual Report looked forward to reducing some parts of Barnardo's child care and developing work for physically handicapped, educationally subnormal, maladjusted and emotionally disturbed children.

All the changes in administration of those years were designed to take account of the children as people in their own right rather than little strays to be rescued and reformed. In the past, destitution or moral danger had been the criteria for admission. Over the years, the definition of destitution was modified as pensions were introduced for war orphans and widows; small payments were made either through those means, from custody orders or, occasionally, from Boards of Guardians (parish authorities). After the Second World War, parents who wanted to send their children to Barnardo's were assessed on their financial position, with other factors such as health and stability of character taken into account.

By 1967, the focus was child-centred. Only if admission to Barnardo's was 'the best possible thing for the child' and the child was kept close to family and childhood surroundings would admission be granted. Parents who sincerely wanted their children to be placed in Barnardo's care received special consideration, as did children with complex, deprived backgrounds, boys and girls born as a result of rape, incest or extra-marital or pre-marital unions. 'Compassion and tradition require that we do not lightly turn a child away.'[21]

Until 1967, a Barnardo rule insisted that Superintendents were not allowed to pass on the children's histories to their staff. This meant that houseparents, the people closest to them, behaved as if the boys and girls had no past before Barnardo's. The secrecy, intended no doubt to protect the most vulnerable from gossip, tended in practice to depersonalise the children and to reinforce the 'Barnardo' identity.

A former social worker from Scotland remembered:

We tended to lose parents with great facility; it was seen as better for the child. The idea was that you always protected children from things that made them unhappy. If you didn't put ideas into children's heads about their past, then they wouldn't remember. We didn't have enough staff to handle children who had tantrums or wet beds. They were supposed to be ideal little children. They always had their photographs taken at meal times or tucked up in bed with a teddy bear.[22]

Senior staff at Barnardo's now recognised the dangers of denying the past: 'It is damaging to a child if a shutter is closed on the past. Residential staff may say: "How well that child has settled, she never talks about her home." Unwittingly they entered into a conspiracy of silence about the past and continue to repress all that is really important . . . not only the facts but her feelings about the past.'[23]

Carol McAllister, sent to the Girls' Village Home at the age of five in 1952, suffered from just such a cut-off from her past. Although she occasionally heard from her family in Ireland, the address was removed from the letters. In 1957, at the age of ten, Carol was fostered by a family in Suffolk. 'They were an elderly couple, quite warm and affectionate, but I had to call them "Mum" and "Dad" and that was hard, because I was always wondering about my own family. I had an insatiable longing to know about them. To this day I'd like to know the colour of my Dad's eyes.'

Carol could not bring herself to call her foster-parents 'Mum' and 'Dad' and that became an issue. A Barnardo social worker, who used to visit every six months, took Carol out for a meal and tried to resolve the problem. But her foster-mother could not accept being called 'auntie' and Carol could not compromise.

'They tried to make me and I was very unhappy . . . People always think they can manipulate a child in its ways and ideals. But basically they were a good family and very affectionate. I'd never had a cuddle in the homes and I was terribly embarrassed at first.'

Carol left that family when her foster-mum's father was ill and Barnardo's tried unsuccessfully to find her new foster-parents. She stayed in the Village at Barkingside and had a happy time during her teenage years.

We had marvellous meals, plenty of fruit, we were better off than most families. Every year we'd go away for holidays, sleeping in church halls, in sleeping-bags. But I didn't like Christmas. You never got what you really wanted. You never got a present that somebody had chosen with a really personal interest. It sounds silly, but I'd always wanted a teddy. There were cottage teddies and general toys in the locker but I'd never had my personal teddy and when I was twenty-one my husband bought me my own teddy as a present. My daughter's got it now.[24]

When she was sixteen Carol was told, to her amazement, that she had two sisters living in Ireland. Barnardo's paid her air fare to visit her mother, who had been ill, and her sisters. By then it was almost too late.

It didn't mean very much after all those years. My mother looked far older than her years and she had a vacant look about her. I think she was totally oblivious to who I was. She went to shake hands with me. My sister gave me a cuddle and wept a few tears and that felt more real. I stayed at a children's home in Ireland and I couldn't wait to get back to Barnardo's.

All in all, I think they took very good care of me. When I left I lodged nearby with Auntie Rose, a cleaning lady who worked for Barnardo's. I've been back there to work and I've fostered a child for them for three years. But nowadays I don't need the security of going back. I've no regrets about living in Barnardo's but I do regret the fact that they split our family up.

The working parties, the committees, the endless meetings did have real meaning in children's lives. By the late 'sixties no girl, however sad her history, would ever be in ignorance of her family and no boy would be labelled 'black or coloured'.

Throughout the 'sixties, Barnardo's were constantly reassessing their role. In the early days, stray children had been rounded up by Barnardo himself and as the homes grew in reputation and respectability, referred by clergy, magistrates, welfare workers, parents and guardians, concerned that children should have a home and a Christian upbringing. With the 1948 Children Act, the duty to care for deprived children became a state responsibility and voluntary societies acted as the agents of local authorities. The number of 'private' children had fallen steeply from 1948 to 1967 and the number of children in Barnardo's paid for by the local authorities had climbed steadily. By 1967, well over half of the children in Barnardo homes were council children. Without them the homes would have had to close. From 1962 to 1967 the numbers of children 'in residence' in Barnardo's had dropped by 500, a clear sign that the charity had to change course.

Since 1965, Mr Cornish and his staff had been preparing for the change by gathering information and assessing the child-care scene. Barnardo's work in child care took place against a background of divorce, rising illegitimacy, a bulging baby population and a mood of social unrest. The new pop culture gripped the teenage generation and heroin came on the scene in the late 'sixties. With more schoolgirl mothers, with restless youngsters drifting into the cities, with more severely handicapped babies surviving due to improved post-natal and surgical techniques, the demands on those caring for children became increasingly complex and diverse.

One area where Barnardo's had been falling behind was in the care of babies and toddlers, housed in residential nurseries. 'Self-respecting local authority children's departments were closing their residential nurseries mindful of the harmful effects of institutional care in the 1950s,' wrote the present Senior Director.[25] Barnardo's, by contrast, was still opening and building new ones in 1967.

To pave the way for change a fact-finding survey of sixteen Barnardo nurseries with a population of 432 babies and toddlers was carried out.

The fundamental question asked in the survey was: did the Barnardo nurseries meet the needs of the small children deprived of mother and home life? Over half the Barnardo babies came into the homes before their first birthday and were looked after by a succession of nursery nurses in training and the survey hinted that, despite devoted care, the babies might be emotionally deprived.[26] At the same time, the Barnardo Council made a grant to Professor Jack Tizard and his wife, Dr Barbara Tizard, to research into the development of the pre-school child in care. Two other children's societies were also involved but Barnardo's was the principal sponsor. By the 1970s, the residential nurseries were at last phased out.

To take stock outside Barnardo's was the next step. Mr Cornish asked the Home Office Inspectorate to help him to assess Barnardo's work in the context of the needs of all the deprived children in the country. Through Home Office eyes, Mr Cornish and his deputy, Miss Roundell, looked dispassionately at the large Barnardo homes for children sited mainly in scenic areas in the prosperous south, and at the greatest centres of need for deprived children: the inner cities. 'The two maps didn't match,' explained Douglas Smyth who was a Home Office official at the time.[27]

By April 1968, Mr Cornish with Miss Roundell had produced 'The Review of Child Care and Special Education Services in the UK and Republic of Ireland', outlining the new directions in which the charity must move.

About the same time, Barnardo's were due to leave their familiar grimy headquarters in Stepney, another wrench with the past.

Although many of the arguments had been heard, in Council, at Staff Conferences, and in policy documents, the extent of the changes only gradually dawned on those involved.

Mr Cornish had planned his strategy for child care to provide help where it was needed, taking into account the provision of Children's Departments and other voluntary societies. He had paved the way for co-operation in the future.

The nub of his argument concerned the need for Barnardo's to site their work where need was greatest. By 1968, the charity was spending over a million pounds for child care work in the south and less than a third of that figure in the north. The new review planned a deliberate removal of many Barnardo services from outer London, the Home Counties and the south-west to the industrial midlands and the north. The shift away from the affluent south towards the midlands and the north, he stated boldly, 'may cause a fall in financial support' which would necessitate a contraction in child care operations. This was revolutionary. Since the first home in 1870, the emphasis had always been on expansion.

Barnardo's other priority was to specialise according to local need, to move from considerations of quantity of children to those of quality of service. For all ages, from babies to school-leavers, changes in methods would be necessary. Nurseries would develop day-care and informal teaching groups for mothers. The charity would increasingly provide for mentally and physically handicapped as well as difficult and disturbed children. Branch homes would become more flexible with an increase in day care, play centres and holiday homes.

Whether anyone, even the author of the report, realised just how radical the changes would have to be seems doubtful. To implement them would mean children leaving, staff losing their jobs, homes closing and properties, funds and popularity threatened in the short term. (Sometimes, as in the case of closure of the sea school at Parkstone, it was necessary to honour the terms of a trust by opening a similar 'character-building' programme. Two small adventure training courses, one in Scotland and one in Wales, were started in the late 'sixties with that aim.)

In the homes, staff particularly felt threatened and insecure with so much change in the air. Council members, too, were filled with uncertainty as they realised the implications of reorganisation. To one or two with homes in their neighbourhood, it appeared that Barnardo's were going downmarket, from the squirearchy to the slums. From caring for babies in loving batches and catering for childhood in structured stately homes, the charity would move to planning programmes with parents and children, giving short-term care to problem children in specialised units and day centres, moving from the scenic south to the concrete jungle of the inner cities.

Perhaps most agonising of all was the sense, in some members of Council and some Superintendents of branch homes, that the children were slipping away. Barnardo's would no longer have the all-powerful, benevolent paternalism and missionary control over young lives. As Sir Arthur Smith, an upright gentleman and ardent Evangelical, remarked in Council, 'it was in the Residential Homes that we had been able to do our greatest Christian work'. To some Barnardo loyal supporters, it seemed that not only were children's homes to be moved and closed down after years of devoted service but a whole way of life was closing down.

For Nan Fyfe, a former teacher who joined Barnardo's as a welfare worker in 1967, the charity seemed a world away from everyday life. 'Barnardo's was highly secretive; it was rather like getting into a monastic order. You always had a feeling they were looking over your shoulder. It was almost as if God ran the organisation.' She was interviewed first by Miss Dyson, a professional social worker, then by the Chairman, General Sir Arthur Smith.

> He was a very deaf gentleman and he had a stick. He kept poking me with it.
> 'Are you a Christian?'
> 'Yes.'
> 'Would you be prepared to take tracts to meet a need if someone is in difficulty?'
> 'No. I wouldn't go out to evangelise. I hadn't conceived of it in a social work job.'
> 'Well, missy, you'd better have a word with Miss Dyson.'[28]

Nan Fyfe got the job as social worker at £870 a year and stayed with the charity for twenty years. But the attitude of the Chairman and a number of like-minded colleagues on the Council, sincere both in their Evangelical faith and in their concern for deprived children, sometimes made for difficulties both in recruiting professional staff and in effecting change.

Unfortunately the upheaval in the 'sixties took place against a background of a divided charity. Since Barnardo's day, the charity had been split into those who raised the funds and those who spent them. Over the years, there had been a rivalry and a lack of understanding which grew into enmity in the 'sixties. As child-care staff became trained professionals rather than devoted helpers, they distanced themselves from the fund-raisers, speaking in professional jargon and keeping themselves apart. They were at pains to separate their children from any hint of 'exploitation'. Barnardo rallies and fêtes at the homes had been a tradition; children slept in beds with donors' names framed above them. Frequently, posters asking for help for charity were pasted on the walls and always a photograph of the founder. To conduct their campaign successfully, fund-raisers tended to emphasise the wretchedness of the children and the need to 'rescue' them from wicked parents. The new social workers mistrusted this approach.

The General Secretary responsible for Finance and Fund-Raising, Mr Potter, a chartered accountant, held considerable influence; he was the opposite number to the General Superintendent in charge of Child Care, Mr Cornish. He had been with Barnardo's for twenty-five years when Mr Cornish arrived. Much respected in the charity, he had played a valuable part in building up Barnardo's finances. After the Second

World War when new homes were needed, Mr Potter always insisted on purchasing the land adjacent and that land has proved a magnificent asset. He also had influential friends in the City and in the legal profession and his groundwork helped to increase legacy income. Mr Potter had also played an active part in the child care policy as well as in financial matters and had been Chairman of the organisation of Chief Children's Voluntary Societies, the national association of children's homes. Until Mr Cornish came, he was regarded virtually as Barnardo's personified, lobbying in political matters and acting as spokesman. He lunched weekly with the Chairman and had his ear. Mr Potter also had a close relationship with several Council members and could recall the days when individuals from Council had helped with private staff problems out of their own pockets. When Mr Cornish came into office, he was warned: 'Don't let Potter bounce you.' Inevitably rivalry and mistrust grew between the new reformer and the long-serving head of finance.

To this day the participants in the struggles of the 'sixties are somewhat at a loss to explain the hurts and passions aroused inside Barnardo's. The roots lie partly in the idealism of all concerned, partly in the structure and partly in the adulation paid to half-understood traditions. For example, in 1960 Mr Potter had been appointed 'Chief of Staff' in succession to Mr Lucette who was in charge of Child Care. The title, to describe a general administrator, dated back to Dr Barnardo's day.

After Barnardo's death, the Chief of Staff became the 'Secretary to the Managers', 'a title apt in its vagueness' and puzzling even to senior staff in the 1930s.

By 1947, the title 'Chief of Staff' was revived but with the head of Child Care in that post. In 1960, Mr Potter became Chief of Staff. His duties included resolving the differences between heads of departments and calling joint staff meetings on matters of policy, a kind of ombudsman. Although, on his appointment it was expressly stated that this in no way altered the relationship between the General Secretary (Mr Potter) and his opposite number, the General Superintendent (now Mr Cornish) and the Council, understandably Mr Potter came to see himself as the key figure in Barnardo's.

The Finance Committee was trying to build up Barnardo's finances, encouraging the charity to invest wisely, urging fund-raisers to become cost-effective. The Finance Committee and Mr Potter were on one side and the Management Committee and Mr Cornish on the other. Staff and Council were split between the two camps. Child Care staff were barely speaking to their colleagues in Appeals and certainly were not prepared to allow them to see their work. Fund-raisers were frustrated and annoyed. Yet everyone, from the Chairman of Council to the cleaners in the homes, worked with tremendous commitment 'for the sake of the children'.

John Hillyer, still a member of Barnardo's Council, eventually proposed that an Executive/Finance Committee be found to bridge the division. That is the system today.

By the time Mr Cornish's revolutionary 1968 report on the new Barnardo's came out, Mr Potter had retired and a new General Secretary, Mr Peter Hunt, had taken over. At first, he welcomed the changes and was confident that all would be well, given the 'fantastic goodwill of the public', although he recognised, a little ruefully, that teenage hostels did not have such a 'romantic appeal' as babies' homes. However, he was convinced that child-care staff and fund-raisers would get to know and understand each other better as a result of the new methods.[29]

In the event the proposed reforms produced the opposite effect. For five years, from its appearance in 1968, Barnardo's seethed with insecurity as homes moved or closed down, staff were made redundant and senior officers resigned.

The need to improve staff morale was urgent and in 1969, Douglas Smyth, the Home Office Inspector who had helped Mr Cornish to plan the changes within Barnardo's, was asked to explain the purpose of the reorganisation at a Staff Conference.

> Superintendents realised that homes would be closing, matrons understood that their nurseries would be shut. But what would it do to their kids? Their schooling? This was a tremendous upset but there was a very fundamental feeling that painful though it was for them, if it was right for Barnardo's, they must go along with it. There was a missionary zeal about it all, which was commendable but at the same time rather frightening.

A detailed plan for the reorganisation of the Child Care Department was prepared by a staff working party in 1969. Both Child Care and Appeals staff were to work from offices in urban centres, throughout the country. Unfortunately for Barnardo's there were interminable delays; they were attempting to settle into new regions and open new work programmes in 1969, at a time when a great upheaval was taking place in social services throughout the country. The Children and Young Persons Act of 1969 introduced a new approach to emotionally disturbed and delinquent young people summoned before the courts and called for treatment rather than punishment. The old Approved Schools were transformed into Community Homes with Education and required to admit emotionally damaged as well as delinquent children. 'Intermediate treatment' was developed as an alternative to residential treatment for the latter. Within the new framework, Barnardo's had to decide on the status of its own homes and former Approved Schools and to consider whether they would join the scheme or remain outside it as registered voluntary children's homes. New Regional Planning Committees were to be set up to assess the needs of all deprived and handicapped children all over the country in order to plan residential and other care.

As a result of two important Government reports, the Redcliffe Maud Report and a planned reorganisation of the social services (the Seebohm Report), new boundaries for local authorities and a new role for social workers within those authorities further complicated the picture. They made it extremely difficult for Barnardo's to plan carefully in localities where so much was uncertain.

Meantime, the fund-raisers, the public relations staff, the architects were becoming increasingly irritated by the endless uncertainty, which entailed loss of revenue and public support. The Finance Committee chafed at the endless delay due to the 'everchanging ideas of modern child care'. They were plagued by the feeling that Barnardo's were always 'waiting for some report from some expert'. Gillian Wagner remembers that when she joined the Council, Mr Cornish remarked: 'There is blood under the carpet in Barnardo's and nobody has noticed.'[30]

A decision to work with mentally handicapped children, 'sub-normal but trainable', was taken in October 1970 by the Council. Not since the nineteenth century had Barnardo's admitted severely mentally handicapped children. The proposal heralded important change but first the crisis had to be resolved.

The Council was concerned to protect the reputation and future of Barnardo's, anxious about the loss of public support and the tension inside the charity. The staff came to doubt and to ask themselves painfully whether parts of their work, far from saving the children, might have been damaging. Appeals staff felt excluded from the new developments and the Child Care side were concerned to wait for the right moment to open new projects, explore new possibilities to build for the future carefully.

In the end, the Council decided early in 1970 to consult yet another team of management consultants to look into the structure of Barnardo's and the relationships between Council, committees and senior staff.[31]

Every Monday afternoon, the Council met to try to resolve the crisis of confidence inside Barnardo's. They spent hours poring over reports, telephoning, taking time off from their offices, businesses and families;

they even spent a weekend in Windsor together in an attempt to find a solution.

Mr Cornish urged the staff to welcome the forthcoming report of the management consultants as a 'medical check up'[32] but wrote more forthrightly in his report to Council: 'For too long Barnardo's has been a house divided and has paid the price ... in terms of poor communications, confusion and friction.' He criticised the Council's policy of 'divide and rule', and suggested that it might be a defence against their own lack of clarity.[33] He also expressed the hope that in the future Council members would not be involved in 'the kind of executive functions which are more appropriate to the professional staff'.

The tone was not conciliatory and the tension was still high between the lay people running Barnardo's and the divided professional staff. The management consultants issued a series of reports, some of them deliberately challenging, culminating in the spring of 1971. They suggested that Barnardo's should engage principally in fund-raising and grant-aiding, giving money to others to do the work. The name Barnardo's was, they concluded, a priceless asset. If they adopted that proposal, it would mean Barnardo's giving up their long history of pioneering child care and, not surprisingly, the Council turned it down. However, they did grasp at one suggestion for resolving the split between the two sides of the organisation. The consultants, Messrs McClintock, Mann and Whinney, suggested that a Chief Executive be appointed to head the organisation, with the Directors of Child Care and Fund-Raising subordinate to him. They also proposed that a separate Finance Department be established under a third Director on an equal footing with the other two. That was the kind of initiative that the Council was looking for. John Hillyer the acting Chairman, had always favoured the 'pyramid structure' and the Council as a whole felt that, at last, the new structure would help to heal the rift.

To the consternation of some of the staff, the new post of Chief Executive was advertised externally, as well as inside Dr Barnardo's. Principal officers had advised against it and in their frustration the heads of Barnardo Divisions all over the country threatened to resign on the grounds that it would undermine the present leadership. Although he was not trained in child care, Mr Cornish had won their loyalty and respect. It was Mr Cornish himself who persuaded the staff to accept the situation.

There were only two applicants on the short list for the top job in Barnardo's in 1971, Dr Herbert Ellis, a medical doctor with an excellent record in industry but no previous knowledge of child care, social work or charity, and V. L. Cornish, a trained administrator with eight years' experience in Barnardo's as well as a successful career overseas.

Perhaps a new face was needed, perhaps too many shibboleths had been broken. In any event, by September 1971, Dr Herbert Ellis was appointed to the newly created post, now termed Director General. At the time, the Council believed that only an outsider, not committed to either the child care or fund-raising side of Barnardo's, could heal the breach.

Very quickly, Mr Cornish resigned from his post as Director of Child Care and Miss Roundell, his deputy who had worked closely with him on the reorganisation, also decided to take early retirement.

The reasons given were that Mr Cornish felt that a child care professional should head the team in which he had worked so hard to raise professional standards, and Miss Roundell, with only two years before her retirement, felt that it would be wrong for her to fill a senior post in the new Barnardo's. Mr Hunt, General Secretary, also resigned.

Douglas Smyth, the Inspector from the Home Office who had joined Barnardo's at Mr Cornish's invitation in 1970, was promoted from Deputy to Director of Child Care, in Mr Cornish's place.

Reverberations from those years of flux echoed in the charity for years. A hint of what may have distressed Council so much in Mr Cornish's forthright, intellectual approach may be found in Dr Ellis's first report to the council (1971-72): 'In talking of change,' he wrote, ' . . . we should take care not to destroy all illusions about our past work, as, for example, the association of the name of Dr Barnardo with orphans. There is an indispensable place for myth and legend in any healthy functioning nation state.'[34]

Dr Ellis headed that nation state and that triumvirate of Directors for just fifteen months. Then he resigned. According to senior staff he simply did not have the experience or knowledge to speak for Barnardo's and answer questions on child care with authority. Although he was personally popular, by uniting the two opposing sides to join forces against him, Dr Ellis had accomplished his task. Douglas Smyth, Director of Child Care, felt convinced that the new head of Barnardo's should be both Director of Child Care and Chief Executive, committing Barnardo's to give priority to the care of the children. The Council, on the other hand, was concerned to see that financial and fund-raising issues should be given equal weight. After several months of delay, Mr Smyth was offered the post of Chief Executive and Director of Child Care, but at that stage felt he could not accept. In June 1973 Mr Smyth, too, decided to resign to take up the post of Director of Social Services in Ballymena in Northern Ireland. In the space of two years, five top posts in Barnardo's were vacated, three in Child Care, one the former General Secretary and one the Director General.

The post of Director General was not resuscitated after Dr Ellis resigned. Barnardo's were fortunate in securing the services of Mary Joynson, a former Child Care Officer, forthright, determined and able. She joined the charity in 1970 and took over the post as Senior Director and Director of Child Care in the autumn of 1973 until her retirement at the close of 1984. Her appointment introduced a period of stability and development after those turbulent years. Roger Singleton, her deputy, succeeded her and in 1986 became the Senior Director of Barnardo's with three Directors, Child Care, Finance and Fund-Raising, working under him. At last Barnardo's had a head to the pyramid.

Despite the upheaval, not a hint of the internal strife reached the press or the outside world. Even in the divisions, staff were not aware of the 'revolution' taking place, an indication of both the tremendous loyalty inside Barnardo's and the smothering instinct to close ranks and cover up.

In 1978, after two years of discussion, the child care aim of Barnardo's, 'a re-statement and elaboration of aims laid down in 1969', paid indirect tribute to the author of the revolutionary report. Although Mr Cornish had left Barnardo's years since, he had cleared the path for progress.

14

The Rock Foundation

'My heart's desire and prayer to God for the children is that they might be saved, not only for the present life but for the life to come.'

T. J. Barnardo,
Something Attempted – Something Done

'Dr Barnardo was referred to by all his staff as the Director. The control of everything was in his hands. Every section of the vast organisation under his supervision was his own creation and every detail had received his personal consideration.'
Barnardo of Stepney
A. E. Williams (Barnardo's personal Secretary)

Thomas J. Barnardo, Dr Barnardo, died over eighty years ago. Yet his influence over the charitable empire he created was so penetrating that his homes did not change significantly until fifty years after his death. His faith was his dynamo and no aspect of the work bears his imprint so strongly as the religious upbringing of the children; to this day his personal legacy of intense idealism harnessed to a fiercely competitive spirit can be felt in the charity.

From the beginning the young Barnardo yearned both to serve God and to make his name. His religious conversion propelled him into teaching ragged children and visiting the poor: 'A fellow labourer with God' is how he described himself. He began his mission, not principally to rescue ragged children from the wretchedness of the slums, but to redeem them from ignorance, to save them from spiritual damnation. What would be called the social work element in modern jargon, clothing, feeding, educating the children, teaching them a trade, started as a by-product of his religious intent. In the East End he was known as preacher before teacher and teacher before social reformer.

His first concern for the rough young boys and girls of the streets was to draw them from sin, from the roistering life of the tap room and the penny gaff, the drinking and dancing and gambling, to lead them to Sunday school and to salvation.

That he saw himself as divinely inspired, as the earthly father of his huge flock, is revealed in a Christmas message to the boys of Mittendorf House, Epsom, in 1899:

My dear boys,
I hope you are all very jolly . . . Christmas comes but once a year and when it comes it brings good cheer.
Don't forget your Great Father in Heaven who supplies all His children with such beautiful hands; and don't forget your small father in London who loves you very sincerely.[1]

In his ardour, his mass appeal, his use of the Christian press (the only vehicle of communication open to him at the time) Barnardo resembles no one so much as the secular, but no less ardent, Bob Geldof. Barnardo's first platform was, however, not the podium at a pop concert but a chair in the street. He drew his spiritual strength and support from his Evangelical faith. At first his zealous commitment seemed so self-righteous, so cocksure as to be laughable to his elders. But it was this very quality of recklessness – or faith – that appealed to some supporters.

The stories that are told of him as a young medical student suggest that he was so strict an adherent of the Plymouth Brethren as to be utterly intolerant of other people's opinions and somewhat insufferable. Yet when he spoke to the men and women of the street he seemed to have an instinctive knowledge of human psychology which enabled him to reach out to them.

One of his great gifts was his ability to adapt other people's ideas and methods and make them his own. The American revivalist Dwight Moody came to London the year after Barnardo, and Barnardo, much impressed, heard him preach and watched his ability to organise and publicise. Through the network of Evangelical Protestants, Barnardo found his financial support, the staff for his homes, his trustees and Committee. Although he spoke in the language of the Evangelicals his words sounded new and fresh:

. . . dear reader,
Whether you send much or little, above all pray for us; give us, our work and our arrangements, a place in your petitions daily when at the Throne of Grace.[2]

'Will you pray for us and this work with all its vast responsibilities?' he entreats soon after he had opened his first home for boys, 'we need burning, unselfish love for souls; we want true, single-eyed zeal for the

Master; we require spiritual wisdom, much grace and great mental and physical endurance.'[3] His homes, he declared, were 'houses of prayer, where war must be waged on both the heartless principles of secularism and the effects and corrupt forms of a merely Sacramental Christianity'.

In almost forty years of working for the poor, Barnardo pursued at least half a dozen careers, any one of which would have fulfilled a lesser man: he was preacher and journalist, doctor and administrator, social worker and fund-raiser and a not inconsiderable showman. As the years advanced he did not lose sight of the spiritual dimension, but his life became more and more taken up with worldly matters as he grew into the well-known, the controversial, the litigious Dr Barnardo. Not long after the arbitration case, he left the Plymouth Brethen to join the Church of England and in his later years he became a lay reader.

By the 1880s the homes were beginning to assume an important role in national life, and to be patronised by the Establishment. The Lord Chancellor, Lord Cairns, was the President and Barnardo's eminent trustees included three titled Evangelicals. Royalty, in the personage of the Duchess of Teck, attended Barnardo fêtes and, by 1890, he was staging mass rallies at the Albert Hall with pomp and panache.

A distinguished friend, Lord Radstock, who had been a spiritual influence on Syrie Barnardo and on Barnardo himself in the early days, felt concerned:

> When you first began your work I felt that your waiting on God only was a means of great blessing, not only to the dear children, but to the Church of God – and I often used to speak of the way the money came in for the 'Edinburgh Castle' as a lesson to us all. Since then it appeared to me you had been tempted to lean more on man and to get the help of people who were more 'influential' with the world than with God ... Of course I feel how blessed it is to minister, even to 'one of those little ones', but as you know, we need not only to do God's work but to do it in His way and I have feared that you might be tempted, as so many are, to think that the work must always be large.

Lord Radstock, disturbed at the debts owing, urged Barnardo to cut down on expenses and 'to wait more on God'.[4]

Barnardo replied that he now had 'a larger grasp of God's word, a truer knowledge of first principles and, I hope, also a truer knowledge of the Master whom I serve. I often wish I had unmarred the zeal of early days.'

'As to the details mentioned in your letter,' Barnardo wrote dismissively, 'I think probably these are less weighty and true than you seem to think: I mean first as to the growth of the work; then as to the financial responsibility.' And Barnardo assured Lord Radstock that he was in God's hand and that the position was 'sound and pleasing to God'.

In this letter Barnardo revealed that he had rejoined the Church of England but added, 'the great work itself, is, as ever, upon a basis where I hope all God's people . . . can join and work'.[5]

He had always believed that the work was too urgent, the plight of the children too dreadful, for him to enter into sectarian controversies. He called his homes 'undenominational', by which he meant that they embraced all the sects of the Protestant Church and he claimed that clergy all over the country as well as non-conformist ministers had written to testify that children from his homes had been confirmed in the Church of England or taken communion and joined non-conformist churches. Uncharacteristically, he did not support his claim with numbers of children 'saved' but contented himself with observing that every single home had received encouragement from changed lives and regenerated hearts. Chapels in the homes were dedicated, not consecrated, so that services could be held by both Church of England clergy and non-conformist ministers. In that way he drew the widest support.

Systematic in every aspect of the work, Barnardo preached and spoke so often that now he numbered his sermons carefully, writing on the place and date where he had preached, sometimes to use them again. From the beginning he had asked for prayers from his sympathisers; as he grew more established, he formalised that sympathy into a Daily Prayer Union. Members who received a membership card pledged themselves to silent prayer for five minutes a day:

> that all the children in our Homes may be led to Christ . . . that wisdom and discernment, patience and physical strength may be given to those who have the chief responsibility in searching out lost children and in dealing with difficult cases . . .
>
> That the hearts of God's people everywhere may be touched by the Lord himself, so that they shall recognise more fully their responsibility towards the Children of the Streets and may minister freely and gladly of their substance . . .[6]

His Annual Reports were always both pious and practical, his appeals for spiritual and financial help indivisible. But thirty years on, his tone had changed dramatically. He was no longer entreating the public for funds; now, he threw down the gauntlet: 'To the scornful taunt of unbelief and the sickly plaint of pessimism, I reply by marshalling the unanswerable facts of thirty years ... Our records are studded with tokens of Divine favour, with special providences, with answers to prayer.'

Pressed as he was for funds, Barnardo declared: 'I feel no qualms about apparently magnifying my office as a chronicler of this Divine work ... it is one of the evidences of Christianity and it is not too much to say that in its success or failure may be seen a gauge of the Christian impulse.'[7]

After the controversy with the Roman Catholics in the 1890s, Barnardo was careful to point out that he did not admit children with a view to proselytise and always consulted both Roman Catholic and Jewish authorities before admitting their children. Then, of course, they were brought up as Protestants. His extreme prejudice towards the Catholics never diminished. Children in boarded-out homes who went to a village school where a crucifix was hung on the wall, or pictures of the Virgin Mary or of the saints displayed, were taken away however favourable or otherwise the district might be.[8] He was fearful, he wrote, of the impression left on young minds. Not until after the Second World War did Barnardo's Homes begin to employ Roman Catholics and only in very recent times has the effect of Barnardo's prejudice begun to dispel. Even today, no Roman Catholic has been elected a member of Council although they are eligible for membership. However, the charity works with both Catholics and Protestants in Northern Ireland and principally with Catholics in the Republic of Ireland.

In his early years, Barnardo's direct appeals to the public for money and his annual sales of goods aroused stern criticism in the Christian community. His critics were afraid that he would resort to raffling his wares. By the end of his life, when the charity was well known, promoters of dances, balls, card parties and theatricals frequently pressed him to accept part of their proceeds. Barnardo refused his 'semi-worldly, semi-benevolent benefactors', convinced that they were misguided and that the spiritual work would be damaged by accepting funds from what he saw as questionable sources.

After his death, the restrictions on moneys raised by 'things doubtful' were gradually lifted. By 1932, the Council of Barnardo's was prepared to countenance fund-raising by private dances and dramatic entertainments provided they were suitably supervised. They did not, however, approve of public entertainments. By the 'sixties only Sunday dances and enter- tainments were banned, although any form of gambling and the 'display or disposal of alcohol' was still vetoed.

In 1984 a grand ball in aid of Barnardo's was held at Blenheim Palace in the presence of Princess Margaret; it was a worldly, glittering, champagne occasion and it is difficult to imagine that Barnardo would have disapproved. He always managed to convey the impression that his charity was specially sanctified and any inconsistencies were, therefore, permissible.

To interpret Barnardo's prohibitions on fund-raising in changing times was one thing; to interpret his religious aspirations for the children in a changing world quite another. Two world wars, the influence of the radio, cinema and television, as well as the changing nature of the population, all helped to transform social patterns and led the charity gradually to adapt their Christian outlook to meet the new realities.

The passion of Barnardo's personality and his forcibly expressed commitment to Christian ideals became legendary in the charity after his death and made any changes in the religious life of the institution very painful. His first successor, William Baker, an earnest Christian and formerly Chairman of Council, made it clear that, like Barnardo, he saw the work as primarily spiritual:

Whatever else it may be, it is Christ's work and therefore the work of Christ's Church. The work we do is not merely laying hold of somebody else's boys or girls who are not cared for at home. These Homes fall into line as one department of the whole Church in action and their charter yields in importance, in majesty, in positive sublimity to no other commission which our Saviour has laid upon His disciples.[9]

On his death in 1920, Baker was succeeded by a paid Director, Rear-Admiral Sir Harry Stileman. Sir Harry possessed all of Barnardo's religious zeal but lacked both his instinct for public relations and his genius with people. He believed, quite literally, that his call to direct the charity came from God. Therefore, he argued, he must have absolute control. His quarrel with the lady Governors of the Village arose partly from social differences but also from his censorious attitude towards their religious life. He criticised the ladies' failure to attend staff prayer meetings and asserted that they had engaged workers whose views 'did not conform with the Protestant Evangelical trend of thought and line of action demanded by those in the care of children in Dr Barnardo's'.

In Barnardo's day it was beyond question that all the staff must be Evangelicals. Very few domestic staff were employed and hardly any expert advisers. Between the wars, in an increasingly secular society, the questions occasionally arose. In the spring of 1922, for example, the Minutes record that it was not considered desirable 'that a lady who was a Jewess should be appointed to the post of Medical Officer for Mental Defectives in the Village'.[10]

Just before the Second World War in their magazine, *Night and Day*, Barnardo's underlined their policy of teaching children religion by example as well as precept. 'We try to place our children in the direct care of men and women of real character and worth. We encourage habits of prayer, of Bible-reading and church attendance.'

During the war, with children scattered all over the country, head-quarters could not adequately supervise religious instruction; some of the junior staff recruited were evidently not of the calibre required. After the war the senior staff agreed that domestic and daily staff must not indicate 'by word or attitude any disagreement or lack of sympathy with the religious upbringing of the children'. According to a survey made at the time, less than half of the boys who left Barnardo's attended church when they first went out to work.[11]

Soon after the war, a Miss Morgan was appointed as Religious Adviser to improve standards of religious education and awareness in the homes. Barnardo's attitude towards Roman Catholics at that time was still extremely cautious. In 1948, a Miss Jones, a staff member in charge of young children, was discovered to have converted to Roman Catholicism. The Council debated the matter carefully and although they acknowl-edged that Miss Jones, a well-respected member of staff, would never consciously attempt to proselytise, they decided to remove children over five from her care. The following month they reaffirmed an earlier decision insisting that all new recruits to Barnardo's residential staff must be of the Protestant faith.[12]

For almost a century the religious training of the children in Dr Barnardo's Homes remained virtually unchanged. Superintendents car-ried on the missionary work from generation to generation and from decade to decade. Children were brought up to Stepney in a group to be formally farewelled on Tuesday mornings before they left the homes. The ritual included a question-and-answer session on their own family history; a handing over of the birth certificate and any other official documents in a presentation wallet containing Dr Barnardo's notes on his last devotional address to his family and a photograph of the Doctor; a short service in the Chapel taken by a member of Council or a Senior Officer; and the presentation of a fountain pen and a Bible or another suitable devotional work.

The religious atmosphere in the homes was robustly described in the Barnardo Book in the mid-'fifties. 'The Family is still the backbone of the nation. A true spirit of worship in the Home will have far-reaching results.' To promote this spirit, family prayers, Bible reading and private prayer were part of the child's daily routine. On Sundays, children from four upwards were expected to go to church (the very young attended Sunday school). In the afternoons the children attended either Sunday school or Bible classes and some of the older ones were expected to attend evening service. Activities suggested to help boys and girls enjoy the day ranged from letter-writing or reading to walking. Even if they were being taken out for a treat on a Sunday by their parents or local benefactors, the children were required to go to church first.

The Barnardo Book also reveals the idealism implicit in what may appear to be a rather narrow attitude towards the children's religious training:

> To the outside world the name 'Barnardo' conjures up the vision of a haven where a homeless child will be certain to receive something more than an institutional training; a place in which he or she is considered as an individual whose characteristics have to be studied and to whom real affection must be given; where unkindliness is left outside, while inside security is felt. 'For Christ is Head of the House.'[13]

That sense of pride and self-confidence in their role had always kept Barnardo's vision bright. But, by the mid-'fifties and early 'sixties, the gap between the Victorian certainties of a child's life in Barnardo's and the explosion of pop culture in the multi-racial cities was growing dangerously wide. And, with parents' rights now upheld by law, the children could not remain entirely insulated, thus the serenity of the Barnardo world was somewhat threatened.

'What can be done about parents and relatives who make a practice of visiting their children on a Sunday?' asked a Barnardo child care worker at a Staff Conference in the 'sixties, ' . . . taking them to places of amusement and making a general holiday of Sunday.'[14]

Until the 'seventies, the Barnardo staff were required to play a part in the missionary process. Their express task was 'to bring up children in the Christian faith and to endeavour to lead each to a personal knowledge of Jesus Christ as Saviour'. In a multi-racial society, that goal restricted the intake of children, since the 1948 Children Act stipulated that a child in care must be given 'a religious upbringing appropriate to the persuasion to which he belongs'. In practice, it happened that many of the country's neediest children were ineligible for Barnardo's help. And not only were immigrant children of the Eastern religions barred, but Roman Catholics of the Christian Church, too, and that at a time when the ecumenical movement was growing in the country. (In the past, once a Catholic child was admitted after prior consultation with Catholic authorities, that child was brought up as a Protestant. That now was against the law.)

In 1965 an exception was noted in the Minutes. A physically handicapped Catholic girl was admitted to Hollins, a Barnardo home for the handicapped, and for the first time in history a Roman Catholic priest was permitted to visit a child in a Barnardo home.[15]

At that time, the Council numbered several crusading Evangelicals, including the Chairman, General Sir Arthur Smith, a much-loved 'character' in the charity, alarming to newcomers from his habit of poking them in the ribs to ask peremptorily, 'Are you saved?' When Billy Graham came to England in 1966 the Council encouraged superintendents and senior staff to attend his mass rallies. Despite a recognition of changing times, in the official literature urging staff 'to make sure that the religious practices in their Homes were appropriate to the child's experience in the outside world' and even a hint that family prayers might be modified, many staff and Council members clung to the first principles of their founder.

To suggestions from child care staff that the religious training in Barnardo's marked their vulnerable children off from others, Sir Arthur Smith countered with his usual vigour:

> Surely we do not want our children to be brought up like the many – indeed, majority – who have no Christian training at home. We want them in this respect to be different and to be taught that they must expect to face opposition as Christians . . . Let us beware lest Barnardo's is too protective. We should train our boys and girls to have character and guts.[16]

However, by 1969, when Sir Arthur wrote that letter, changes in the wider world had already begun to impinge on the traditional nature of Barnardo's. The charity found it increasingly difficult to retain its Protestant stronghold at a time when 'the increasing acceptance by Catholics and Protestants of one another called into question Barnardo's claim to be a Christian Society while its practice excluded one part of Christendom, the Roman Catholics'.[17] In Scotland, which enjoyed a degree of autonomy, a number of children from other faiths were already admitted and in the charity generally a handful of Catholic staff was employed, but always in junior posts and always with special permission. The situation was growing increasingly uncomfortable. By the end of the 'sixties, Barnardo's itself had reorganised and changed radically in the process. Many of their traditional homes in the countryside had closed and Barnardo social workers were beginning to work with children in inner cities such as Leeds, Birmingham and Liverpool. They could hardly be unaware of the high concentration of deprived immigrant families in ghetto slums. Soon, the anomaly of Barnardo's position became painfully clear. Their reputation was based on more than a hundred years' work with the most neglected children in Britain. Their guiding principle as a Protestant foundation was a commitment to bring children up in the Christian faith. Could they afford to turn their back on either the non-Christian children in their midst, or their Christian principles?

The division in both staff and Council touched on some of their deepest feelings. On the one hand there were those who had joined Barnardo's because it was an Evangelical Protestant charity, committed to employ the work with children as 'an opportunity and a vehicle for sharing the Christian message'. On the other, there were those who saw Barnardo's in the modern world as a child care agency with a Christian basis, whose faith would be demonstrated in their care and love for children.

In 1970 a working party of senior staff investigating Barnardo's help to families asked Council to face the questions: 'Should Barnardo's help Muslim and Hindu families knowing that if we do we must respect their religious faith and practice?' Or should they refuse to help those in need on religious grounds? Not surprisingly, at the time few immigrant children or families were referred to Barnardo's, nor was the charity attracting the trained social workers it needed. The Council was also asked to consider Barnardo's attitude towards the appointment and promotion of Roman Catholic staff and the question of the charity's Christian responsibility towards adoptive parents.

After wrestling conscientiously with the problem for more than a year, they decided in 1971 to widen their doors to admit non-Christian children and to help those families without attempting to change their beliefs or interfere with their culture. 'Our attitude towards such families . . . should be that of the good Samaritan who was moved to help his neighbour without any other motive.' The report contained the merest hint that Barnardo's were reluctant to renounce their traditional missionary role:

In the case of immigrant families, our witness will mainly lie in the mere acceptance of the family as people, particularly if the family is well integrated within the religious culture of the racial group. There may be some families who are on the fringe of their own community and great sensitivity will be required . . . to know whether they should be encouraged to participate more fully with their own religious group or whether they should be encouraged to join the Christian community. While we consider the latter course to be the better, it may be possible only in a few cases where members of the family themselves first express the wish to take this step.[18]

Barnardo's agreed to admit Roman Catholic or Jewish children if their own religious authorities could not cater for them. Their approach towards employing Roman Catholic staff in Barnardo's was, however, still very guarded: the Roman Catholics were to continue to be appointed to junior posts on the understanding that they could not be promoted beyond a certain point, deputy head of a Barnardo home, for example, or teacher in a Barnardo residential school. Individual Catholic social workers were not to be employed because they would be acting as Barnardo agents. '. . . appointment to prominent positions in our Society would be widely misunderstood and would confuse many of the loyal supporters and staff of this Protestant Society,' the Committee judged. They noted that the policy of Roman Catholic societies towards Protestants was similar.

Two years later, in 1973, the line had softened. Roman Catholics were accepted on the staff on an equal basis and Barnardo's guiding principle had altered to become more tolerant, if somewhat anomalous: 'Our Guiding Principle is to communicate the Christian Faith and a personal knowledge of Jesus Christ to the children and families for whom we care, whilst respecting the religious beliefs and traditions of those specifically belonging to non-Christian faiths.'[19]

For many of the staff, united by their faith, their endurance, their work for the children, Barnardo's became a way of life. The great majority were evangelical Protestants who looked on their employment as a way to give meaning to their lives and relate earning a living to their religious beliefs. To this day, ex-members of staff keep in touch with each other, their former charges and the organisation to a remarkable extent. 'Barnardo staff are much alike wherever they are,' a senior officer's report in the 'sixties commented: 'the same loyalties – the same enjoyment in "get togethers"; staff meetings; school leavers' services, etc., are evident.' Dr Barnardo himself wove the web. He stood at the head of the 'Barnardo family' and for sixty-five years after his death the staff and Council embraced that family with the 'Barnardo spirit', a proud and conscious tradition.

For the children, the family feeling held many advantages. They enjoyed remarkable continuity of care, since staff stayed for years and they remained stamped with a strong Barnardo identity all their lives. However, the family could be stifling and inward-looking and by the post-war years inevitably the ties began to weaken in the face of the new world. The trend for all voluntary societies was to become more businesslike and, to some extent, more bureaucratic and professional. Barnardo's was one of the first of the large charities to 'rationalise'.

By the 1970s, those changes were evident in their recruitment of staff, and in the kind of children they were beginning to help and in their attitude towards them. Even when he had catered for 7,000 children Barnardo had behaved as if they were all his own family. As a result, for years the homes were run on the strict, religious lines of his day. After social workers and offices moved into the big cities, that approach was no longer viable. Dr Barnardo's became a truly interdenominational organisation, more flexible in the demands it made on the religious life of both staff and children, less institutional, less judgemental. Rigid rules for Sunday observance were abandoned, staff were asked to exercise their discretion: 'children will normally accept one session at Church or Sunday School or Bible class as reasonable'.[20] The only positive injunction was to vary the routine and make Sunday a 'happy, care-free day, when there is time to enjoy the countryside or seaside if nearby'.

Until that time, Barnardo's policy was 'to adopt children into Christian families only'. When a boy or girl joined a new family through their services, they saw an opportunity to exhort new parents to deepen their faith. Adoption Officers were expected to keep a list of suitable books available to help adoptive parents to teach their children the Christian faith. A Barnardo book of children's prayers is often given to parents at the court hearing or the baptism.

Today, since Barnardo's place mainly older or handicapped children, social workers are asked to explore the resources of the Christian community first but are more concerned about the family's philosophy of life and values than about formal church attendance. In Bradford, with its multi-cultural and religious community, the Barnardo new family project states explicitly that they are a 'Christian child care association whose purpose is to express the love of God by serving those in need, irrespective of their beliefs'.

Very gradually during the last decade Barnardo's have begun to care for non-Christian children. By 1976, nineteen boys and girls from disparate backgrounds were living in Barnardo homes: one agnostic; two Hindus; one Jew; two Jehovah's Witnesses; three Mormons; one Seventh Day Adventist and two Sikhs. (Nowadays they no longer count the numbers although the overall impression is that there are still very few non-Christian children.) By 1978, a Jew was appointed as head of the Village.

Clearly that kind of ecumenism would have been impossible when Barnardo's were committed to bringing up the children as Evangelical Protestants. But today the vast majority of children living in their homes (now called units) are referred by local authorities for a limited period; they include difficult or delinquent children and the mentally and physically handicapped. Also, many of the children and families they help live in their own homes and for all these reasons Barnardo's original aim of bringing up a child to a trade and a religion is no longer appropriate.

Although idealism is not lacking, the outward trappings of the 'rock foundation', the missionary zeal, can barely be traced. The days when each home would display a photograph of Dr Barnardo, when the children sat silent during meals and marched to church in crocodile, two or three times on Sundays, have gone for ever. Today some of Barnardo's most exciting ventures with unemployed or delinquent teenagers take place in beaten-up church halls, a poignant reminder of the origins.

Timothy Lawson, who chaired the committees on Barnardo's religious outlook throughout the 'sixties and 'seventies, believes that the charity has found the means to retain their faith 'that God can transform the lives of those who put their trust in Him'. He recognises that 'the main expression of the Christian motivation of Barnardo's in the multi-racial society will be in the quality of our caring'.

Some of the old-timers in the charity regret the past and regard the changes and reforms as a loss. Certainly Barnardo workers in the homes in the old days did not know the meaning of overtime or unsocial hours and would have regarded themselves as privileged rather than exploited. Yet commitment to the children and Christian concern are not lacking in the charity. A religious faith is seen as an asset in Barnardo's and the number of churchgoers among present-day staff would almost certainly be higher than the national average. In recent years, the weekly staff service at headquarters held at lunchtime on Tuesdays in the Children's Church has been sparsely attended, despite the devoted efforts of those concerned. In the past, some staff felt that they needed to be seen to be devout and that pressure has now gone.

The Christian basis of Barnardo's throughout the country seems to depend on the attitude of the Divisional Directors and their staffs. Some Barnardo groups work closely with local churches and youth clubs; others have no involvement. Staff in some regions meet regularly for study, prayer and retreats. As to the future, Barnardo's are planning to link more closely with local churches and work with them; one group of staff is also anxious for Barnardo's to build more bridges to other faiths. Only in very recent years has such a democratic approach been possible.

Barnardo imprinted his organisation with an indelible image of rescuing orphans or abandoned children from a ruinous background and restoring them to respectability and a religious faith. His genius and his vision saved thousands, yet even in the beginning that image was highly coloured. For a hundred years, staff and Council reaped the benefits of his image-making and the drawbacks as well. Until after the Second World War parents were regarded as a threat to the children and the charity jealously guarded their charges. Only in very recent years has the ideal of rescuing and re-creating a child in the Barnardo image given place to working with children and their families to overcome handicaps and help a child explore his full potential.

In today's world the staff feel concerned that some of the public still think of Barnardo's as orphan homes. The simple powerful religious message of the past proved so fruitful that the charity is only just gaining confidence to re-direct the public to the complexities of their present-day work and to focus more sharply on new directions.

15

The New Jerusalem

'I wonder will the connected history of this work for God ever be written! I am afraid not. It would almost be too large an effort for anyone to attempt.'

Barnardo and Marchant, 1907

In the range of their work in size and in wealth, Barnardo's dominate the world of children's charities and rank high in the top twenty charities in the United Kingdom. Until the reorganisation, their homes and schools remained landmarks in their localities for a hundred years. From the day that Barnardo invited the rough lads and lost girls of Stepney to a free tea meeting, however, the work has been characterised by change. The great change at the end of the 'sixties released new dynamism and enthusiasm as the charity gained confidence in a modern vision.

By 1973, the reorganisation which had riven Barnardo's was almost complete and the Barnardo map moved northwards. Large traditional homes in the south had been closed or contracted, children referred to other care and staff retired or transferred. In the eight divisional offices throughout the United Kingdom, Child Care and Appeals staff worked side by side within reasonable distance of Barnardo children in schools, day centres and foster-homes. The London Division (twice as big as the others) was sited at Barkingside, next door to headquarters.

A large, faceless, four-storey office block at Barkingside has replaced Old Man Stepney, as the elderly headquarters was affectionately termed; in 1984 a plaque to Dr Barnardo was unveiled in Stepney Causeway. The new headquarters stands in Barnardo heartland, once the Girls' Village Home, surrounded by cottages and smooth lawns where generations of girls grew up. Gone is the high wall enclosing the Village, the swimming pool and the Australasian Hospital. Children still live in a corner of the grounds in the remaining ivy-clad cottages but their existence could scarcely be imagined by the old-timers. Nearby, at the Children's Church, staff still worship weekly and from the picture windows their offices overlook, at a respectful distance, a brooding memorial to the founder. The bronze monument, flanked by semi-circular stone seats, depicts at the top a motherly figure of Charity embracing two babes, at the centre a medallion of Barnardo in profile and at the base a cluster of three little girls modelled at the time of Barnardo's death. One of the models was Emily Runcie, whose widower, Arthur, lives close by in the grounds in a modern bungalow building for local senior citizens.

Some links with the past have gone. The waxwork figure of Barnardo to whom new staff were introduced at Stepney was passed to Limehouse Public Library. Today the figure of 'Doctor B' appears as a smiling Pickwickian cartoon character on publicity, his influence at last diminished. In some offices the portrait of Barnardo has been replaced by a photograph of today's President, Her Royal Highness the Princess of Wales. The very real sense of awe for Barnardo and his work that caused Council and staff at Stepney to ask themselves, 'What would the founder have done?' has been replaced by a corporate nostalgia.

Gone, too, is the paternalistic style of government in the modern, managerial Barnardo's. For years after Barnardo's death, the Chairman and members of Council stood as head of the family, distant but benign. Respect for elders and betters was not limited to the children and individual Council members might show a sign of favour or displeasure to individual staff members ('Barnardo servants') as well as to boys and girls. The preference for senior staff with military or colonial experience to take charge of the children lingered for years. An Army officer, Lieutenant-Colonel Atkins and his lady were in charge of the Village until 1964. That year the Annual Report underlined the importance Barnardo's attached to giving 'ordinary children' love, encouragement and Christian example in their hundred homes. Within a decade the character of the children, the staff, the methods of care and management had all changed.

Part of the change came from the reorganisation and the decision to concentrate on especially disadvantaged children in run-down areas of the country. Barnardo's task was made more complex by changes in legislation and Government attitudes towards those children.

Since the Second World War, Barnardo's had established three Approved Schools run on behalf of the Home Office. The 1969 Children and Young Persons Act placed all children in trouble, whether from neglect or delinquent behaviour, in the care of the local authority. The Community Homes with Education, the new title for the old Approved Schools, now took in both the bad and the sad (a principle implicitly applied by Barnardo when he opened his first Boys' Home to shelter destitute children and to save young delinquents from a life in prison). By 1970 Regional Planning Committees composed of grouped local authorities were established to decide on provision for children in their area. Like other voluntary associations, Barnardo's were invited to join in the public system but after a long period of indecision resolved in 1973 to preserve their independent status. (Had they joined the public scheme they would have had to share the management of their homes but they could have claimed all building costs.) Remaining independent made them more vulnerable to closure than homes within the public system. In recent years, however, all children's homes both statutory and voluntary have been closing down.

At that time, in 1973, Barnardo's were buoyant and eager to expand and modernise. An ambitious new centre for the physically handicapped near headquarters was planned and the old barrack-style Approved School at Druid's Heath was to be transformed into a modern Community Home with Education. New homes for disturbed children were to be built. In 1974–5 £2.25 million was set aside for development.[1]

Only a year later raging inflation and social services budgets priced many Barnardo plans off the drawing board. Painful cutbacks were inevitable. The development of new homes for emotionally disturbed children in London and the north-east was abandoned, and the rebuilding of schools in the Midlands and Kent was delayed. Cost-effectiveness became the watchword and Barnardo's grew cost-conscious as never before. A detailed monitoring of budgets in all Barnardo buildings was introduced. Residential homes by the 1970s were expected to be almost entirely self-financing, with each child referred and paid for by the local authorities.[2] With social services departments struggling with smaller budgets and anxious to keep their own children's homes occupied, the children they did refer to Barnardo's were either severely handicapped or deeply disturbed, many of them children who had been in and out of other forms of care. They describe themselves as 'the kids nobody else will take'.

To care for those kids meant that Barnardo senior staff had to forge links with senior civil servants in Government Departments and with directors of social services all over the country to research, plan and obtain finance either through grants for day care work or fees for children in homes.

Political, economic and social conditions impinged increasingly on the once-private world of Barnardo's Homes. Senior child care professionals (as in the other helping professions) have become more and more caught up in administration, policy and seeking funds. In the 'sixties, the General Superintendent, Mr Cornish, was sometimes consulted about an individual child. In the late 'seventies, Mr Singleton, Deputy Director of Child Care, remarked that it was 'an anomaly of the work that rarely does one hear about a child. It is difficult to know whether to be proud or ashamed of this.'[3] Mr Singleton expressed pride in the knowledge that today responsibility in Barnardo's is delegated from the Child Care Director at headquarters, through the Divisional Director to the Project Leader. His shame came from the knowledge that he was so distanced from Barnardo's essence: the children. The sheer size of Barnardo's sometimes leaves the uncomfortable impression that the cart is pulling the horse.

Yet that impression is quickly dispelled by a visit to work in progress. Although the superstructure is so remote from the Doctor's one-man-band control, and the carefully planned monitored budgeting a world away from his creative debts, Barnardo would certainly have recognised the kind of children that Barnardo's seeks to help today. They still come from a world of high unemployment, vandalised and run-down neighbourhoods, poverty and despair.

These potted biographies, from the casebook of a West Country Barnardo hostel for older teenagers, compare in drama with anything the founder ever met:

Linda aged eighteen: in care with her sister, subsequently homeless. Admitted to mental hospital on a compulsory order. Discharged, slashed her wrists. On trial at the hostel.

Sam aged sixteen: in care all his life. Fostered at fifteen. Rebelled, pilfered, sexually assaulted a little girl. Took lock off hostel door, broke in, stole petty cash, TV and electric kettle. Put fists up to (female) warden.

Barnardo in his day would certainly have spotlighted the cases of young people like this to raise funds. Today the charity chooses to focus on 'the happy ending' for their fund-raising. An aura of gentility, a whiff of Enid Blyton surrounds their public image.

Yet the people helped by Barnardo social workers all over the country are families in trouble. Whether they are abused, violent or distressingly handicapped children, families so disruptive that the children cannot live safely at home, or harassed parents, unable to cope, they present problems which are not always easy to solve and human tragedy which cannot be pigeonholed. To its credit, Barnardo's management select staff who are, in the main, skilful, sensitive and extremely devoted. By tradition, extra effort is asked and often given by their workers.

Since the great Children Act of 1948, finding new families, in other words fostering or adopting children, rather than placing them in institutions has been favoured by Government.

In the 'fifties, Barnardo's found it hard to compete with the more numerous local authority Child Care Officers throughout the country in finding suitable homes for their children. By the 'sixties, when Home Office reports revealed that a high proportion of foster-children had had to leave their new homes and were thus rejected again, enthusiasm for substitute families flagged. By the 1970s with the recession, cost became a vital factor. To keep a child in a children's home costs local authorities about seven times more than paying a foster-parent for upkeep. (Once a child is adopted successfully those local authorities who are not themselves registered adoption agencies pay an outright fee to the voluntary agency in the region of £5,000.) Also the new mixed homes which took in both delinquent and neglected children meant that such a home might not be suitable for a 'normal' child, in care because of a family crisis. On humane grounds, the solution seemed preferable. If fostering or adoption prove successful, it offers a child the experience of a normal childhood and a happy family life.

From the early 'seventies the work has become much more skilled as the children needing new families became more complex. About that time, the kind of babies everyone wanted to adopt or foster, healthy, fair-haired, blue-eyed children, had almost disappeared from the scene. Now the children who needed loving parents might be as old as eleven or twelve; physically or mentally handicapped; black; many with years in a children's home or successive foster-homes; some with medical or legal complications in their background. Ten years earlier they would not have been considered for a place.

As early as 1973, Barnardo's had noted that their welfare workers were asked to take on complicated children with difficult problems for adoption and fostering. All over the country in the 'seventies, their Divisions began to specialise in placing 'difficult' children. Their work in the field is respected and in some cases emulated. A Barnardo's New Families' Shop in Colchester, the first in the country, displays attractive posters in the window written by the children themselves with their photographs, asking for the kind of families they would like.

In 1979, a cottage in the Girls' Village Homes, Barkingside, used a hundred years earlier to transform lost girls into Barnardo handmaidens, became the unlikely launching pad for nine 'hard to place' children. The children arrive at times of crisis, usually after an unsuccessful spell in a children's home or with foster-parents. The boys and girls who come to be resettled are muddled, frightened children. Eight out of ten of them have been roughly handled by their own parents. Most are on the register which local authorities keep of children discovered to have a 'non-accidental injury'. The past is often tragic.

They were children forced to bear the brunt of their parents' problems.

Jean, a little girl of five with a deformed face, kept asking why her mother did not want her. She did not want to hear the answer.

David, aged seven, was blamed by his mother for quarrels with her lover: 'if it wasn't for you we wouldn't be quarrelling'. His mother is an alcoholic but David feels guilty.

Not a few have been badly abused. A boy of five was made to stand in an electric fire until his legs burned. He still remembers the pain. A little girl had a pan of boiling water thrown over her. A three-year-old was sexually abused by her father.

Since the children have had such shattering experiences great care is taken to ease them into their new life. When a child is referred to a cottage in the Village, the person appointed to befriend the child, the key worker, visits the children's home or foster-home to get to know her.

Tracy is a pretty little girl with blonde hair and blue eyes. When she came to the Village she had had sixteen moves in her four years. Her foster-mother was pregnant so Tracy had to move again. Pat, the social worker, visited to find Tracy extremely restless. 'She was up and down all the time: "Can I have a cuddle?" "May I have a sweet?" "Can I have a glass of water?" ' After two or three hours Pat realised that she could not get Tracy's attention and she left. Tracy visited her new home with her foster-mother to help her to get used to the idea of moving. But when the little girl saw the room that was to be her bedroom she realised what was happening and clung to her foster-mother. When she did arrive it was 'quite an ordeal' for the rest of the little community. Seven of the children were playing a game when Tracy dug a nail in a child's smock. She was told to sit on the bottom of the stairs. 'It must have been horrific for her,' Pat commented. (Physical punishment of any kind is forbidden by Barnardo rules.)

As Tracy settled in, it was gradually explained to her that she was to have a new family. At times when Tracy was relaxed, at bath-time or in the kitchen, she was gently helped to unravel her own complex past. With the help of Pat, her key worker, she began to make her own life story book. (Pat had already looked at Tracy's file and discovered that her mother was in prison. Tracy was not taken to see her mother in prison but she did visit three sets of foster-parents.) She wrote down her birthday, her first address, her mum's name, 'My mum didn't look after me properly', and she began to feel that she would like to have a new family.

She was encouraged to make a poster, showing what sort of family she would like. In common with many other children in care, Tracy displayed certain habits which might have caused trouble in a family setting. She did not pull the chain after going to the lavatory, she slammed doors and jumped on furniture. Meantime, a Barnardo home-finding team looked for a suitable family for Tracy and prepared them for the task of looking after her.

Usually children in the cottages (there are now four in the Village) are ready to leave in six to nine months. Because she had such a troubled history it was almost eighteen months before Tracy was ready to move to her new foster-parents. The prospective parents were told the whole story and then Tracy was introduced to them in her cottage, on her own ground. During a courting period which lasted about a month, Tracy visited her foster-parents three times and stayed overnight. Her foster-mother came to the cottage and bathed Tracy and put her to bed.

Once she was placed, her key worker visited her within the first week and she had other visits from social workers (one from the local authority and one from Barnardo's home-finding team.) Gradually Pat, the key-worker, withdrew from the scene. But Barnardo's offer a twenty-four-hour telephone service for worried parents. Tracy's new mother rang up one day to say that the little girl had started to pinch her father on the cheek quite hard. She had done the same thing to Pat at the cottage. The family was advised to tell her that that 'was not a very nice way to say "I love you".' Tracy is now going to school. She has been adopted by her new family and has been able to accept the news that her parents are planning to adopt another child. For a little girl who has moved seventeen times in five years, she has settled remarkably well.

The new look in Barnardo's was intended to focus services on es-pecially vulnerable children in areas of need. From looking after babies with starched and loving care in large nursery homes Barnardo's moved to day centres, nursery schools, playgroups and toy libraries for young children. In recent years the charity has become more open and flexible involving parents and asking them what they want! Nowhere are the needs of mothers and children more pressing than in Belfast, a city beleaguered by sectarian bigorty, killings and bombings. Barnardo's care for children across the religious divide is a development Barnardo himself could not have foreseen.

As early as 1970, a Barnardo day centre was opened for under-fives on the ground floor of a mother and baby home in a Belfast suburb. At first the nursery took in local children of single parents, but over the years the children they care for have become increasingly troubled. Today young children are referred by local authorities from 'ghetto' districts, both Protestant and Catholic, of Belfast. Most have a disrupted home life. They suffer from lack of sleep at night. Many of the fathers of the twenty children at the nursery are unemployed; some are in prison.

Three or four-year-olds talk of shooting, of soldiers and of seeing 'bad men'. One four-year-old witnessed the shooting of his father. 'They don't talk about it as much as they should,' commented a young member of staff, 'because it's become a way of life.'

The staff sometimes notice babies or toddlers with unexplained bruises and marks on their bodies. When that happens nursery staff will request local authority social workers to arrange a medical but the process may take time. Partly through Barnardo's efforts in Belfast in the 'seventies, special consideration is now given to children suffering from 'non-accidental injuries'.

Inside the nursery is bright, equipped with a sand pit, tiny chairs, woolly toys, bright pictures on the walls. No set routine is imposed. Books and toys are put out and the staff have lunch and tea with the children. 'We let them feel that they can trust us; that we're going to be there and not knock them about. Some children are aggressive and noisy. Others, like the little boy of two, strapped in his chair all day at home, don't want to play or be touched. Sometimes it takes a year before a child will cry for the first time or just cuddle up to you. That's when you see the real person. You've always got to realise that they're going home to arguments and fights,' explained a nursery officer.

In working with the children, the staff soon discovered that many of their mothers were deprived themselves, women in their twenties and thirties who had been 'literally trailed up'. They were being asked to give the kind of care and affection they had never had themselves.

To work well, the day nursery must create a friendly atmosphere and help the mums to feel that they are not being judged. A Christmas party is held for them. One year a mother who had injured her child came in to cook the dinner, a buffet supper. The women watched a weepie on the video and for many it was the most relaxed evening they had spent all year.

Although Barnardo's is recognised as a Protestant agency, families from both communities are so deeply embroiled in their own personal difficulties and their need is so great that they are glad to come to the nursery. 'There are no religious differences here, although one half's parents are in one prison and the rest in the other,' a staff member commented wryly.

At four o'clock a Barnardo minibus driven by a staff member and four taxis (paid for by the local authorities) with escorts take the children home through the rubble-littered streets. At times of high tension they have to pass Army blockades which frighten the children. They always take the children into their homes. If nobody is in, the child is never left; a staff member will care for the small boy or girl until it is safe to go home. 'Anybody who works in this unit has to be dedicated,' a young helper remarked. If children need extra help and attention 'caregivers' are found for them, usually good mothers themselves with grown children who have worked as nurses or childminders in the past. These 'caregivers' look after the child during the day, befriend the mother and attend regular sessions at the nursery as well as the reviews of the child's progress held every six months. They act as day foster-mothers.

From working with very deprived families, the staff at the nursery soon became convinced that in certain cases the mother as well as the child needed help. Barnardo's opened a Family Centre in Belfast in 1980, funded jointly with the local authority to help the mother to regain her self-respect and self-confidence and, through the process, to learn to grow closer to and cope better with her child.

In the rambling, redbrick Victorian house near the centre of the city fourteen families a week come for help. The parents are often despairing, the majority single or separated, mothers living chaotic lives on the poverty line, with children crying all night and debts piling up. A third of the parents (either mothers or fathers) have been psychiatric patients; a third of the children have been injured by their parents. Without help the spiral would continue. According to the project leader, about 60 per cent of parents who abuse children were themselves abused in childhood. Violence appears to breed violence and when small children begin to shout at their dolls and push them around, it acts as a warning signal to the staff. Children are discreetly checked every day for bruising.

Bruce, the Project Leader, a bearded, kindly man explains:

The parents are not deliberately wanton or callous, they are young immature people. Before they come here we try to make sure that they take some responsibility and feel some remorse. What needs to happen is a personal change in the parent, so that the parent can care for the children.

Care has become a dirty word but in terms of healing it can be the most important way in to help the family ... What we find when working on child behaviour problems is that it sparks off memories of how parents were treated. One girl who had bruised her own baby was brought up by a father in the Forces. Her father would line up the seven children with the tallest on the right, the shortest on the left. Then he would take the buckle end of his belt. She was the fifth of seven children and even before he touched her she was so frightened that she had wet herself.

Most of the families come from the north and west of Belfast, the most deprived areas of the city, and once they are referred (usually by social services or health visitors) two members of staff visit the family. If they are willing, the family then comes to the Centre. Most of the parents are single mothers but if husbands or men-friends are living with the family they are obliged to attend at first.

Each person, each family, presents a different problem and different programmes are worked out on the basis of family needs. The 'treatment' usually takes about a year.

Flash points in troubled families often occur at meal-times, at toilet or bath-time. With the use of a video, the mothers at the Centre are helped to 'see' themselves with their children. A mother who had beaten her toddler with a wooden spoon while she was in the bath was aided by a re-enactment of the crisis. As she bathed her little girl at the Centre a member of staff talked her through, encouraging her to play with the child and enjoy the event.

Play is important and staff look after the children in a bright, spacious playroom. They take care to see that when toys are put out mother is not forgotten. Pat, a twenty-eight-year-old married woman suffering from post-natal depression, couldn't reach out to her year-old son. She felt nervous at being filmed with him and sat reading when he was trying to find out how to use a new toy. Just seeing herself helped her to realise the problem. Another mother, in for assessment, lay on top of her four-year-old son and put a pillow over his face 'in play'. That child is now permanently removed from her care.

An important part of the programme for the mothers is the support, encouragement and close involvement of the staff. Doreen came to the Centre with her youngest child, Michael, after she had confessed to her health visitor that she felt like killing her baby. She has three other children, two boys and a girl, aged eight, six and three. At the time, Michael was nine months old, crying all day and all night.

My confidence was at its lowest ebb when I first came to the Centre. I was shouting at the other children and biting the head off Paddy [her husband]. Michael had to be on my knee, he wouldn't stop crying and he clung and clung. I had a lot of problems, marriage problems, I really contemplated suicide.

I said to myself, if I kill myself, I know my mum will take care of the kids. We were over our heads in debt, rent and electric, and if I done away with myself all our debts would be cleared. But you love your kids that much you don't want to leave 'em.

Patricia [Doreen's key worker] was gently probing to find out why

I felt aggressive. I was able to talk to her more openly than I'd done in my whole life. Patricia seemed to understand me right away, to pick up my moods. I could never sit down with my own sisters. I felt they had enough troubles of their own. At the Centre I had the freedom to talk. I felt it was confidential, they listened to me and were interested. The fact of saying things makes it clear to you. I had so much in my head going round and round and it all got on top of you. Paddy and myself, our marriage was at rockbottom and he drank quite a bit. There were things in the background, too. I had a brother that died and in our house no one talks about it, it's sort of a sacred subject.

Patricia helped me to sort things out. She really helped me, talking about the way I coped with Michael. We worked out a programme. If I felt aggressive I put him in his cot, locked the door and put TV on, and it worked. I put him in bed at seven and didn't go into him at all.

I supposed I was a bit ashamed before. I couldn't go out to the kitchen to make a meal without him crying. For months, whenever we had our meals Patricia took him off our hands. It was the only bit of peace we had. She made me see that it wasn't all Paddy's fault, that I was to blame, too. Bruce [the project leader] went out to see Paddy about our marriage and how it affected the baby. I realise now I played as big a part as he did.

When I came here I was getting anti-depressants from the doctor but they just seemed to make me tired. I took myself off them soon after I came. I had Tricia and Bruce's home numbers and I could have rung them if I ever felt the need. Sometimes I just sat beside the telephone and cried. I came twice a week for over a year. Patricia helped me to see about rent arrears and make weekly payments. At least we were doing something to get the debt paid off.

After a year at the Centre Doreen felt ready to leave. She and her husband went to a marriage guidance counsellor and she is now looking for a part-time job. She must be counted as one of the 50 per cent successes. One-third of the very troubled mothers who come to the Centre drop out of the programme and the strain on staff who carry the problem is high. In a report on the Centre written for Barnardo's, Dorothy Birchall of the National Children's Bureau commented that it 'is providing a valuable service for a considerable number of highly disadvantaged families, due in no small measure to the deep commitment of the small group of dedicated staff'.[4]

In his day, Barnardo had believed, with some justification, that the only chance for neglected or badly treated children was to snatch them away from their parents to safety. Until twenty or thirty years ago, the children's families were allowed to split up and disappear. Today, Barnardo's approach embraces the whole family; they reach out to isolated and disadvantaged parents as well as their children. That is the direction of their work with all children, especially the under-fives. Local and national needs and customs make for variations. The imaginative work with Catholic families centred in Dublin includes a popular children's bus, a bright yellow Barnardo's double-decker which travels to Dublin's grimmest slums to offer the children a hot meal, a story, painting, plasticine and creative play. Mothers are encouraged to climb aboard, too, and gradually to learn to take over the task of play leaders. Some of those mothers gain the confidence to take courses in play-leadership themselves and start their own playgroups, arrange meetings and attract the finance and publicity. After a time the bus moves on, to encourage other deprived children and parents (gypsies on one site) and give them a chance to learn to play.

In 1970, with the support of the Department of Health and Social Security, Barnardo's took over the work of the Family Institute in Cardiff, a pioneering family therapy service which developed a programme of practice, teaching and research which was internationally acclaimed. The Institute, with a team of clinical psychologists and social workers, explores family problems through the interaction of all the members, using video tapes and role play. Although administratively a Barnardo unit, the Family Institute stands outside the mainstream of Barnardo work in method, staffing and clientele. Over the years many family therapists have trained there and it has proved a useful resource for the social work profession. Unfortunately, the grants for students from the Central Council for Education and Training in Social Work ceased this year and the Student Training Unit has closed.

Barnardo himself began his work partly to prevent juvenile delinquency by housing the wretched children of the streets. Just before the Second World War, the charity was asked by the Home Office to administer Approved Schools for children in trouble. They always regarded those schools as distinct from their charitable work with children: the young tearaways were safely contained within them and the costs met by the Government. The public knew little of them.

When the Government transformed the Approved Schools in 1969 into Community Homes with Education, they also suggested an alternative scheme to avoid sending children away from home. 'Intermediate Treatment' was an option for the courts. It is a broad term which included training, treatment and recreation that might mean giving a boy or girl in trouble a change of scene and keeping them out of mischief. Local authorities could either set up such schemes themselves or ask voluntary societies to do the work on their behalf. Barnardo's set up their first scheme for boys at risk in 1974 in a large old house in the centre of Yorkshire. Today they have Intermediate Treatment Centres (or IT Centres as they are usually called) all over the country. All are different. Some look superficially like 'sixties-style youth clubs with drama, art, disco dancing, guitar, keep-fit and swimming as part of the programme.

At an IT Centre in Cardiff, boys and girls from ten to sixteen who are in trouble and persistently truanting from school receive daily lessons in living with other people as well as in the more conventional subjects in the school curriculum. Despite a court order, they themselves 'contract' to attend and are gradually weaned back from the runaway life. For almost all of the children involved, learning in a small and friendly setting makes a welcome change from the huge schools they attend. The IT staff keep in close touch with the local schools and the children must attend their ordinary school at least one day a week. The luxury of a listening ear (either a social worker or a teacher is on hand) is paramount for these children.

'They've got time for you,' said Iris, a tall fourteen-year-old who attends the second biggest school in the city. 'They phone up the court to see if you are all right.' Children like Iris who have gained a reputation for wrongdoing in their brief lives, get a second chance, and often value it. 'They makes you feel trusted,' she blurted out, 'they trust you, because they leave money about.' Even if that trust is occasionally abused, the children's gain is incalculable. But it can be hard on the staff.

In January 1980 a Barnardo IT Centre was due to open in a drab suburb of Liverpool but vandals broke into the building and set it on fire. The first group of children was meeting temporarily in a church hall and the new building opened in December. Despite padlocks and a barricaded building, the Centre is broken into regularly. Like much of the city, the area looks run-down and shabby, a disintegrating community with an air of desolation in the streets. Barnardo's initiated the Intermediate Treatment programme in Liverpool with a 50 per cent grant from the Social Services Department, housed in Barnardo's well-used and abused building. The co-operation works well, with all those concerned with local youth involved, the local police chief, social services officers, local magistrates and representatives from Education and Probation Departments as well as local residents.

The problem for young people is acute in an area of 50 per cent unemployment, with the local secondary schools teaching mainly at remedial level and their teaching staffs dwindling. The local IT Centre makes a brave effort to redress the balance. Ordinary youth club activities are held from banger-racing to working with computers, from music and drama to five-a-side football, netball and canoeing in order to attract youngsters not yet in trouble.

Their main priority, however, is youngsters referred from the courts, who range in age from fourteen to seventeen and have committed offences such as taking and driving away, shoplifting, wounding. The court order may require them to spend several nights away from home and this usually means going camping or staying in a cottage in the Welsh mountains. The first two nights with a group usually begin with a big battle over the ground rules. If the boy (it is nearly always a group of boys) does not stick it or attend the group meetings two nights a week, Barnardo's takes him back to the court. That has happened in one case.

Their second priority is borderline children, boys and girls in danger of committing a crime or being placed in care without help. Many of them come from appalling home backgrounds and Barnardo's visit the children and parents at home with a local authority social worker to try to help resolve the fights and the truanting which may lead to more serious trouble.

On Monday evenings a small group of young offenders meets to discuss the issues of delinquency and its effects. Paul, an ex-convict in prison for two years and formerly on a community service order, is a full-time volunteer. His life revolves around the Centre. His practical experience of prison life and his knowledge of the youngsters make him invaluable. 'So many people are slagging the kids off and nobody is praising them,' he says. Praise and reward (a monthly night out ice-skating, roller-skating, a visit to the cinema or a meal out) beckon those who behave well.

In the group the reasons for committing a crime are debated: broke, bored, or 'my mates do it' are phrases often heard. 'I have had a row with me dad,' says another lad. With the exception of Pete, who is big for his sixteen years and had been thrown out of his school, the 'criminals' look small and rather frightened, despite their spunky talk.

Pete is in trouble for passing forged notes, theft and wounding (he was found with a knife at three in the morning). He lives with his mother who has a rich boyfriend. His dad is a bouncer in a local men's club. On his first overnight camp where the boys' behaviour in a group is noted, Pete caused trouble, smashed some equipment and smoked cannabis.

Fourteen-year-old Simon's brother has recently died from an overdose of heroin. Since then Simon has been in a lot of trouble: in front of the magistrates for burglary and abusive, insulting behaviour. He was recently remanded in custody for car theft.

Tony, aged fifteen, was also thrown out of school. He has appeared on a 'burglary with assault' charge. The only delinquent in his family, Tony nicks from his mother's purse at home.

The group was smaller than usual as it was holiday time. Paul, the volunteer, and a social worker try to point out the moral and practical issues involved in crime to the boys. In an area of such high unemployment, those who 'have' are regarded as fair game. It is rare to find a youngster who thinks shoplifting is wrong. A list of crimes is drawn up on the blackboard. The boys call out what they:

Would do
Screw a club
Shoplift
Take-and-drive-away

and what they

Wouldn't do
Child molesting (the most unpopular crime among these youngsters)
Murder
Kidnap
Rape

in that order.

It is difficult to assess the success of the project since the policies of both policing and sentencing vary so greatly that crime figures are hard to interpret.

Significantly Barnardo's have opened three new IT Centres in the north-west. Central Government supports Intermediate Treatment enthusiastically and in 1983 gave local authorities a strong inducement to work with voluntary agencies. For local authorities who work in partnership with the voluntary societies to set up Intermediate Treatment, the Government provided an extra grant of fifteen million pounds over a period of three years.[5] At present Barnardo's have twenty IT Centres throughout the country.

Barnardo saw education and training for the young as a cure for juvenile delinquency. By the early 'seventies, however, all vocational training save the small printing school at Hertford with twenty-five living-in apprentices, had been closed. The need for help to find work, it was justifiably assumed, was no longer a priority.

Recession and unemployment changed the perspective. Barnardo social workers in the inner cities had begun to notice the stress suffered by families in areas of high unemployment and the despair and disaffection of young people who might never find a job. The charity was faced with two options: either to train the young and help them to get work or to encourage teenagers to develop interests that would enrich a life without work.

In Newcastle, Barnardo's have tried both strategies. In 1975 they opened a Day Centre for children and families and young people on a vandalised post-war housing estate, made up of high-rise council flats, maisonettes and houses. Today the Youth Centre, enlarged and in separate premises, includes an advice centre and club for the unemployed with darts, a disco, ping-pong and pin-tables. Weekend camping, hill-walking and outings to swimming pools and skating rinks are on the programme. A local further education college offers courses in woodwork and carpentry. During the day the scene is fairly quiet. A handful of children over twelve act as part-time leaders. Inside the club two long-haired youths in leather jackets play pool and share a packet of Woodbines. 'It's somewhere to hang about,' said one. 'There's nothing else here. A job. What's that?'

Only one in three of the youths is likely to find work according to local social workers. The club does offer another focus to young people whose lives are bounded by the telly and the Social Security office. Despite the distractions offered and the football pitch at the back, they dream of more exotic activities: racing cars, scuba diving, hang gliding.

Barnardo himself began his work training young people for a trade. High unemployment, financial cutbacks in the social services and a declining child population caused Barnardo's in Newcastle to go back to its nineteenth-century origins. Once more the charity has decided to become a training agency for young people.

On the coast outside Newcastle, a residential hostel for young people was converted into a Youth Training Scheme in 1982, funded by the Manpower Services Commission and managed by Barnardo's. The scheme now schools up to 140 young people a year in domestic, clerical, retail and warehousing work. The youngsters come in daily for thirteen weeks. Recently the EEC Anti-Poverty Programme has agreed to provide a grant and with the additional funding Barnardo's will be able to help trainees who complete the course successfully yet still fail to find work. Training youth to find work is today a growing part of Barnardo's work and a handful of schemes exists already.

A hundred years ago, Barnardo was opening large new homes for children year after year. Today his charity presents as active and restless a picture as in the past, with new projects constantly opening and others closing. Now, however, two-thirds of Barnardo's work consists of keeping children out of institutions. The only growth in residential work is with the mentally (and usually multiply) handicapped. The difference is that until twenty or thirty years ago the children came in for their entire childhood. Today each girl or boy enters a Barnardo home with a definite treatment programme worked out and the prospect of going back either to their own homes or to a foster-parent's.

A passionate commitment to giving mentally handicapped children and their families a better chance in life combined with careful planning has contributed significantly to the whole field. The commitment originated principally in the north-west (Liverpool), one of the last Divisions to be re-organised after the great shake-up.

In 1970 Alan Kendall (now the Divisional Director for Barnardo's in the north-west) had just joined the charity from a post with the local authority. He began to tour Barnardo's older homes in the area, in Llandudno, Chester, Liverpool and Southport to discover that they were half-empty; at the same time he was constantly hearing from local authority colleagues of the urgent need for suitable homes for mentally handicapped children. To build special homes for those children would take time as well as money and Alan Kendall wondered whether those mentally handicapped children could not share their lives with the 'ordinary' children in Barnardo's homes.

At the time Barnardo's housed their mentally handicapped children in two small homes. In the past they had been chary of expanding in the field. At first reservations were expressed about integration: staff might spend too much time on the handicapped and neglect the 'normals' or 'normal' boys and girls would feel the stigma of living with their handicapped fellows and be ashamed to invite other children to the home.[6] A later study in Liverpool revealed that living with handicapped children had made the normal children more tolerant and understanding and helped the handicapped to learn to master eating with a knife and fork, as well as other social skills. (Barnardo himself had put forward cogent similar arguments for integrating the handicapped.)

At the time, a handful of individuals in Liverpool, both inside Barnardo's and in the social services was concerned to transfer mentally handicapped children from the often grim, longstay sub-normality hospitals to a more homely atmosphere. Pilot fostering schemes were set up for a few severely subnormal children (usually measured as children with an IQ below fifty-five). When Barnardo's launched their scheme offering full support to foster-parents, transport and a lifeline to social workers, the natural parents of mentally handicapped children elsewhere responded through the *Guardian* newspaper by saying that if they had been given that kind of support fostering would not have been necessary.

Listening to parents and acting on their needs became the way forward for Barnardo's in their crusade to better the lives of mentally handicapped children and their families. By the mid-'seventies, the head of Barrow's Green, a Barnardo home in the Lake District, retired and the home was converted into a holiday residence for mentally handicapped children, to give parents a vital break during the long summer holidays. Meeting those parents and hearing of their difficulties contributed to the Division's experience. They were meeting families with a child who screamed all day long, mothers with a doubly incontinent child and no washing-machine and an increasing number of families with multiply handicapped children.

The decision to work with families in their own homes, to set up support services for the mentally handicapped, came as a natural consequence. Barnardo's in the north-west decided to start work in Chorley, where they had links with the social services and an office not too far away. They wanted to get in touch with every single parent with a mentally handicapped child in the locality. Through meticulous planning they enlisted the co-operation of all the statutory and voluntary bodies concerned with the mentally handicapped and held a meeting of parents in Chorley's Special School.

With parents' consent, Barnardo social workers visited the families to find out what they wanted. Information was perhaps the first priority. Many parents lacked knowledge or information about their child's handicap. Often doctors would not give a diagnosis, they reported, and parents simply did not know where to turn. They were missing out on welfare rights or attendance allowance. One of Barnardo's biggest tasks was to help parents to use the system to learn what to ask for and where to get help. From this contact came a parents' workshop with talks from local specialists: educational and clinical psychologists, occupational therapists, speech therapists, geneticists. Although a few parents resented the intrusion into their lives, most found help, support, companionship through the activities.

The social workers also discovered that although the children often had plenty of toys of the soft, cuddly type they might benefit from more stimulating play. A toy library was set up with attractive toys designed to help the child's development. Often parents find themselves isolated because of their child's handicap and the library, as well as the parents' workshop, serves as a meeting place for parents who can share experiences and companionship.

Every year social workers run a play scheme when the schools are on the long summer holidays, taking the children on outings to local parks and beauty spots, organising painting and craftwork, a Punch and Judy show, birthday parties. Volunteers from local schools, colleges and voluntary groups are recruited. The volunteers form an important part of the service since they work closely with the children, escorting, baby-sitting, as well as helping with transport and manning the toy library; they must all be cleared by the police as well as giving two personal references.

Barnardo's Chorley project takes an overall view of families with handicapped children. They have involved brothers and sisters of the handicapped in an imaginative play scheme, both to help them to feel a part of the service and to assess the impact of handicap on 'normal' children. Working with all those seeking to help handicapped families has made a significant contribution both locally and countrywide inside and outside Barnardo's.

Alan Kendall's work for mentally handicapped children has won him respect in this country and abroad. He has twice visited America to study the methods of caring for profoundly handicapped children in the community. In recent years all governments have been convinced of the need to care for hospital patients in the community on both humane and economic grounds. In the case of the mentally handicapped, however, it was always assumed that a hard core of very severely handicapped children would have to be nursed in hospital wards. To challenge that assumption, Barnardo's built four bungalows near Liverpool for eight children and the necessary staff. Their experiment was supported and mainly funded by the Department of Health and Social Security.

Before the children were transferred to the bungalows, Barnardo psychologists and social workers worked for weeks on the wards of the hospital selected. They assessed suitable children and helped to ease the transition by learning to nurse the children, to feed them, to put them to bed and wake them in the morning. The children chosen suffered from both mental retardation and physical disability. Some could neither walk nor speak; some were doubly incontinent. Diagnostically they were labelled as suffering from cerebral palsy; spastic quadraplegia; profound deafness; blindness and hydrocephalus. When they transferred to the new bungalows they were deliberately known by their names and not by their handicaps.

Barnardo's decided to discriminate positively for these very handicapped children. The four bungalows were built on a pleasant, modern, middle-class housing estate near the city. Inside they are bright and cheerful with cream walls, a Dralon settee and family photographs on the mantelpiece. The dining room has a cork-tiled floor and the kitchen is modern and well equipped. Part of the challenge was to prove to the neighbours that mentally handicapped people are pleasant to be with and visits were encouraged. But the main purpose was to introduce children used to a fifteen-bed ward and all the regimentation of hospital routine to a more homely and friendly environment. In hospital the children were woken at 6 a.m. In the Intensive Support Unit (an ugly name for a humane enterprise) the children are woken at 7 a.m. on schooldays and allowed to sleep late at weekends. In hospital all the children's food was liquidised to make it quicker and easier to feed them. They were spoken to and treated as helpless babies.[7]

At home in the bungalows, the staff put enormous effort into helping them to develop individual tastes, to express, in some form, likes and dislikes.

Michael, aged eleven, lay in a permanent spasm in hospital. He was wheeled to school in the mornings in a 'horrendous' Victorian pram, plumped on a bean bag and left. He has recently learnt to enjoy hydrotherapy, a new experience, to laugh, cry and develop a taste for chocolate.

Shirley, who is ten, clamps her teeth when eating. (One of the nurses in the hospital had to have stitches after Shirley bit her.) In the hospital all the food arrived on a trolley. In the bungalow Shirley is gradually learning to recognise the smell and sound of food being prepared. She has physiotherapy every day and is beginning to relax her jaw and to chew. Every weekend she goes home to her family who are delighted with her progress. 'I can kiss my daughter now,' said her mother.

Phyllis, aged six, was treated like a baby and classed as profoundly deaf. Nobody really talked to her. Now she has a hearing aid. When Phyllis had to have a feeding tube passed from her nose down the back of her mouth to her aesophagus, her 'link' worker tried it herself. 'She doesn't like it,' she said, 'and I don't blame her.' The tiniest movement brings an enthusiastic response from the staff. Peter held his head up for ten seconds. Phyllis followed a volunteer round the room with her eyes.

With such handicapped children who need medical care as well as constant attention, the staff ratio must be high. For the eight children there are ten social workers and five night staff as well as eight young girl trainees, fourteen volunteers and two part-time domestics.

After a year most of the children were sitting at the dining-table eating or being fed solid or semi-solid food. After two years, three of the children had been fostered and all had improved. A research worker from the University of Hull monitored the project carefully. 'In view of the extent of the children's handicaps and the ill-health that they experience, this is a remarkable achievement.'[8]

Through workshops, working parties and papers, the North-West

(Liverpool) Division and Barnardo's Research and Development team disseminated knowledge of the new ways of caring for the mentally handicapped. Today every Division of Barnardo's is involved in some aspect of the work.

Dr B's Kitchen, another imaginative project with handicapped young people, arose out of a visit social worker Ian Booth made in 1983 to the Donut Shop in San Diego, an eaterie where handicapped youngsters learn to make and sell the product. Ian studied training schemes in the USA and Canada and from his visit came an English adaptation. In Harrogate, Barnardo's Yorkshire Division opened Dr B.'s Kitchen, a clean, attractive café especially adapted for handicapped apprentices and selling home-made country fare. The cash till in the café can be operated from a wheelchair and a stairlift carries the young people to the first floor, where they are trained and counselled. Gardner Merchant, a division of Trust House Forte International, committed to helping the disabled to find employment, contributed to the design of the café and kitchen, advised on catering equipment and recruited supervisors. The first four trainees, aged from nineteen to twenty-one, a girl with a visual handicap and three mentally retarded young people, have all done well. The Manpower Services Commission paid their training wage and part of Barnardo's management costs. Barnardo's subsidise the Kitchen to the tune of £35,000 a year: not cheap but it does live up to their aim 'to extend knowledge and improve practice' in their child care work.[9]

These are but a small sample of some of the best of Barnardo's 140 – 150 child care projects all over the country. Schools like New Mossford in the Village, near the founder's first honeymoon home, tend physically handicapped children with high tech and human concern. In the decade since the home opened the difficulties of the children coming into the home have increased. Many have multiple handicaps and a few do not have long to live. The Project Leader sees a part of his work as helping the parents to face their death. In his first hospital Barnardo took in dying children so the school stands well in the Barnardo tradition.

In all their homes and schools the needs of the children have become more acute. Wherever possible today children are cared for in their own homes or with foster-parents. In schools for the maladjusted and the educationally subnormal, Barnardo's are offering a chance to children at the end of the line. The task grows more difficult as the number of local authorities who can or will afford the fees for the service diminishes. Yet there will always be children with severe problems who need a sheltered and caring environment. If Barnardo's do not care for them, it is difficult to know who will.

The variety of Barnardo's work within the sphere of child care is extraordinary: from helping widows and widowers to cope with their grief and bring up their children in Newcastle, to divorce conciliation in Liverpool and Kent; from working with chronically sick children suffering from cystic fibrosis in Birmingham, to tackling drug misuse on Tyneside. Yet the cumulative effect of building up specialist knowledge and concentrating on the needs of one group of children has proved important. In Liverpool a new plan has been made to ensure the future for mentally handicapped children living with their families by an Advocacy/Trustee Scheme. That will take an enormous burden from the parents.

Diversity has its difficulties. In Barnardo's day, with his brilliance with words, it was relatively simple to stamp the charity with an image: the image of orphan children. That image has never been completely dislodged from the minds and hearts of the nation. Yet it is not easy to characterise Barnardo's many facets in a phrase or a picture today. Within the charity the quest for a new image has been going on for at least two years. Barnardo's has so many roles: Christian child care agency, property owner, publisher, film maker, retailer and extremely successful non-profit-making business. Barnardo's fund-raising has always been commendably powerful and effective. But as in earlier times, the thrust to expand, the pomp and ceremony of the Barnardo occasion, sometimes tends to obscure the fine work and the main direction of the charity. Does Barnardo's exist to raise money primarily and then to find needs to meet, or to find needs which must be funded?

Careful husbandry by Council and staff since the years of recession has meant that funds and investments look remarkably healthy. Barnardo's income in 1987 was £47.3 million, their expenditure £44.7 million of which £36 million was spent on child care.

Council and staff have been debating how best to spend some of that growing income, selecting new directions for Barnardo's for some time. Many would like to see Barnardo's attack the problems of homelessness and drugs on a larger scale. Others would prefer Barnardo's to help children in the Third World and there are those who feel that the charity should be working with the very poorest families in this country.

In recent years they have worked closely with local authorities as well as with central Government. That was their intention on reorganisation. Unfortunately they are caught in the political crossfire between a Government who would like social services to co-ordinate and facilitate welfare services rather than providing them, and certain local authorities who suspect all voluntary work as privatisation. Some authorities want to see welfare services provided as a right and not as a charity; they may include those with the families in the greatest need. To care for those children and their parents, Barnardo's would have to find a means of independent action: to go it alone. Once again the responsibility of raising standards and meeting new needs for children has fallen back on the large voluntary societies.

In recent years Barnardo's has gained a high reputation for careful and systematic management and administration. Their present Senior Director, Roger Singleton, is committed both to expand Barnardo's and to maintain their high professional standards. He is initiating an independent inspection for all their work. The sheer size and hierarchical structure of Barnardo's makes it difficult for the charity to act quickly. Plans mature over years and piles of papers. To rule over Barnardo's, to decide on priorities when so many needs are pressing, demands patience, caution, wisdom and professional skill and perhaps one other quality which the founder of Barnardo's possessed in abundance: passion.

Any organisation dealing with children must have rules and Barnardo's rules on the care and control of children are models of concern and compassion. In the torrents of paper which make up their Policy and Procedure guide they also include rules on the minutiae of corporate life: from the amount of time needed to clean a child's bedroom (seven minutes a day for a bedroom for one child, ten minutes a day for two children) to the right season to hold a gala evening (the autumn) and the number of the form needed to apply for a Barnardo car loan. The guide omits any mention of sexual instruction for children. Even though there are discussion documents on the subject, the omission seems extraordinary in a voluntary society with over 1,000 children in residence. Is it fanciful to imagine that the constraints of their Puritan past still haunt the Village?

Barnardo's has always attracted committed and concerned individuals both as staff members and honorary officers. Lady Wagner took a diploma in Social Administration in order to become more effective in her work for Barnardo's. During the years of reorganisation Mr Hillyer and Mr Lawson gave innumerable hours from their business and professional commitments to help resolve the dilemma. The present Chairman of Barnardo's, Norman Bowie, devotes endless time to committees, functions, and fund-raising occasions. To be a member of Barnardo's Council is rightly regarded as a privilege and a cachet. For many years, Council members have come from similar worlds and similar backgrounds. Over sixty years ago in April 1925, the Executive Committee raised the question of inviting a working man's representative to serve but that was shelved. Today the charity seeks to include people from Ireland and the ethnic minorities as well as clients or their families, to broaden the nature of Council and reflect modern Barnardo's.

The sheer size of Barnardo's achievement is staggering. During its history, the charity has absorbed seven other organisations which cared for children: the John Curtis Charity; the Liverpool Sheltering Homes; the Macpherson Homes; the Reformatory and Refuge Union of which the Children's Aid Society was a part; St Matthew's Orphanage and Miss Sharman's Homes.

In Australia today the charity supports and keeps families together and helps with the handicapped; in New Zealand they provide mother-care flats for vulnerable young women, family support and foster care. In the future they plan to sponsor a conference in Malaysia in co-operation with Voluntary Service Overseas on the needs of handicapped children. In 1987 Barnardo's in the Republic of Ireland plan to became an independent charity.

Today as in the founder's day there are great chasms in society, neglected children, uncaring parents, poverty and ignorance. Barnardo's does co-operate with the other major voluntary children's charities as well as with the local authorities and central Government. But provision for the children remains patchy. For over a hundred years Barnardo's has influenced Government and public opinion; their history places them in a unique and powerful position. If Barnardo's could spearhead a coalition of children's charities, identifying the most acute needs and planning a comprehensive cover to supplement state provision, that would seem a fitting role for the children's champion. The undertaking would be vast, difficult and costly, but with the increased responsibility for child welfare placed on charity in recent years and the social deprivation so prevalent in our cities, a major initiative is needed. Anyone who gets caught up in the Barnardo operation becomes infected with enthusiasm and concern. And no one can doubt their commitment, their vitality, their resolve to do their best – for the sake of the children.

Notes

NOTE ON SOURCES

I have drawn largely on primary sources in this book, on Barnardo's very extensive archives housed in Liverpool University and in their library at head-quarters in Barkingside.

In the early years Barnardo's Annual Reports and Accounts were dated irregularly and often appeared months late. 'The First Occasional Record of the Lord's Dealings in connexion with the East End Juvenile Mission' was dated July 1868; the second Annual Report was dated December 1869; the third March 1871. After that they were dated 31 March until the accounting system changed at the end of 1888. From 1889 to 1963 the institutional year was dated from 1 January. Then the date was changed back to April to coincide with the local authority practice. Today the Report and Accounts are drawn up by the end of March, approved by Council in July and issued at the Annual General Meeting in October.

The title of the institutions has changed several times: originally it was entitled the 'East End Juvenile Mission'; after the arbitration in 1878 the name was changed to 'Dr Barnardo's Homes and East End Juvenile Mission'; in October 1899 after incorporation, the organisation became the 'National Incorporated Association for the Reclamation of Destitute Waif Children otherwise known as Dr Barnardo's Homes'; after Barnardo's death, the title was changed yet again to become 'Dr Barnardo's Homes: National Incorporated Association'; on 1 January 1966 the title was changed to the present-day 'Dr Barnardo's', the name by which the public has known it for over a century. The Executive Committee, too, changed its name several times; so did the different fund-raising schemes.

In two lengthy Annual Reports, 1874–5, entitled 'Rescue the Perishing' and 1887–8, entitled 'Something Attempted, Something Done!' (published in 1890 in book form) Barnardo included a great deal of institutional history. Since he wrote so prolifically, identical material often appeared in Annual Reports and in his magazines, particularly *Night and Day*. His use of figures in his publicity was sometimes very exaggerated.

CHAPTER 1: ORIGINS

1. Barnardo and Marchant, *The Memoirs of the Late Dr Barnardo*, Chapter 1
2. Wagner, Gillian, *Barnardo*, Chapter 1
3. Somerville Large, Peter, *Dublin*
4. ibid.
5. Barnardo and Marchant, *Memoirs*, Chapter 2
6. ibid.
7. Wymer, Norman, *Father of Nobody's Children*, Chapter 1
8. Barnardo and Marchant, *Memoirs*, Chapter 2
9. ibid.
10. ibid.

11. Wagner, Gillian, *Barnardo*, Chapter 1
12. Barnardo and Marchant, *Memoirs*, Chapter 2
13. ibid.
14. ibid.
15. ibid.
16. Taylor, Dr and Mrs Howard, Hudson Taylor and the China Inland Mission, Vol. 1

CHAPTER 2: THE OPPORTUNITY

1. Barnardo, T. J., *Sermon Notes on St Paul's Letters*
2. Taylor, Dr and Mrs Howard, *Hudson Taylor and the China Inland Mission*, Vol. 1
3. ibid.
4. The First Occasional Record of the Lord's Dealings in connexion with the East End Juvenile Mission, 1867–8.
5. Barnardo and Marchant, *Memoirs*, Chapter 4
6. Barnardo, T. J., *Sermon Notes*, December 1874
7. Barnardo and Marchant, *Memoirs*, Chapter 3
8. ibid., Chapter 4
9. ibid.
10. First Occasional Record, 1867–8
11. Wagner, Gillian, *Barnardo*, Chapter 2
12. ibid.
13. ibid.
14. Denison, Edward, Letters and other writings
15. The First Occasional Record, 1867–8
16. Annual Report, 1870–71
17. Barnardo and Marchant, *Memoirs*, Appendix B., Wagner, Gillian, *Barnardo*, Chapter 2
18. Barnardo and Marchant, *Memoirs*, Chapter 6
19. Perkin, Harold, *The Origins of Modern English Society, 1780-1880*, Chapter 4
20. Barnardo and Marchant, *Memoirs*, Chapter 8
21. ibid., Chapter 10
22. ibid.
23. Annual Report, 1874–5

CHAPTER 3: AN UNCHARITABLE AFFAIR

1. Annual Reports, 1868, 1874
2. Annual Report, 1874–5
3. Perkin, Harold, *Origins of Modern English Society*, Chapter 8
4. Wagner, Gillian, *Barnardo*, Chapter 6
5. *East London Observer*, 4 September 1875
6. ibid., 11 September 1875
7. ibid., 18 September 1875
8. *Tower Hamlets Independent*, 25 September 1875
9. *East London Observer*, 2 October 1875
10. Wagner, Gillian, *Barnardo*, Appendix
11. *Night and Day*, May 1877
12. *Tower Hamlets Independent*, 25 August 1877
13. *Night and Day*, May 1885
14. *Tower Hamlets Independent*, Supplement, 20 October 1877

15. *The Times*, 20 October 1877
16. Wagner, Gillian, *Barnardo*, Chapter 10; Pollock, John, *Shaftesbury*, Chapter 19

CHAPTER 4: A DREAM HOME

1. *Night and Day*, June 1879
2. Perkin, Harold, *The Origins of English Society*, Chapter 9
3. *Night and Day*, June 1879
4. ibid., March 1886
5. ibid., June 1880, Address by Lord Cairns
6. ibid., 1881, Article 'A Village Home' reprinted from *The Quiver*
7. Atkins, Lt.-Col. S. H., *Forum*, July 1965
8. *Night and Day*, June 1888
9. ibid., 1881, 'A Story of the Barkingside Village Home'
10. Barnardo, T. J., *Something Attempted, Something Done*, Chapter 7
11. ibid.
12. Barnardo and Marchant, *Memoirs*, Chapter 10
13. Interview with author
14. ibid.
15. Picton-Turbervill, Beatrice, *Memoirs of the Girls' Village Home 1920-41*
16. ibid.
17. Stileman, Rear-Admiral Sir Harry, Controversy between the Council and the Director, 1923
18. ibid., Minutes of Council and Executive, November 1921–May 1923
19. Annual Report, 1922. (Section based also on Council Minutes 16 November 1921–May 1923, and Executive Minutes of same period)
20. Picton-Turbervill, *Memoirs of the Girls' Village Home*
21. Rules, Girls' Village Home, 1927
22. Interview with author
23. ibid.
24. ibid.

CHAPTER 5: A NEW HEAVEN AND A NEW EARTH

1. Parr, Joy, 'The Home Children. British Juvenile Immigrants to Canada, 1868–1924, Ph.D. thesis, 1977. From Report to the Rt. Hon. the President of the Local Government Board by Andrew Doyle Esq., local government Inspector, as to the emigration of pauper children to Canada.
2. *Night and Day*, May 1879
3. ibid., September 1879
4. ibid., December 1880
5. Annual Report, 1881–2
6. Smith, Samuel, *Nineteenth Century*, May 1883
7. *Night and Day*, 1882, 'Our First Emigrants'
8. *Night and Day*, October 1883
9. ibid., August 1884
10. ibid., December 1883
11. ibid., June 1884
12. Barnardo and Marchant, *Memoirs*, Chapter 12
13. *Night and Day*, November 1885
14. Barnardo and Marchant, *Memoirs*, Chapter 12
15. Wagner, Gillian, *Barnardo*, Chapter 14

16. Parr, Joy, *Labouring Children*, Chapter 5
17. ibid., Chapter 6
18. Boys' Canada Register, Series I
19. ibid.
20. ibid.
21. *Night and Day*, December 1895
22. Wagner, Gillian, *Children of the Empire*, Chapter 8
23. *Ups and Downs*, 1 July 1898
24. Letters to the author
25. Parr, Joy, *Labouring Children*
26. Loveday, J., Letter to Mr Owen, 27 January 1900
27. Ingram, A. G., Letter to Owen, 12 May 1900
28. Cummings, Laura, Letter to Mr Owen, undated
29. Minutes of the Executive, 14 December 1910
30. Black, G. H., Letters to Mr McCall, 16 and 23 November 1916
31. ibid., Letter to Rev. W. J. Mayers, 17 November 1916
32. McCall, William, Letter to G. H. Black, 8 December 1916
33. Letter from Rev. W. J. Mayers to Mr Black, 5 December 1916
34. Hobday, J. W., Confidential Report, 1919
35. Minutes of the Executive, 12 January 1921
36. Minutes of the Council, 15 March 1922
37. Annual Report, 1923
38. Minutes of the Executive, 18 July 1931
39. Interview with author
40. *Night and Day*, Spring 1939

CHAPTER 6: ANY BEGGAR'S BAIRN

1. Annual Report, 1910
2. Barnardo and Marchant, *Memoirs*, Chapter 13
3. *Something Attempted, Something Done*, Chapter 23
4. Barnardo and Marchant, *Memoirs*, Chapter 22
5. *Something Attempted, Something Done*, Chapter 23
6. Heywood, *Children in Care*, Evidence of Miss Mason to Mundella Committee on Poor Law Schools
7. Barnardo and Marchant, *Memoirs*, Chapter 41
8. Annual Report, 1896
9. *Night and Day*, November 1897
10. Barnardo, T. J., *A Problem Solved*, Pamphlet, 1891
11. Barnardo, T. J., Letter to Dr Sinclair, 28 January 1903
12. Barnardo and Marchant, *Memoirs*, Chapter 8
13. Annual Report, 1911
14. Minutes of the Executive, November 1929
15. Dr Barnardo's Homes, Staff Conference Report, 1937, address by P. T. Kirkpatrick
16. ibid.
17. Letter to the author
18. Interview with the author
19. ibid.

CHAPTER 7: THE LITTLE SUFFERERS

1. Abstract of British Historical Statistics, 1962
2. *Night and Day*, April 1883

3. ibid., June 1884, Personal Notes
4. Barnardo and Marchant, *Memoirs*, Chapter 17
5. *Something Attempted, Something Done*, Chapter 18
6. Bowder, Bill, *Children First*
7. *Night and Day*, December 1897
8. ibid., December 1898
9. ibid., December 1894
10. Barnardo and Marchant, *Memoirs*, Chapter 20
11. T. J. Barnardo, Letter to J. W. Godfrey, 16 November 1904
12. Annual Report, 1896
13. *Night and Day*, March 1902
14. Minutes of the Executive, 14 December 1910
15. *Night and Day*, June 1911
16. Annual Report, 1922
17. Annual Report, 1937
18. Annual Report, 1928
19. *Night and Day*, July 1928
20. Picton-Turbervill, Beatrice, *Memoirs of the Girls' Village Home*
21. Minutes of the Executive Committee, 2 January 1936
22. Benson, John, *Working Class in England*
23. Interview with author
24. ibid.

CHAPTER 8: A START IN LIFE

1. *Something Attempted, Something Done*, 1888, Chapter 3
2. Annual Report, 1873–4
3. *Something Attempted, Something Done*, Chapter 20
4. Annual Report, 1874–5
5. Letter from Lord Cairns, Barnardo and Marchant, *Memoirs*, Chapter 20
6. *Night and Day*, 1882, Advertisement
7. *Something Attempted, Something Done*, Chapter 40
8. ibid., Chapters 13 and 14
9. Barnardo and Marchant, *Memoirs*, Chapter 10
10. *Night and Day*, January–June 1902, June 1903
11. Annual Report, 1925
12. Council Minute, July 1924
13. Letters to the author
14. Board of Education, Report of H.M. Inspectors on Watts Naval Training School, 1935
15. *Ups and Downs*, September 1899
16. Annual Report, 1922
17. Executive Minute, 7 March 1928
18. Interview with author
19. Annual Report
20. ibid.
21. Minutes of the Council, 8 June 1940
22. Annual Report, 1942
23. Committee of Management Meeting, January 1947; Annual Report, 1947

CHAPTER 9: PASSPORT FOR LIFE

1. *Night and Day*, December 1886
2. *Something Attempted, Something Done*, Chapter 3
3. ibid.
4. Dr Barnardo's Homes, Conference Report, 1928
5. ibid., 1937
6. ibid.
7. *Something Attempted, Something Done*, Chapter 10
8. ibid.
9. Annual Report, 1898
10. ibid.
11. Annual Report, 1925
12. Minutes of the Executive, 13 April 1938
13. *Night and Day*, January–March 1938
14. Annual Report, 1894
15. ibid., 1898
16. *Night and Day*, 1883
17. Annual Report, 1933–4
18. Annual Report, 1937
19. Interview with author
20. ibid.

CHAPTER 10: WAIFS IN WARTIME

1. Annual Report, 1940
2. Central Statistical Office, Annual Abstract of Statistics
3. *Night and Day*, Spring 1939
4. ibid.
5. Annual Report, 1943
6. Interview with author
7. Report of the Care of the Children Committee, Section 2, 1946
8. ibid.
9. Minutes of Executive, 21 August 1940, 6 March 1941
10. *The Children's Advocate*, 1873
11. Interview with author
12. Boarding Out, Inspectors' Report, January - June 1941
13. *Forum*, December 1966
14. Appeals Department, File on Little Bardfield; Wilson, Stanley, 'The Mayor and the Matron'
15. Interview with author
16. Letters to author
17. Barnardo Book, 1944
18. Mr Tetley, Special Meeting of Council, March 1946

CHAPTER 11: 'WHOSE CHILDREN?'

1. Dr Barnardo's Homes, Conference Report, 1957
2. *The Times*, 15 July 1944
3. Allen of Hurtwood, Lady, 'Whose Children?' Pamphlet, 1945
4. Minutes of the Executive, January 1945
5. Interview with author
6. *Forum*, April 1946

7. Barnardo Report on the Care of the Children Committee, 1946
8. Memorandum from Miss Dyson on the Care of the Children Report, January 1947
9. Letter from Lady Blackford, 17 October 1947
10. McCauley, Duncan, *Behind the Scenes at Wimbledon*
11. Annual Report, 1948
12. Children Act, 1948, Part II, 12
13. ibid., Part 1, 3
14. Memorandum on Reorganisation, 9 July 1952
15. Interview with author
16. Dr Barnardo's Homes, Staff Conference Report, 1953
17. Council Meetings, 25 June 1947, 12 November 1947
18. Special Meeting of Council, 20 March 1946
19. Council Meeting, 12 November 1947
20. Dr Barnardo's Homes, Staff Conference Report, 1953
21. Responses from Superintendents of homes to question of mixing boys and girls, November 1955
22. Interview with author
23. Letter to author
24. Interview with author
25. Dr Barnardo's Homes, Staff Conference Report, 1953
26. Report of Sub-Committee on Auxiliary Boarding Out, 1953
27. Dr Barnardo's Homes, Conference Report, 1957
28. Report of S. J. Noel-Brown and Co. Ltd., appointed February 1958

CHAPTER 12: WITH A GRATEFUL HEART

1. Annual Report, 1874 - 5
2. *Night and Day*, May 1879
3. Barnardo and Marchant, *Memoirs*, Chapter 16
4. Barnardo, T. J., Letter to Advertising Agents dated 9 April 1903
5. Annual Report, 1894
6. *Night and Day*, April 1878
7. ibid., July, August, December 1880
8. *Night and Day*, March 1886
9. ibid.
10. Barnardo and Marchant, *Memoirs*, Chapter 15
11. ibid., Chapter 20
12. *Night and Day*, July and August 1880
13. ibid., December 1880
14. ibid., February 1885
15. Letter to accompany Musical Party, 1891, from John Ruffels Archive, Australia
16. Barnardo and Marchant, *Memoirs*, Chapter 17
17. *Night and Day*, April 1898
18. Barnardo and Marchant, *Memoirs*, Chapter 10
19. *Night and Day*, January, September, December 1906, March, December 1907
20. Bentham, Effie, Letter to Mr Potter, September 1967
21. Annual Report, 1937
22. ibid., 1981
23. *Forum*, January 1964

CHAPTER 13: THE YEARS OF FLUX

1. Interview with author
2. ibid.
3. Report on a Visit to Kenya, 1970, Appendix A
4. Childcare Problems in Kenya, 1956
5. Special Meetings of Council on Kenya, 15, 18 July, 17 September 1956
6. Appendix I to Report on The Work of Dr Barnardo's in Kenya, 1965
7. ibid., Appendix II
8. Report on a Visit to Kenya, 1970
9. Dr Barnardo's Homes, Staff Conference Report, 1965
10. Minutes of Committee of Management, May 1959
11. Noel-Brown Report, Sheet 114
12. Racial Integration Report, 1966
13. Interview with author
14. Racial Integration Report, 1966
15. Interview with author
16. Origins of Family Social Work, Edinburgh (undated)
17. Special Meeting of Committee of Management, 31 May 1962
18. *Goldonian Magazine*, 1967
19. Minutes of the Executive, 14 December 1908
20. Cornish, V. L., A Statement of Policy, 1965
21. *Forum*, Spring 1968
22. Interview with author
23. Meetings of Area Executive Officers, 1967
24. Interview with author
25. Singleton, Roger, *Barnardo News*, November 1976
26. A Residential Survey of Dr Barnardo's Nurseries, 1967
27. Interview with author
28. ibid.
29. General Secretary's Report to Council, 1968
30. Interview with author
31. Messrs Mclintock, Mann and Whinney Murray appointed in February 1970
32. *Forum*, Autumn 1970
33. General Superintendent's Report to Council, 1969–70
34. Director General's Report to Council, 1971–2

CHAPTER 14: THE ROCK FOUNDATION

1. Barnardo, T. J., Letter to Boys of Mittendorf House, Epsom, 22 December 1899
2. First Occasional Dealing (First Barnardo Report), 1867–8
3. Annual Report, 1871–2
4. Barnardo and Marchant, *Memoirs*, Chapter 16
5. ibid.
6. *Something Attempted, Something Done*, Chapter 32
7. Annual Report, 1895
8. *Night and Day*, February, April 1903
9. Annual Report, 1906
10. Minutes of Executive Committee, March 1922
11. Report of a Sub-Committee on Religious Upbringing, 1952
12. Committee of Management Minutes, 1, 28 July, 11, 18 August, 15 September 1948
13. Barnardo Book, 1955, 'Religious Training'

14. Dr Barnardo's Homes, Staff Conference Report, 1961
15. Committee of Management Minutes, 5 October 1965
16. Smith, General Sir Arthur, Letter, *Forum*, Spring 1969
17. Bywaters, Nancy, *Barnardo News*, November 1976
18. Report of the Committee on the Christian Outlook, 1971
19. Second Report of the Committee on the Christian Outlook, 1973
20. Christian Belief and Practice in Barnardo's, Report, 1974

CHAPTER 15: THE NEW JERUSALEM

1. Staff Report to Council, 1972/3
2. ibid., 1979/80, 1980/81
3. ibid., 1978/9
4. Barnardo's Antrim Road Family Centre, Belfast. Report by Dorothy Birchall of the National Children's Bureau
5. Staff Report to Council, 1982/3
6. A Review of the Integration Policy in the North-West, 1970–80
7. General Information on the Intensive Support Unit, Croxteth Park, 1983
8. Croxteth Park Project, 1986
9. Dr B.'s Kitchen, July 1985

Select Bibliography

Barnardo, Mrs, and Marchant, James, *Memoirs of the late Dr Barnardo*, Hodder and Stoughton, 1907

Benson, John, ed., *The Working Class in England*, Croom Helm, 1985

Best, Geoffrey, *Mid-Victorian Britain*, Fontana, 1979

Bloom, C. V., *Children are our Concern*, Dr Barnardo's, 1969

Booth, Charles, *Life and Labour of the People of London*, Macmillan, 1902

Booth, William, *In Darkest England and the Way Out*, Cooper Budd, 1890

Boss, Peter, *Exploration into Child Care*, Routledge and Kegan Paul, 1971

Bowder, Bill, *Children First*, Mowbray, 1980

Bready, J. Wesley, *Doctor Barnardo*, Allen and Unwin, 1930

Burnett, John, ed., *Destiny Obscure*, Penguin, 1984

Cunnington, Phyllis and Lucas, Catherine, *Charity Costumes*, Black, 1978

Denison, Edward, *Letters and Other Writings*, Bentley, 1871

Dyson, D. M., *The Foster Home*, Allen and Unwin, 1947

Dyson, D. M., *No Two Alike*, Allen and Unwin, 1962

Goffman, E. *Asylums*, Penguin, 1961

Gorst, Sir John, *The Children of the Nation*, Methuen, 1906

Harrison, Phyllis, *The Home Children*, Watson and Dayer, Winnipeg, 1979

Heasman, Kathleen, *Evangelicals in Action*, Geoffrey Bles, 1962

Heywood, Jean S., *Children in Care*, Routledge and Kegan Paul, 1978

Hitchman, J. *King of the Barbareens*, Puffin, 1981

Holmes, G. V., *The Likes of Us*, Muller, 1948

Houghton, Walter, *The Victorian Frame of Mind*, Yale University Press, 1957

Inglis, Brian, *Poverty and the Industrial Revolution*, Panther, 1971

Inglis, K. S., *The Churches and the Working Class in Victorian England*, Routledge and Kegan Paul, 1963

Jones, Gareth Steadman, *Outcast London*, Clarendon Press, 1971

Longmate, Norman, *The Workhouse*, M. Temple Smith, 1974

MacLeod, Valerie, *Whose Child?*, Study, Commission on the Family, 1982

Mayhew, Henry, *London Labour and the London Poor*, Oxford University Press, 1961

Middleton, Nigel and Weitzman, Sophia, *A Place for Everyone*, Gollancz, 1976

Norman, Frank, *Banana Boy*, Secker and Warburg, 1969

Owen, David, *English Philanthropy*, 1660–1960, Oxford University Press, 1965

Packman, Joy, *Who Needs Care?*, Blackwell, 1986

Parfitt, Jessie, ed., *The Community's Children*, Longmans Green, 1967

Parr, Joy, *Labouring Children*, Croom Helm, 1980

Perkin, H., *The Origins of Modern English Society*, Routledge and Kegan Paul, 1969

Pinchbeck, Ivy and Hewitt, Margaret, *Children in English Society*, Routledge and Kegan Paul, 1973

Pugh, Elizabeth, *Social Work in Child Care*, Routledge and Kegan Paul, 1968

Reynolds, George, *Dr Barnardo's Homes: Startling Revelations*, Privately Printed, 1876

Somerville Large, Peter, *Dublin*, Hamish Hamilton, 1979

Stileman, Rear-Admiral Sir Harry, *Controversy between the Council and the Director*, Philip Palmer Press, 1923

Stroud, J., *An Introduction to the Child Care Service*, Longmans, 1965

Taylor, Dr and Mrs Howard, *Hudson Taylor and the China Inland Mission*, Overseas Missionary Fellowship, 1919

Thomas, Leslie, *This Time Next Week*, Constable, 1964
Tucker, T. F., *Children without Homes*, Bodley Head, 1952
Wagner, Gillian, *Barnardo*, Weidenfeld and Nicolson, 1979
Wagner, Gillian, *The Camera and Dr Barnardo*, National Portrait Gallery and Dr Barnardo's, 1974
Wagner, Gillian, *Children of the Empire*, Weidenfeld and Nicolson, 1982
Williams, A. E., *Barnardo of Stepney*, Allen and Unwin, 1943
Wilson, Stanley, *The Mayor and the Matron*, Precision Press, 1971
Wymer, Norman, *Father of Nobody's Children*, Hutchinson, 1954

OFFICIAL PUBLICATIONS AND REPORTS

Custody of Children Act, 1891 (Barnardo Act)
Children and Young Persons Act, 1933
Children Act, 1948
Children Act, 1958
Children and Young Persons Act, 1963
Children and Young Persons Act, 1969
Children Act, 1975
Child Care Act, 1980
Foster Children Act, 1980
Report of the Care of Children Committee, 1946 (Curtis Report)
Home Office Memorandum on the Boarding-Out of Children Regulations, 1955
Report of the Committee on Children and Young Persons, 1960 (Ingleby Report)
The Child, the Family and the Young Offender, 1965
Children in Trouble, 1968
Young Offenders, 1980

NEWSPAPERS

The Times, 1877–1987
East London Observer
Tower Hamlets Independent

BARNARDO PUBLICATIONS

Annual Reports, 1868–1986
Barnardo Book, 1944
Barnardo Book, 2nd ed., 1955
Barnardo News, 1963–87
Forum, 1946–71
Night and Day, 1877–1987
Practice Papers, 1985
Reports of Staff Conferences, 1928–65
Social Work Papers, 1977–83
Nowell, J., *The Structure and Organisation of Dr Barnardo's*, 1970
Ups and Downs, 1895–1949
Young Helpers' League Magazine, 1892–1929

UNPUBLISHED THESES

Parr, Joy, 'Home Children', Ph.D. thesis, Yale University, 1977
Wagner, Gillian, 'Dr Barnardo and the Charity Organisation Society', Ph.D. thesis, University of London, 1977

UNPUBLISHED MSS

Adnams, Nora, 'My Memoirs of Dr Barnardo's Home, Barkingside'
Cox, Carol Ann, 'A study of the Girls' Village Home, Ilford', 1874–1938
Gordon, Gillian, 'Dr Barnardo and Social Reform'
Hughes Jones, Rosemary, J. W., 'A Historical Approach to the problem of shortage of staff in Residential Child Care 1946–72'
Picton-Turbervill, Beatrice, 'Memoirs of the Girls' Village Home, 1920–41'
Steel, John Walker, 'Child Care in Barnardo's: a decade of change, 1963–73'
Wagner, Gillian, 'Charity and Self Help in Victorian London'

ARCHIVE COLLECTIONS

Barnardo's
Dr Barnardo's sermon notes; correspondence; publications
Council Minutes; Committee Minutes: 1. Executive Committee 2. Committee of Management 3. General Purposes Committee 4. Executive and Finance Committee. Children's histories. Reports of working parties, sub-committees, committee reviews, tables, etc.
Greater London Records Office
MS minutes of the Charity Organisation Society inquiry into Dr Barnardo's Homes MS papers, letters, reports and press cuttings about Dr Barnardo's organisation, 1883–90, 1904–43

Index